ZATCHBELL!™

ZATCH BELL!
Vol. 4

STORY AND ART BY
MAKOTO RAIKU

English Adaptation/Fred Burke
Translation/David Ury
Touch-up Art & Lettering/Melanie Lewis
Design/Izumi Hirayama
Special Thanks/Jessica Villat, Miki Macaluso,
Mitsuko Kitajima, and Akane Matsuo
Editor/Frances E. Wall

Managing Editor/Annette Roman
Director of Production/Noboru Watanabe
Vice President of Publishing/Alvin Lu
Sr. Director of Acquisitions/Rika Inouye
Vice President of Sales & Marketing/Liza Coppola
Publisher/Hyoe Narita

Published by VIZ Media, LLC
P.O. Box 77010
San Francisco, CA 94107

10 9 8 7 6 5 4 3 2 1
First printing, November 2005

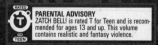

www.viz.com
store.viz.com

ZATCH BELL! ™

STORY AND ART BY
MAKOTO RAIKU

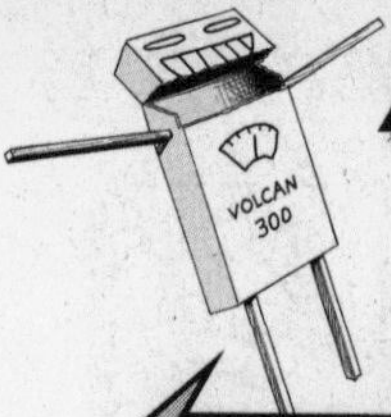
VOLCAN
300

Kiyo Takamine

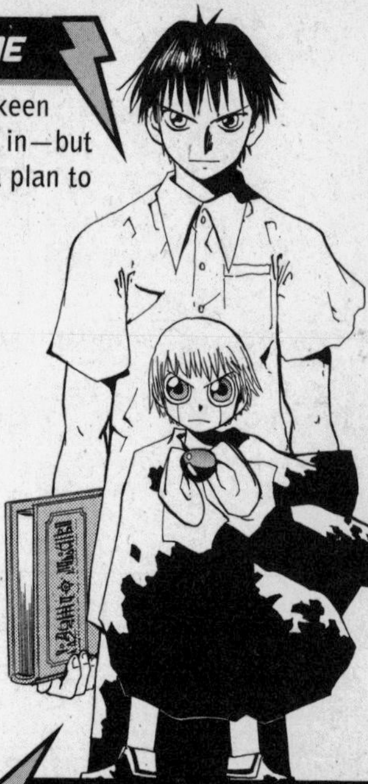

An aloof student with a keen intellect, Kiyo doesn't fit in—but now Zatch is here with a plan to change all that!

Volcan 300

A friend Kiyo made for Zatch. This is already version 3!

Suzy Mizuno

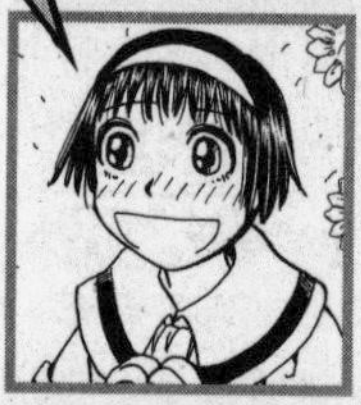

A classmate who likes Kiyo, Suzy is always getting in trouble.

Naomi

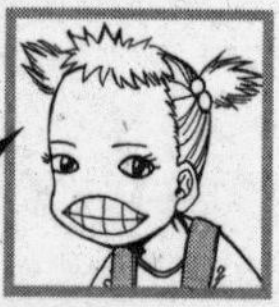

A girl who picks on Zatch in the park.

Zatch Bell

A mamodo kid who came to help Kiyo reform his bad attitude. When Kiyo holds the red book and reads a spell, lightning bolts shoot from Zatch's mouth.

Hana Takamine

Kiyo's mother, nice but strict.

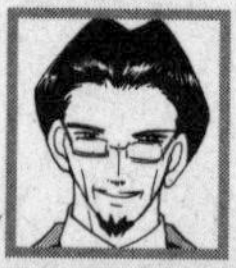

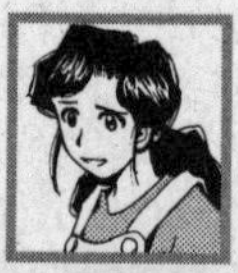

Seitaro Takamine

Kiyo's father, an archaeology professor at a university in England.

Ivy Kinoyama

Botanical garden manager.

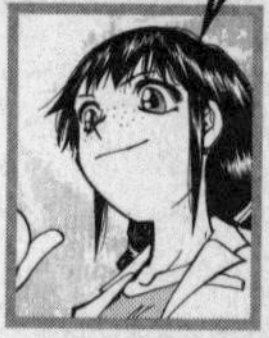

Hiroshi Yamanaka

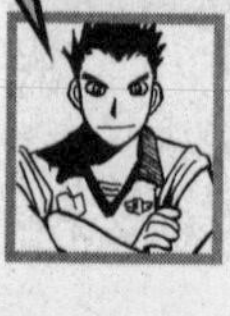

On the baseball team.

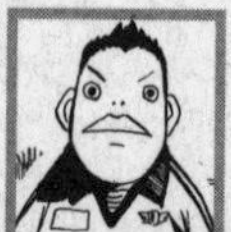

Mamoru Iwashima

A funny guy.

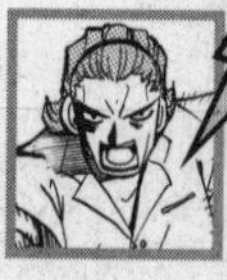

Kane

The class bully.

ZATCH'S PAST OPPONENTS

KOLULU

SUGINO

GOFURE

BRAGO

REYCOM

KANCHOMÉ

ESHROS

FEIN

THE STORY THUS FAR

Kiyo is a junior high student who's so intelligent that he's bored by life and doesn't even go to school. But Kiyo's life changes when his father sends him an amazing child named Zatch as a birthday present. When Kiyo holds Zatch's red book (which only Kiyo can read) and utters a spell, Zatch displays awesome powers.

Soon the duo finds out that Zatch is one of many mamodo children chosen to fight in a battle which will determine who is king of the mamodo world for the next 1,000 years. Zatch is saddened to learn the truth about his situation, but the bond between Zatch and Kiyo deepens as they're forced to fight for their own survival.

After battling with a sweet mamodo girl named Kolulu, Zatch makes up his mind to fulfill her wish that he become a "kind king." So far, Zatch has mastered three spells from the red book, and his battles with other mamodo are getting more and more fierce!

ZATCHBELL! 4

CONTENTS

LEVEL 29: The Fighting Sculptor

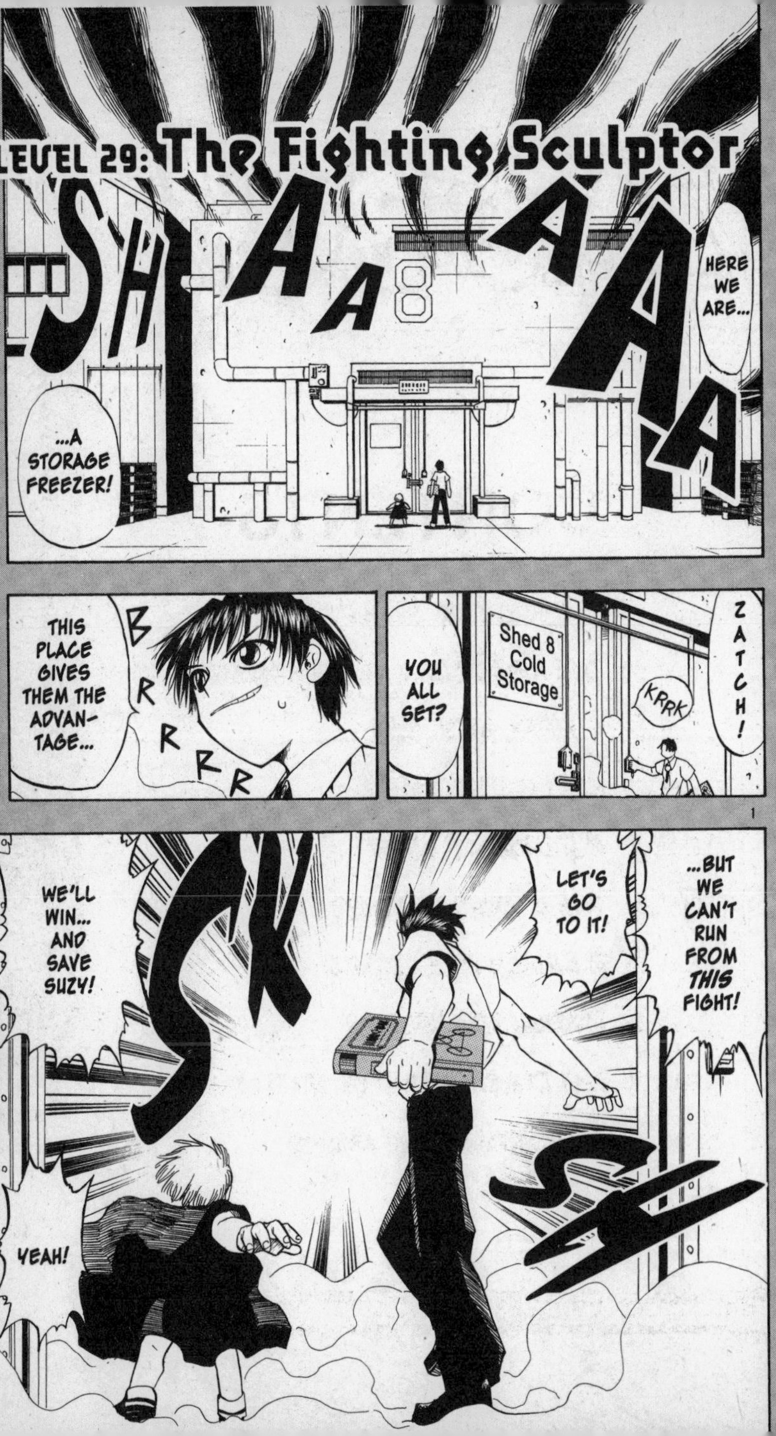
HERE WE ARE...
SHAAAAAAA
8
...A STORAGE FREEZER!
ZATCH!
KRRK
Shed 8 Cold Storage
YOU ALL SET?
BRRRR
THIS PLACE GIVES THEM THE ADVAN-TAGE...
...BUT WE CAN'T RUN FROM *THIS* FIGHT!
LET'S GO TO IT!
WE'LL WIN... AND SAVE SUZY!
SK
SH
YEAH!

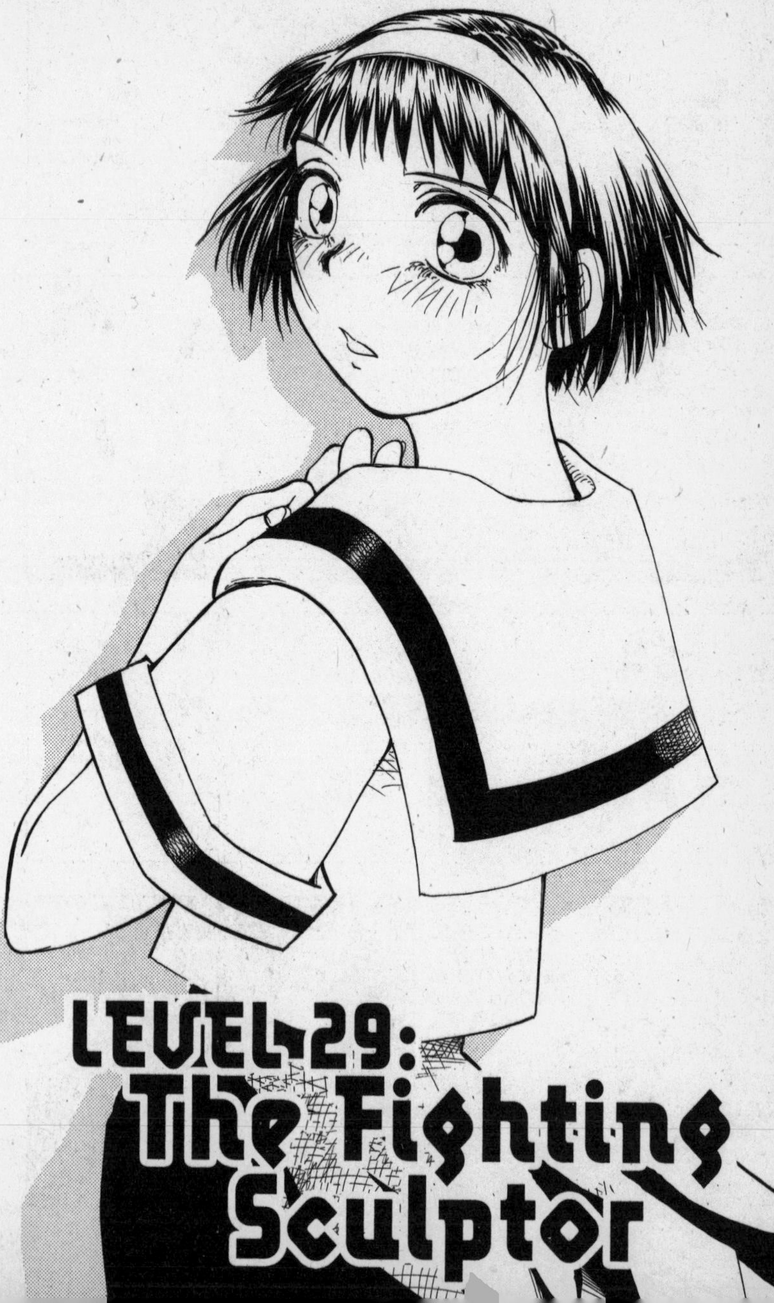

LEVEL 29: The Fighting Sculptor

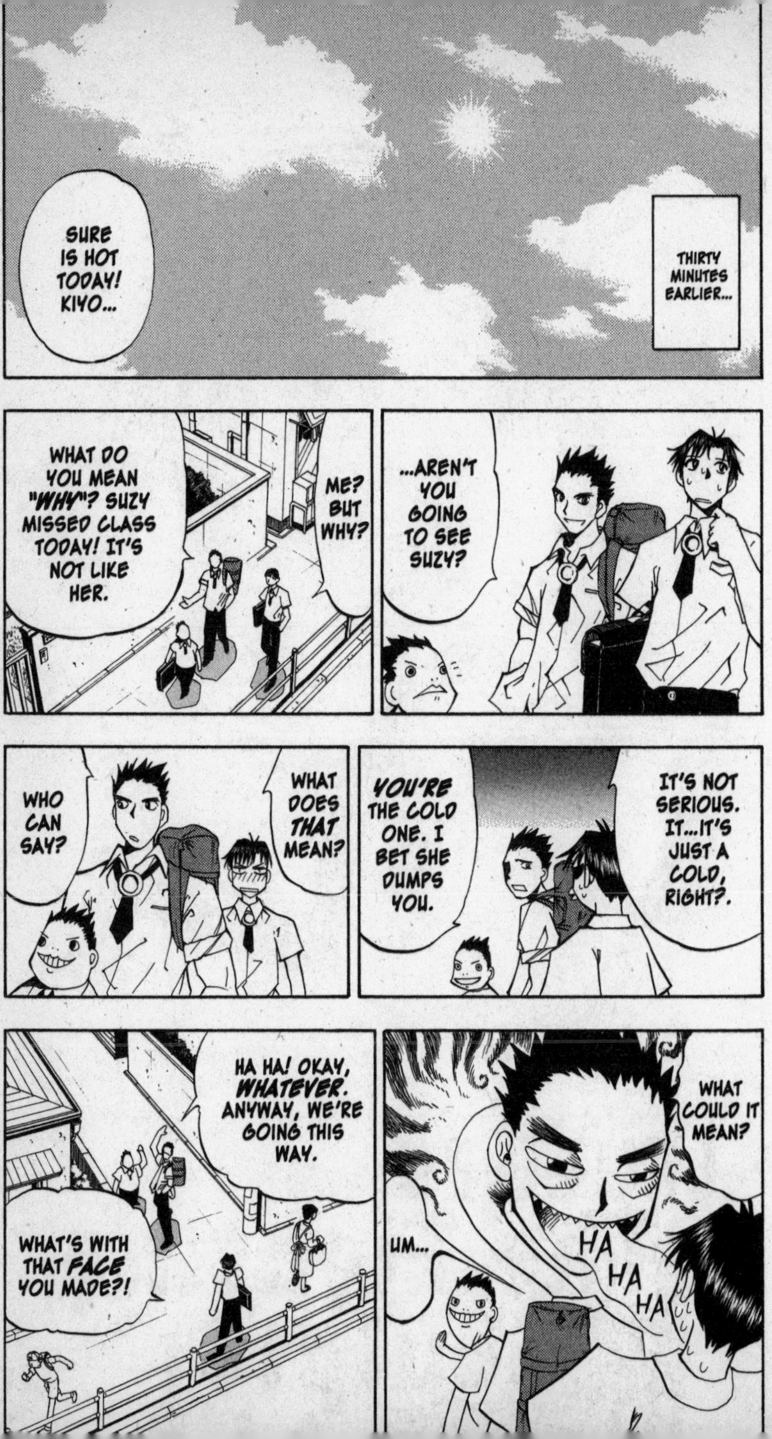
THIRTY MINUTES EARLIER...
SURE IS HOT TODAY! KIYO...
...AREN'T YOU GOING TO SEE SUZY?
ME? BUT WHY?
WHAT DO YOU MEAN "WHY"? SUZY MISSED CLASS TODAY! IT'S NOT LIKE HER.
IT'S NOT SERIOUS. IT...IT'S JUST A COLD, RIGHT?.
YOU'RE THE COLD ONE. I BET SHE DUMPS YOU.
WHAT DOES THAT MEAN?
WHO CAN SAY?
WHAT COULD IT MEAN?
HA HA HA
UM...
HA HA! OKAY, WHATEVER. ANYWAY, WE'RE GOING THIS WAY.
WHAT'S WITH THAT FACE YOU MADE?!

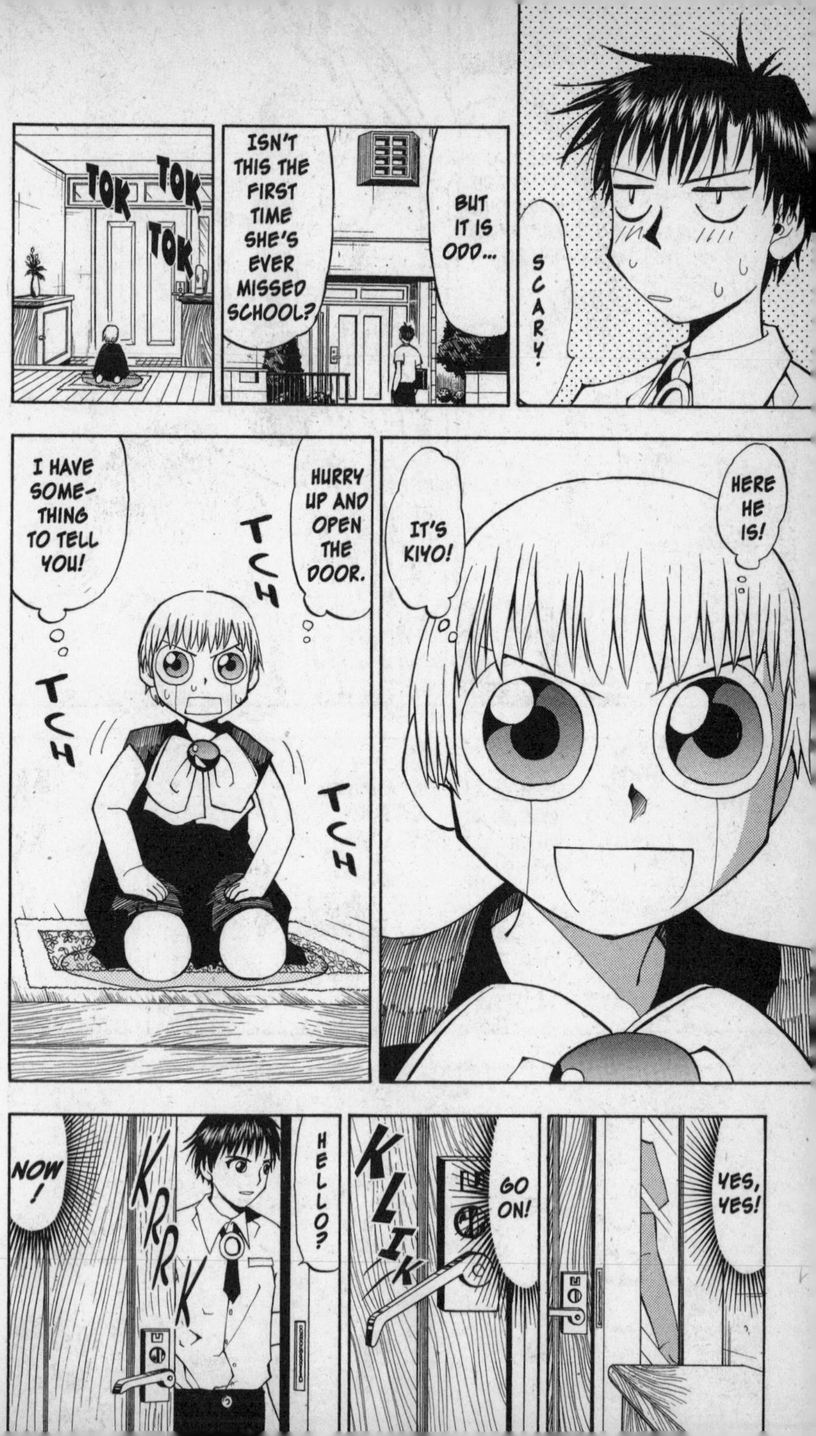
SCARY.
BUT IT IS ODD...
ISN'T THIS THE FIRST TIME SHE'S EVER MISSED SCHOOL?
TOK TOK TOK
HERE HE IS!
IT'S KIYO!
HURRY UP AND OPEN THE DOOR.
TCH
I HAVE SOME-THING TO TELL YOU!
TCH
TCH
YES, YES!
GO ON!
KLIK
HELLO?
KRRRK
NOW!

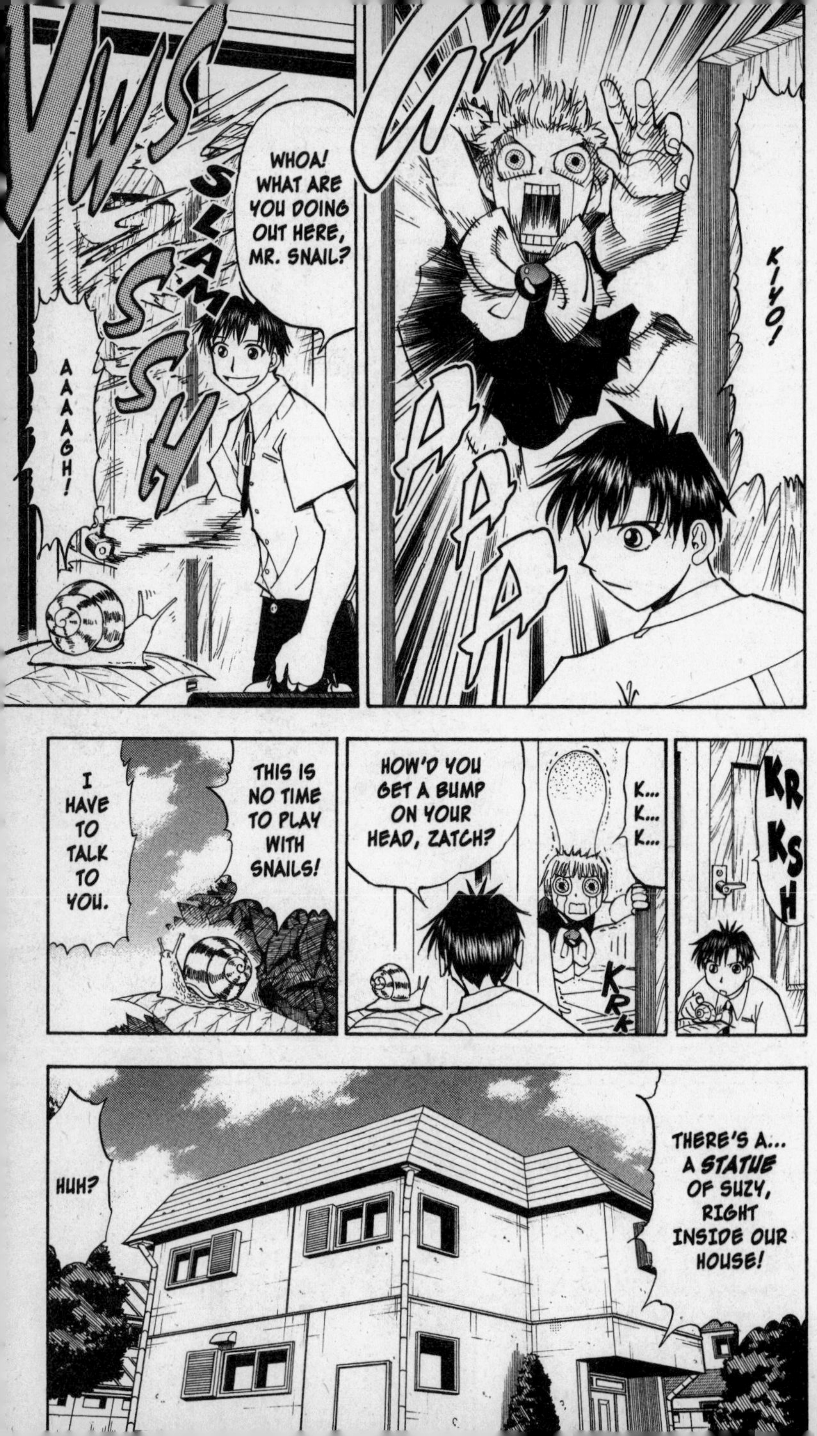
KIYO!
WHOA! WHAT ARE YOU DOING OUT HERE, MR. SNAIL?
SLAM
AAAAAGH!
KRKSH
K... K... K...
KRK
HOW'D YOU GET A BUMP ON YOUR HEAD, ZATCH?
THIS IS NO TIME TO PLAY WITH SNAILS!
I HAVE TO TALK TO YOU.
THERE'S A... A *STATUE* OF SUZY, RIGHT INSIDE OUR HOUSE!
HUH?

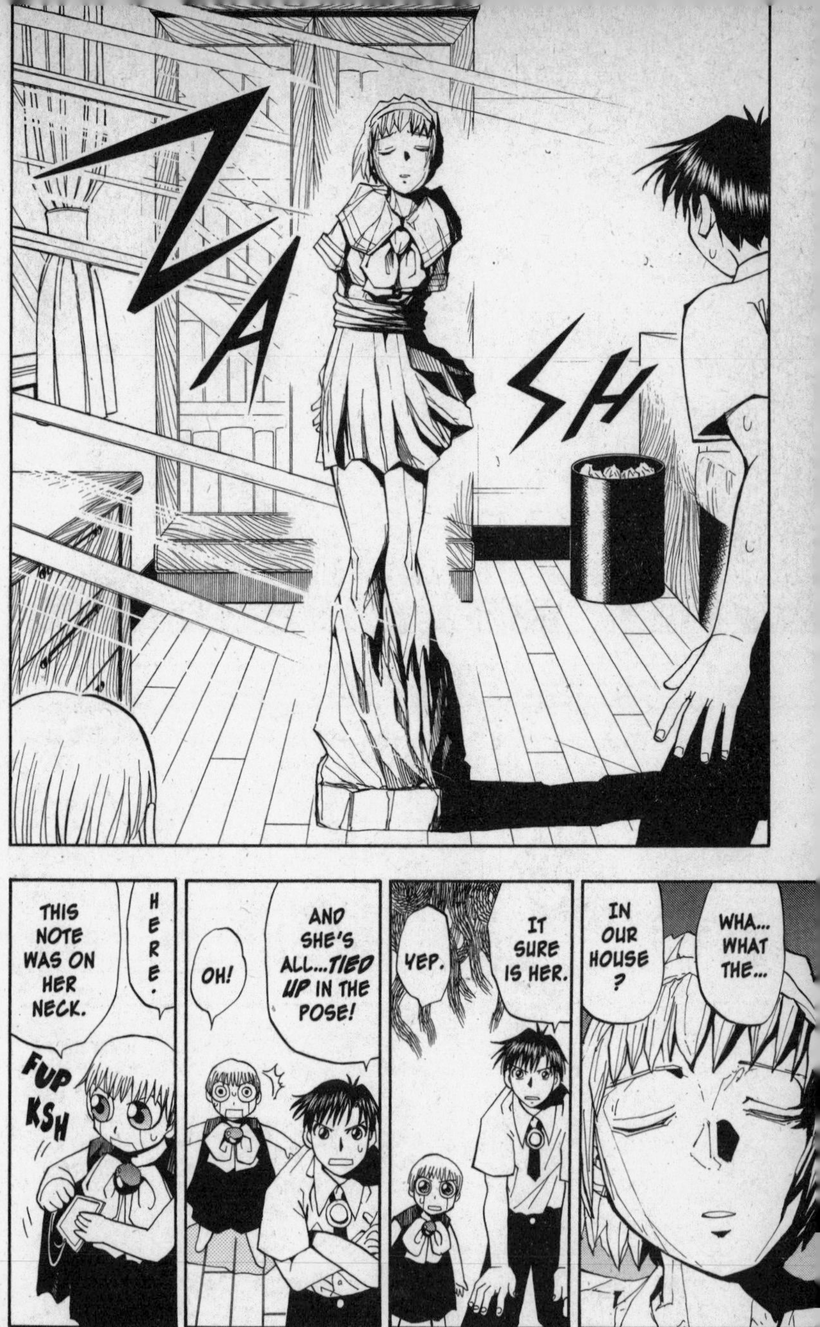
ZA
SH
WHA... WHAT THE...
IN OUR HOUSE?
IT SURE IS HER.
YEP.
AND SHE'S ALL...TIED UP IN THE POSE!
OH!
HERE.
THIS NOTE WAS ON HER NECK.
FUP KSH

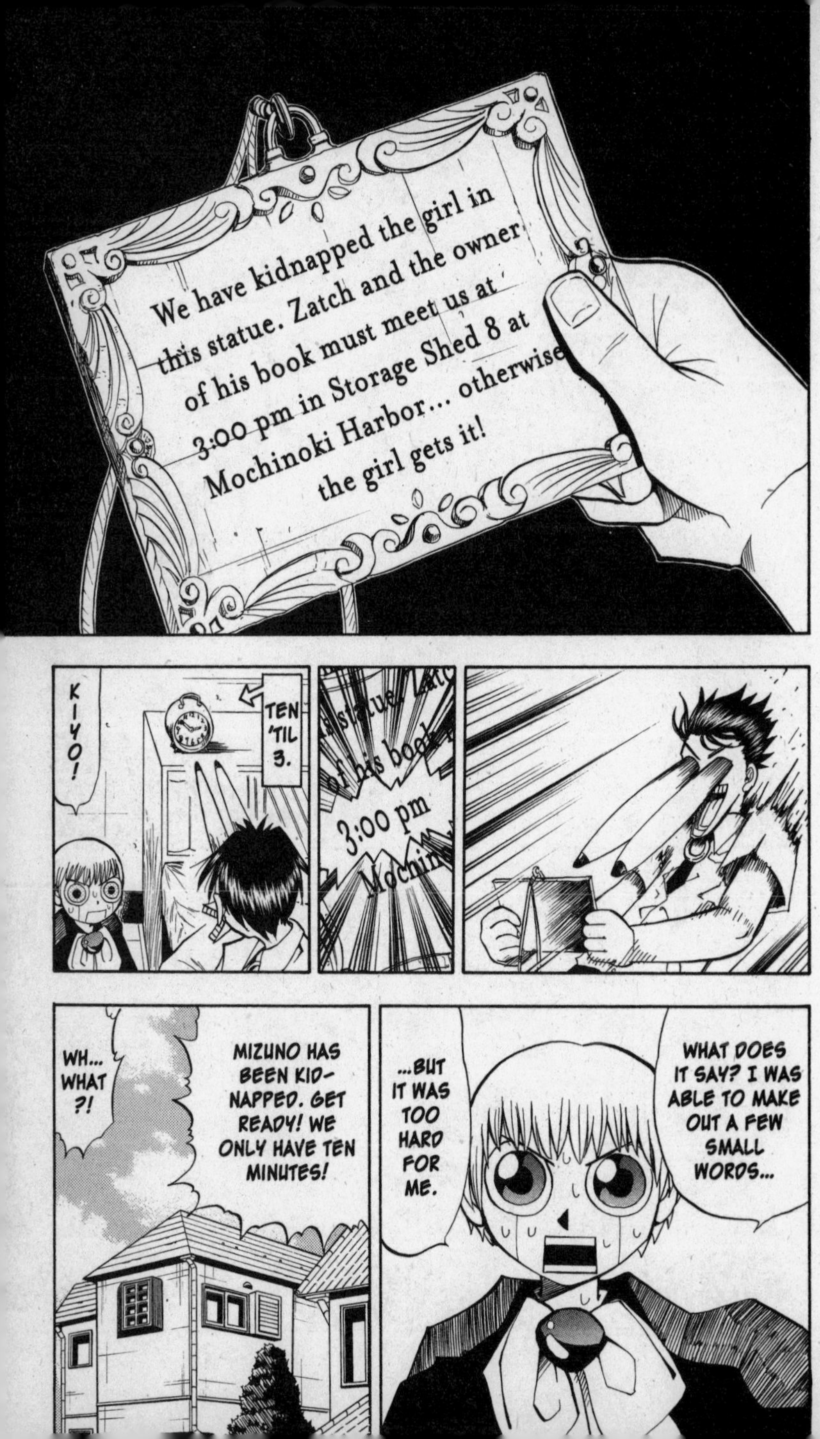

We have kidnapped the girl in this statue. Zatch and the owner of his book must meet us at 3:00 pm in Storage Shed 8 at Mochinoki Harbor... otherwise the girl gets it!
of his book
3:00 pm
TEN 'TIL 3.
KIYO!
WHAT DOES IT SAY? I WAS ABLE TO MAKE OUT A FEW SMALL WORDS...
...BUT IT WAS TOO HARD FOR ME.
MIZUNO HAS BEEN KID-NAPPED. GET READY! WE ONLY HAVE TEN MINUTES!
WH... WHAT ?!

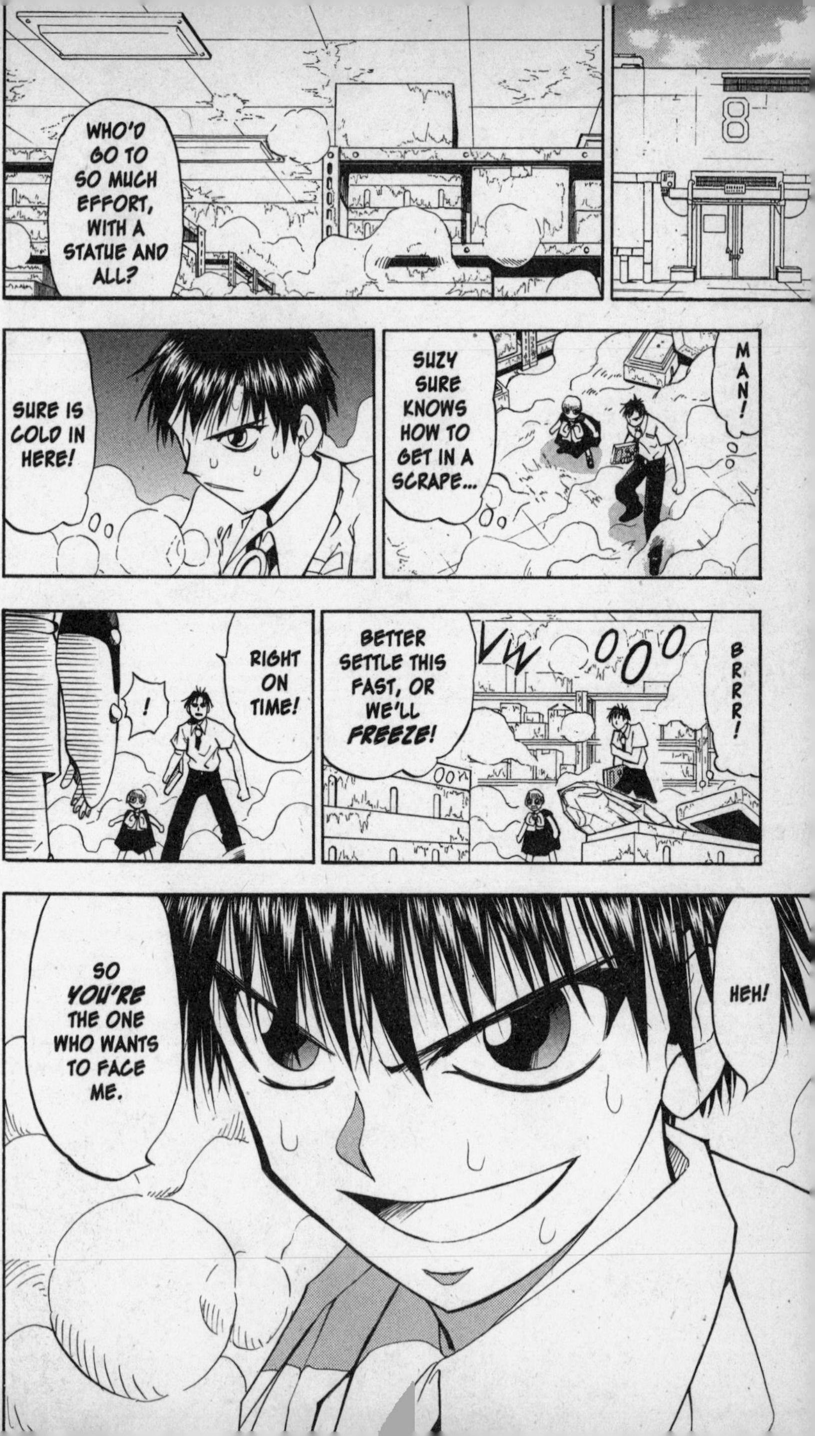
WHO'D GO TO SO MUCH EFFORT, WITH A STATUE AND ALL?
MAN!
SUZY SURE KNOWS HOW TO GET IN A SCRAPE...
SURE IS COLD IN HERE!
BRRR!
VWOOOO
BETTER SETTLE THIS FAST, OR WE'LL *FREEZE!*
RIGHT ON TIME!
!
HEH!
SO *YOU'RE* THE ONE WHO WANTS TO FACE ME.

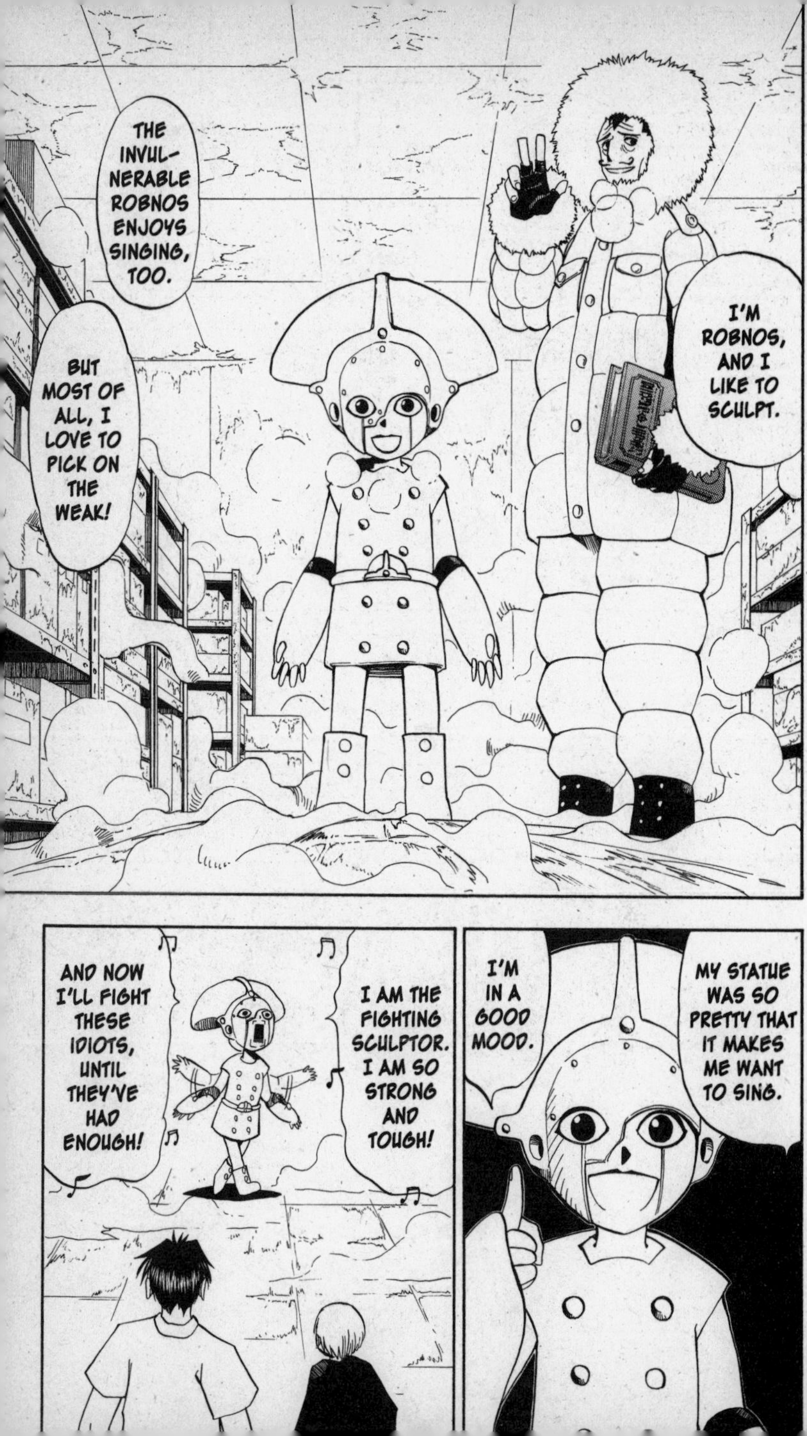
I'M ROBNOS, AND I LIKE TO SCULPT.
THE INVULNERABLE ROBNOS ENJOYS SINGING, TOO.
BUT MOST OF ALL, I LOVE TO PICK ON THE WEAK!
MY STATUE WAS SO PRETTY THAT IT MAKES ME WANT TO SING.
I'M IN A GOOD MOOD.
I AM THE FIGHTING SCULPTOR. I AM SO STRONG AND TOUGH!
AND NOW I'LL FIGHT THESE IDIOTS, UNTIL THEY'VE HAD ENOUGH!

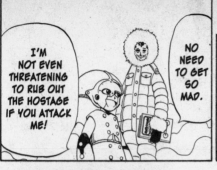

YOU!
OOOH!
NO NEED TO GET SO MAD.
I'M NOT EVEN THREATENING TO RUB OUT THE HOSTAGE IF YOU ATTACK ME!
I CAME TO JAPAN TO MAKE A FOOL OUT OF ZATCH.
THE GIRL... SHE'S JUST BAIT.
ZATCH?
ZATCH IS A SILLY BRAGGART!
AND HE'S WEAK, TOO!
AND THE INVULNERABLE ROBNOS LIVES TO PUNISH THE WEAK!
I'VE LOOKED FORWARD TO THIS SINCE THE FIGHT TO BE KING BEGAN...
I WANT TO HUMILIATE ZATCH WHILE I MAKE HIS TEETH CHATTER!
TEE HEE HEE

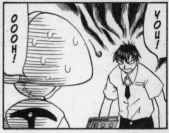

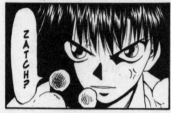

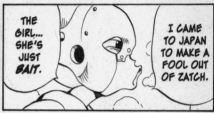

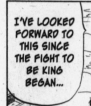

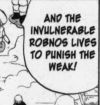

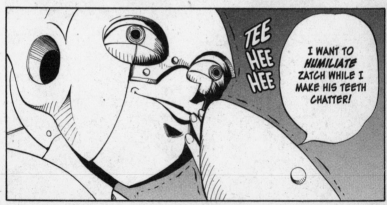

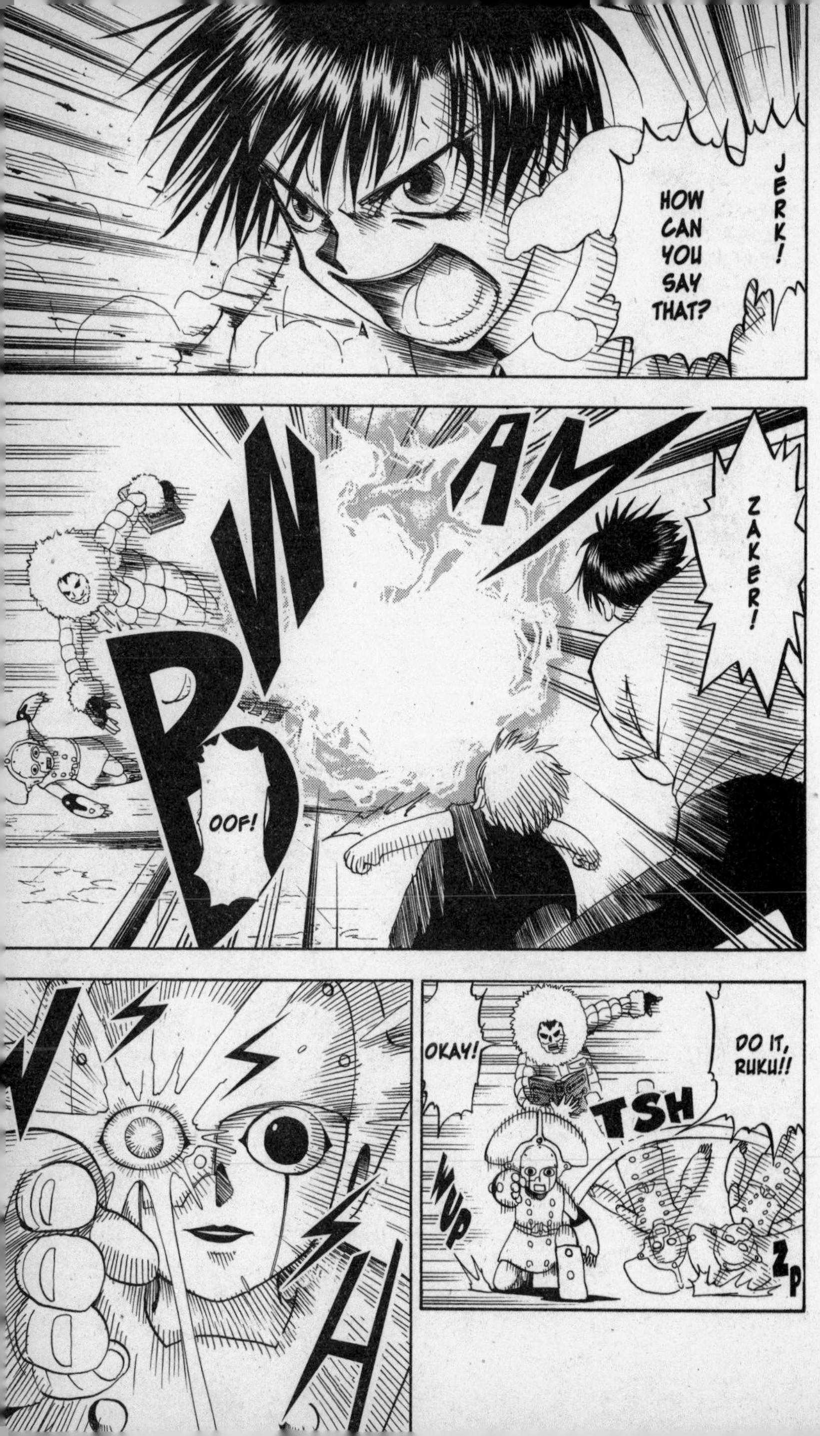
JERK!
HOW CAN YOU SAY THAT?
ZAKER!
BWAM
OOF!
DO IT, RUKU!!
OKAY!
TSH
WUP
ZP

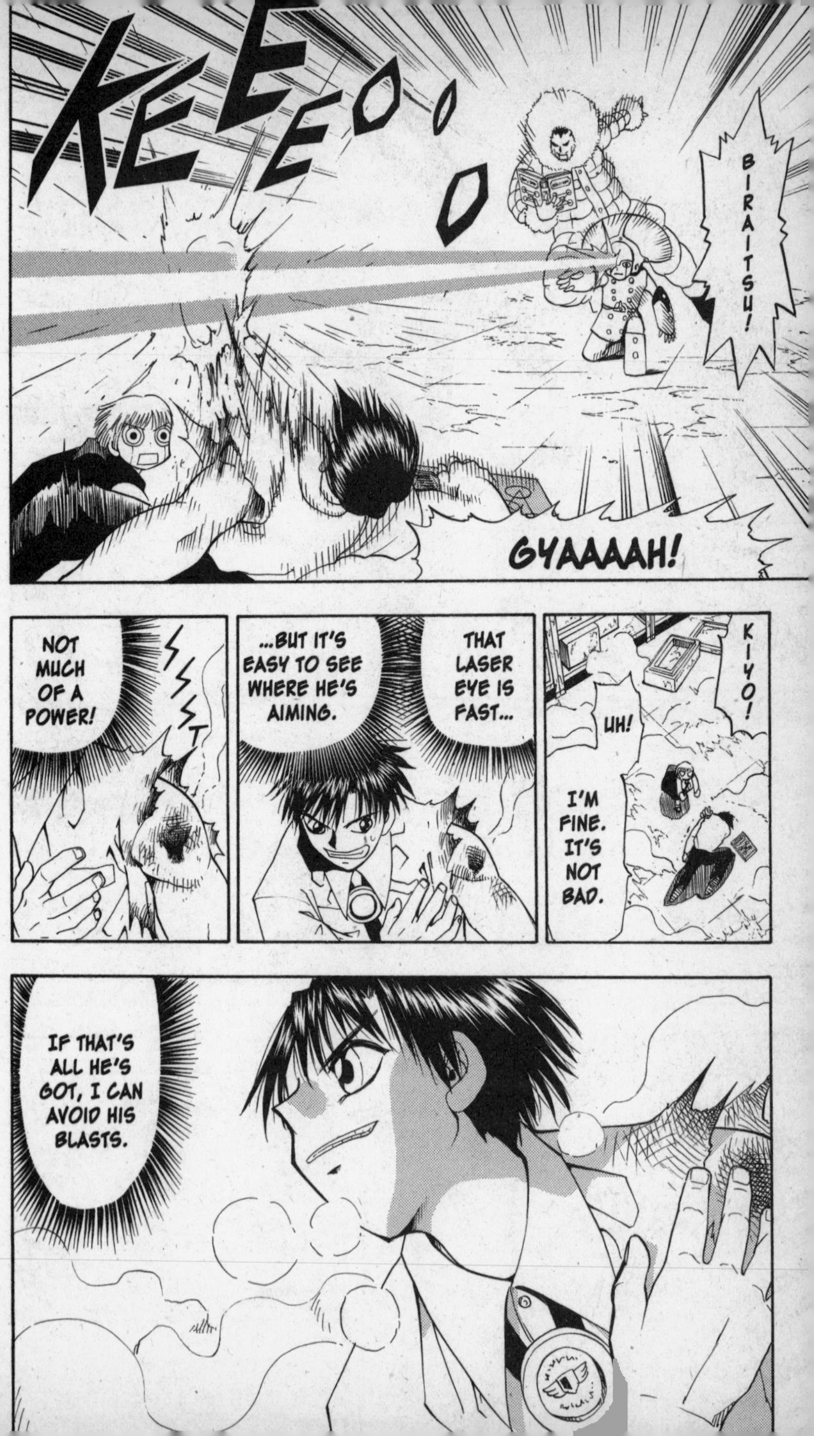
BIRAITSU!
KEEOOO
GYAAAAH!
KIYO!
UH!
I'M FINE. IT'S NOT BAD.
THAT LASER EYE IS FAST...
...BUT IT'S EASY TO SEE WHERE HE'S AIMING.
SSST
NOT MUCH OF A POWER!
IF THAT'S ALL HE'S GOT, I CAN AVOID HIS BLASTS.

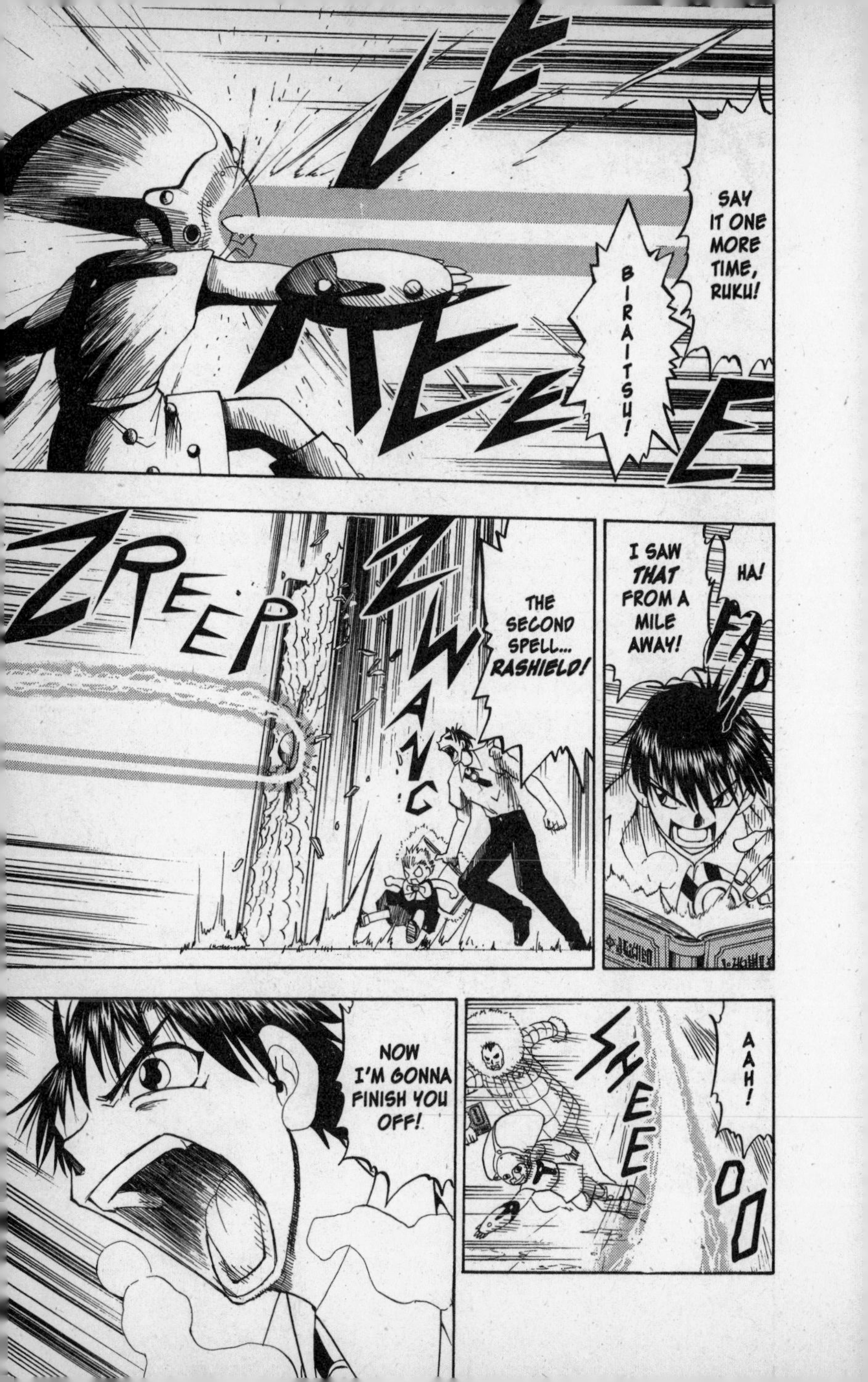
SAY IT ONE MORE TIME, RUKU!
BIRAITSU!
ZZZEEE
HA!
I SAW THAT FROM A MILE AWAY!
FAP
THE SECOND SPELL... RASHIELD!
ZWANG
ZREEP
AAH!
SHEEOO
NOW I'M GONNA FINISH YOU OFF!

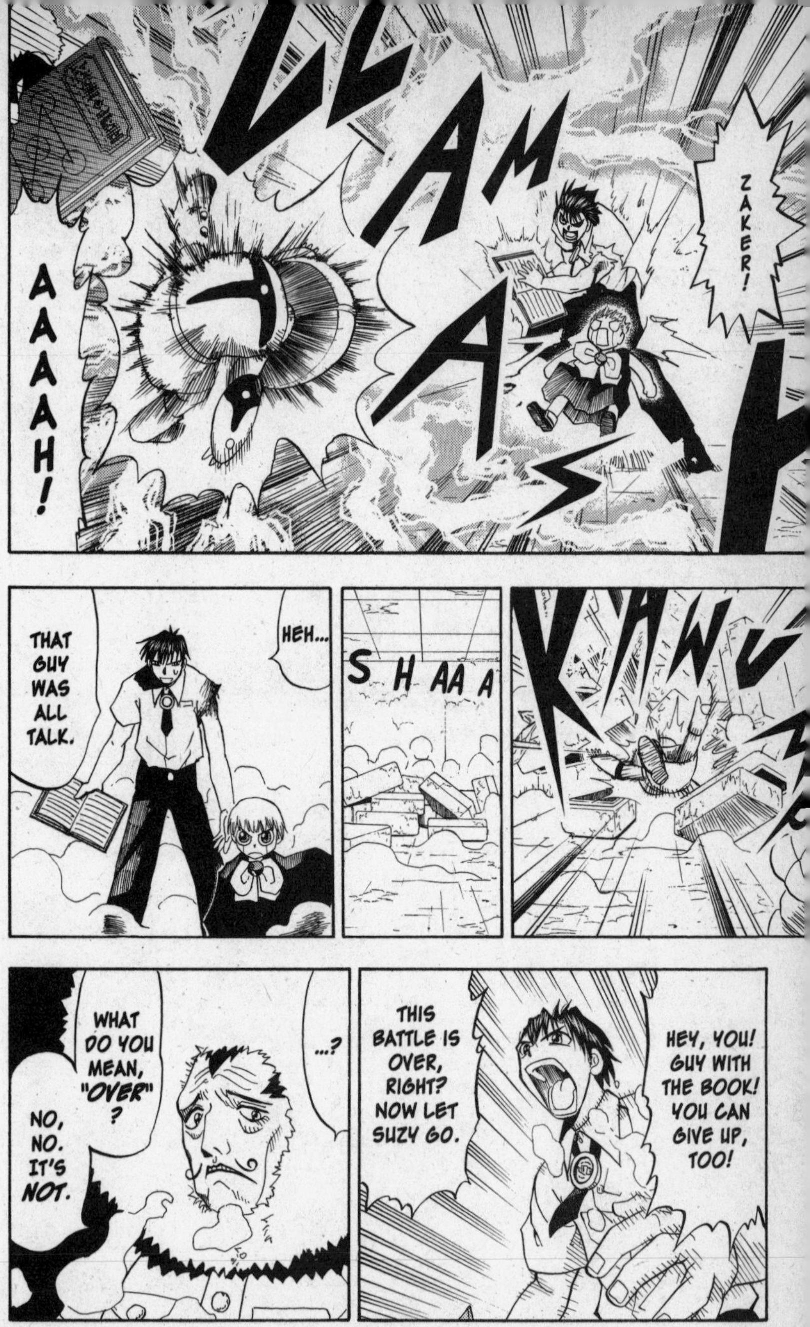
ZAKER!
AAAAAH!
HEH...
THAT GUY WAS ALL TALK.
SHAAA
HEY, YOU! GUY WITH THE BOOK! YOU CAN GIVE UP, TOO!
THIS BATTLE IS OVER, RIGHT? NOW LET SUZY GO.
...?
WHAT DO YOU MEAN, "OVER"?
NO, NO. IT'S NOT.

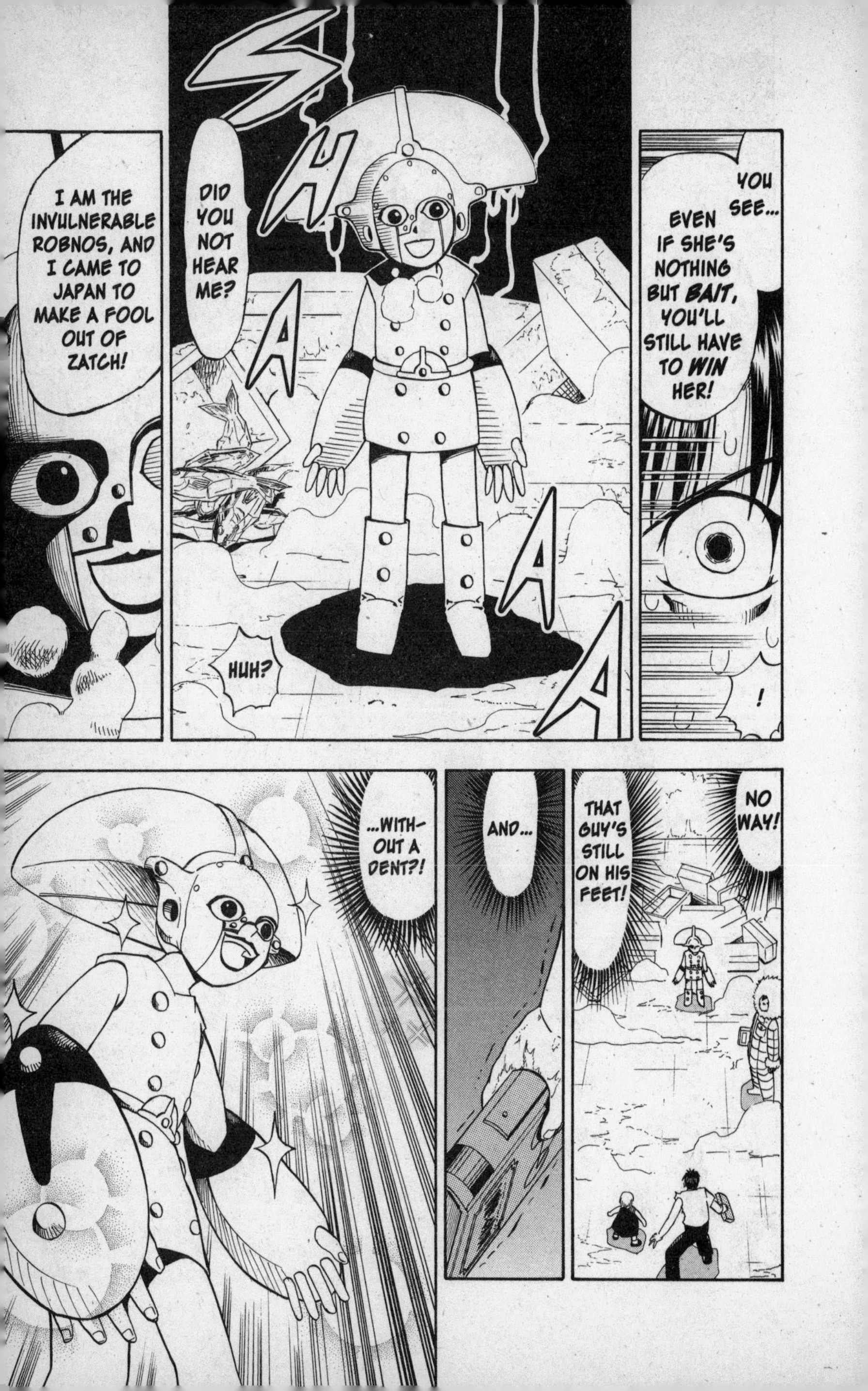
YOU SEE...
EVEN IF SHE'S NOTHING BUT BAIT, YOU'LL STILL HAVE TO WIN HER!
!
SHAAAA
DID YOU NOT HEAR ME?
HUH?
I AM THE INVULNERABLE ROBNOS, AND I CAME TO JAPAN TO MAKE A FOOL OUT OF ZATCH!
NO WAY!
THAT GUY'S STILL ON HIS FEET!
AND...
...WITH-OUT A DENT?!

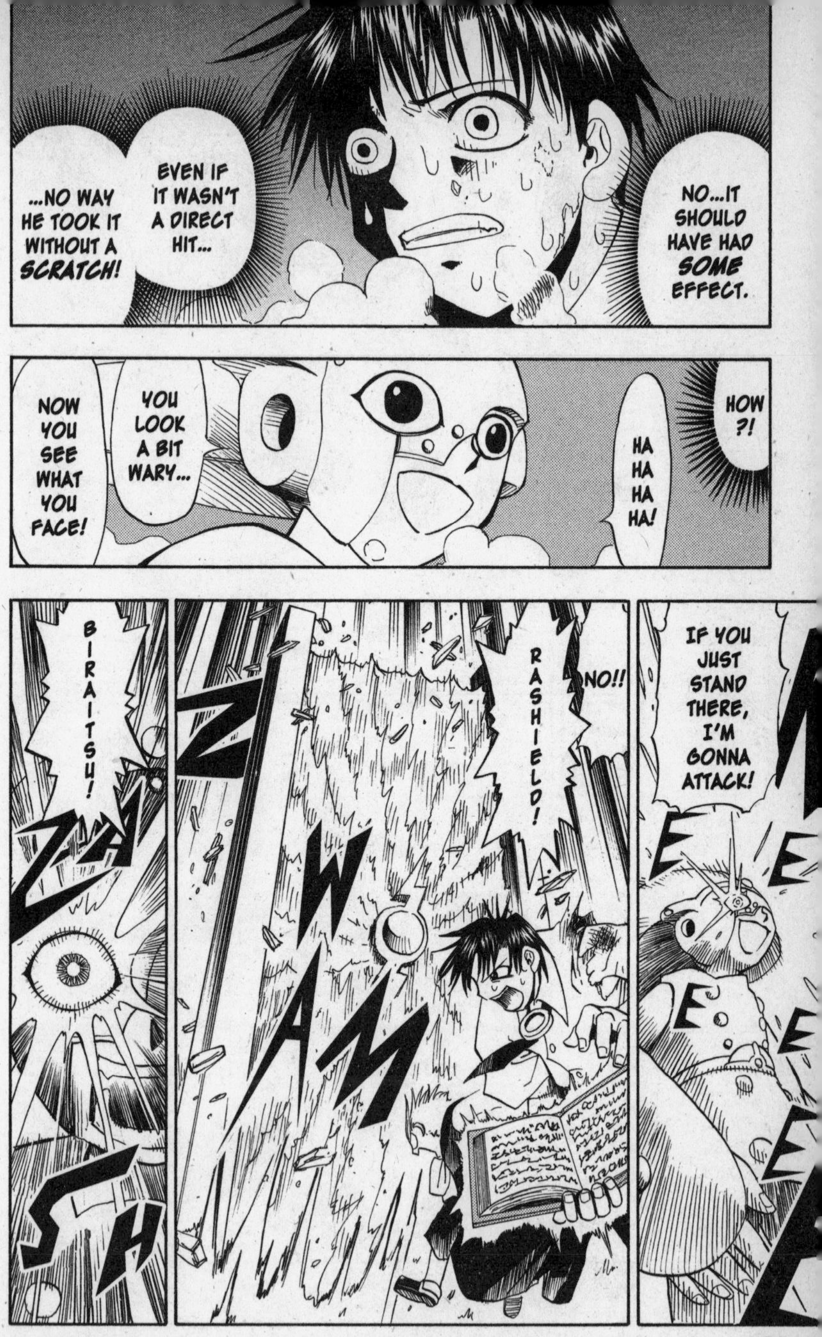
NO...IT SHOULD HAVE HAD SOME EFFECT.
EVEN IF IT WASN'T A DIRECT HIT...
...NO WAY HE TOOK IT WITHOUT A SCRATCH!
HOW?!
HA HA HA HA!
YOU LOOK A BIT WARY...
NOW YOU SEE WHAT YOU FACE!
IF YOU JUST STAND THERE, I'M GONNA ATTACK!
NO!!
RASHIELD!
BIRAITSU!

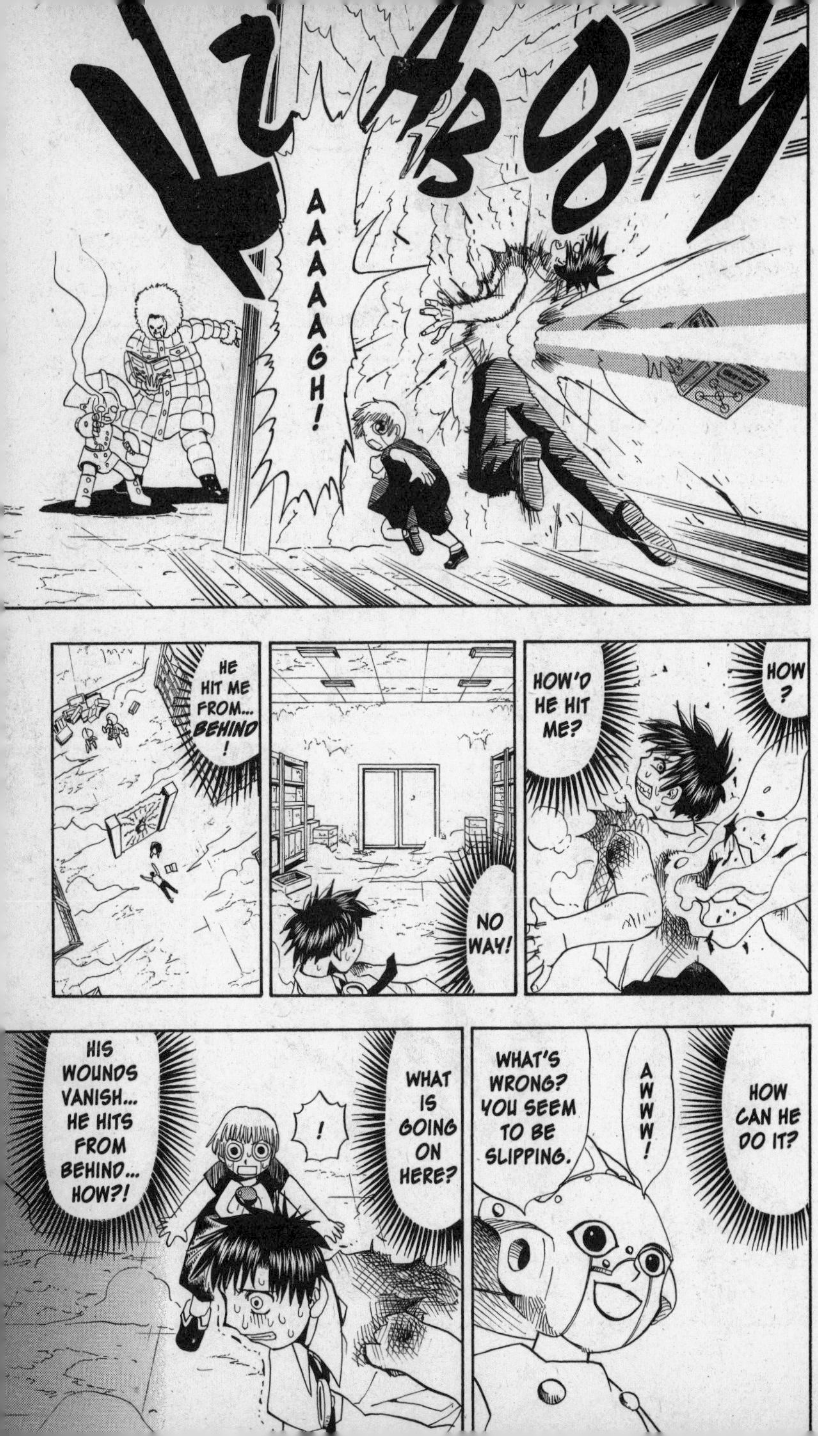
KABOOM
AAAAAAGH!
HOW?
HOW'D HE HIT ME?
NO WAY!
HE HIT ME FROM... BEHIND!
HOW CAN HE DO IT?
AWWW!
WHAT'S WRONG? YOU SEEM TO BE SLIPPING.
WHAT IS GOING ON HERE?
!
HIS WOUNDS VANISH... HE HITS FROM BEHIND... HOW?!

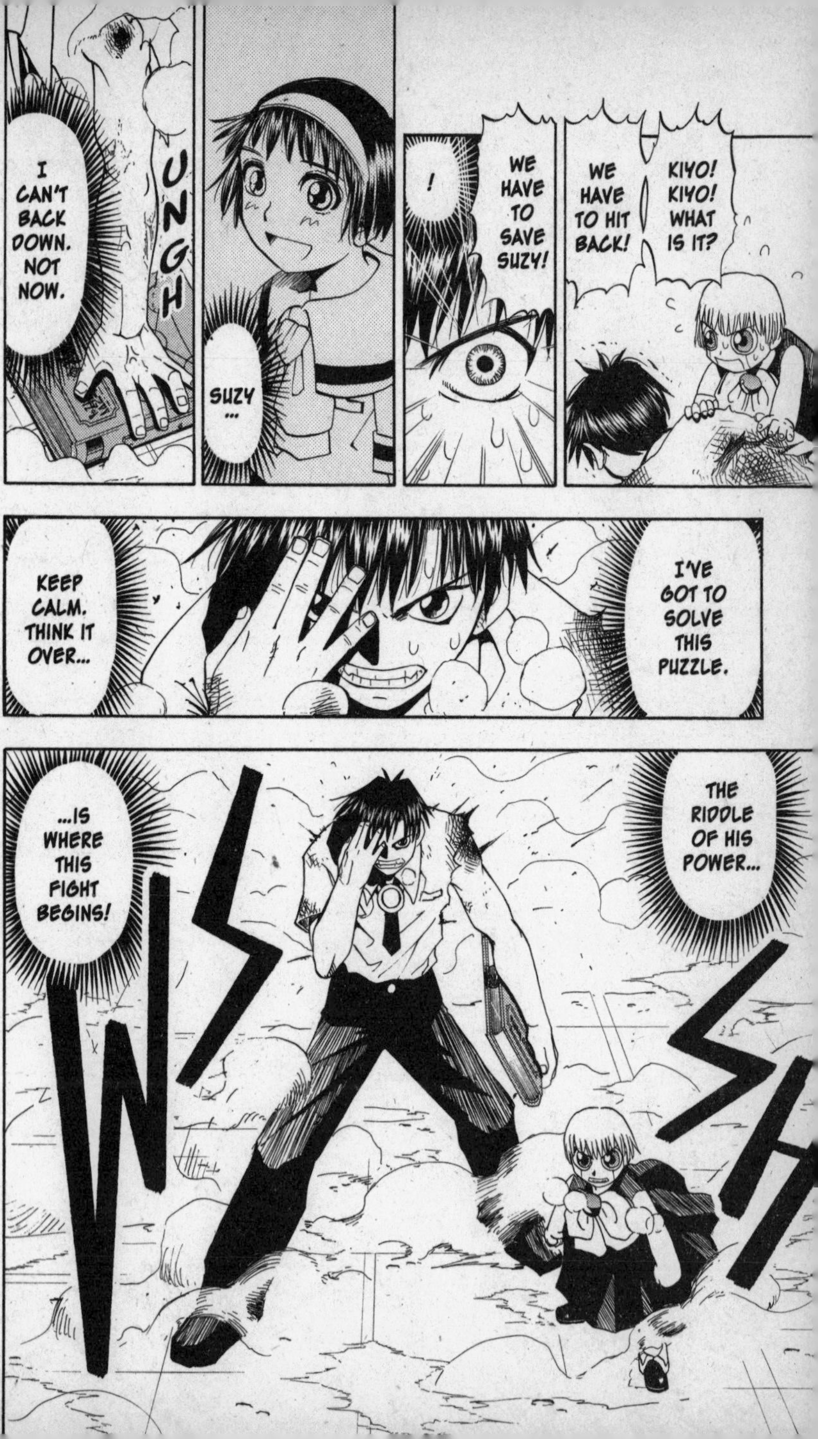
KIYO! KIYO! WHAT IS IT?
WE HAVE TO HIT BACK!
!
WE HAVE TO SAVE SUZY!
SUZY ...
UNGH
I CAN'T BACK DOWN. NOT NOW.
I'VE GOT TO SOLVE THIS PUZZLE.
KEEP CALM. THINK IT OVER...
THE RIDDLE OF HIS POWER...
...IS WHERE THIS FIGHT BEGINS!
WSSH

LEVEL 30: The Riddle of Invulnerability

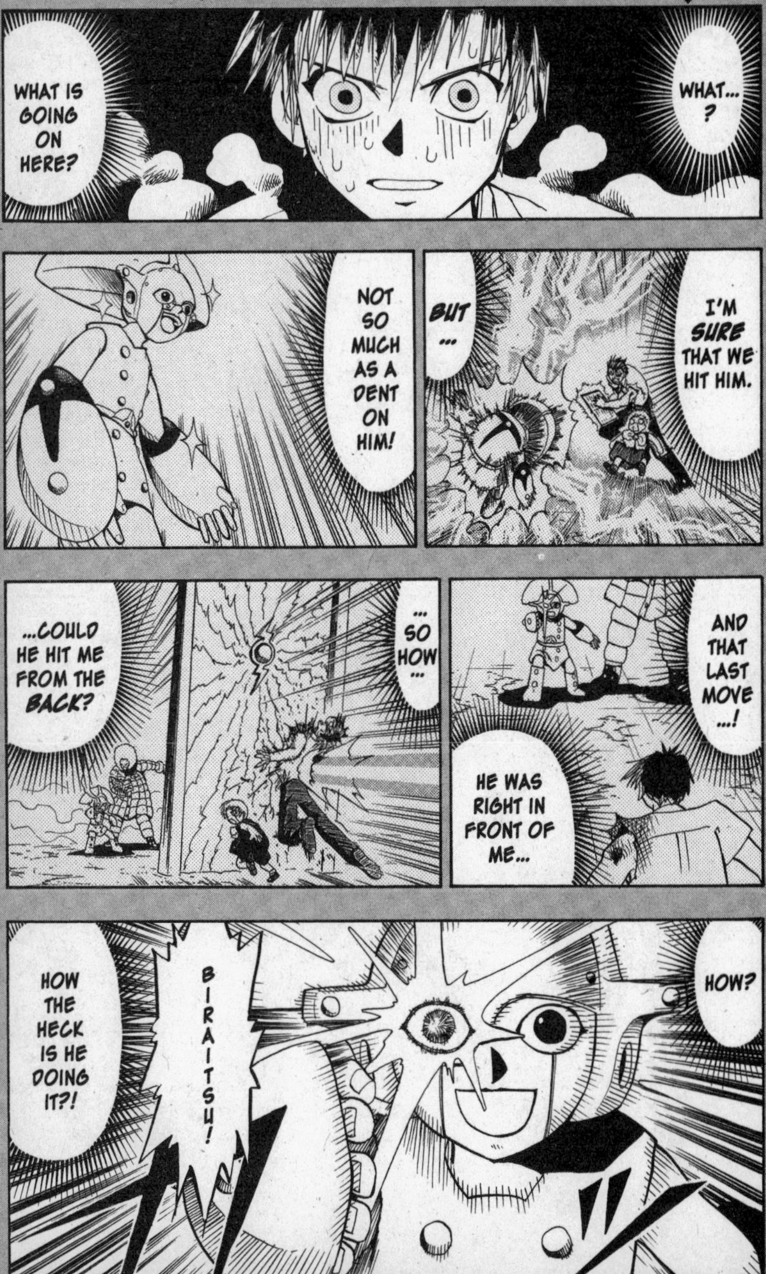
WHAT... ?
WHAT IS GOING ON HERE?
I'M SURE THAT WE HIT HIM.
BUT ...
NOT SO MUCH AS A DENT ON HIM!
AND THAT LAST MOVE ...!
HE WAS RIGHT IN FRONT OF ME...
... SO HOW ...
...COULD HE HIT ME FROM THE BACK?
HOW?
BIRAITSU!
HOW THE HECK IS HE DOING IT?!

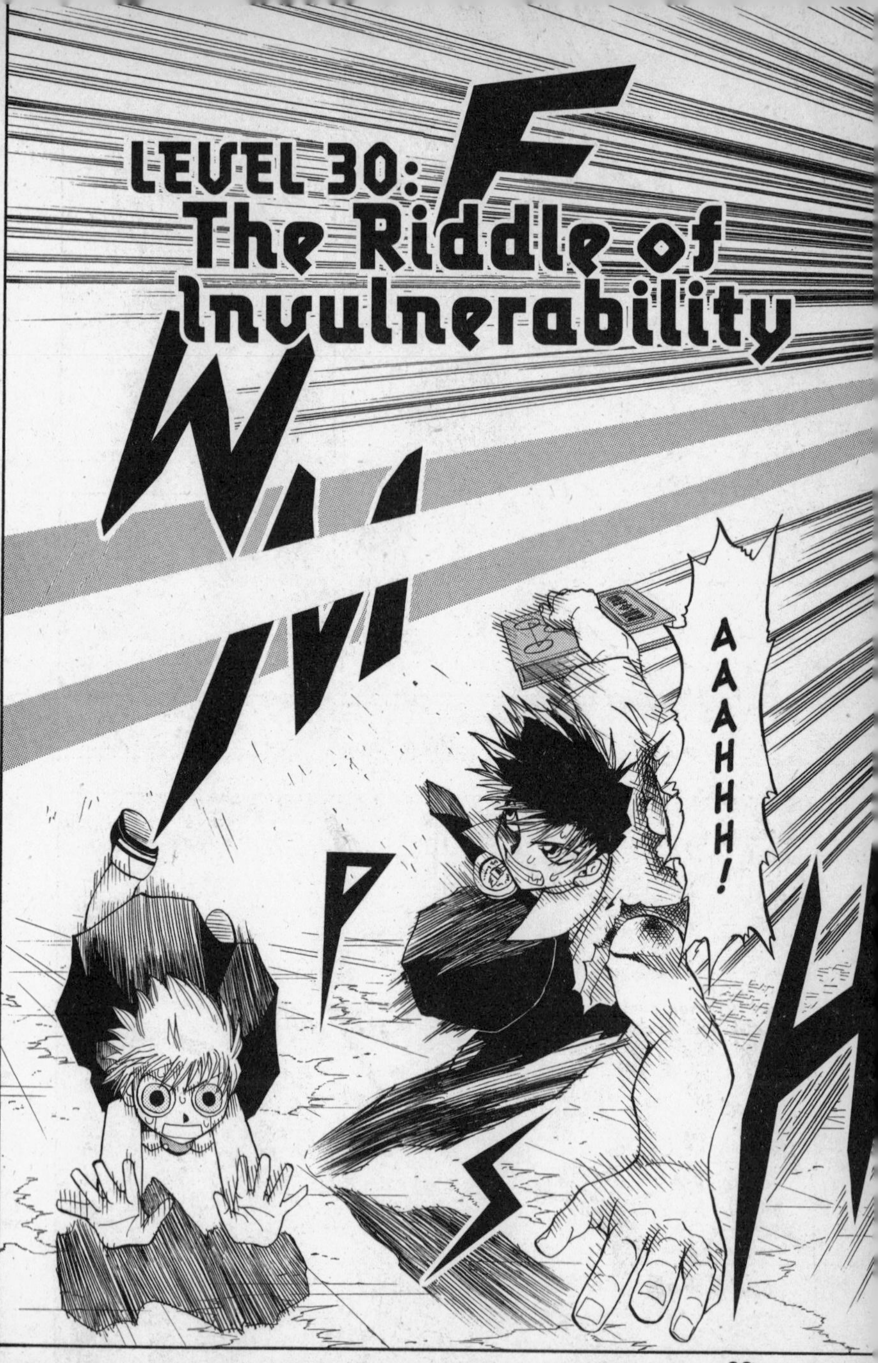
LEVEL 30:
The Riddle of Invulnerability
AAAHHH!

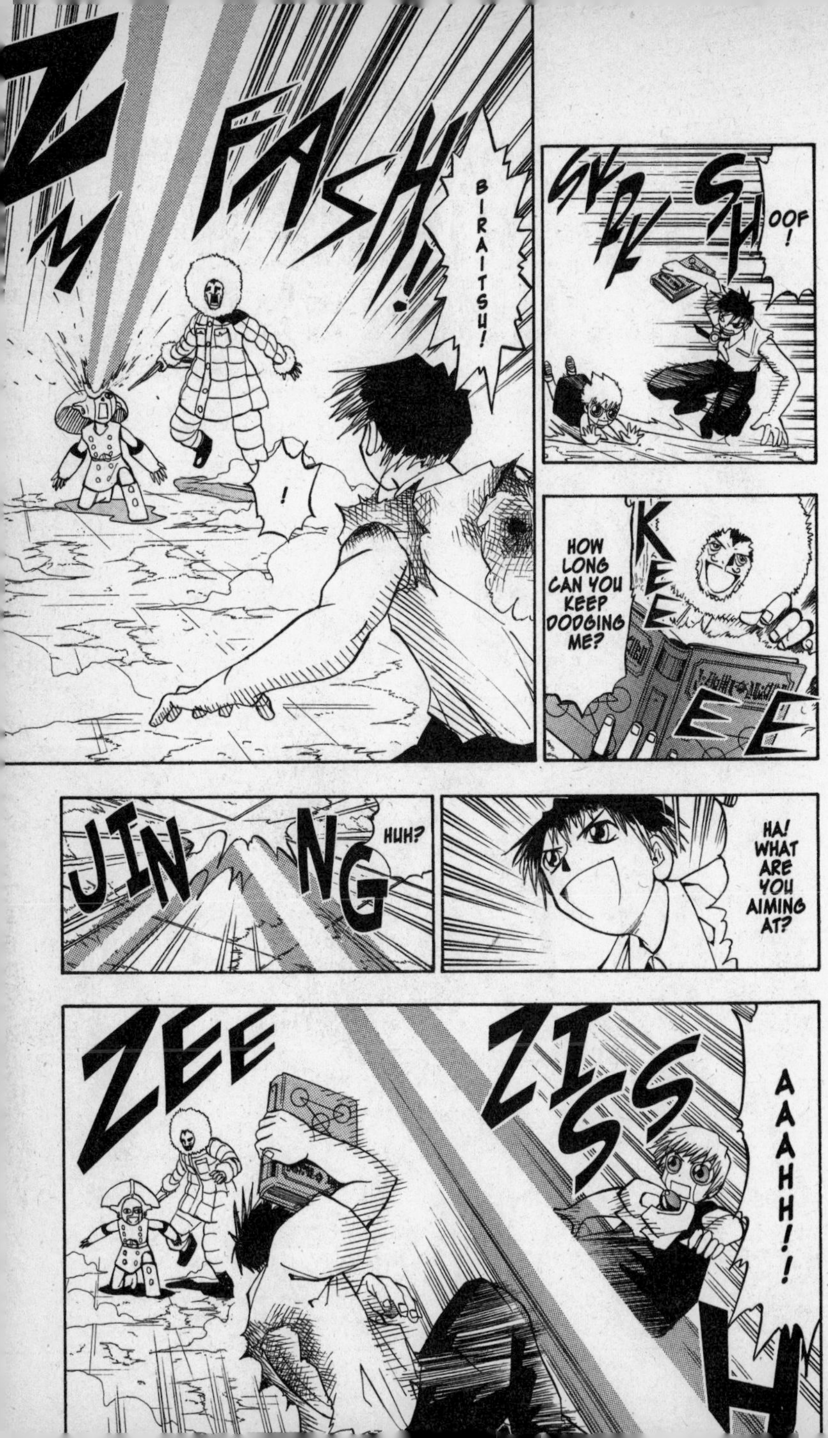
OOF!
HOW LONG CAN YOU KEEP DODGING ME?
KEEEE
ZM
FASH!!
BIRAITSU!
HA! WHAT ARE YOU AIMING AT?
HUH?
JINNG
AAAAHH!!
ZISS
ZEE

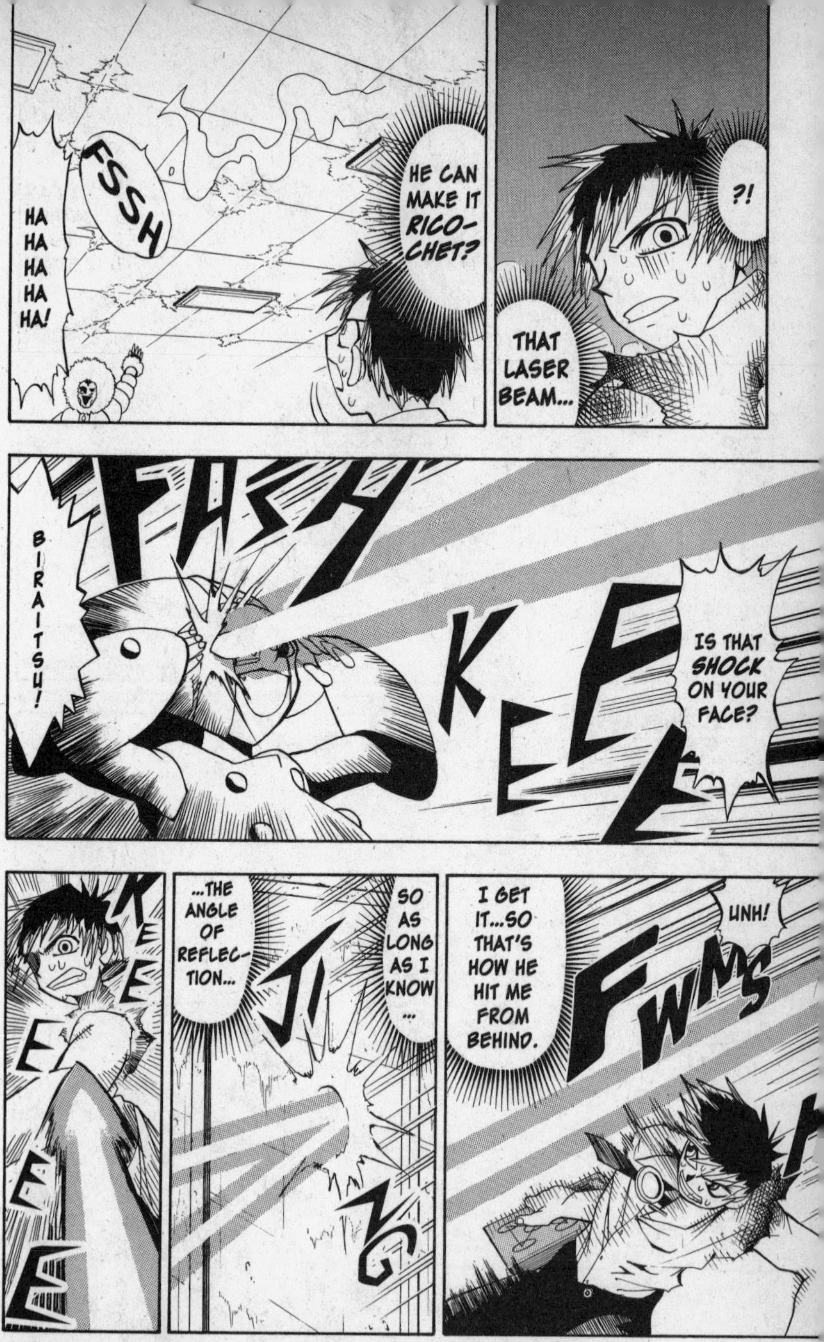
?!
THAT LASER BEAM...
HE CAN MAKE IT RICOCHET?
FSSH
HA HA HA HA HA!
IS THAT SHOCK ON YOUR FACE?
KEEE
FASH
BIRAITSU!
UNH!
FWMS
I GET IT...SO THAT'S HOW HE HIT ME FROM BEHIND.
SO AS LONG AS I KNOW...
...THE ANGLE OF REFLECTION...
JING
KEEEEE

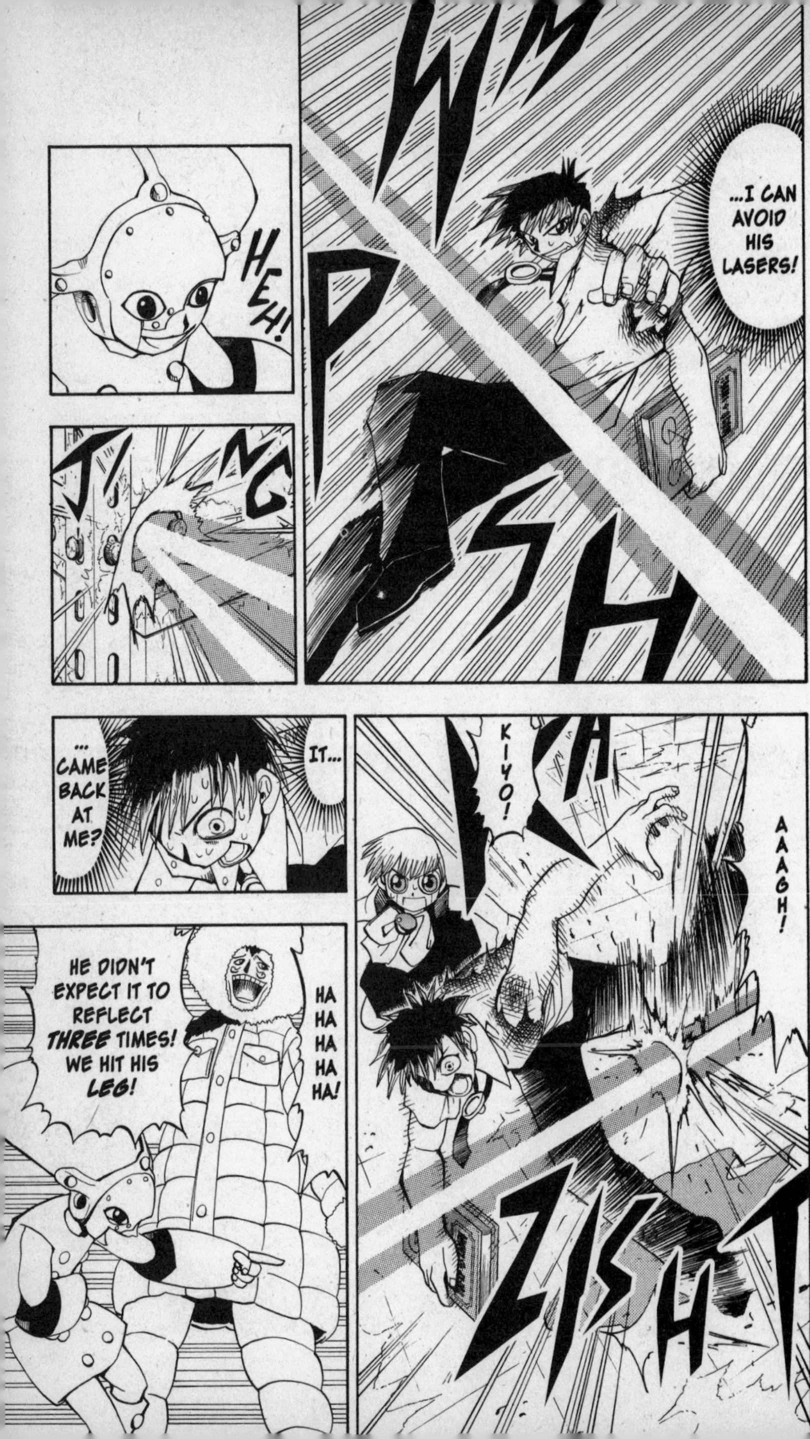
...I CAN AVOID HIS LASERS!
HEH!
JING
KIYO!
AAAGH!
ZISHT
IT...
...CAME BACK AT ME?
HE DIDN'T EXPECT IT TO REFLECT *THREE* TIMES! WE HIT HIS *LEG*!
HA HA HA HA HA!

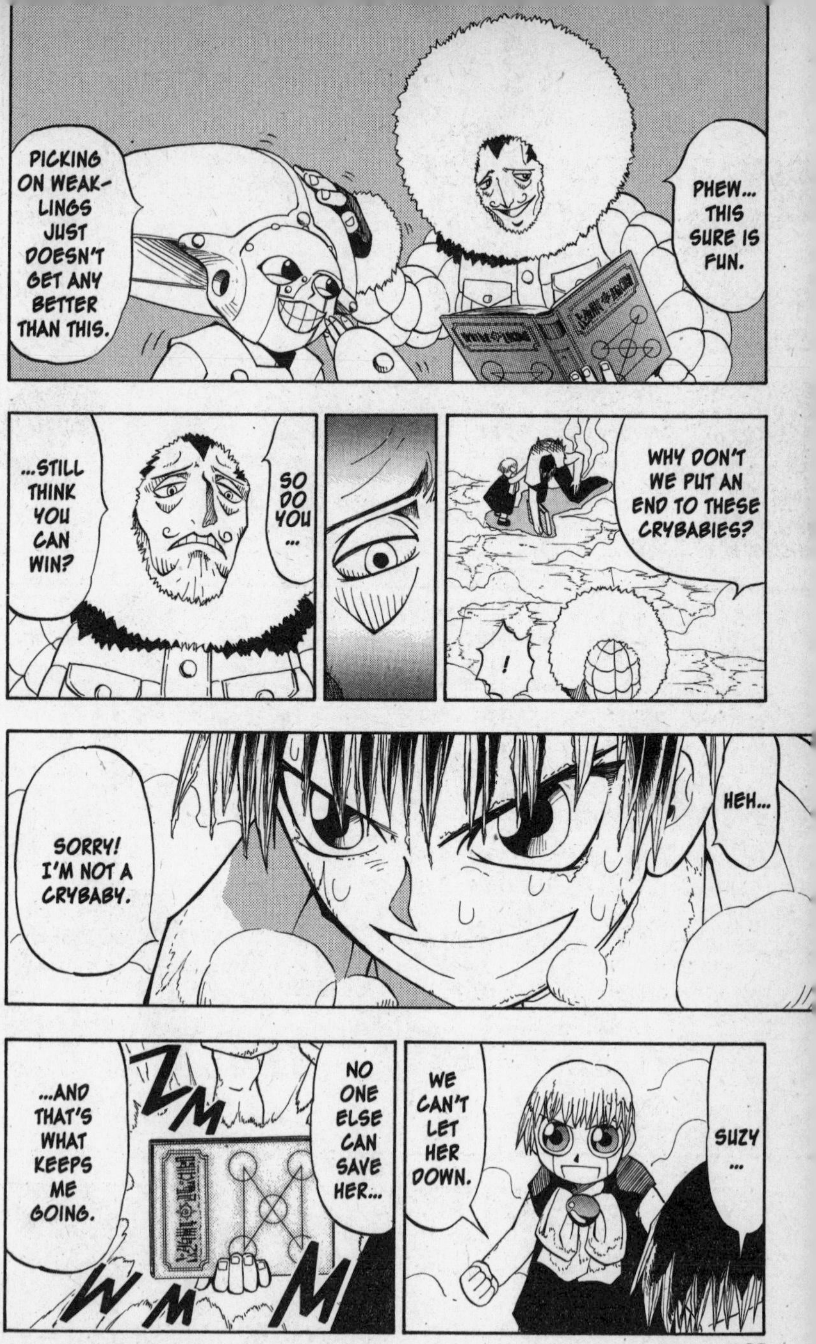
PHEW... THIS SURE IS FUN.
PICKING ON WEAKLINGS JUST DOESN'T GET ANY BETTER THAN THIS.
WHY DON'T WE PUT AN END TO THESE CRYBABIES?
!
SO DO YOU ...
...STILL THINK YOU CAN WIN?
HEH...
SORRY! I'M NOT A CRYBABY.
SUZY ...
WE CAN'T LET HER DOWN.
NO ONE ELSE CAN SAVE HER...
...AND THAT'S WHAT KEEPS ME GOING.
ZM
WMM
M

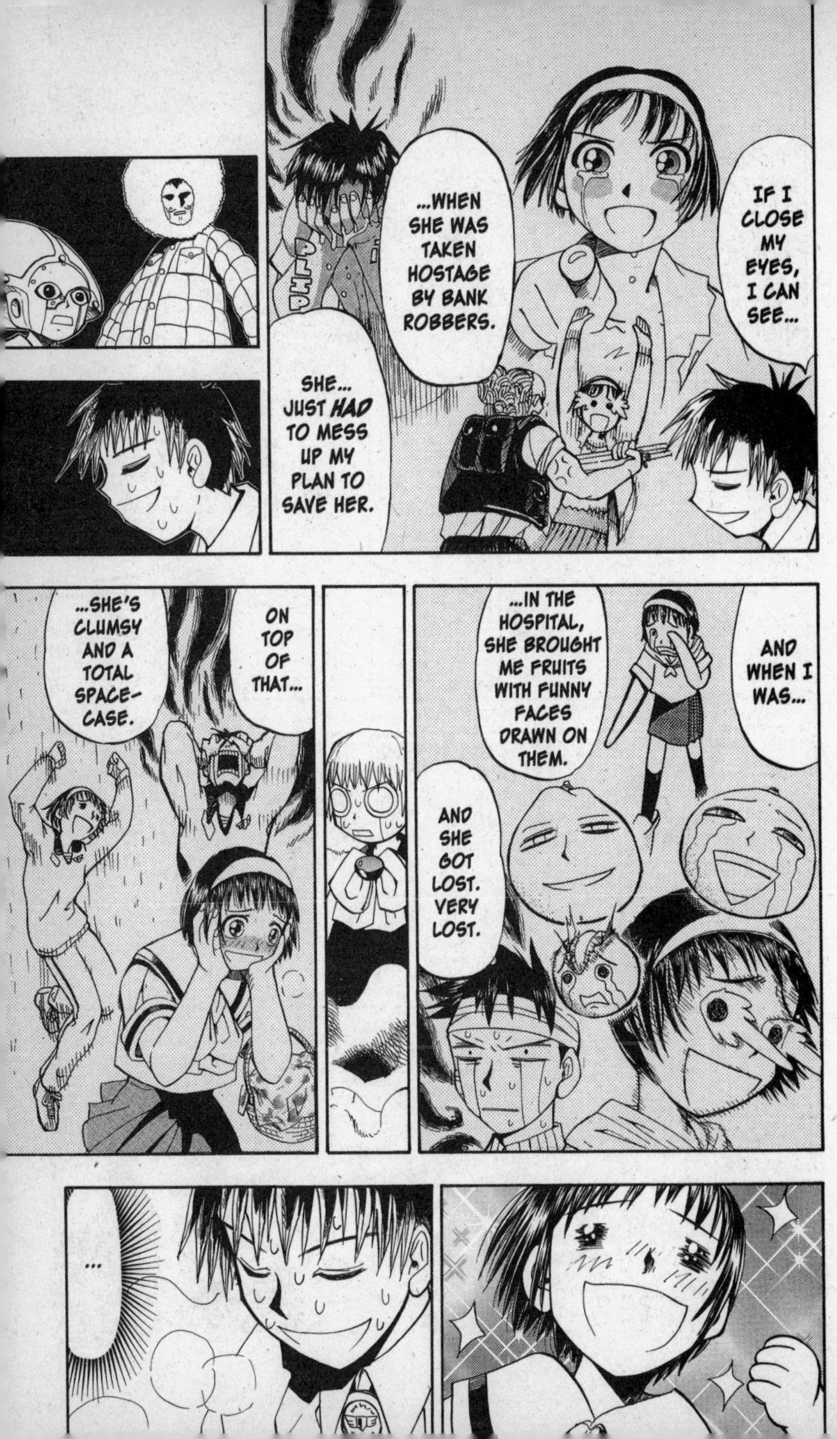
IF I CLOSE MY EYES, I CAN SEE...
...WHEN SHE WAS TAKEN HOSTAGE BY BANK ROBBERS.
SHE... JUST *HAD* TO MESS UP MY PLAN TO SAVE HER.
AND WHEN I WAS...
...IN THE HOSPITAL, SHE BROUGHT ME FRUITS WITH FUNNY FACES DRAWN ON THEM.
AND SHE GOT LOST. VERY LOST.
ON TOP OF THAT...
...SHE'S CLUMSY AND A TOTAL SPACE-CASE.
...

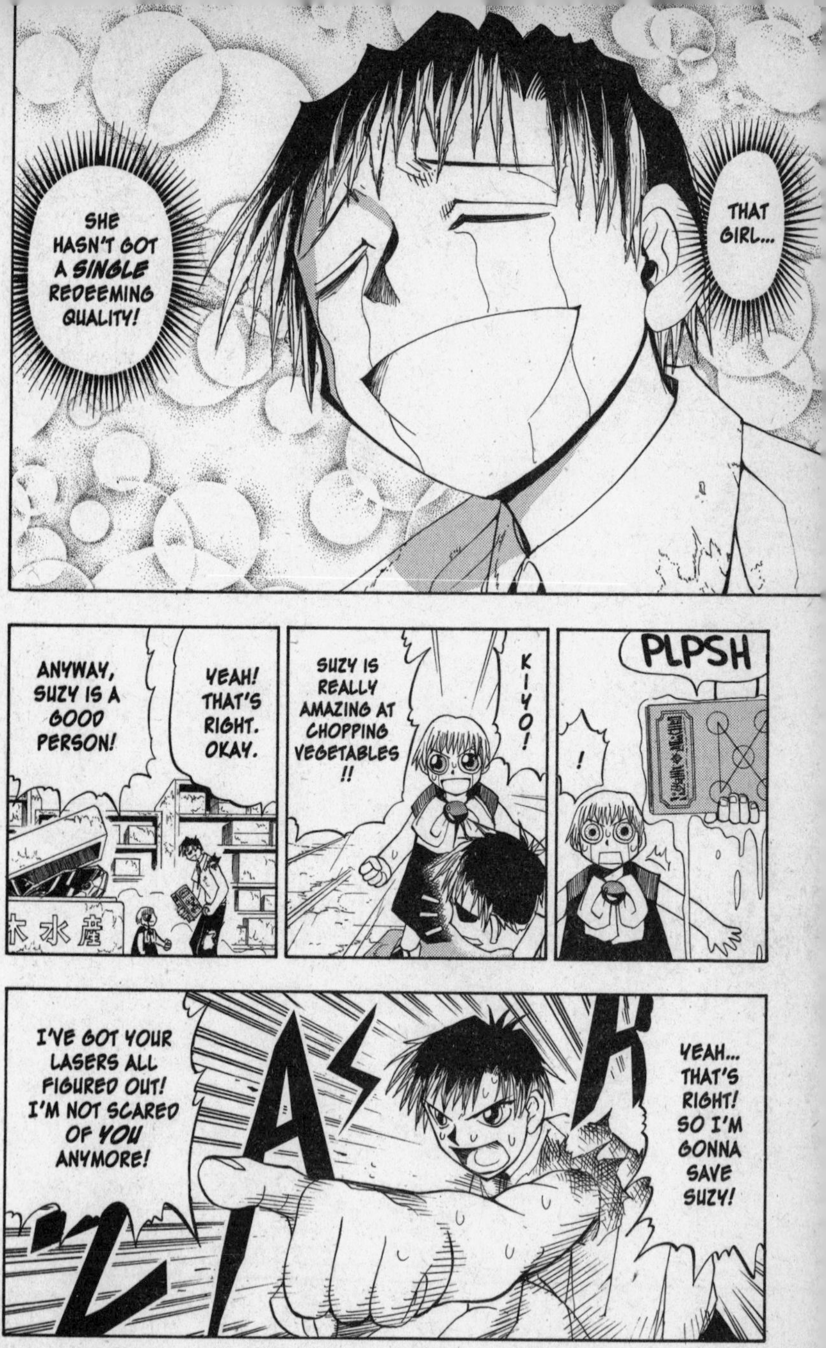
THAT GIRL...
SHE HASN'T GOT A SINGLE REDEEMING QUALITY!
PLPSH
!
KIYO!
SUZY IS REALLY AMAZING AT CHOPPING VEGETABLES !!
YEAH! THAT'S RIGHT. OKAY.
ANYWAY, SUZY IS A GOOD PERSON!
木水産
YEAH... THAT'S RIGHT! SO I'M GONNA SAVE SUZY!
I'VE GOT YOUR LASERS ALL FIGURED OUT! I'M NOT SCARED OF YOU ANYMORE!

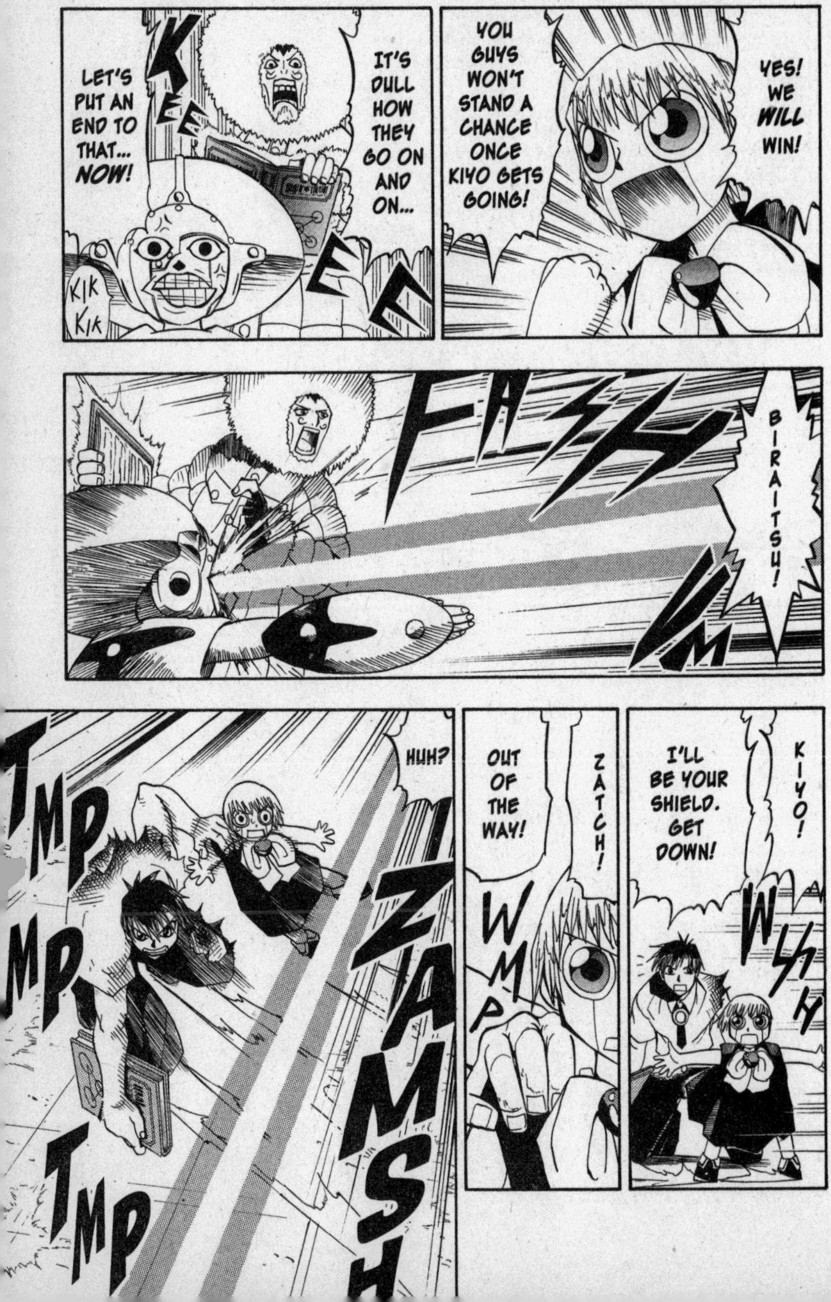

YES! WE WILL WIN!
YOU GUYS WON'T STAND A CHANCE ONCE KIYO GETS GOING!
IT'S DULL HOW THEY GO ON AND ON...
LET'S PUT AN END TO THAT... NOW!
KIK KIK
BIRAITSU!
KIYO!
I'LL BE YOUR SHIELD. GET DOWN!
ZATCH!
OUT OF THE WAY!
WMP
HUH?
ZAMSH
TMP
TMP
TMP

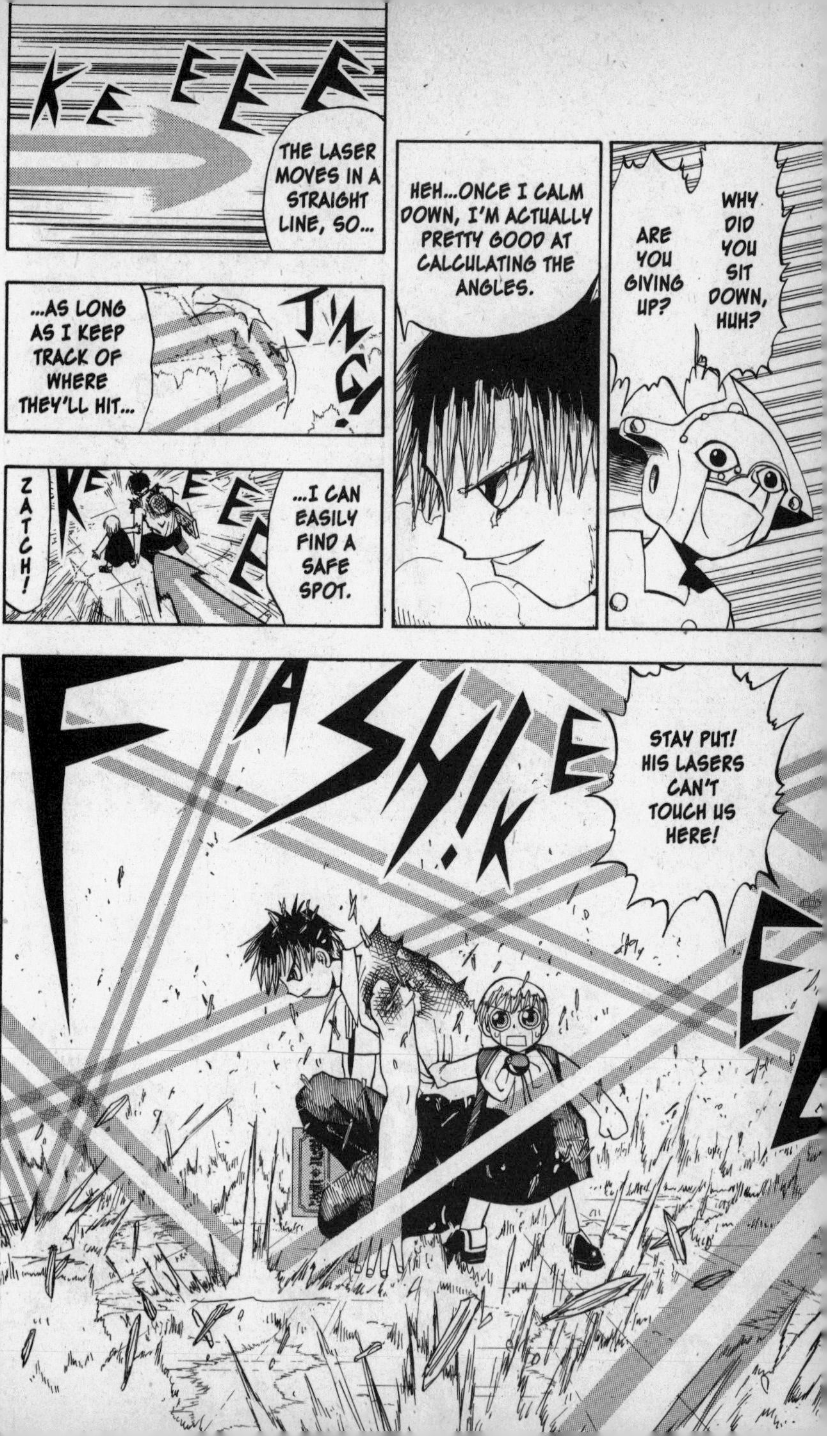
WHY DID YOU SIT DOWN, HUH?
ARE YOU GIVING UP?
HEH...ONCE I CALM DOWN, I'M ACTUALLY PRETTY GOOD AT CALCULATING THE ANGLES.
THE LASER MOVES IN A STRAIGHT LINE, SO...
KEEEE
JING!
...AS LONG AS I KEEP TRACK OF WHERE THEY'LL HIT...
...I CAN EASILY FIND A SAFE SPOT.
KEEEE
ZATCH!
STAY PUT! HIS LASERS CAN'T TOUCH US HERE!
FASHIEK!

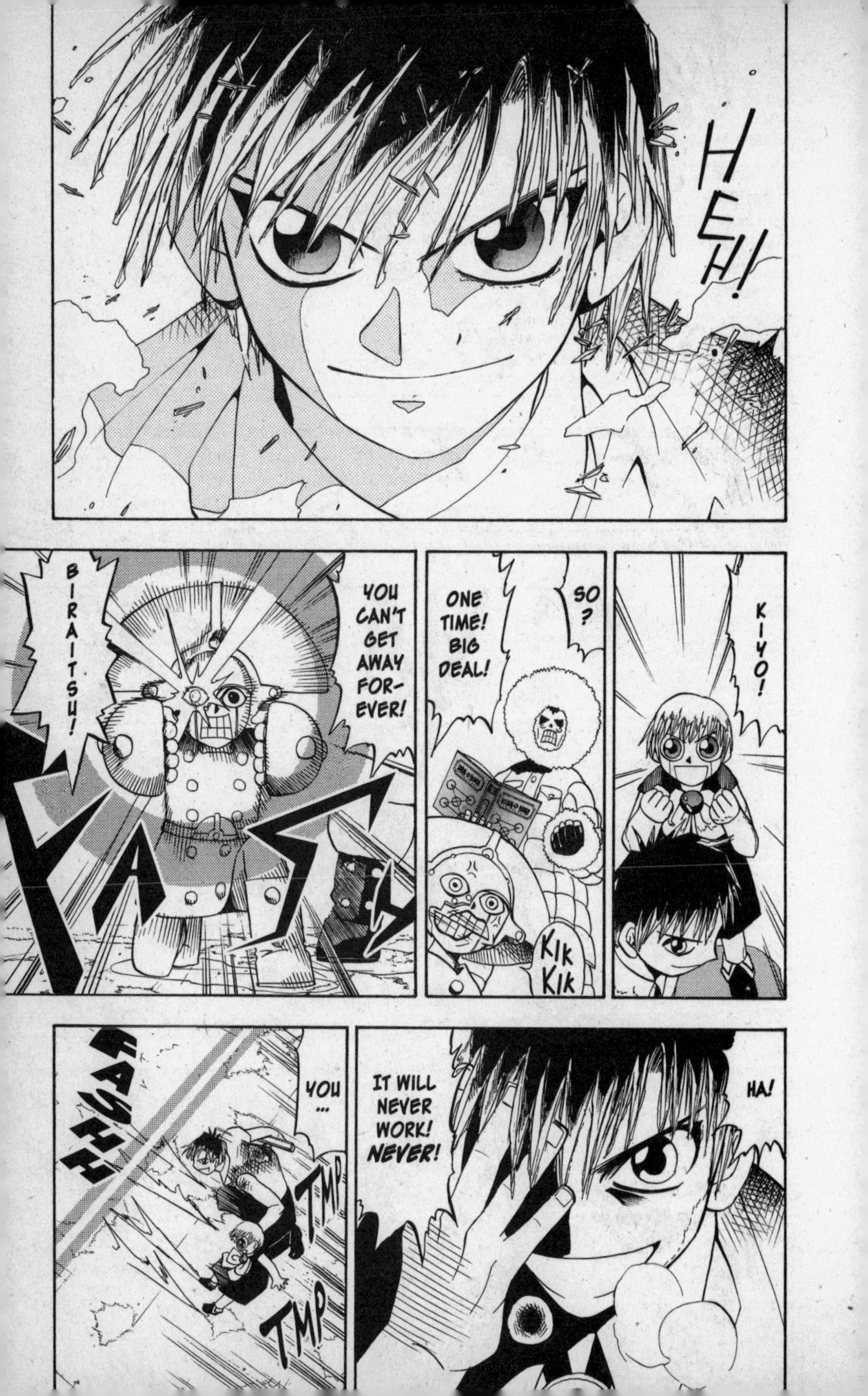
HEH!
KIYO!
SO?
ONE TIME! BIG DEAL!
KIK KIK
YOU CAN'T GET AWAY FOR-EVER!
BIRAITSU!
HA!
IT WILL NEVER WORK! NEVER!
YOU...
TMP
TMP
FASH

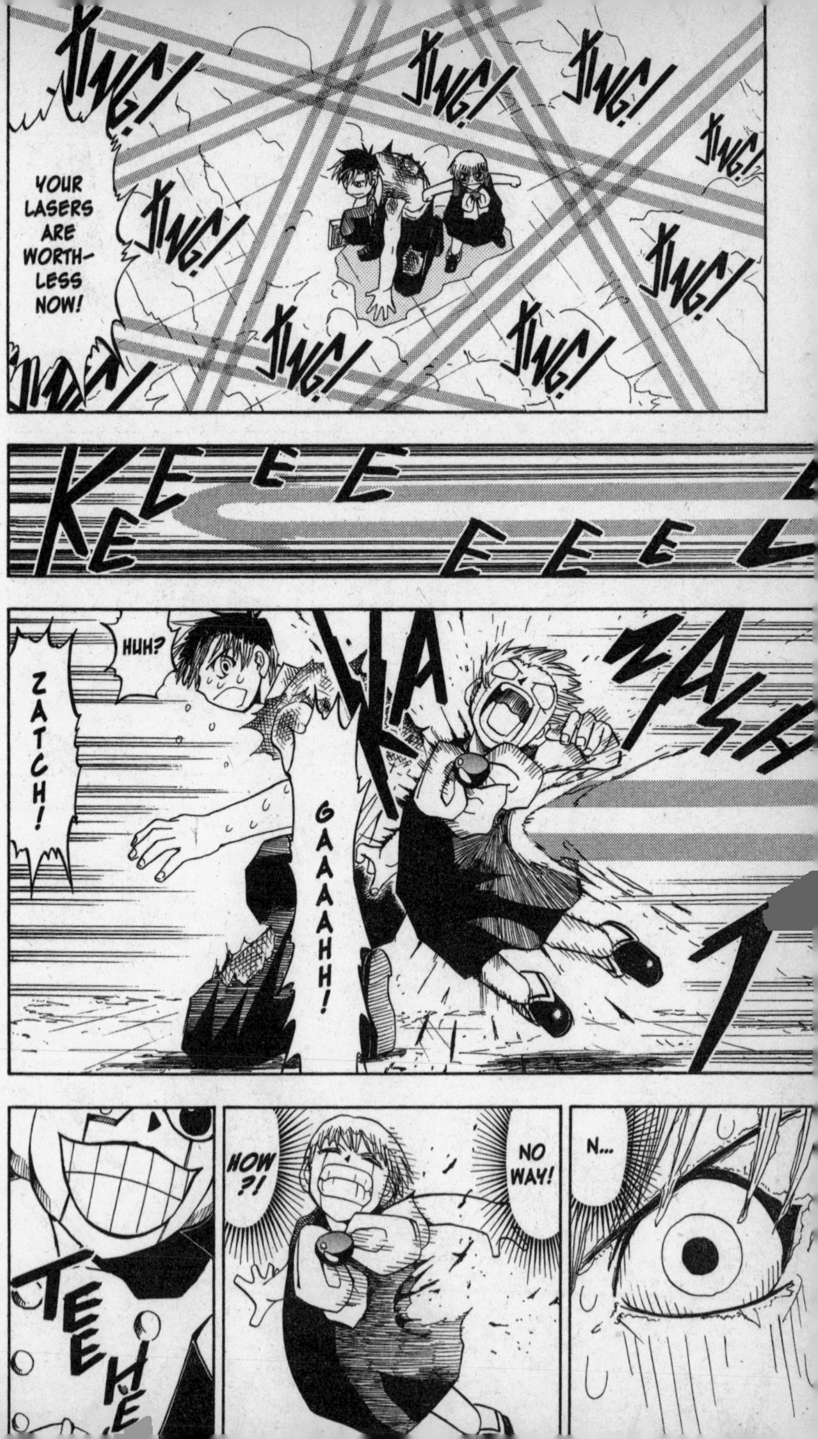
JING!
JING!
JING!
JING!
JING!
JING!
JING!
JING!
YOUR LASERS ARE WORTH-LESS NOW!
KEEEEEEEE
HUH?
ZATCH!
GAAAAAHH!
N...
NO WAY!
HOW?!
TEEHEE

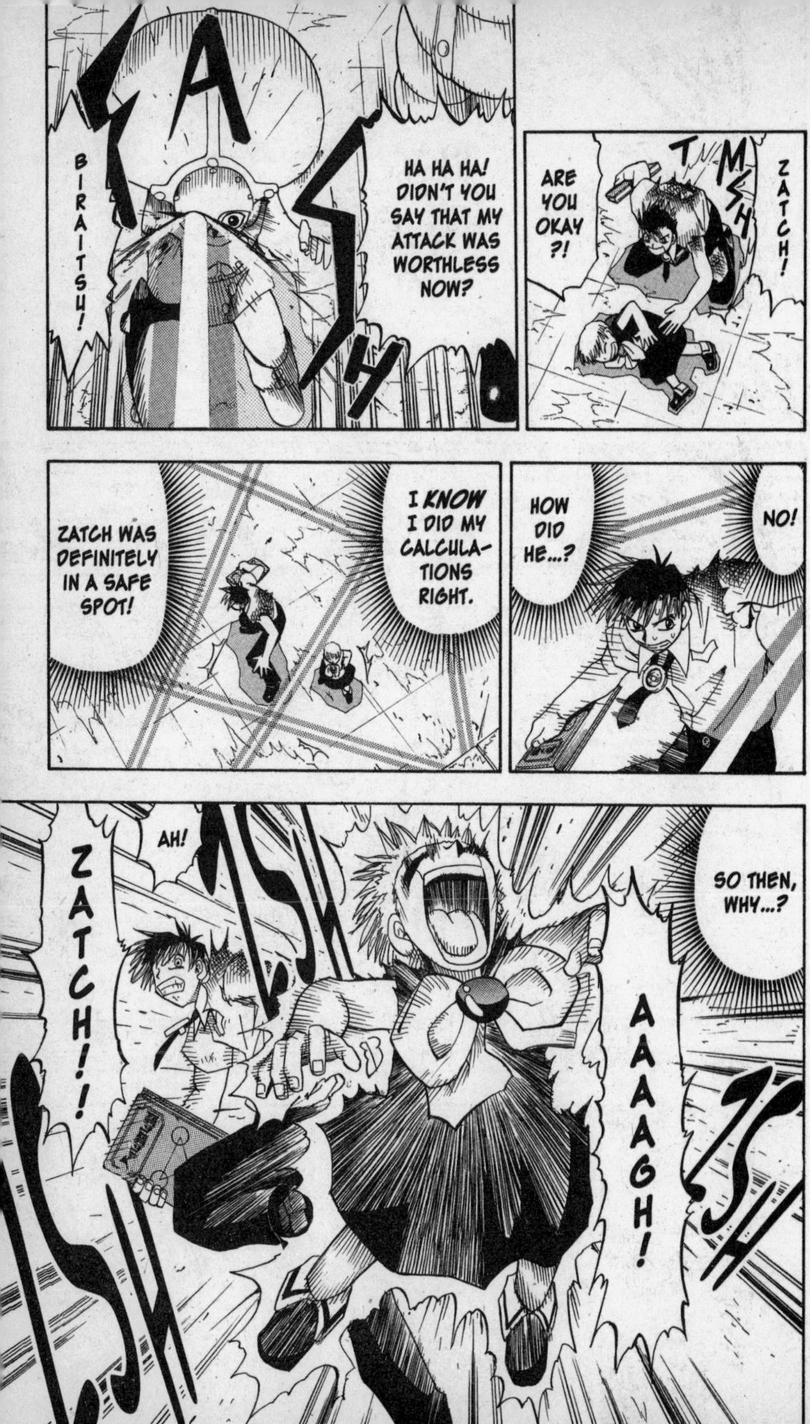
ZATCH!
TMSH
ARE YOU OKAY?!
KASH
HA HA HA! DIDN'T YOU SAY THAT MY ATTACK WAS WORTHLESS NOW?
BIRAITSU!
NO!
HOW DID HE...?
I *KNOW* I DID MY CALCULATIONS RIGHT.
ZATCH WAS DEFINITELY IN A SAFE SPOT!
SO THEN, WHY...?
TSH
AAAAGH!
AH!
ZATCH!!!

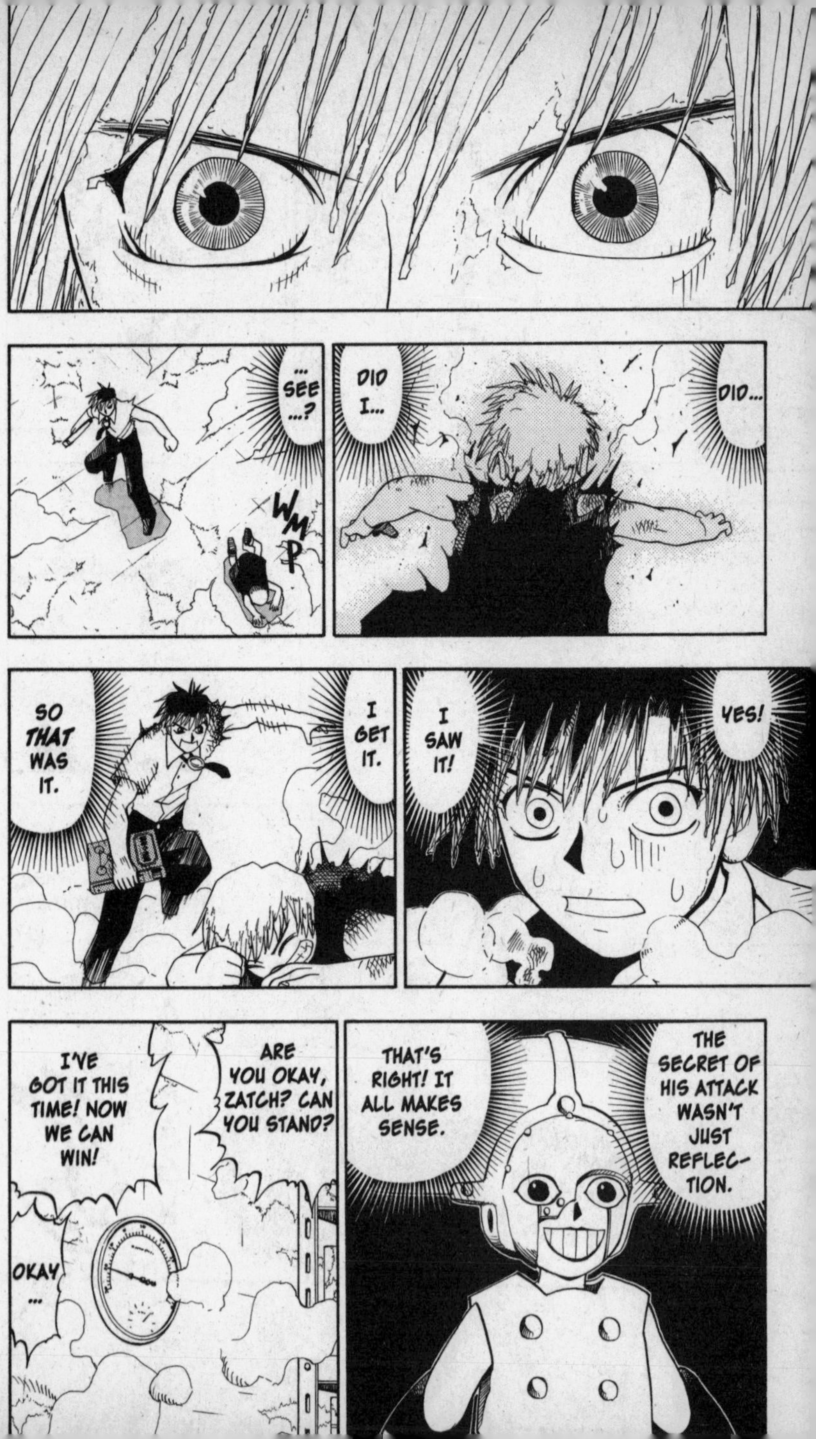
DID...
DID I...
...SEE ...?
WMP
YES!
I SAW IT!
I GET IT.
SO THAT WAS IT.
THE SECRET OF HIS ATTACK WASN'T JUST REFLECTION.
THAT'S RIGHT! IT ALL MAKES SENSE.
ARE YOU OKAY, ZATCH? CAN YOU STAND?
I'VE GOT IT THIS TIME! NOW WE CAN WIN!
OKAY ...

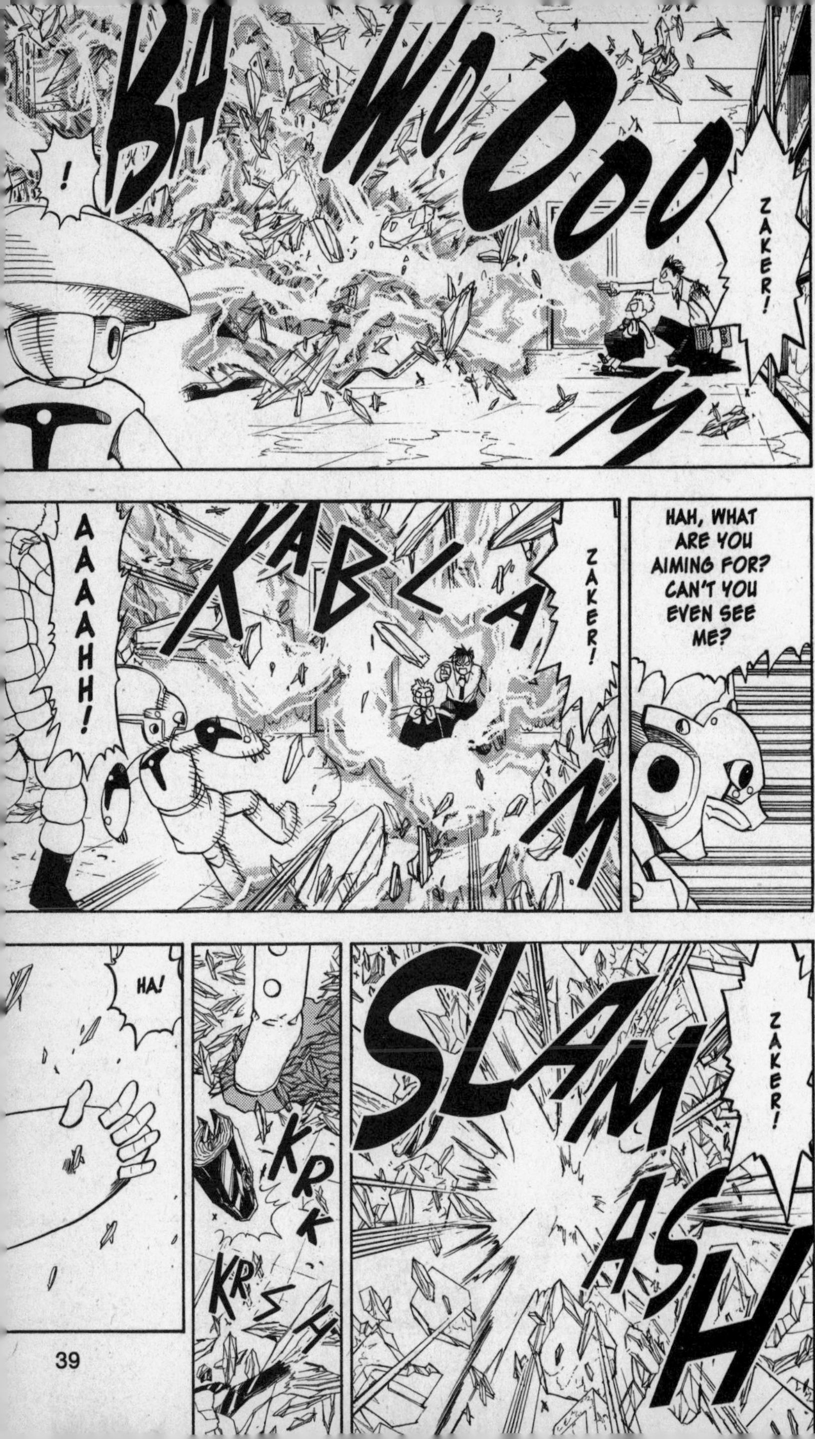
ZAKER!
BA WOOOOM
!
HAH, WHAT ARE YOU AIMING FOR? CAN'T YOU EVEN SEE ME?
ZAKER!
KABLAM
AAAAAHH!
ZAKER!
SLAMASH
KRK
KRSH
HA!

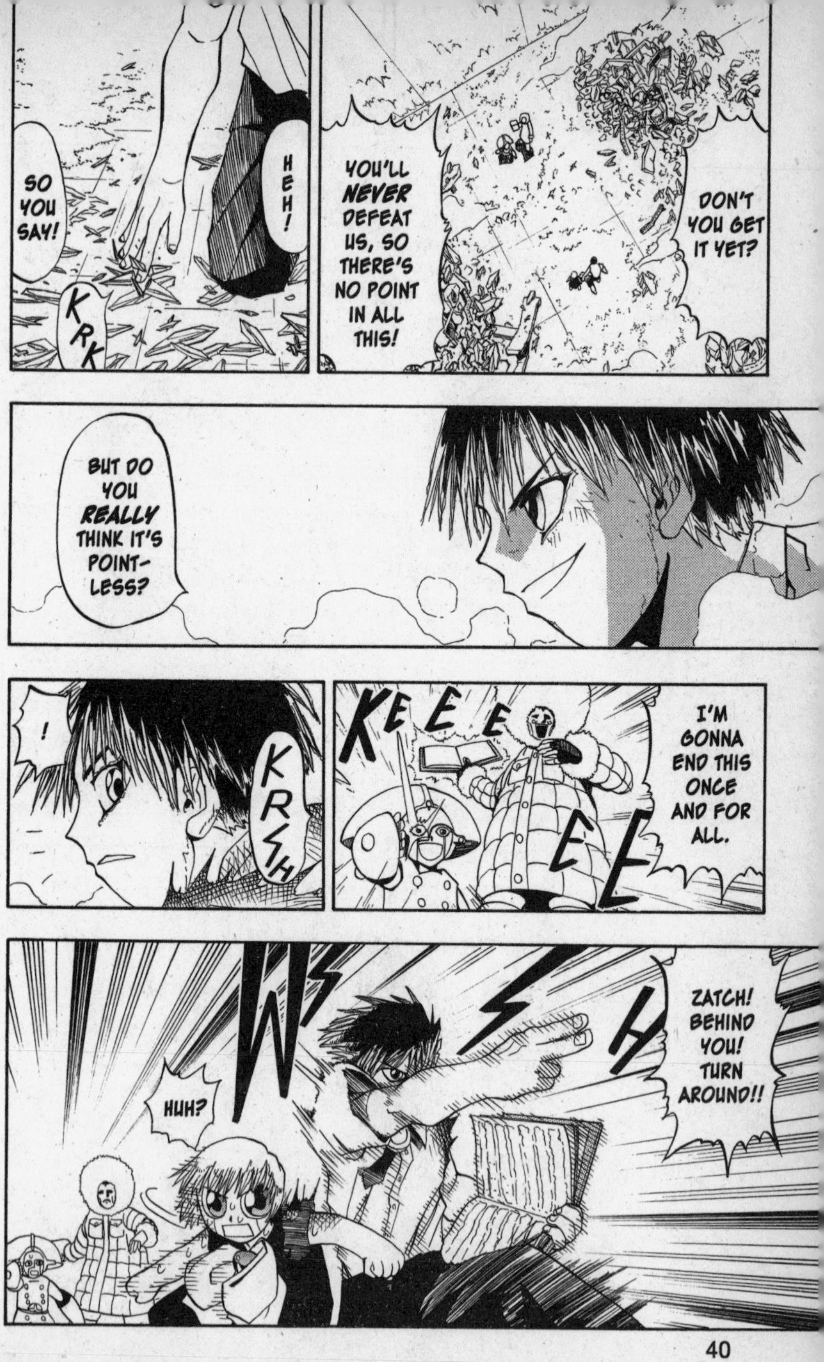
DON'T YOU GET IT YET?
YOU'LL NEVER DEFEAT US, SO THERE'S NO POINT IN ALL THIS!
HEH!
SO YOU SAY!
KRK
BUT DO YOU REALLY THINK IT'S POINTLESS?
I'M GONNA END THIS ONCE AND FOR ALL.
KEEEEE
KRSH
!
ZATCH! BEHIND YOU! TURN AROUND!!
WSSH
HUH?

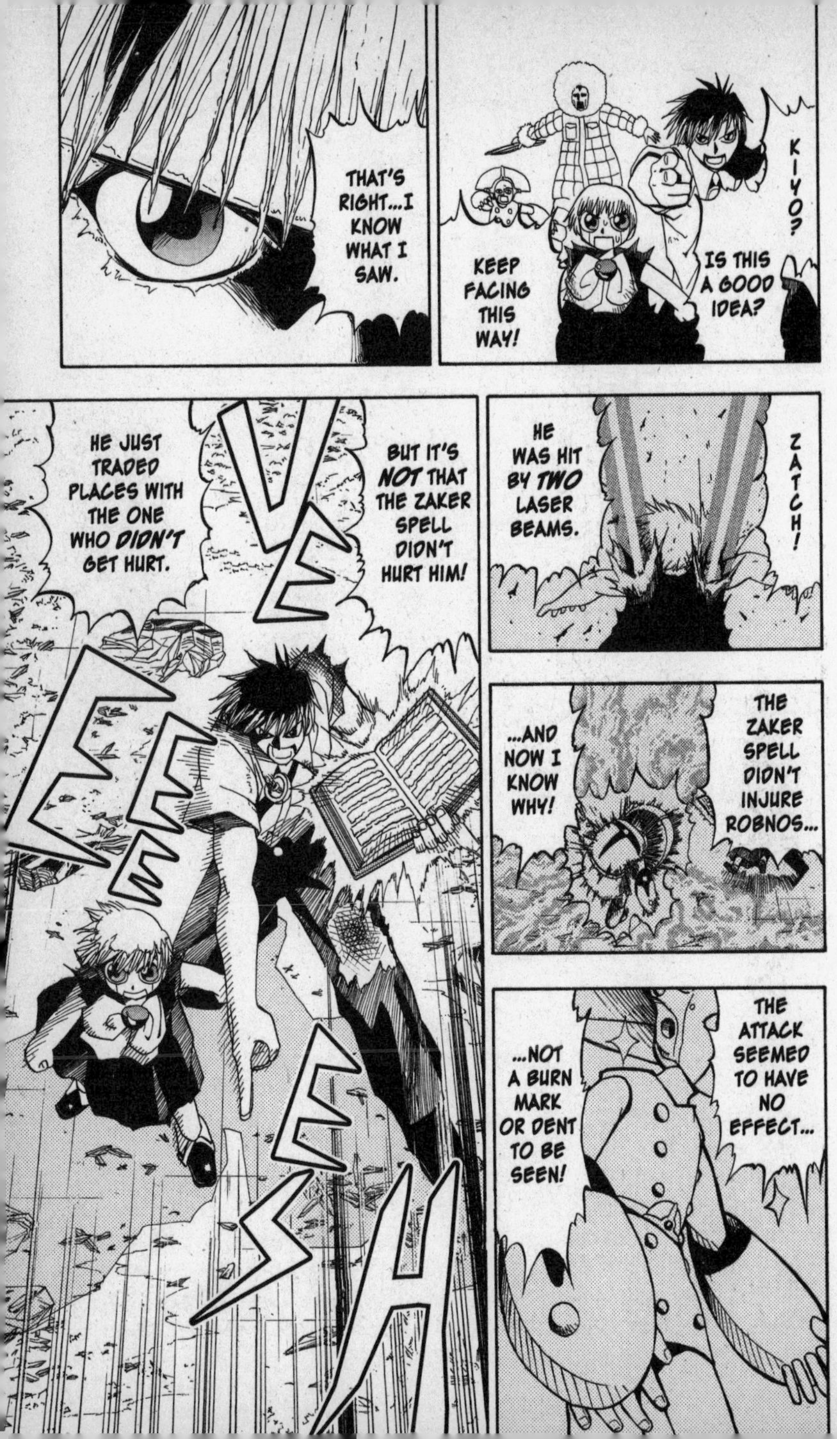
KIYO?
IS THIS A GOOD IDEA?
KEEP FACING THIS WAY!
THAT'S RIGHT...I KNOW WHAT I SAW.
ZATCH!
HE WAS HIT BY *TWO* LASER BEAMS.
THE ZAKER SPELL DIDN'T INJURE ROBNOS...
...AND NOW I KNOW WHY!
THE ATTACK SEEMED TO HAVE NO EFFECT...
...NOT A BURN MARK OR DENT TO BE SEEN!
BUT IT'S *NOT* THAT THE ZAKER SPELL DIDN'T HURT HIM!
HE JUST TRADED PLACES WITH THE ONE WHO *DIDN'T* GET HURT.
VEEEEESH

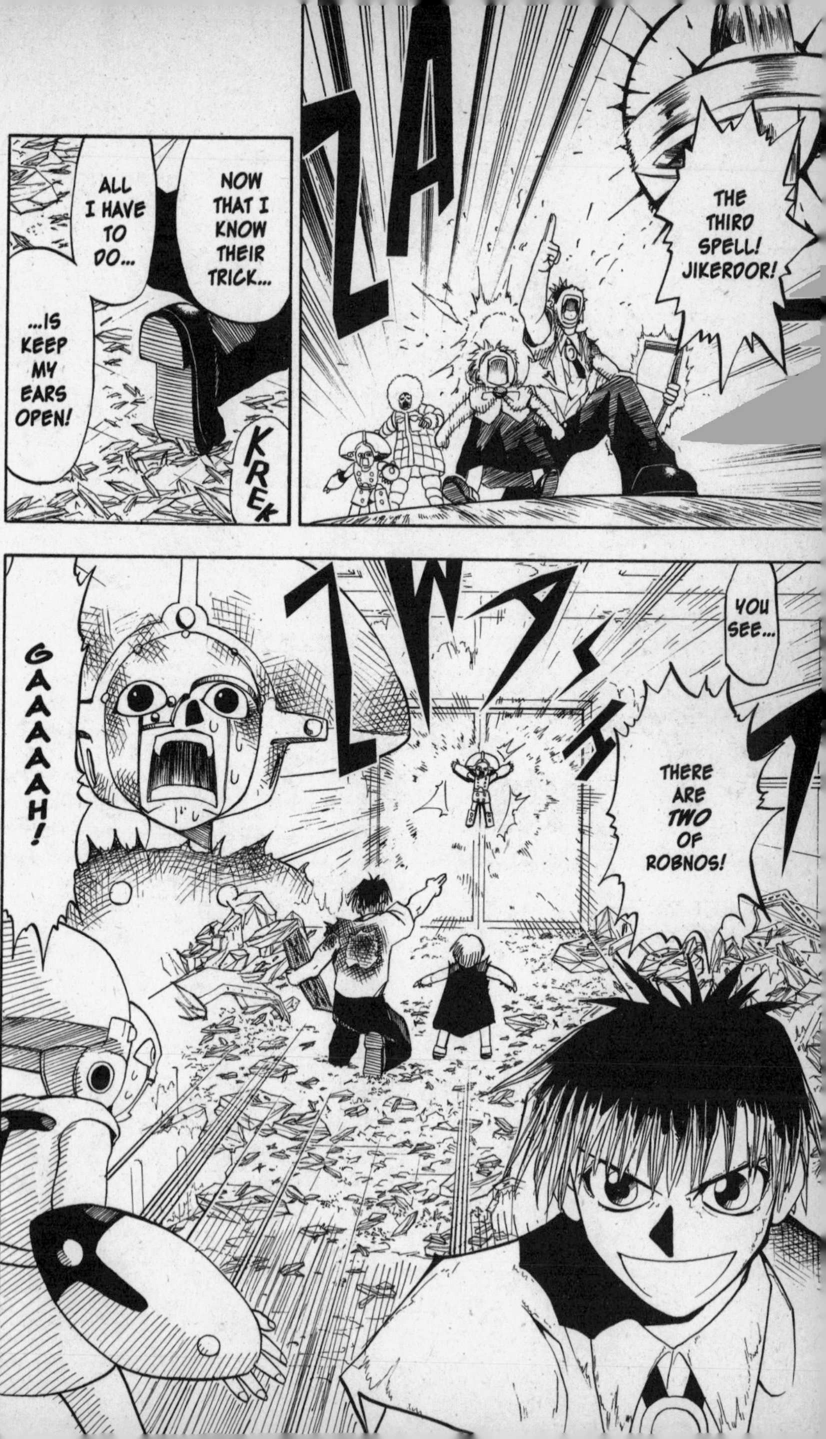
ZA
THE THIRD SPELL! JIKERDOOR!
NOW THAT I KNOW THEIR TRICK...
ALL I HAVE TO DO...
...IS KEEP MY EARS OPEN!
KREK
YOU SEE...
ZWASH
THERE ARE *TWO* OF ROBNOS!
GAAAAAAH!

LEVEL 31: A Final Message

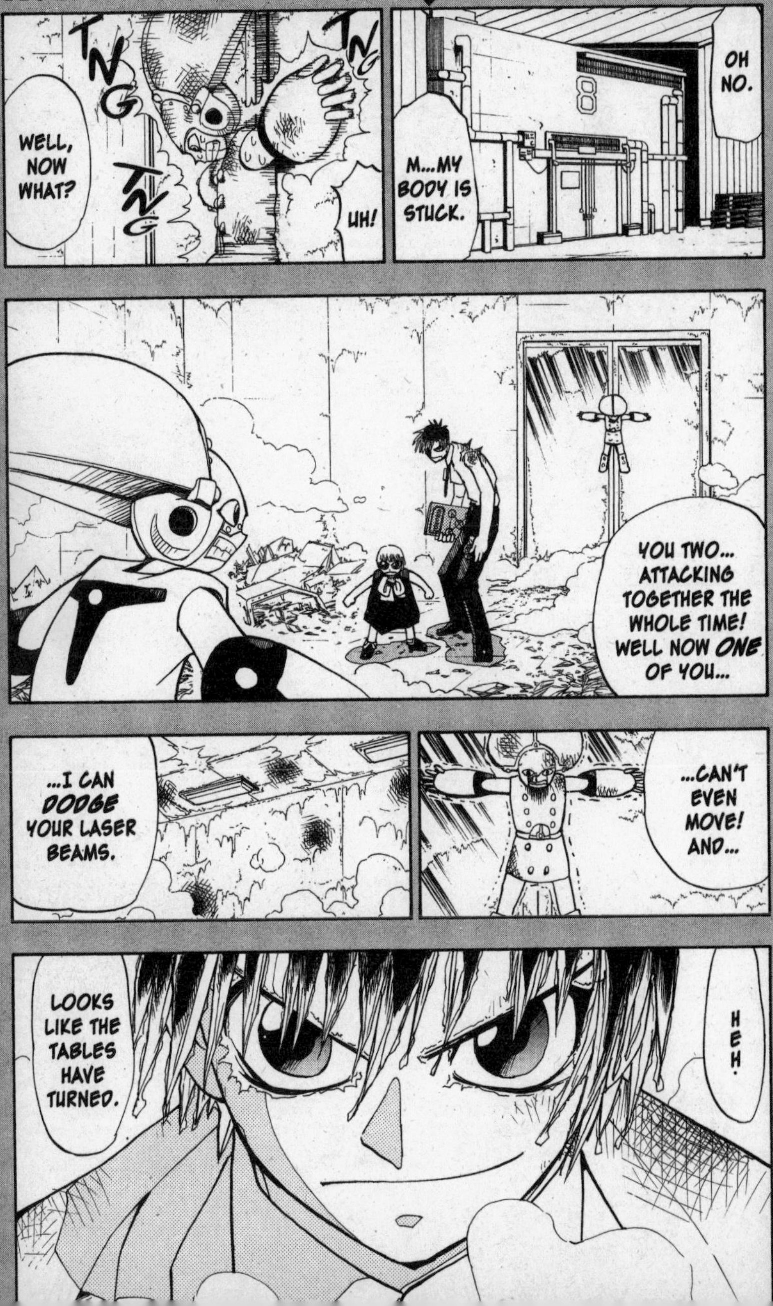
OH NO.
M...MY BODY IS STUCK.
TNG
TNG
TNG
UH!
WELL, NOW WHAT?
YOU TWO... ATTACKING TOGETHER THE WHOLE TIME! WELL NOW *ONE* OF YOU...
...CAN'T EVEN MOVE! AND...
...I CAN *DODGE* YOUR LASER BEAMS.
HEH.
LOOKS LIKE THE TABLES HAVE TURNED.

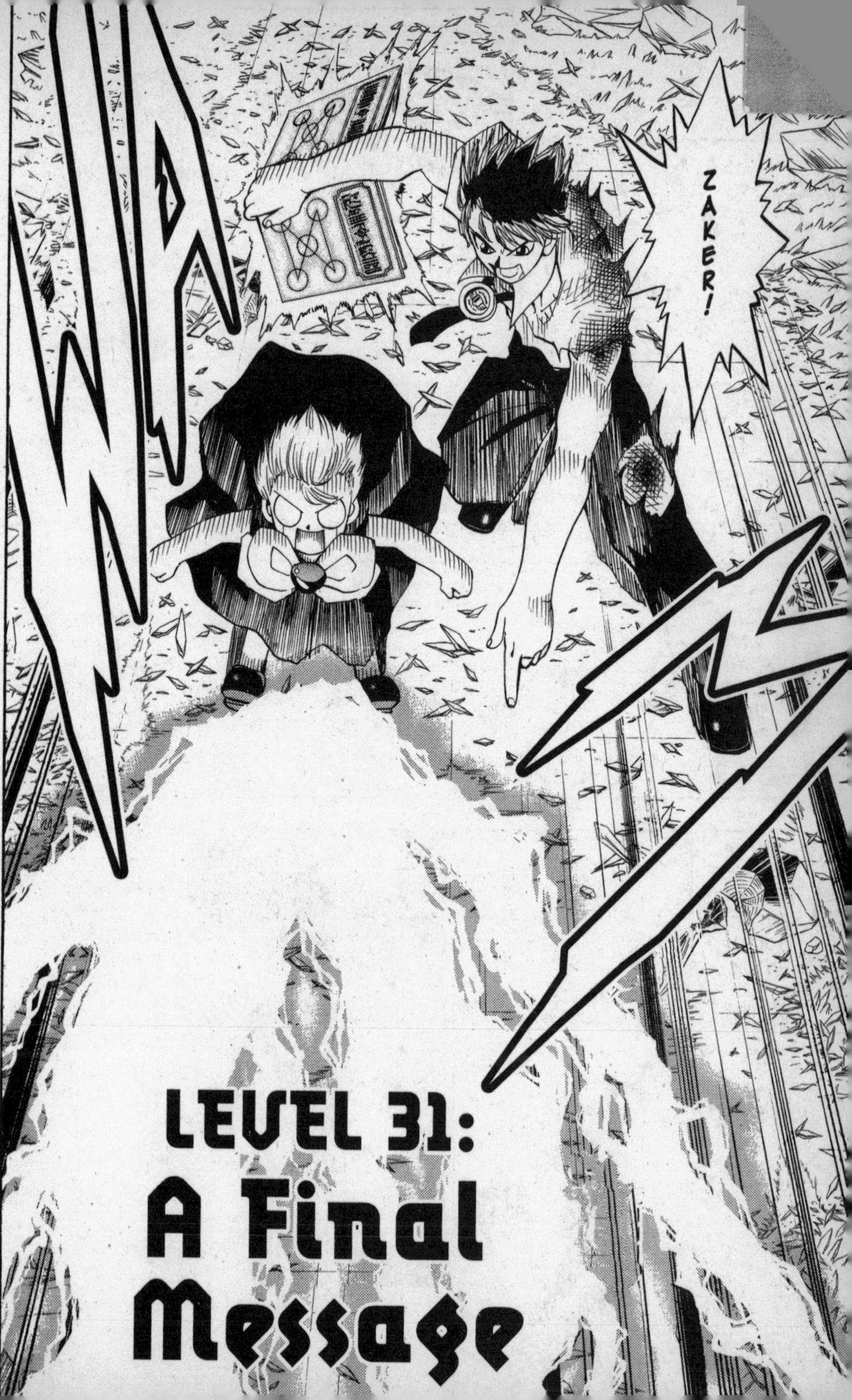
ZAKER!
LEVEL 31:
A Final Message

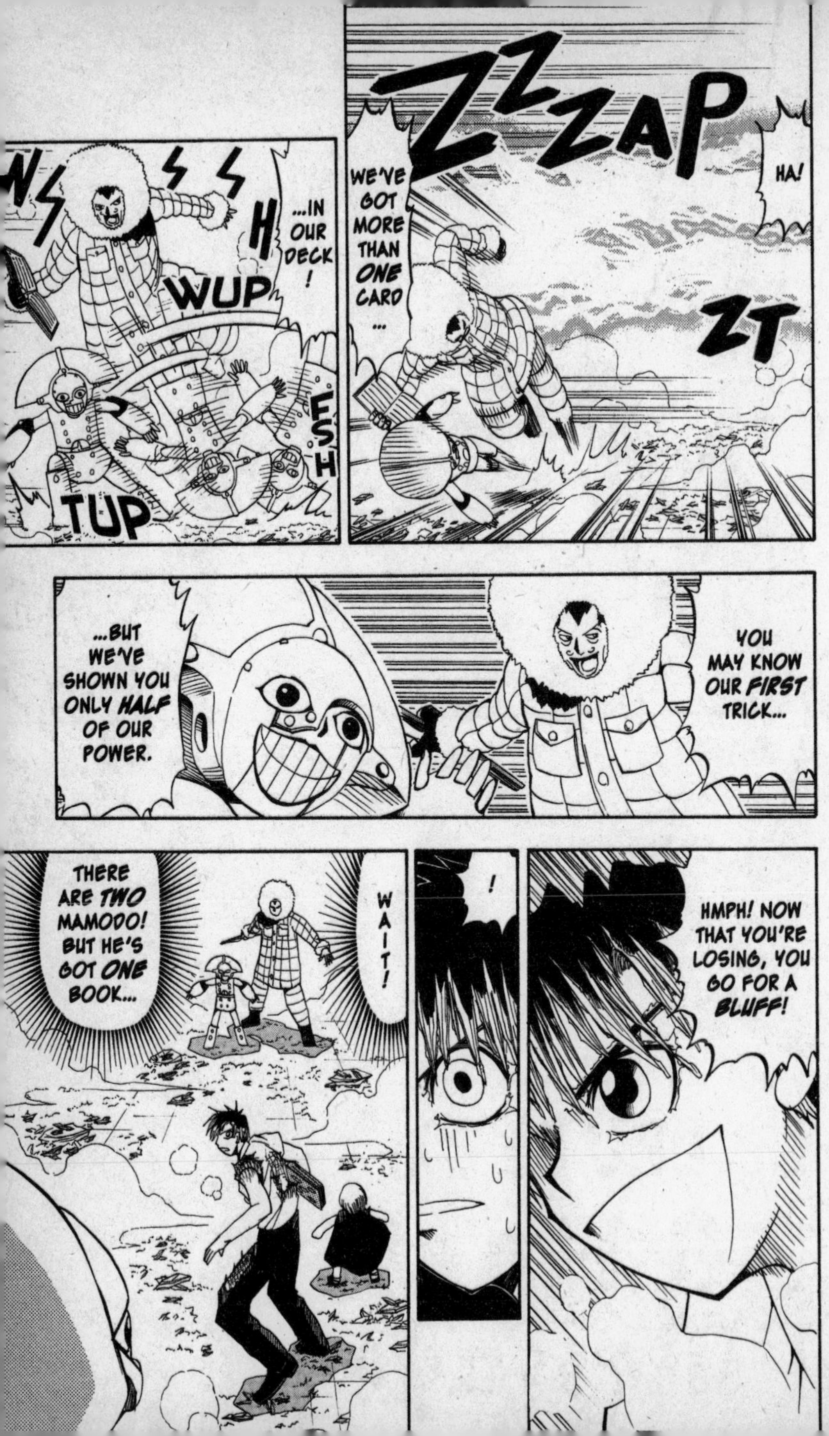
ZZZAP
HA! HA!
WE'VE GOT MORE THAN ONE CARD...
ZT
...IN OUR DECK!
WUP
FSH
TUP
YOU MAY KNOW OUR FIRST TRICK...
...BUT WE'VE SHOWN YOU ONLY HALF OF OUR POWER.
HMPH! NOW THAT YOU'RE LOSING, YOU GO FOR A BLUFF!
!
WAIT!
THERE ARE TWO MAMODO! BUT HE'S GOT ONE BOOK...

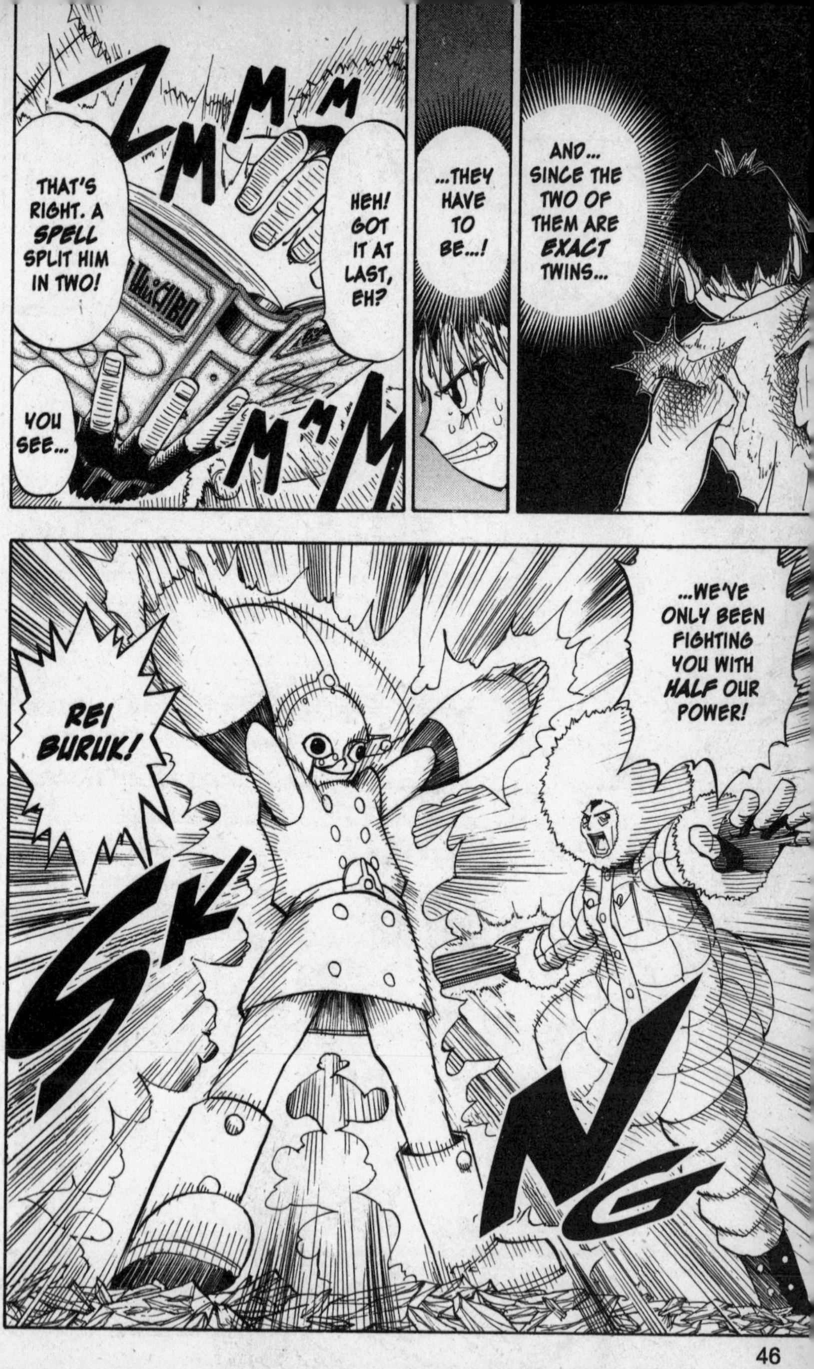
AND... SINCE THE TWO OF THEM ARE EXACT TWINS...
...THEY HAVE TO BE...!
HEH! GOT IT AT LAST, EH?
THAT'S RIGHT. A SPELL SPLIT HIM IN TWO!
ZMMMM
YOU SEE...
MMM
...WE'VE ONLY BEEN FIGHTING YOU WITH HALF OUR POWER!
REI BURUK!
SKNG

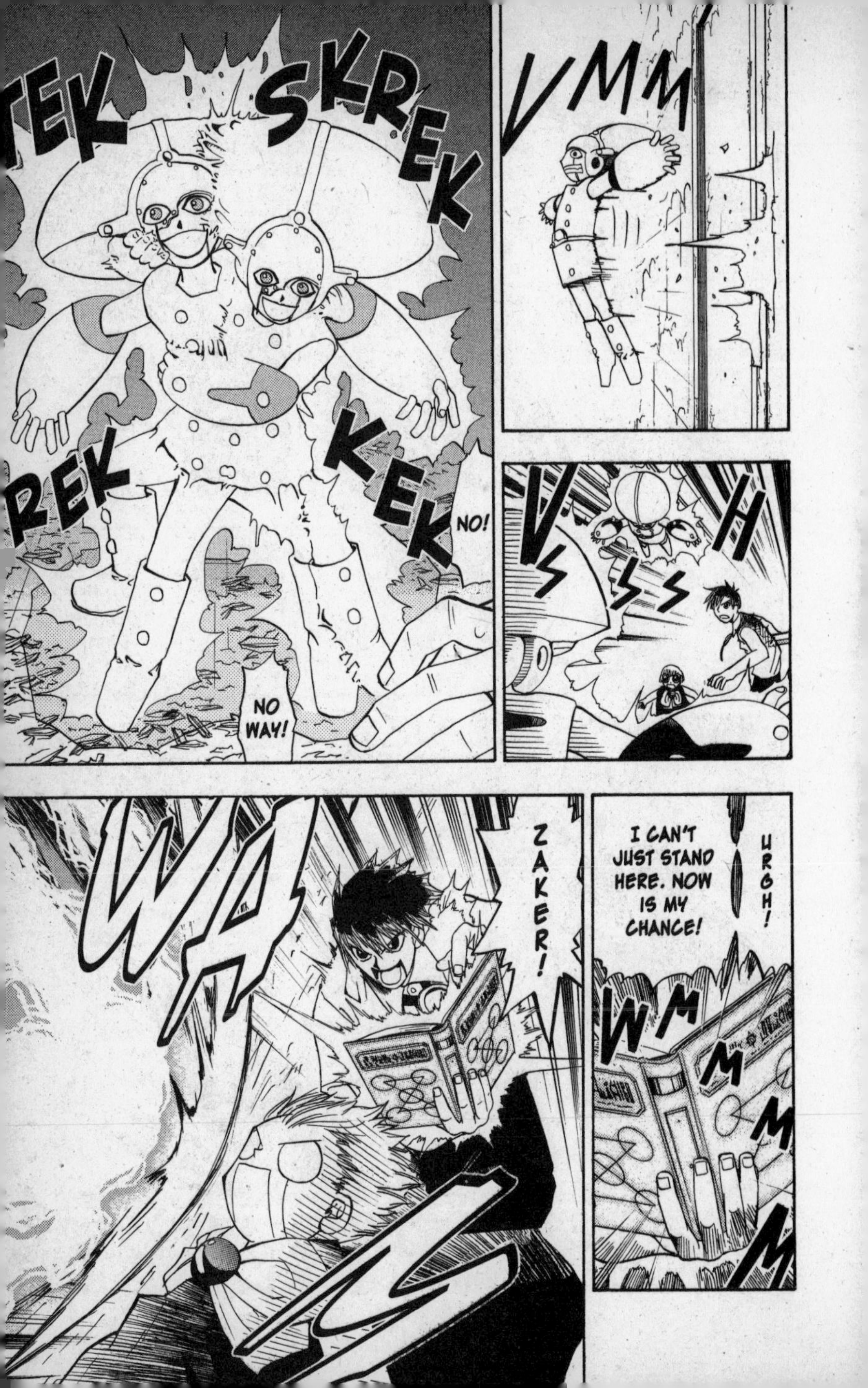
VMMM
V SSS H
SKREK
TEK
KEK
REK
NO!
NO WAY!
URGH!
I CAN'T JUST STAND HERE. NOW IS MY CHANCE!
WMMMM
ZAKER!
WA

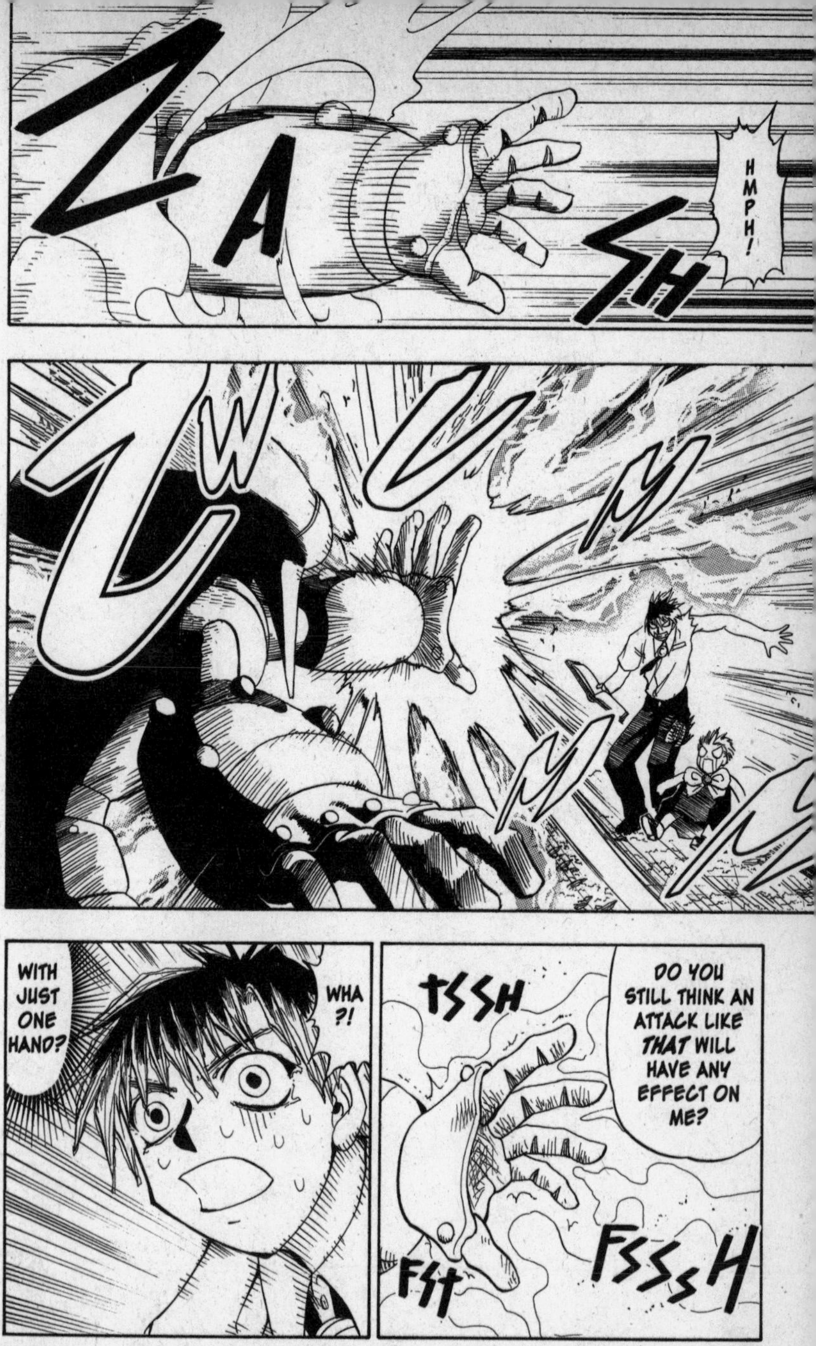
ZASH
HMPH!
ZWUMMM
TSSH
DO YOU STILL THINK AN ATTACK LIKE *THAT* WILL HAVE ANY EFFECT ON ME?
FSSSH
FST
WHA?!
WITH JUST ONE HAND?

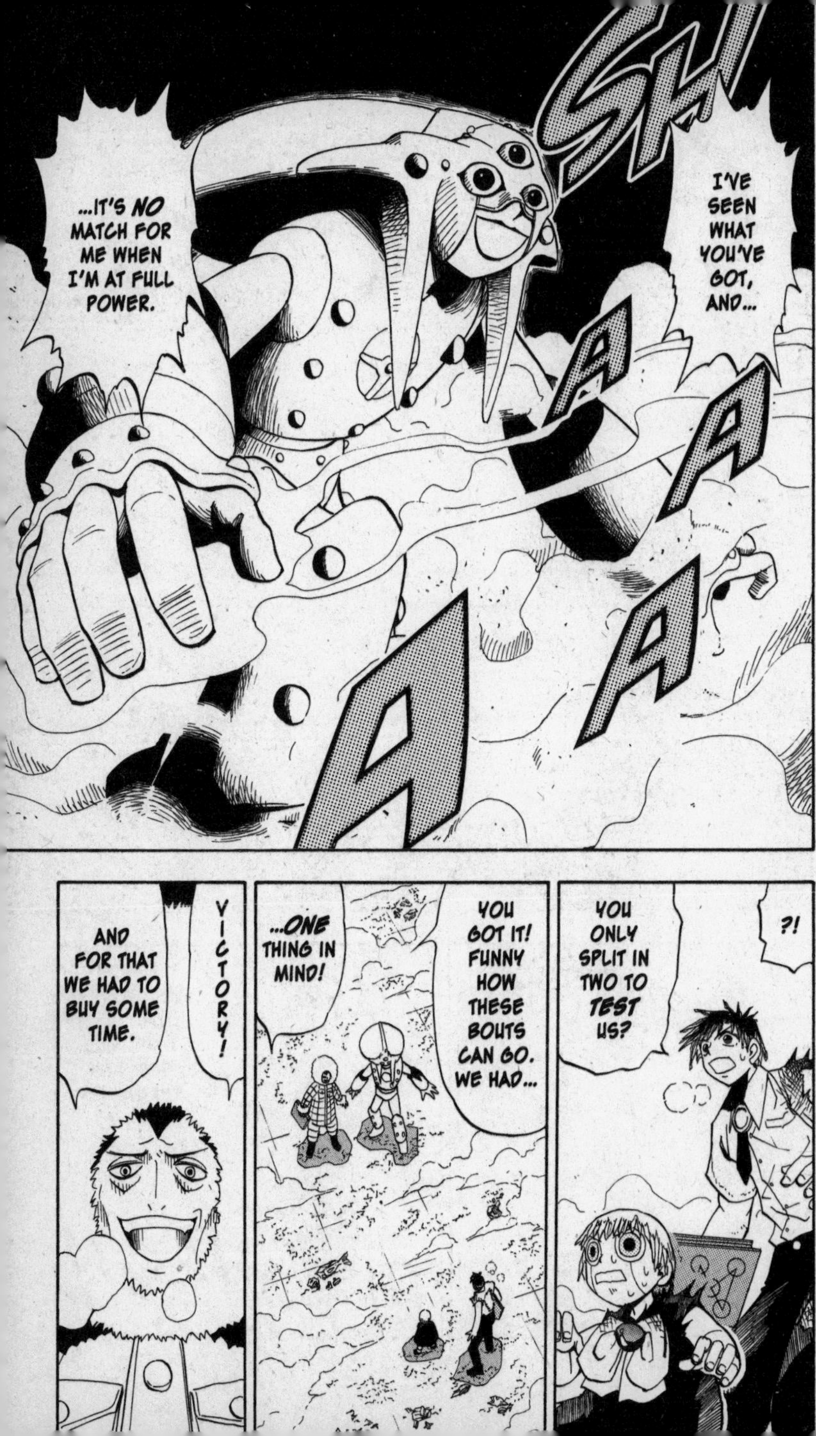
SHAAAA
I'VE SEEN WHAT YOU'VE GOT, AND...
...IT'S NO MATCH FOR ME WHEN I'M AT FULL POWER.
?!
YOU ONLY SPLIT IN TWO TO TEST US?
YOU GOT IT! FUNNY HOW THESE BOUTS CAN GO. WE HAD...
...ONE THING IN MIND!
VICTORY!
AND FOR THAT WE HAD TO BUY SOME TIME.

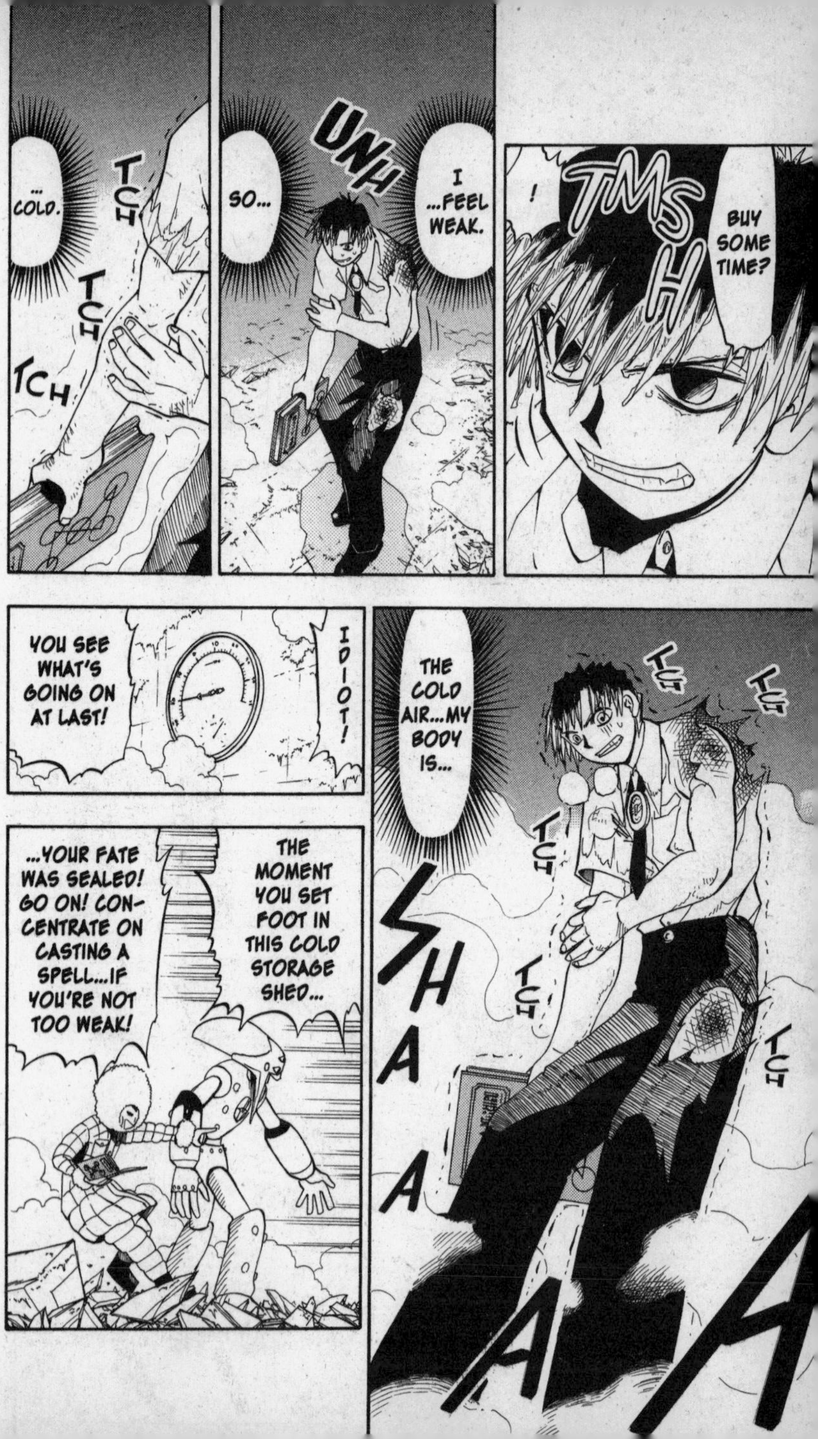
!
TMSH
BUY SOME TIME?
UNH
I ...FEEL WEAK.
SO...
TCH
TCH
TCH
...COLD.
THE COLD AIR...MY BODY IS...
TCH
TCH
TCH
TCH
TCH
SHAAAAA
IDIOT!
YOU SEE WHAT'S GOING ON AT LAST!
THE MOMENT YOU SET FOOT IN THIS COLD STORAGE SHED...
...YOUR FATE WAS SEALED! GO ON! CON-CENTRATE ON CASTING A SPELL...IF YOU'RE NOT TOO WEAK!

IT'S ALL OVER NOW!
VMMMMMMMM
KEEEEE
H-HIS HEAD ...GLOWING.
WHAT-EVER IT IS...
...IT'S BIG!
KIYO! LET'S RUN AWAY... C'MON!
HERE IT COMES!
BIRAITSU!
WAM
GAAAAAAAH!
WAAAAM

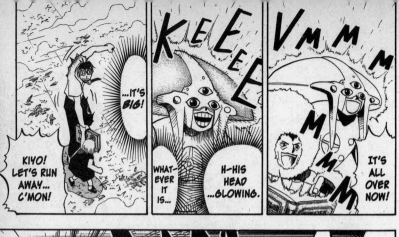

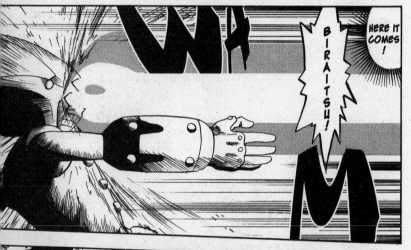

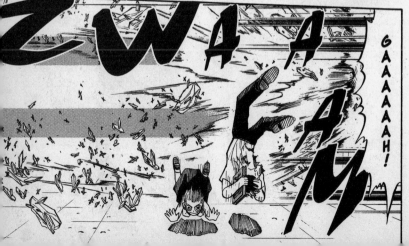

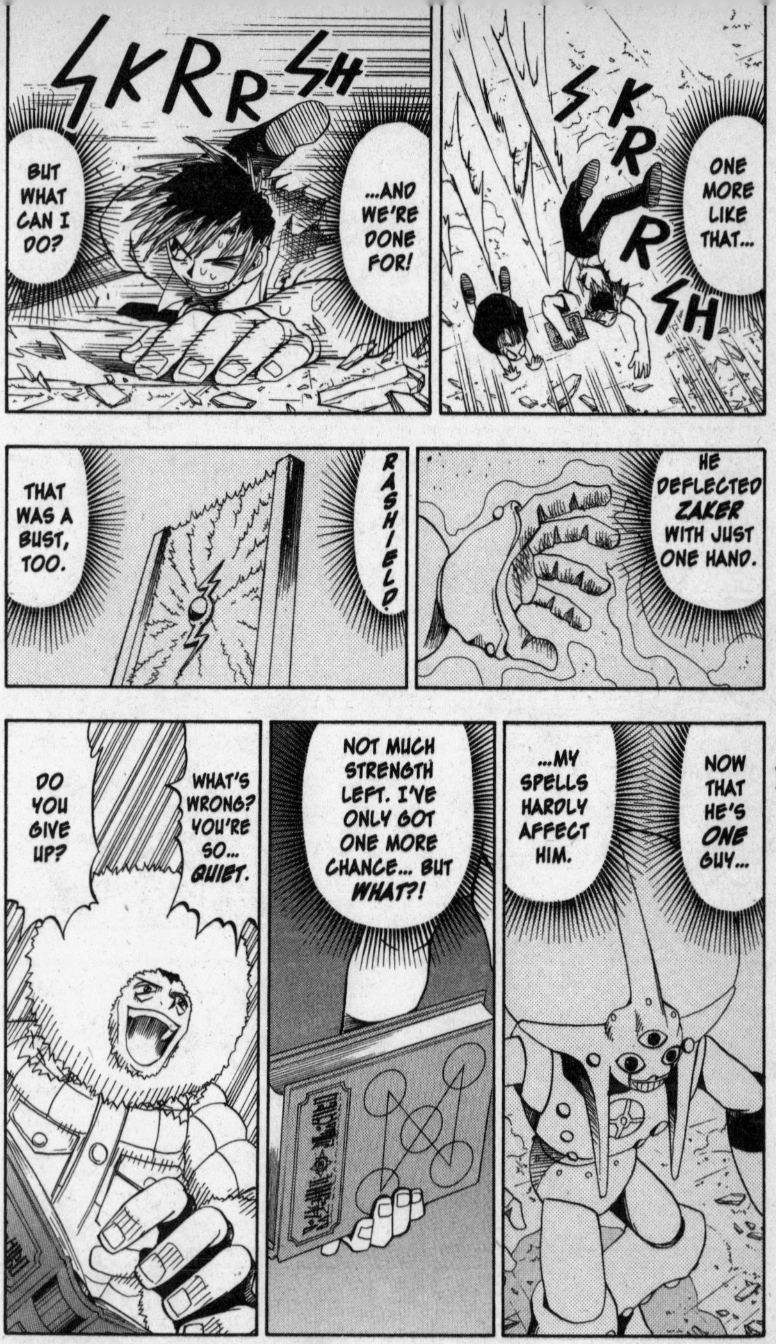
ONE MORE LIKE THAT...
SKRRRSH
...AND WE'RE DONE FOR!
SKRRSH
BUT WHAT CAN I DO?
HE DEFLECTED **ZAKER** WITH JUST ONE HAND.
RASHIELD.
THAT WAS A BUST, TOO.
NOW THAT HE'S ***ONE*** GUY...
...MY SPELLS HARDLY AFFECT HIM.
NOT MUCH STRENGTH LEFT. I'VE ONLY GOT ONE MORE CHANCE... BUT ***WHAT?!***
WHAT'S WRONG? YOU'RE SO... ***QUIET.***
DO YOU GIVE UP?

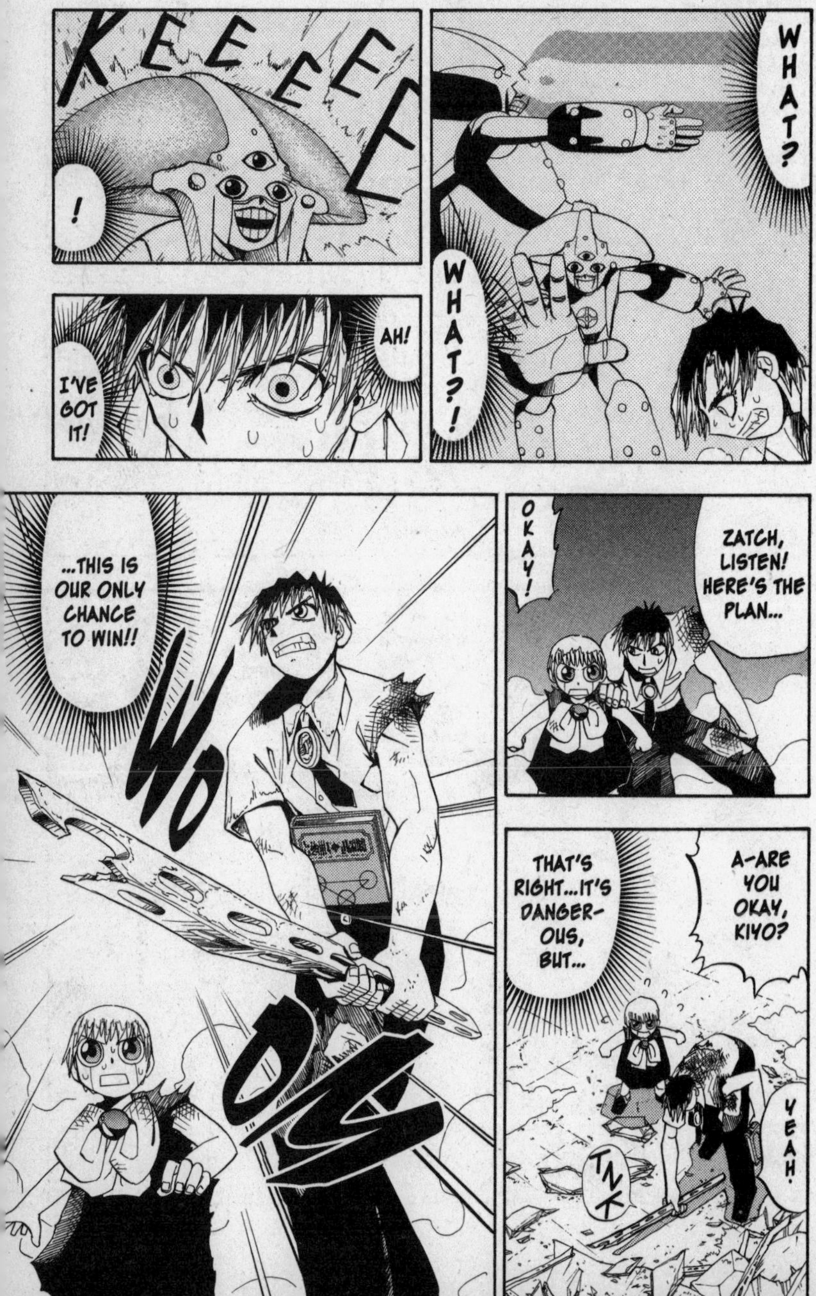
WHAT?
WHAT?!
KEEEEE
!
AH!
I'VE GOT IT!
ZATCH, LISTEN! HERE'S THE PLAN...
OKAY!
A-ARE YOU OKAY, KIYO?
THAT'S RIGHT...IT'S DANGER-OUS, BUT...
YEAH.
TNK
...THIS IS OUR ONLY CHANCE TO WIN!!
WO

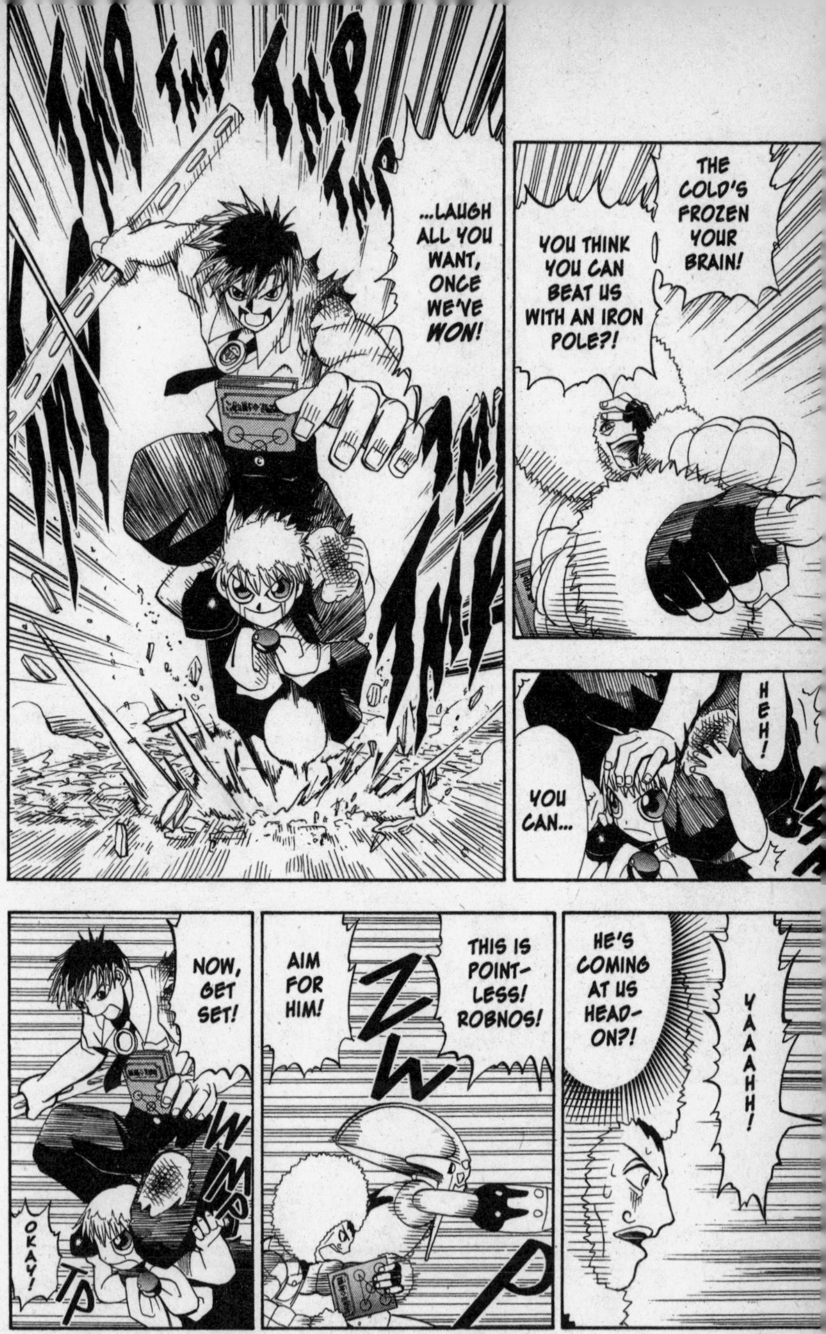
THE COLD'S FROZEN YOUR BRAIN!
YOU THINK YOU CAN BEAT US WITH AN IRON POLE?!
HEH!
YOU CAN...
THP THP THP THP
...LAUGH ALL YOU WANT, ONCE WE'VE WON!
HE'S COMING AT US HEAD-ON?!
YAAAHH!
THIS IS POINT-LESS! ROBNOS!
ZWP
AIM FOR HIM!
NOW, GET SET!
WMP
OKAY!
TP

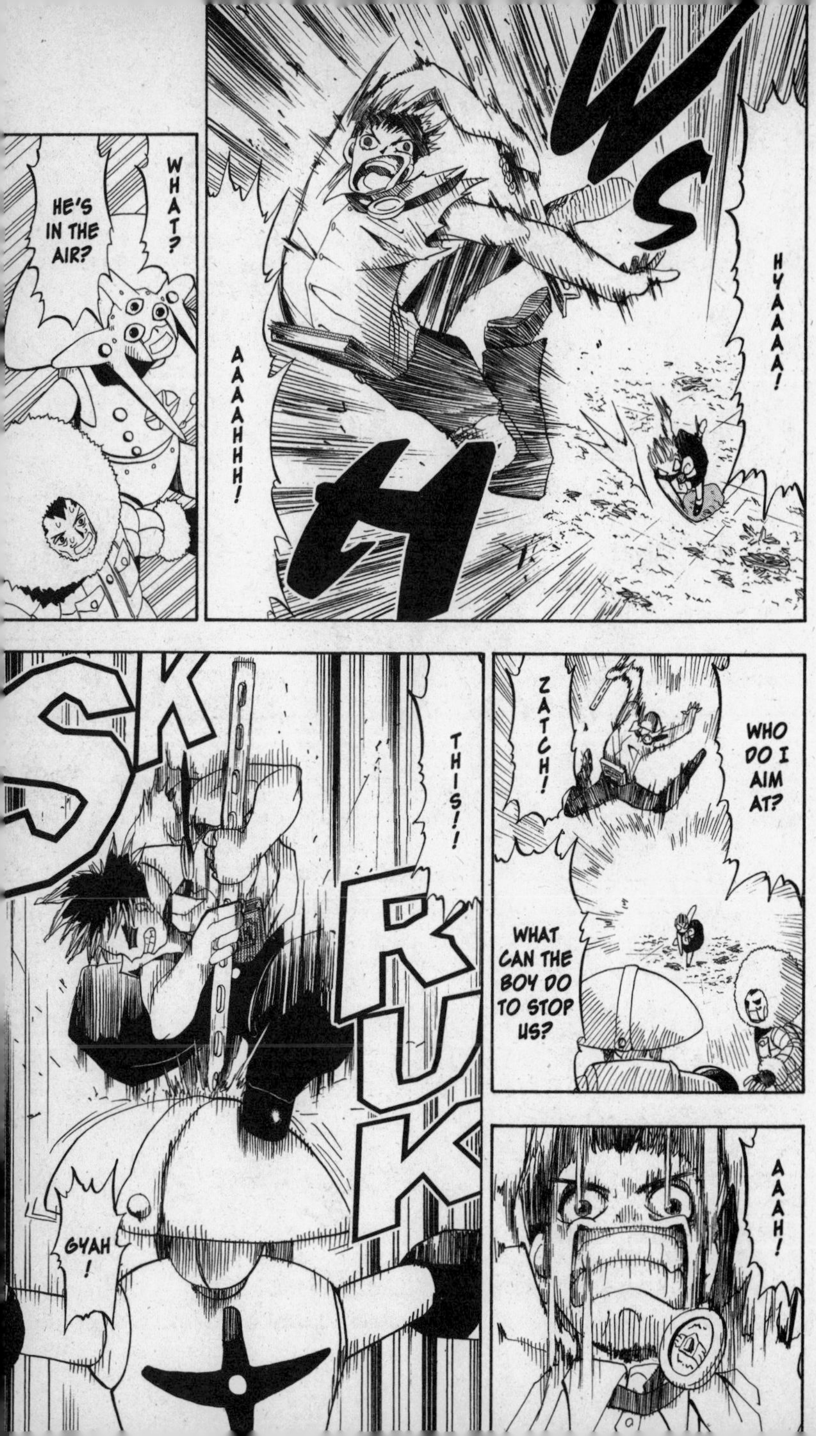
WS
HYAAAAA!
H
AAAAAHHH!
WHAT?
HE'S IN THE AIR?
WHO DO I AIM AT?
ZATCH!
WHAT CAN THE BOY DO TO STOP US?
AAAAH!
THIS!!
SK
RUK
GYAH!

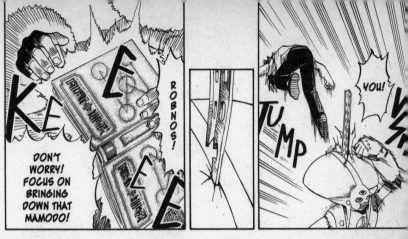

KEEE

ROBNOS!

DON'T WORRY! FOCUS ON BRINGING DOWN THAT MAMODO!

TU MP

YOU!

VS

HIS *HEAD* AMPS UP WHEN HE'S GOING TO FIRE!

YES!

KEEE

YEAH!

FMIS H

ZATCH!

AIM FOR THE IRON POLE!

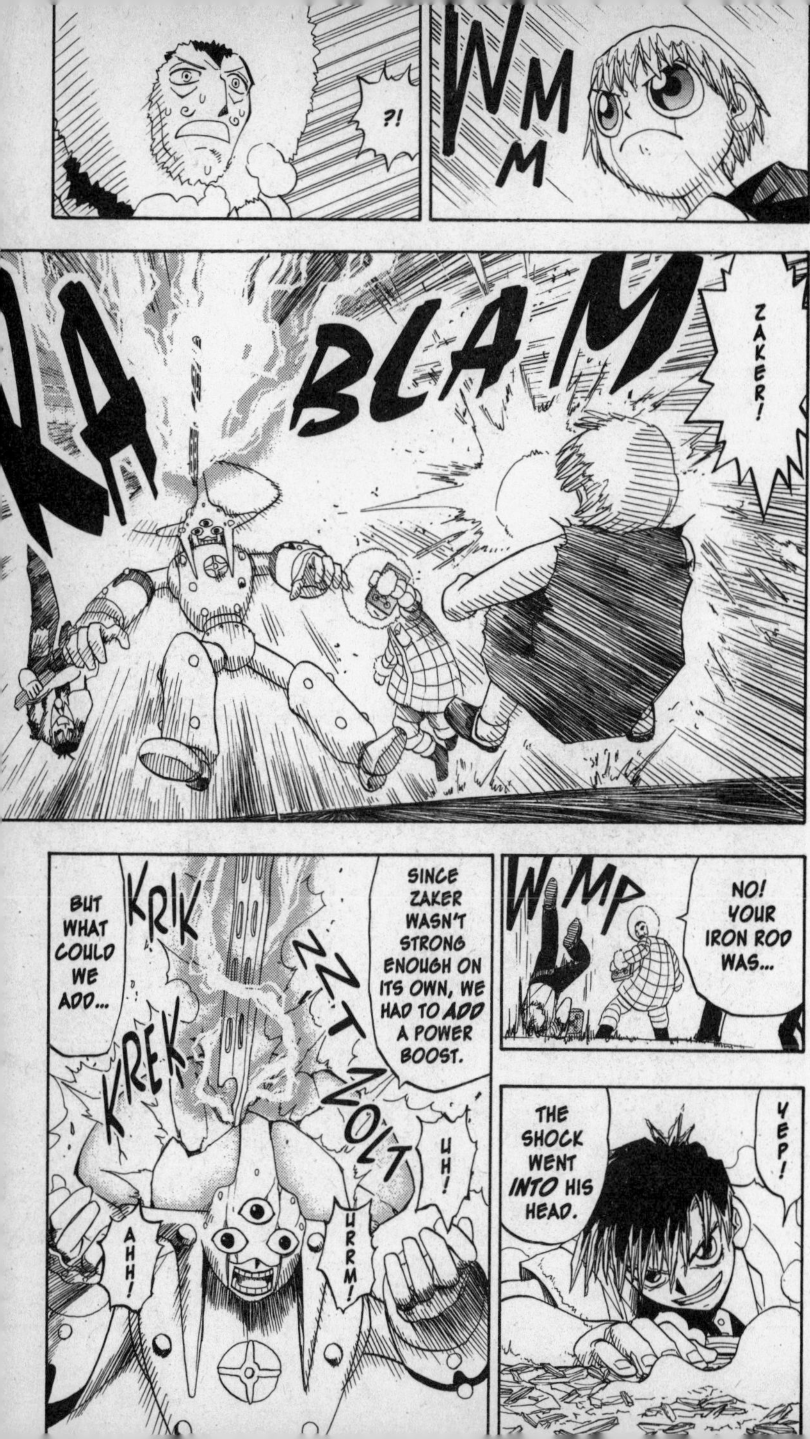
WMM
M
?!
ZAKER!
BLAM
KA
NO! YOUR IRON ROD WAS...
WMP
YEP!
THE SHOCK WENT *INTO* HIS HEAD.
SINCE ZAKER WASN'T STRONG ENOUGH ON ITS OWN, WE HAD TO *ADD* A POWER BOOST.
BUT WHAT COULD WE ADD...
KRIK
KREK
ZZT
ZOLT
UH!
URRM!
AHH!

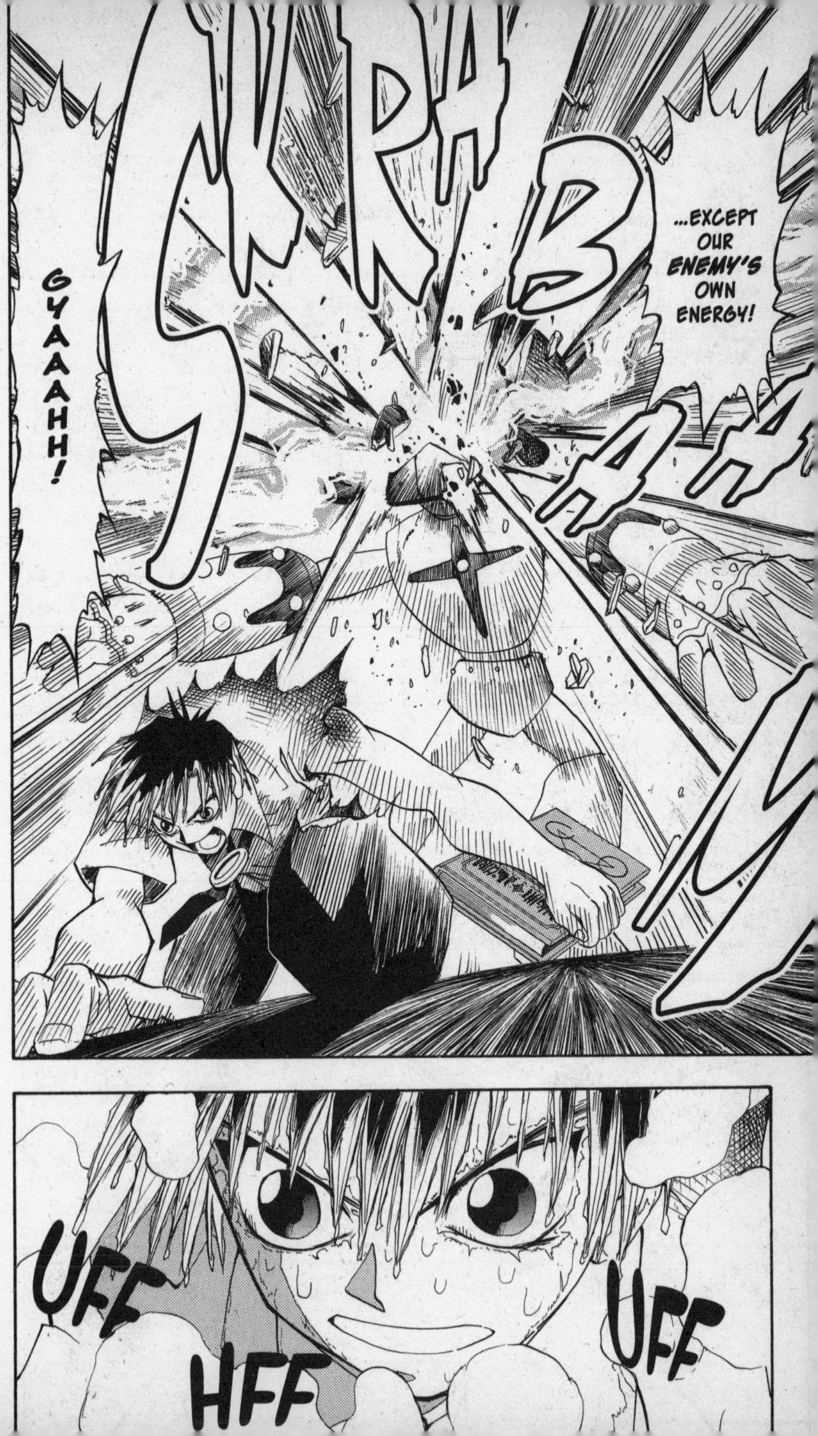
...EXCEPT OUR ENEMY'S OWN ENERGY!
GYAAAAHH!
UFF
UFF
HFF

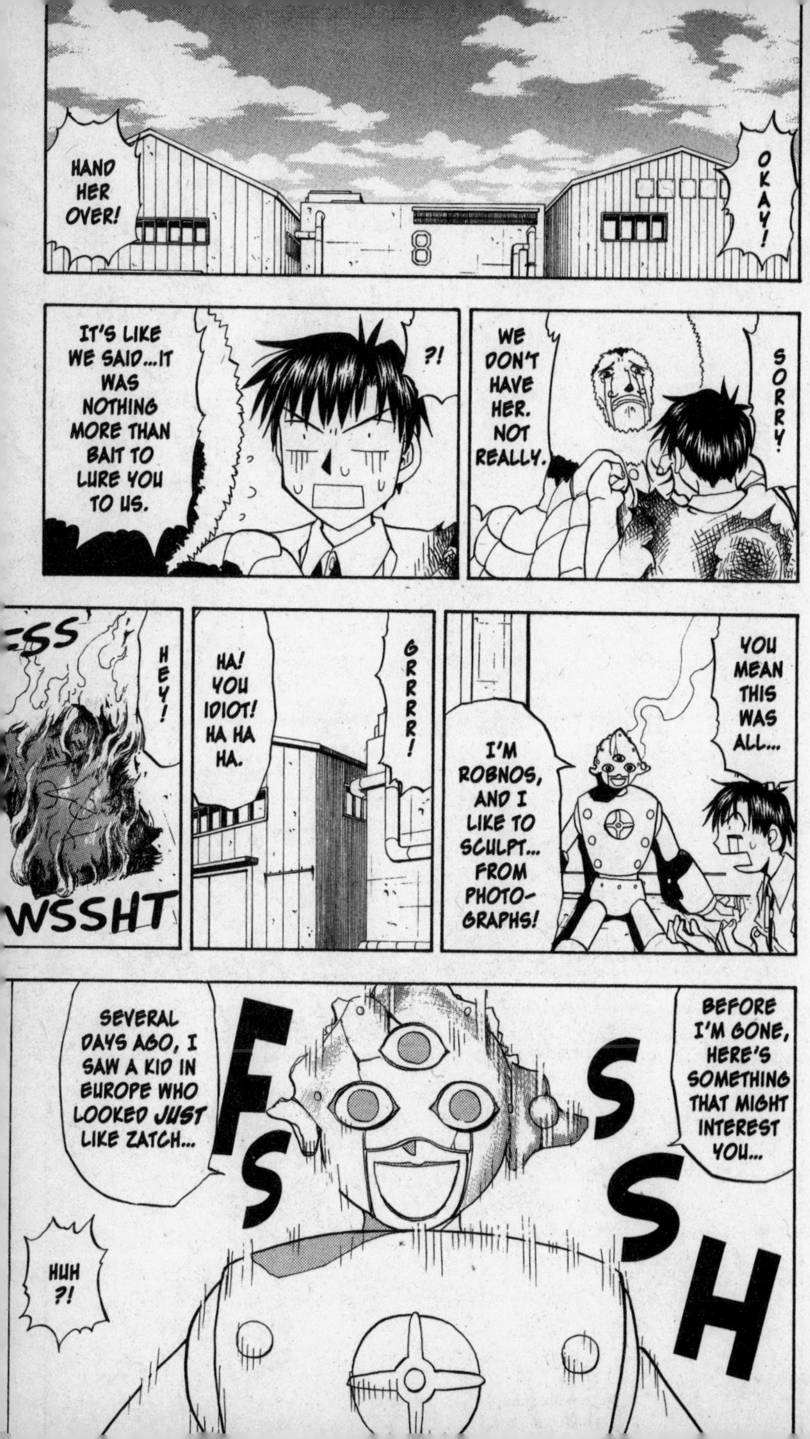
OKAY!
HAND HER OVER!
SORRY.
WE DON'T HAVE HER. NOT REALLY.
?!
IT'S LIKE WE SAID...IT WAS NOTHING MORE THAN BAIT TO LURE YOU TO US.
YOU MEAN THIS WAS ALL...
I'M ROBNOS, AND I LIKE TO SCULPT... FROM PHOTOGRAPHS!
GRRRR!
HA! YOU IDIOT! HA HA HA.
HEY!
SS
WSSHT
BEFORE I'M GONE, HERE'S SOMETHING THAT MIGHT INTEREST YOU...
FSSSH
SEVERAL DAYS AGO, I SAW A KID IN EUROPE WHO LOOKED JUST LIKE ZATCH...
HUH?!

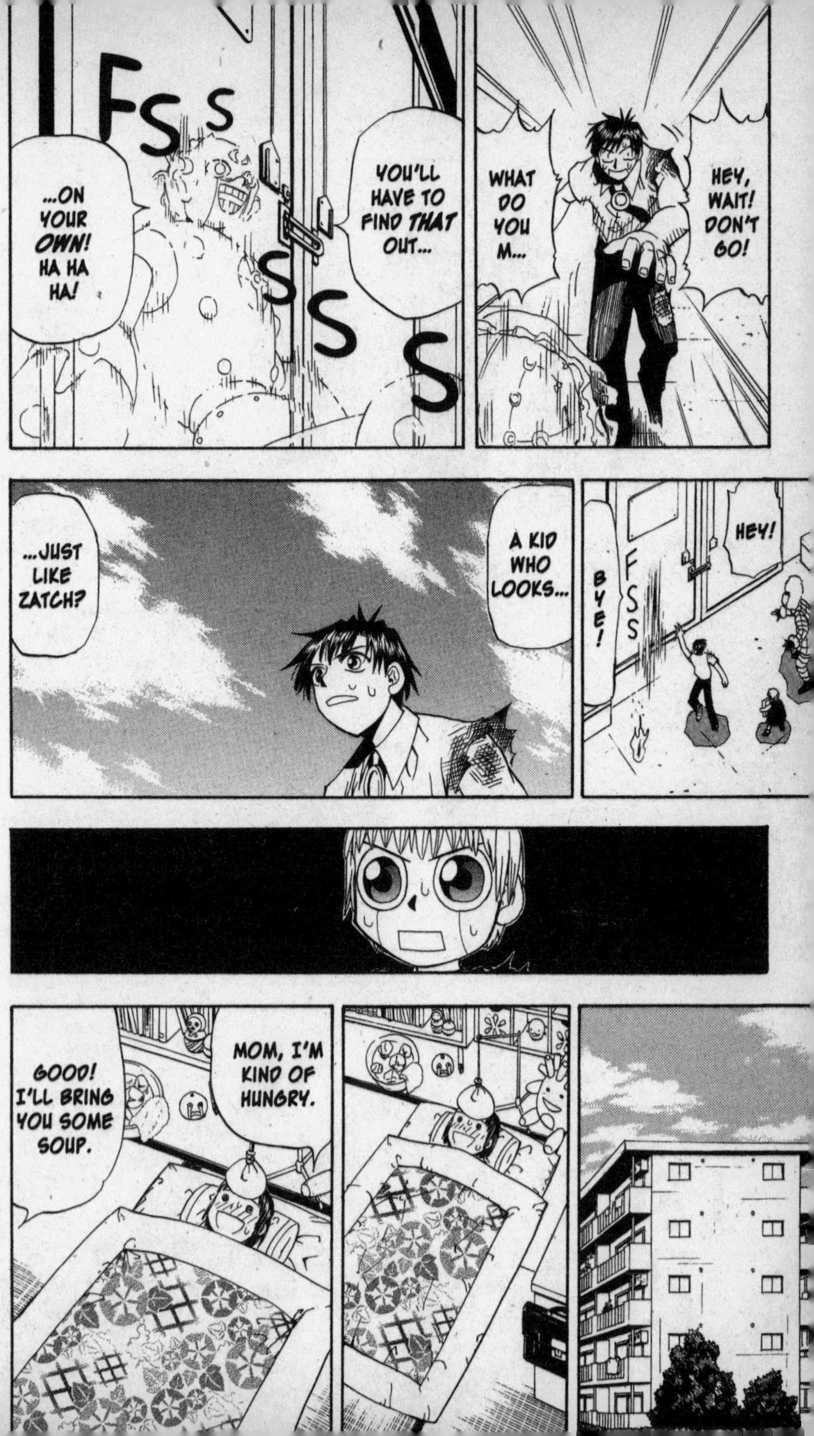
HEY, WAIT! DON'T GO!
WHAT DO YOU M...
YOU'LL HAVE TO FIND *THAT* OUT...
FSSS
SSS
...ON YOUR *OWN!* HA HA HA!
HEY!
FSS
BYE!
A KID WHO LOOKS...
...JUST LIKE ZATCH?
MOM, I'M KIND OF HUNGRY.
GOOD! I'LL BRING YOU SOME SOUP.

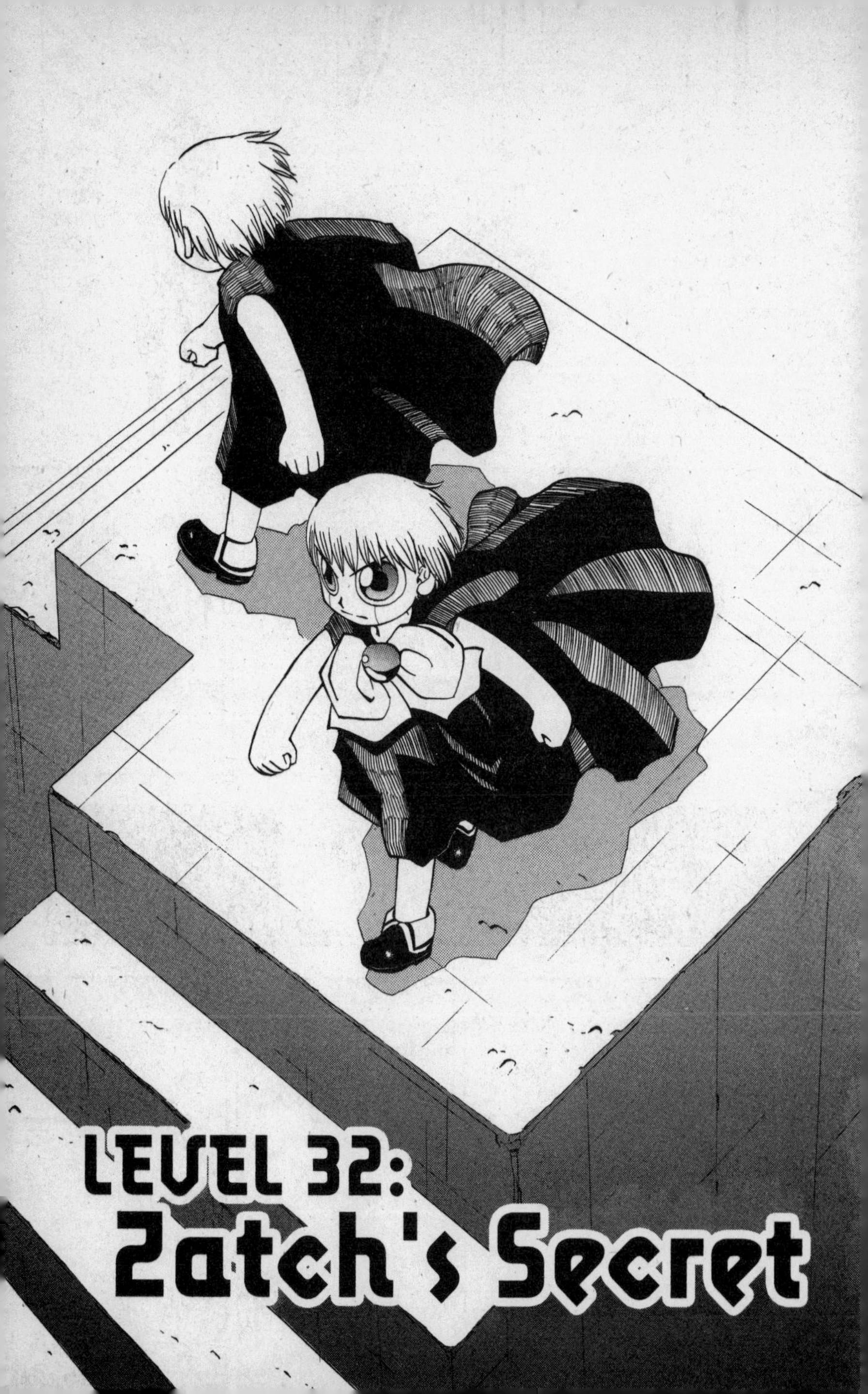

LEVEL 32: Zatch's Secret

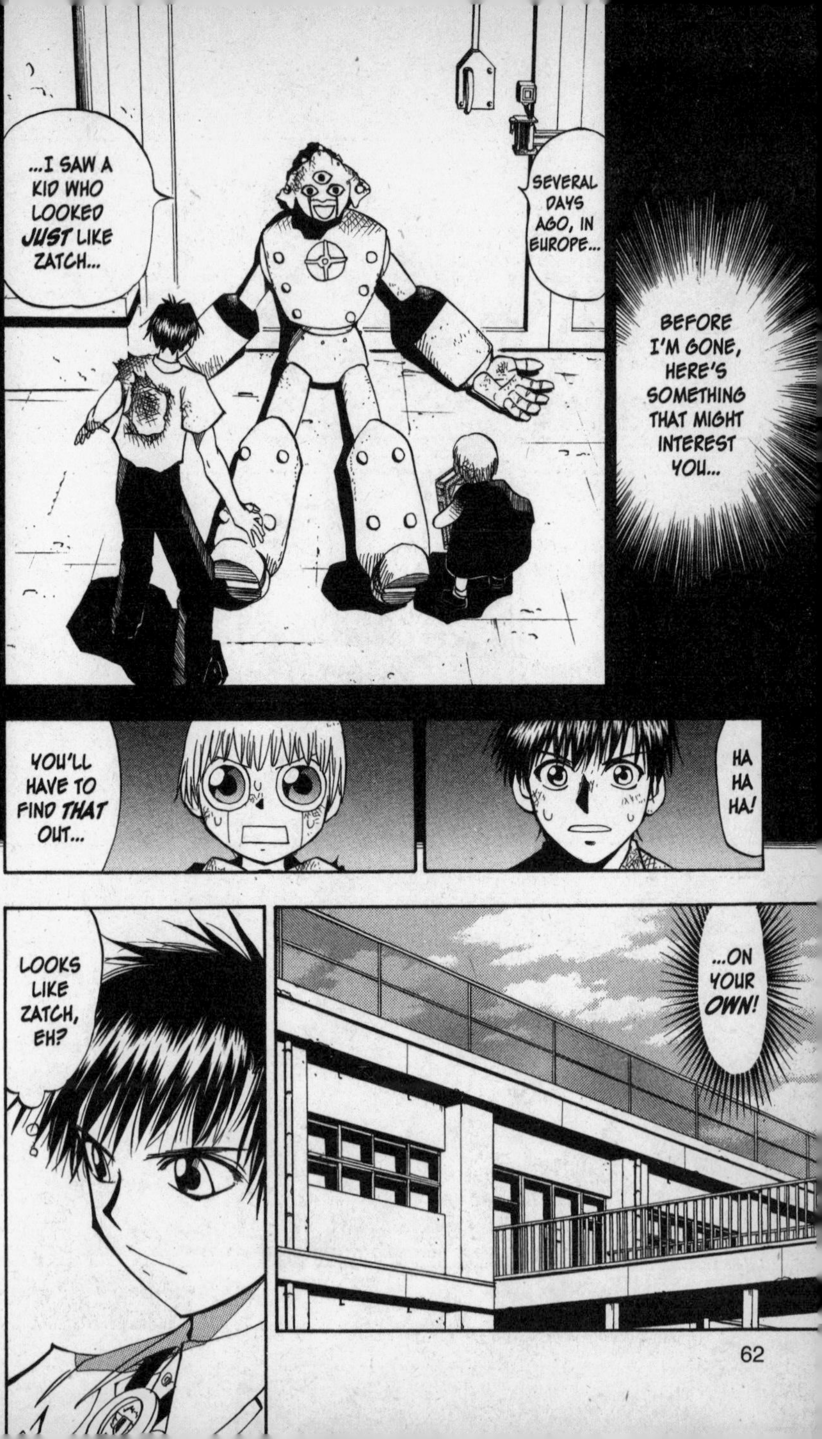
BEFORE I'M GONE, HERE'S SOMETHING THAT MIGHT INTEREST YOU...
SEVERAL DAYS AGO, IN EUROPE...
...I SAW A KID WHO LOOKED JUST LIKE ZATCH...
HA HA HA!
YOU'LL HAVE TO FIND THAT OUT...
...ON YOUR OWN!
LOOKS LIKE ZATCH, EH?

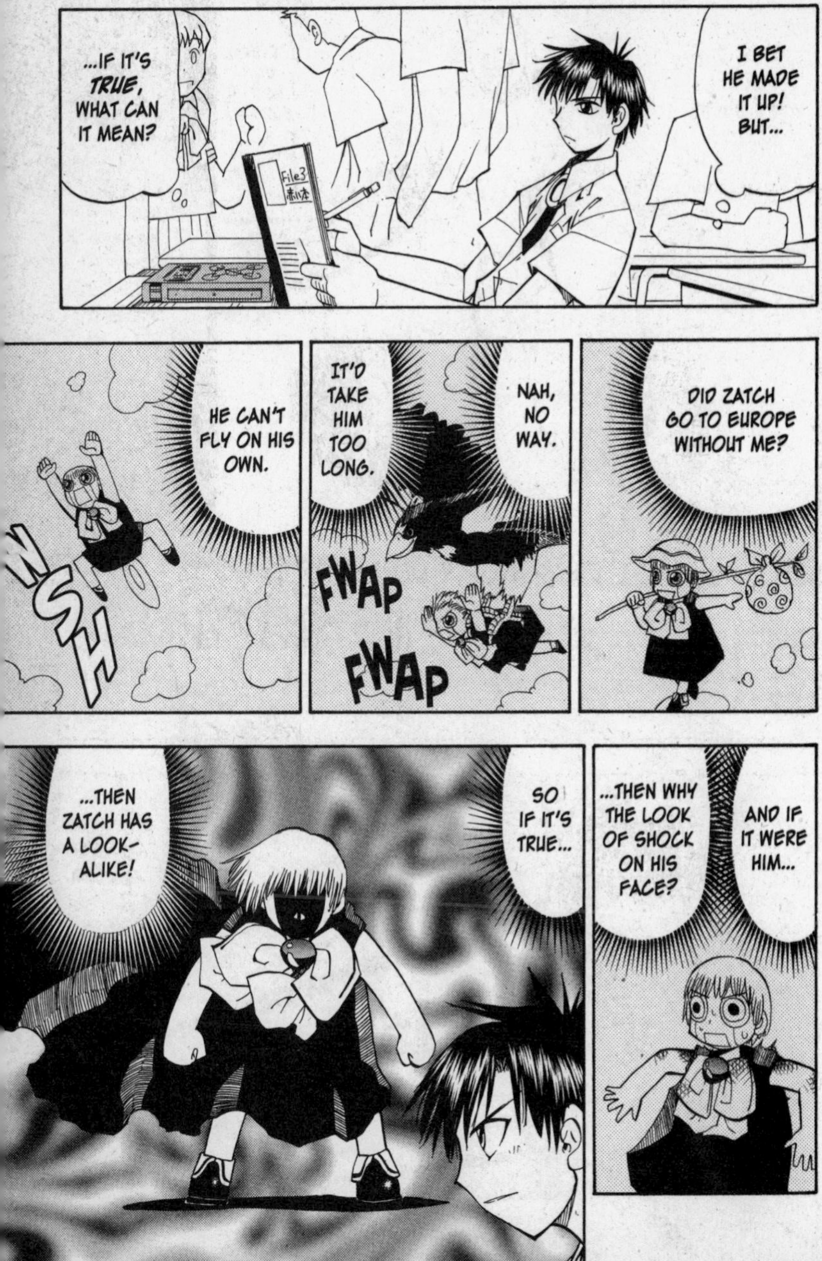
I BET HE MADE IT UP! BUT...
...IF IT'S TRUE, WHAT CAN IT MEAN?
File3
赤い本
DID ZATCH GO TO EUROPE WITHOUT ME?
NAH, NO WAY.
IT'D TAKE HIM TOO LONG.
FWAP
FWAP
HE CAN'T FLY ON HIS OWN.
WSHH
AND IF IT WERE HIM...
...THEN WHY THE LOOK OF SHOCK ON HIS FACE?
SO IF IT'S TRUE...
...THEN ZATCH HAS A LOOK-ALIKE!

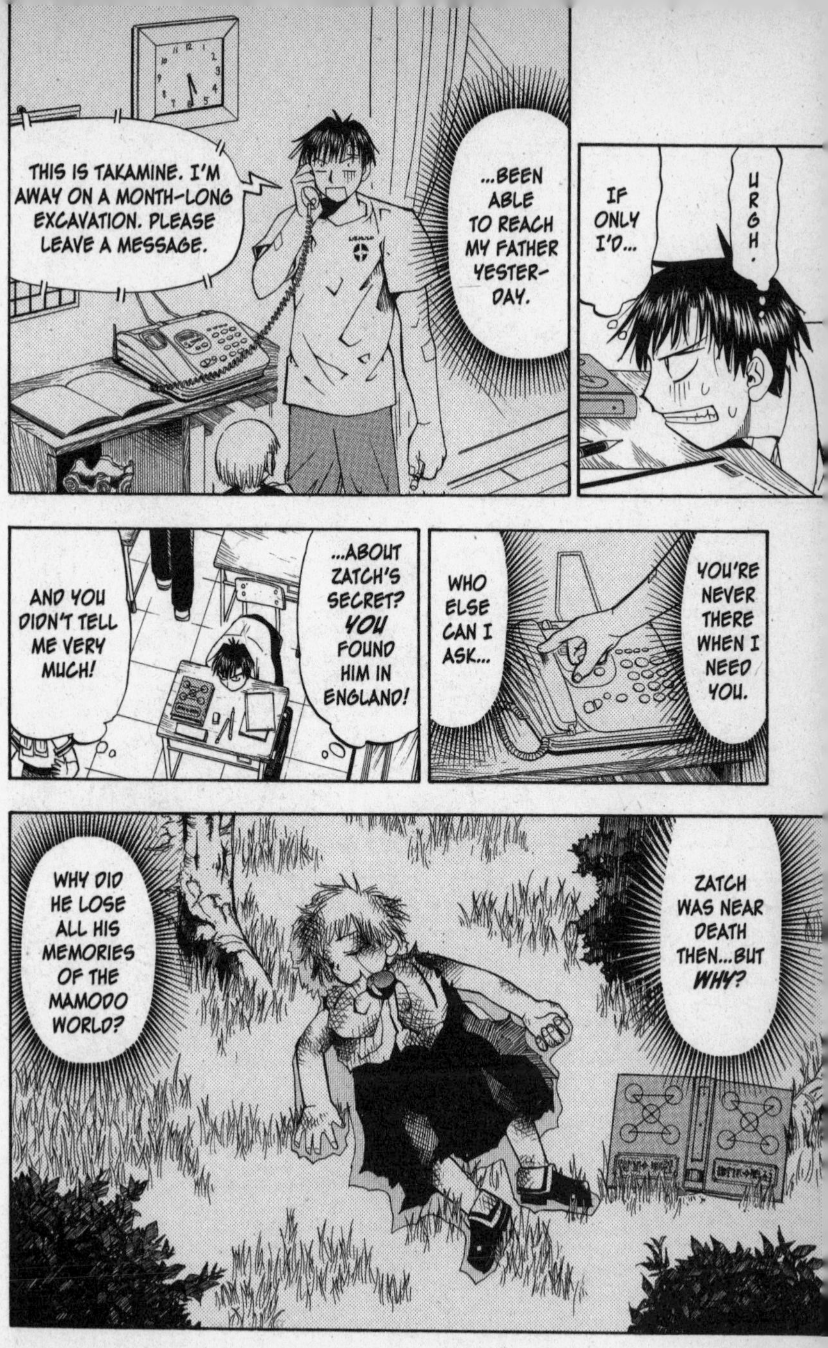
URGH.
IF ONLY I'D...
...BEEN ABLE TO REACH MY FATHER YESTERDAY.
THIS IS TAKAMINE. I'M AWAY ON A MONTH-LONG EXCAVATION. PLEASE LEAVE A MESSAGE.
YOU'RE NEVER THERE WHEN I NEED YOU.
WHO ELSE CAN I ASK...
...ABOUT ZATCH'S SECRET? *YOU* FOUND HIM IN ENGLAND!
AND YOU DIDN'T TELL ME VERY MUCH!
ZATCH WAS NEAR DEATH THEN...BUT *WHY?*
WHY DID HE LOSE ALL HIS MEMORIES OF THE MAMODO WORLD?

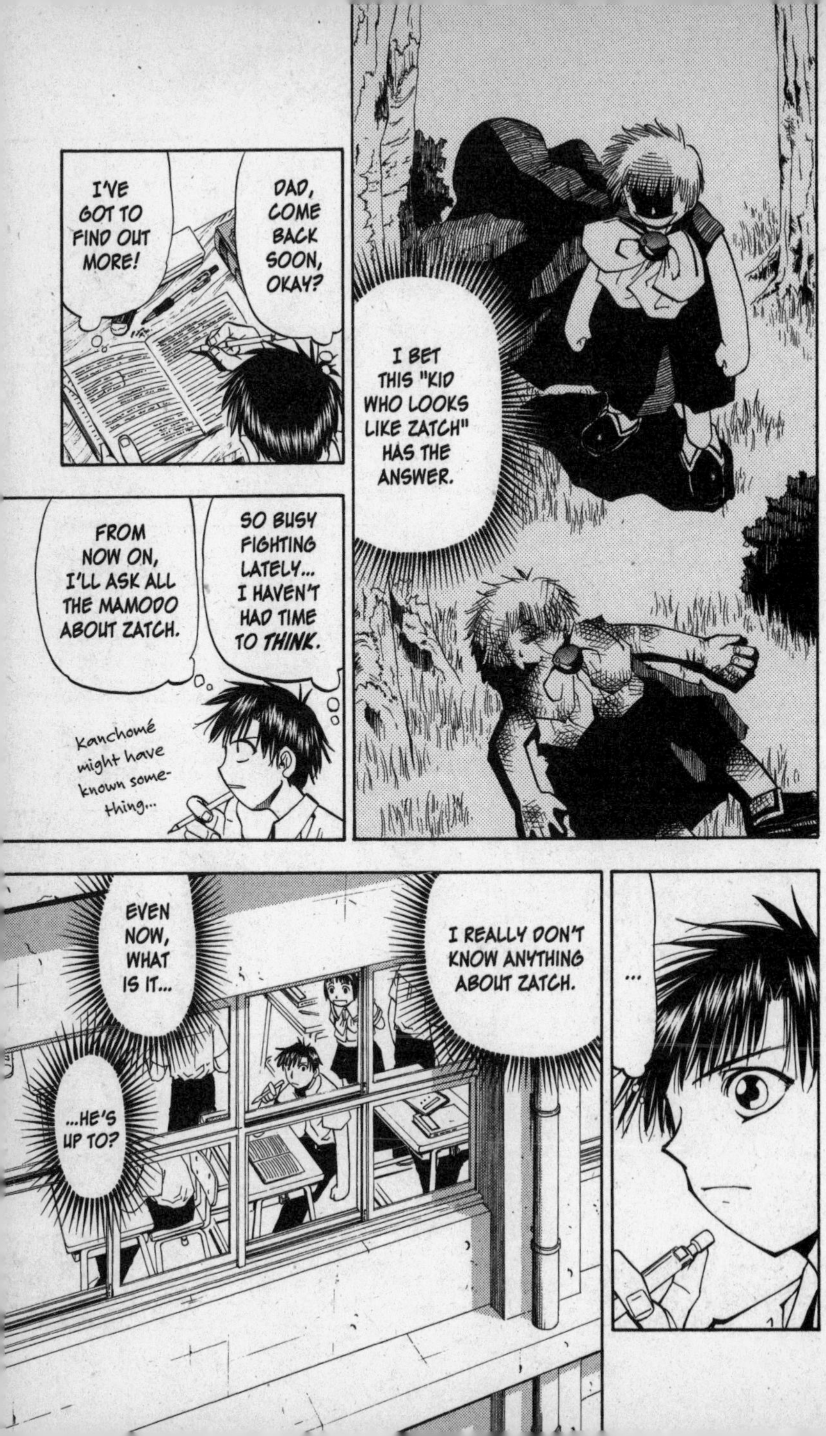
I BET THIS "KID WHO LOOKS LIKE ZATCH" HAS THE ANSWER.
DAD, COME BACK SOON, OKAY?
I'VE GOT TO FIND OUT MORE!
SO BUSY FIGHTING LATELY... I HAVEN'T HAD TIME TO *THINK*.
FROM NOW ON, I'LL ASK ALL THE MAMODO ABOUT ZATCH.
Kanchomé might have known something...
...
I REALLY DON'T KNOW ANYTHING ABOUT ZATCH.
EVEN NOW, WHAT IS IT...
...HE'S UP TO?

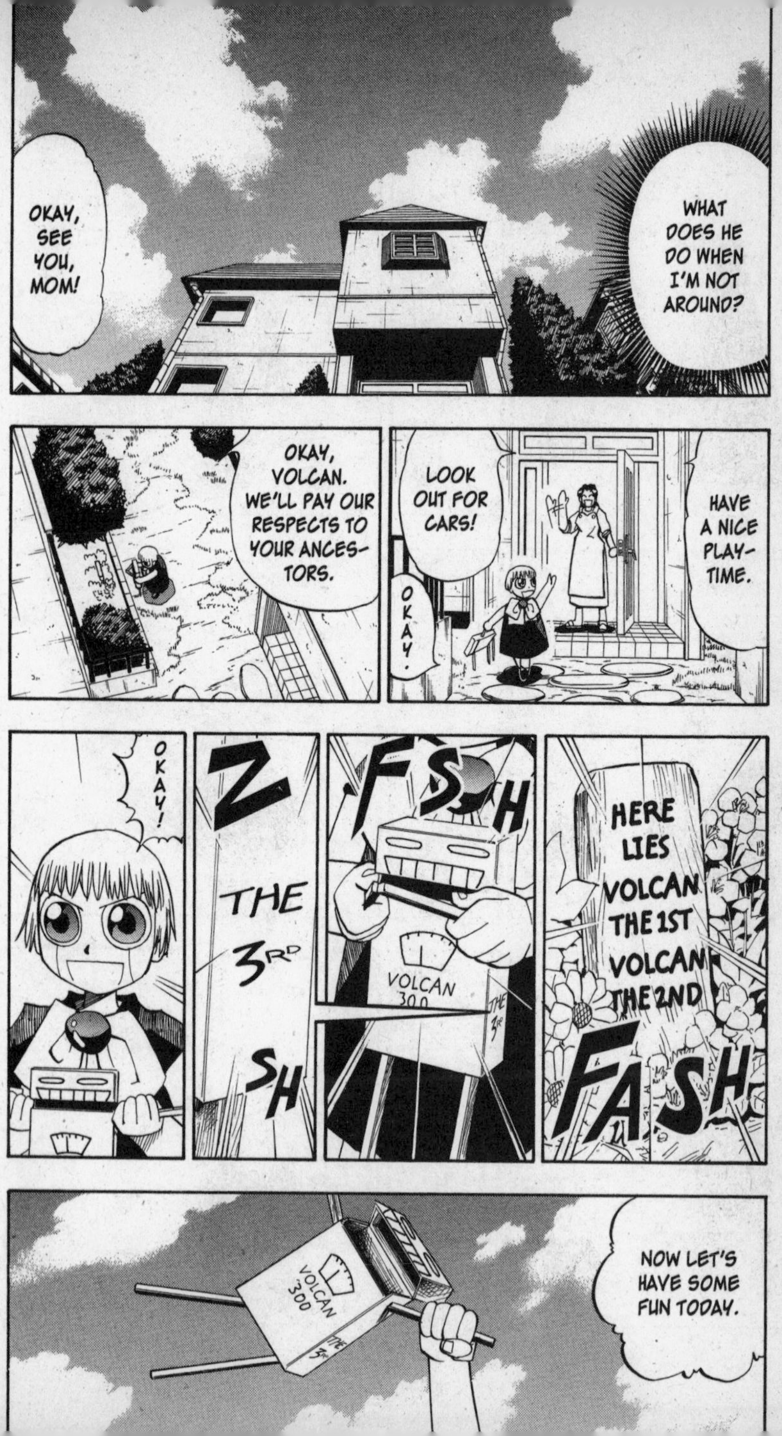
WHAT DOES HE DO WHEN I'M NOT AROUND?
OKAY, SEE YOU, MOM!
HAVE A NICE PLAY-TIME.
LOOK OUT FOR CARS!
OKAY.
OKAY, VOLCAN. WE'LL PAY OUR RESPECTS TO YOUR ANCES-TORS.
HERE LIES VOLCAN THE 1ST VOLCAN THE 2ND
FASH
FSH
VOLCAN 300
THE 3RD
Z
THE 3RD
SH
OKAY!
NOW LET'S HAVE SOME FUN TODAY.
VOLCAN 300
THE 3RD

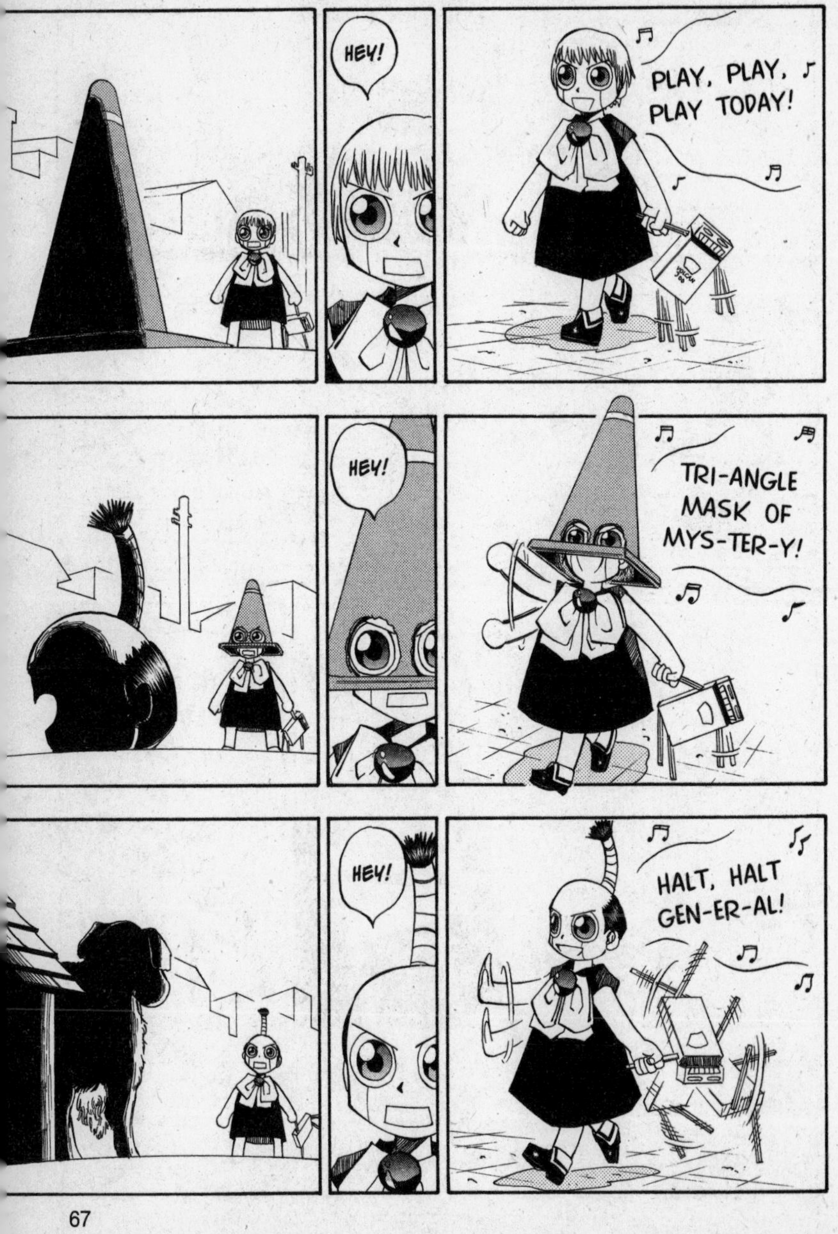
PLAY, PLAY, PLAY TODAY!
HEY!
TRI-ANGLE MASK OF MYS-TER-Y!
HEY!
HALT, HALT GEN-ER-AL!
HEY!

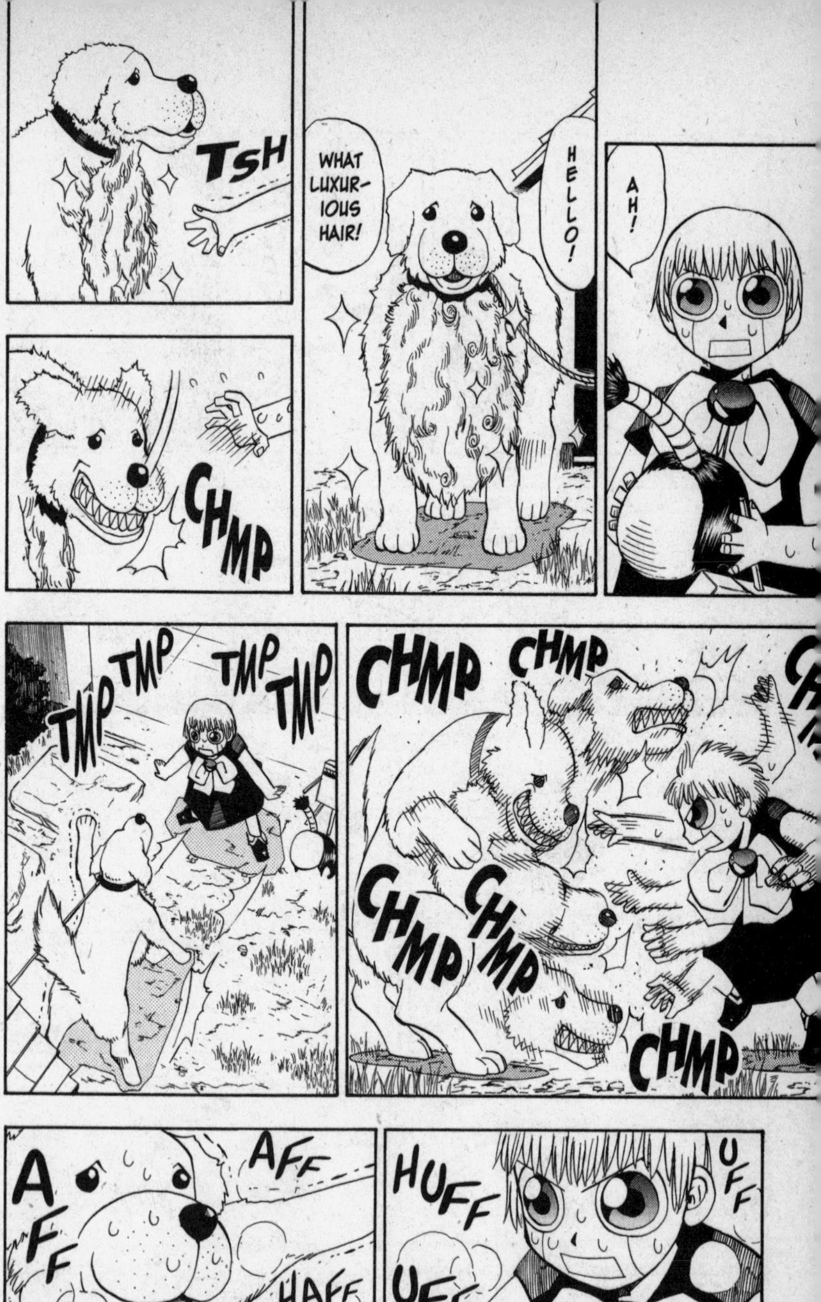
AH!
HELLO!
WHAT LUXUR-IOUS HAIR!
TSH
CHMP
CHMP
CHMP
CHMP
CHMP
CHMP
TMP
TMP
TMP
TMP
UFF
HUFF
UFF
AFF
AFF
HAFF

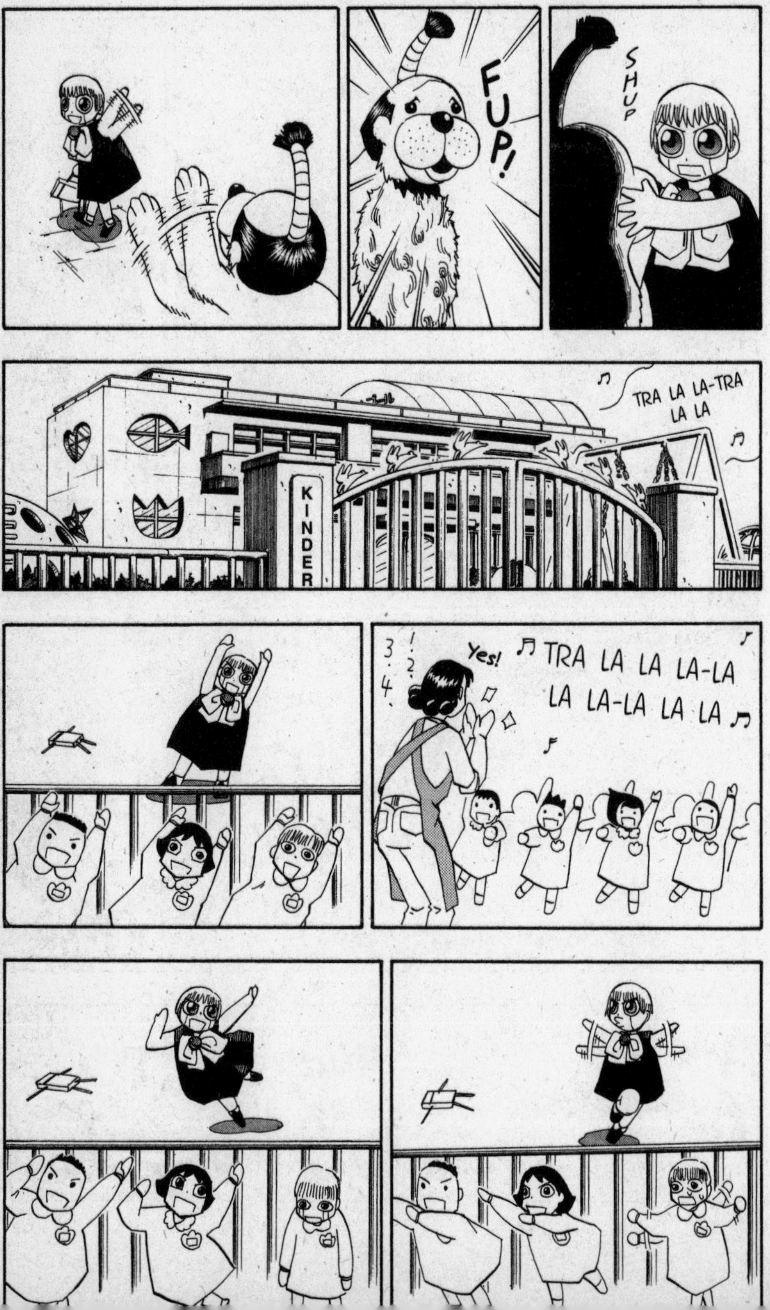
SHUP
FUP!
TRA LA LA-TRA LA LA
Yes!
TRA LA LA LA-LA LA LA-LA LA LA

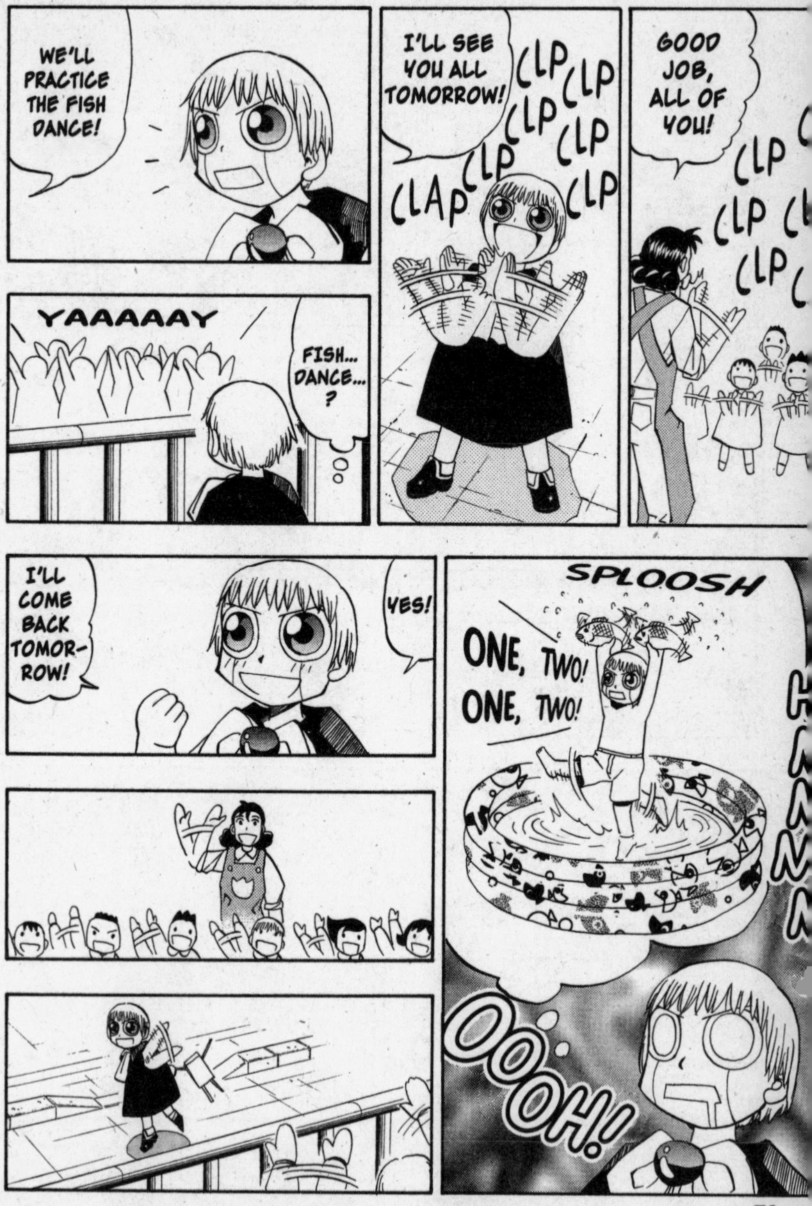
GOOD JOB, ALL OF YOU!
CLP CLP CLP
I'LL SEE YOU ALL TOMORROW!
CLAP CLP CLP CLP CLP CLP CLP
WE'LL PRACTICE THE FISH DANCE!
YAAAAAY
FISH... DANCE...?
SPLOOSH
ONE, TWO! ONE, TWO!
OOOOH!
I'LL COME BACK TOMORROW!
YES!

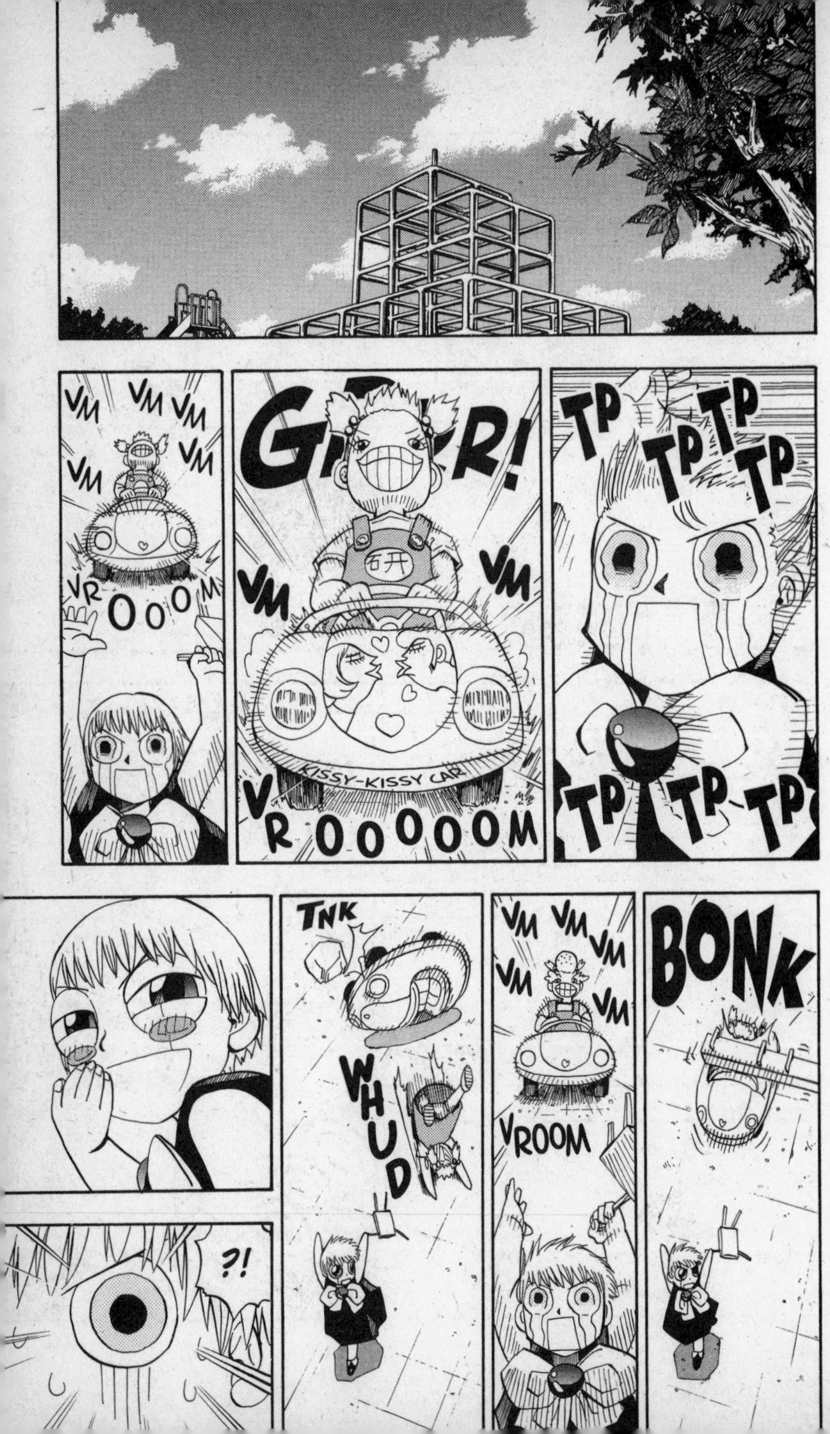
TP TP TP TP
TP TP TP
G R!
KISSY-KISSY CAR
VM VM
VROOOOOM
VM VM VM VM VM
VROOOM
BONK
VM VM VM VM VM
VROOM
TNK
WHUD
?!

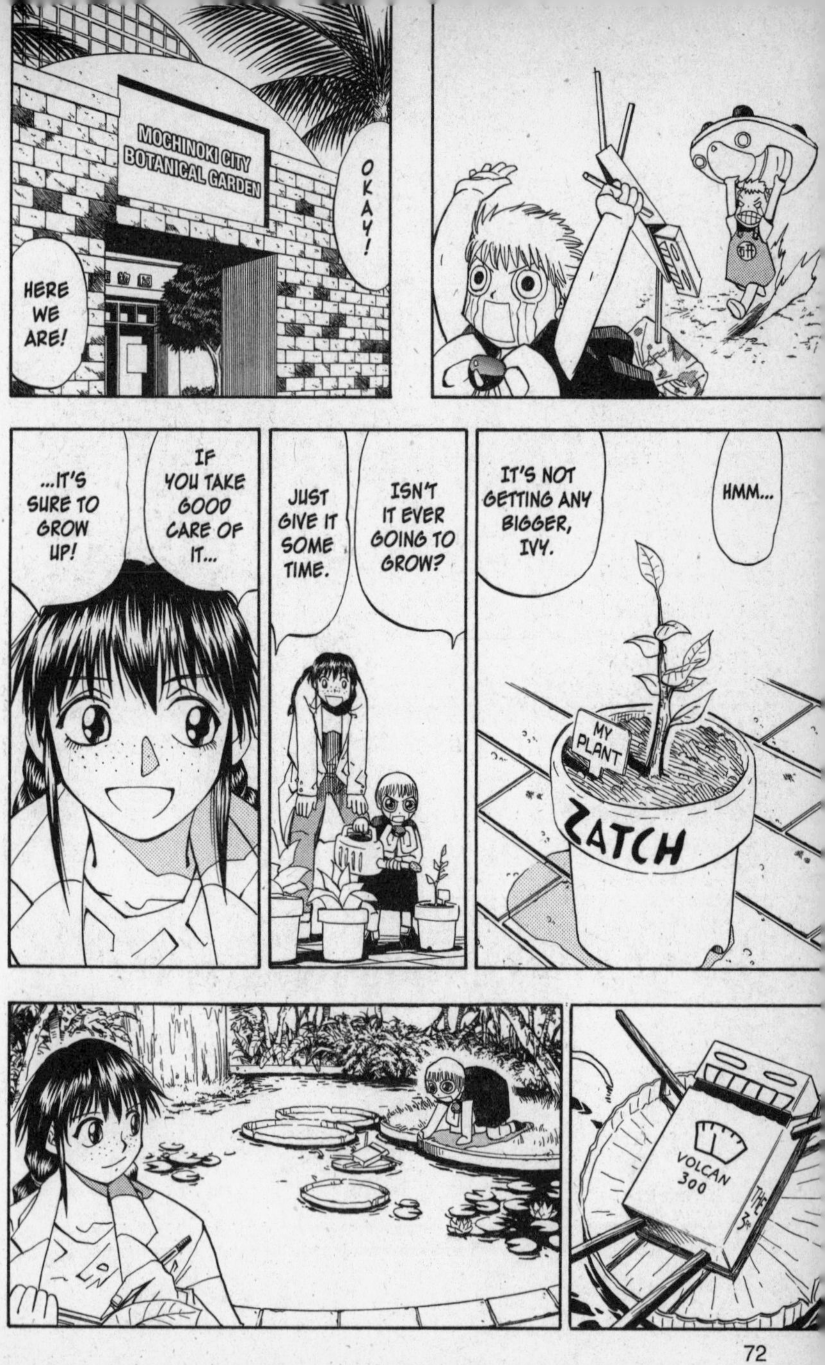
MOCHINOKI CITY BOTANICAL GARDEN
OKAY!
HERE WE ARE!
HMM...
IT'S NOT GETTING ANY BIGGER, IVY.
MY PLANT
ZATCH
ISN'T IT EVER GOING TO GROW?
JUST GIVE IT SOME TIME.
IF YOU TAKE GOOD CARE OF IT...
...IT'S SURE TO GROW UP!
VOLCAN 300

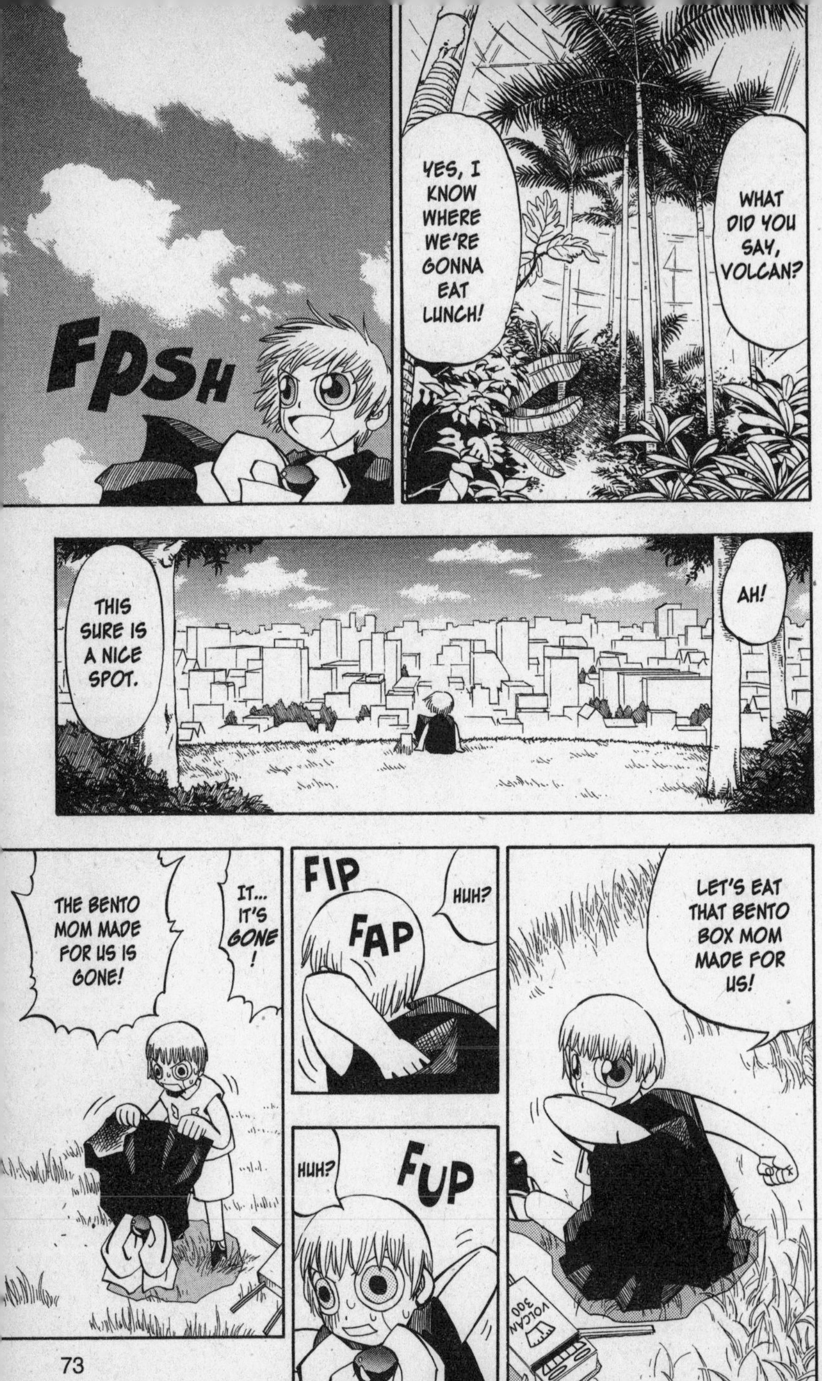
WHAT DID YOU SAY, VOLCAN?
YES, I KNOW WHERE WE'RE GONNA EAT LUNCH!
FPSH
AH!
THIS SURE IS A NICE SPOT.
LET'S EAT THAT BENTO BOX MOM MADE FOR US!
VOLCAN 300
HUH?
FIP
FAP
FUP
HUH?
IT... IT'S GONE!
THE BENTO MOM MADE FOR US IS GONE!

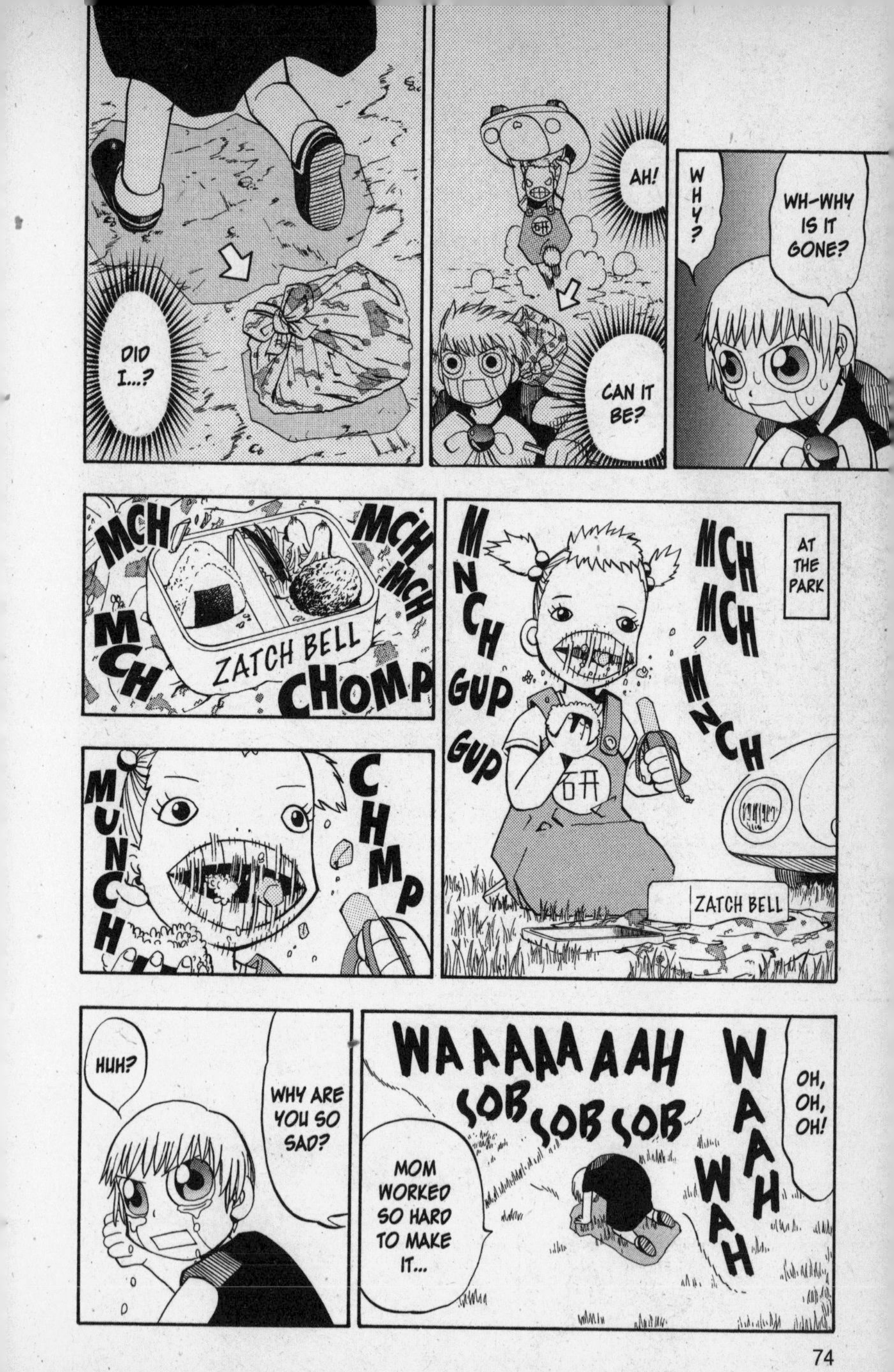
WH-WHY IS IT GONE?
WHY?
AH!
CAN IT BE?
DID I...?
AT THE PARK
MCH MCH MNCH
MNCH
MNCH
GUP
GUP
ZATCH BELL
MCH
MCH
MCH
MCH
CHOMP
ZATCH BELL
CHMP
MUNCH
OH, OH, OH!
WAH WAH
WAAAAAAH
SOB SOB SOB
MOM WORKED SO HARD TO MAKE IT...
WHY ARE YOU SO SAD?
HUH?

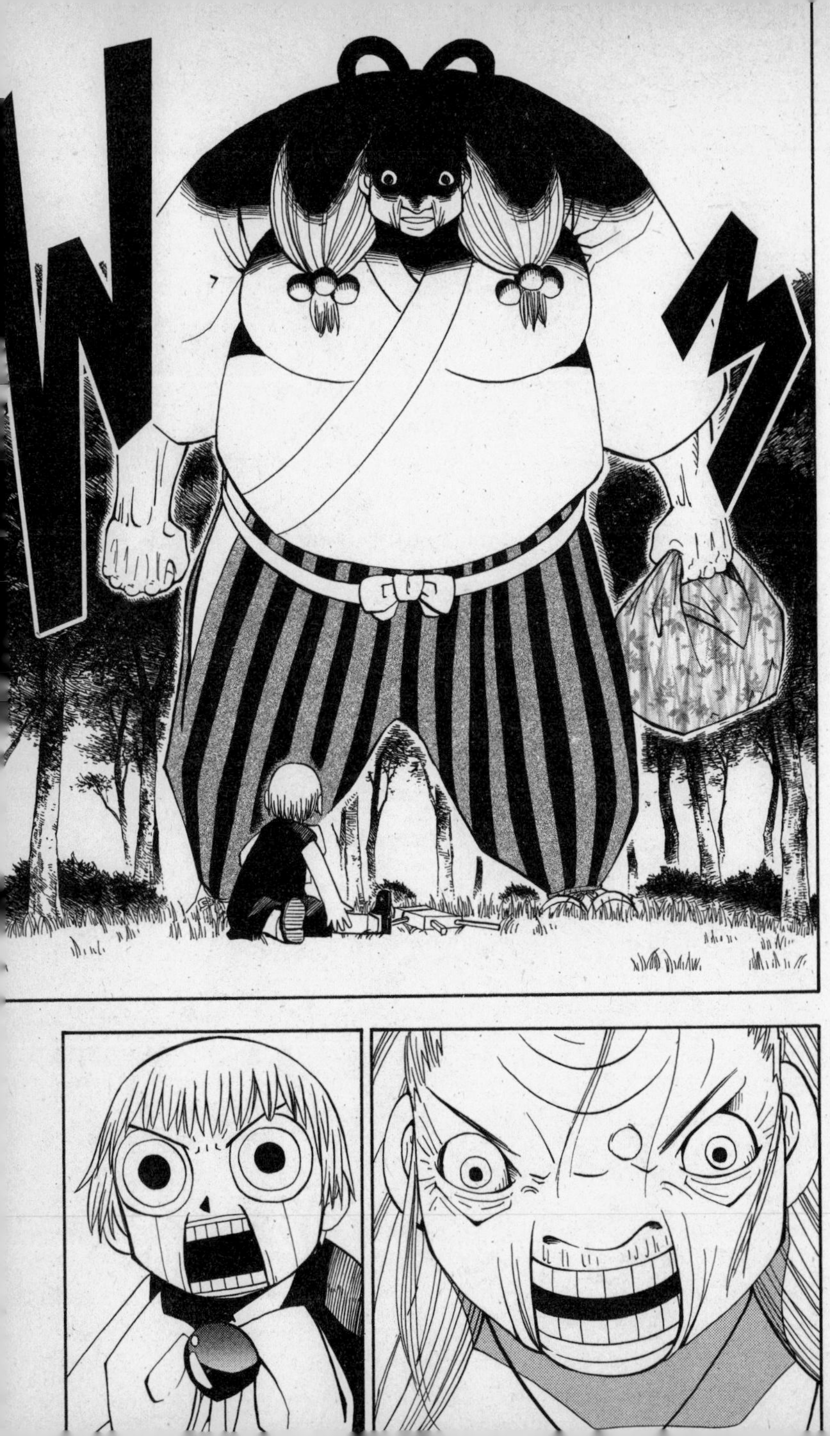

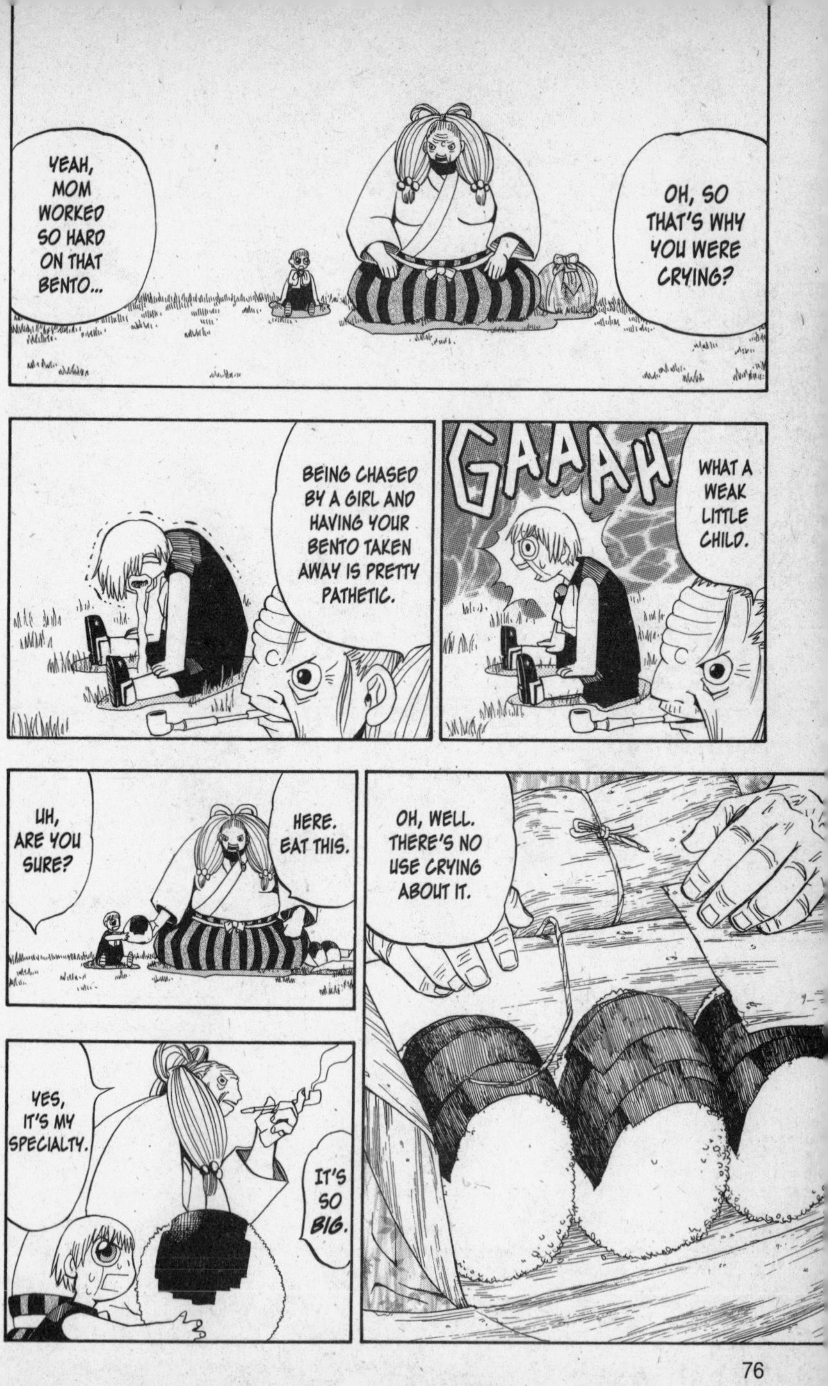
OH, SO THAT'S WHY YOU WERE CRYING?
YEAH, MOM WORKED SO HARD ON THAT BENTO...
WHAT A WEAK LITTLE CHILD.
GAAAH
BEING CHASED BY A GIRL AND HAVING YOUR BENTO TAKEN AWAY IS PRETTY PATHETIC.
OH, WELL. THERE'S NO USE CRYING ABOUT IT.
HERE. EAT THIS.
UH, ARE YOU SURE?
IT'S SO BIG.
YES, IT'S MY SPECIALTY.

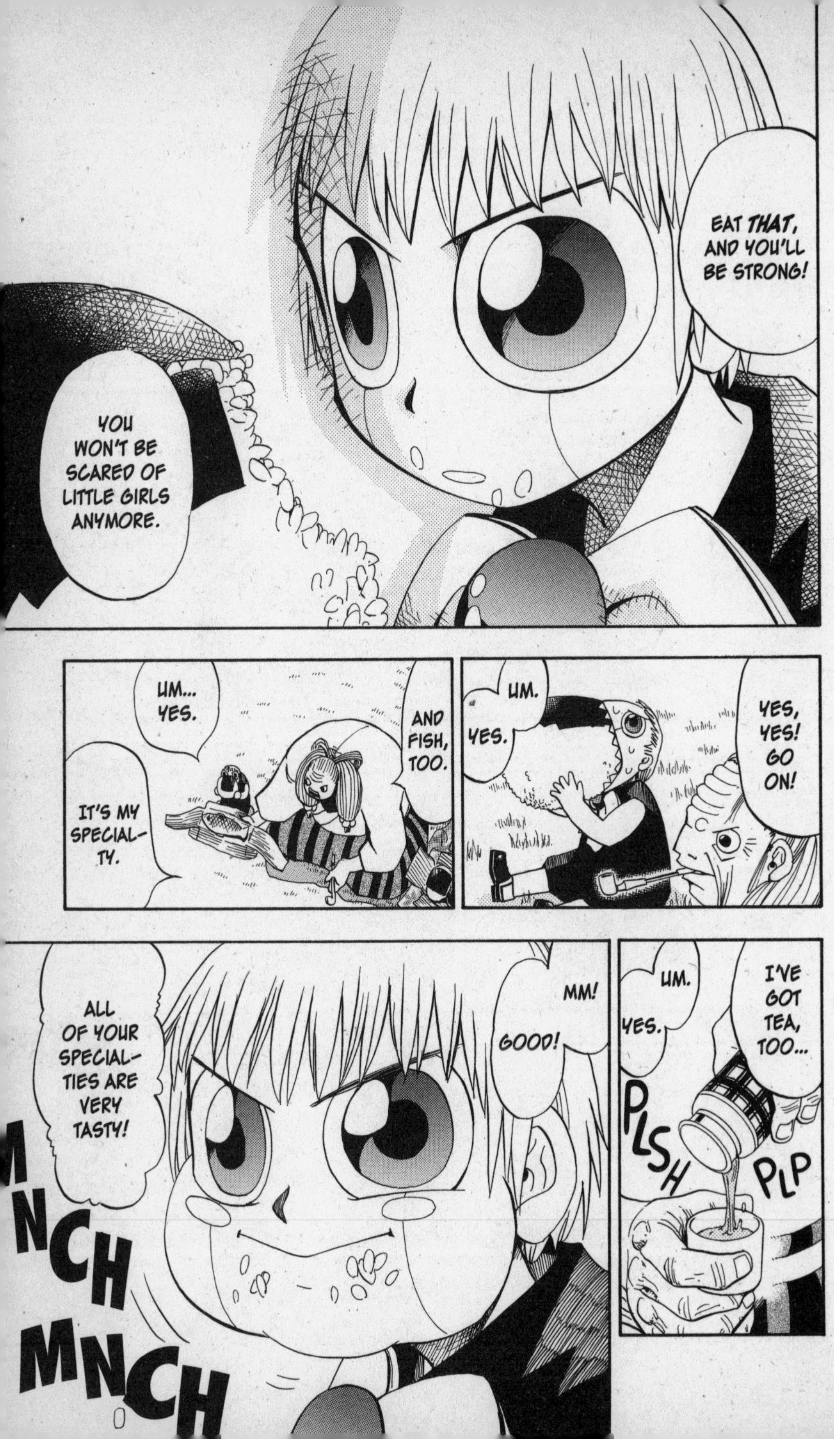
EAT *THAT*, AND YOU'LL BE STRONG!
YOU WON'T BE SCARED OF LITTLE GIRLS ANYMORE.
YES, YES! GO ON!
UM. YES.
AND FISH, TOO.
UM... YES.
IT'S MY SPECIAL-TY.
I'VE GOT TEA, TOO...
UM. YES.
PLSH
PLP
MM! GOOD!
ALL OF YOUR SPECIAL-TIES ARE VERY TASTY!
MNCH
MNCH

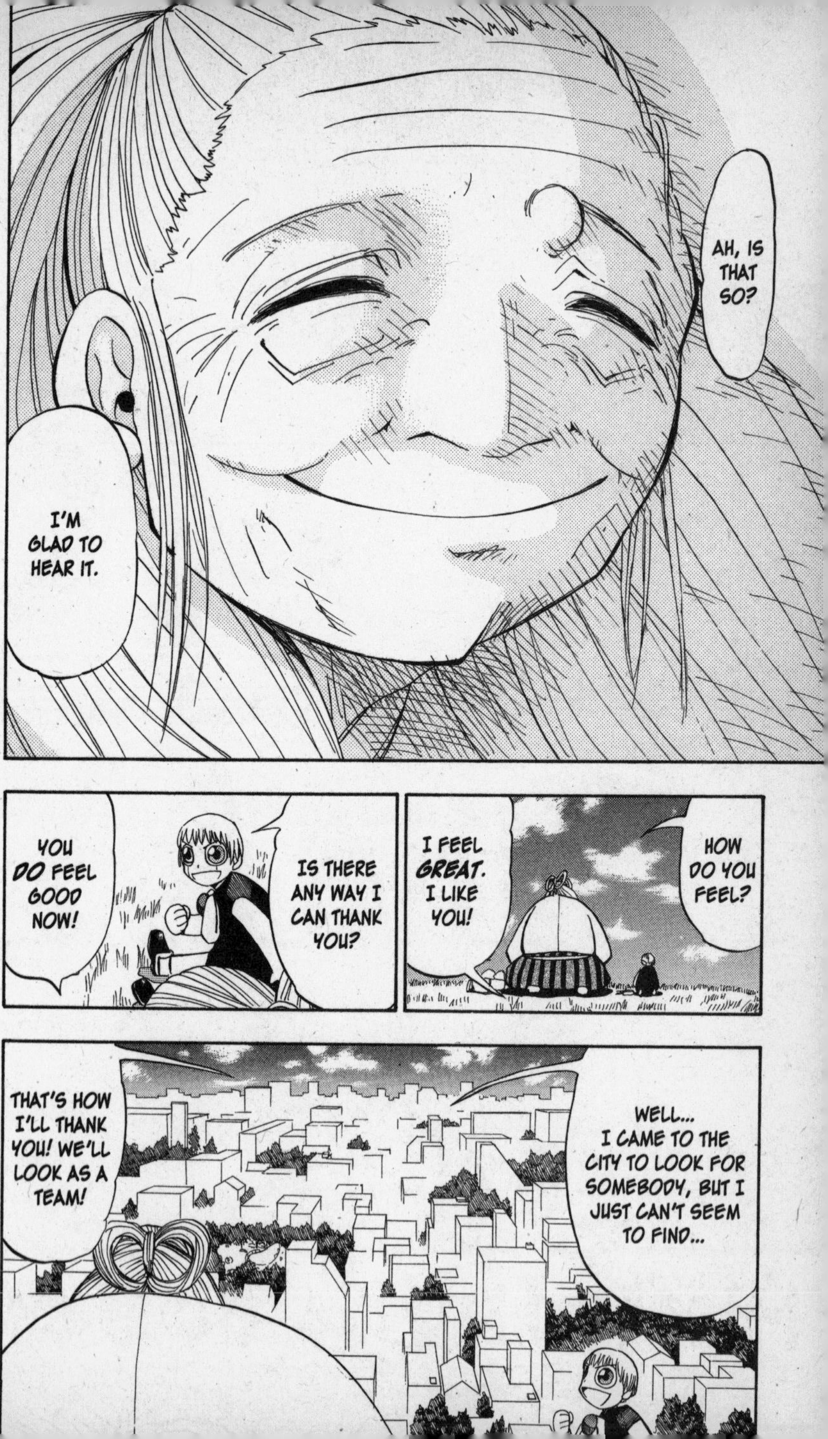
AH, IS THAT SO?
I'M GLAD TO HEAR IT.
HOW DO YOU FEEL?
I FEEL GREAT. I LIKE YOU!
IS THERE ANY WAY I CAN THANK YOU?
YOU DO FEEL GOOD NOW!
WELL... I CAME TO THE CITY TO LOOK FOR SOMEBODY, BUT I JUST CAN'T SEEM TO FIND...
THAT'S HOW I'LL THANK YOU! WE'LL LOOK AS A TEAM!

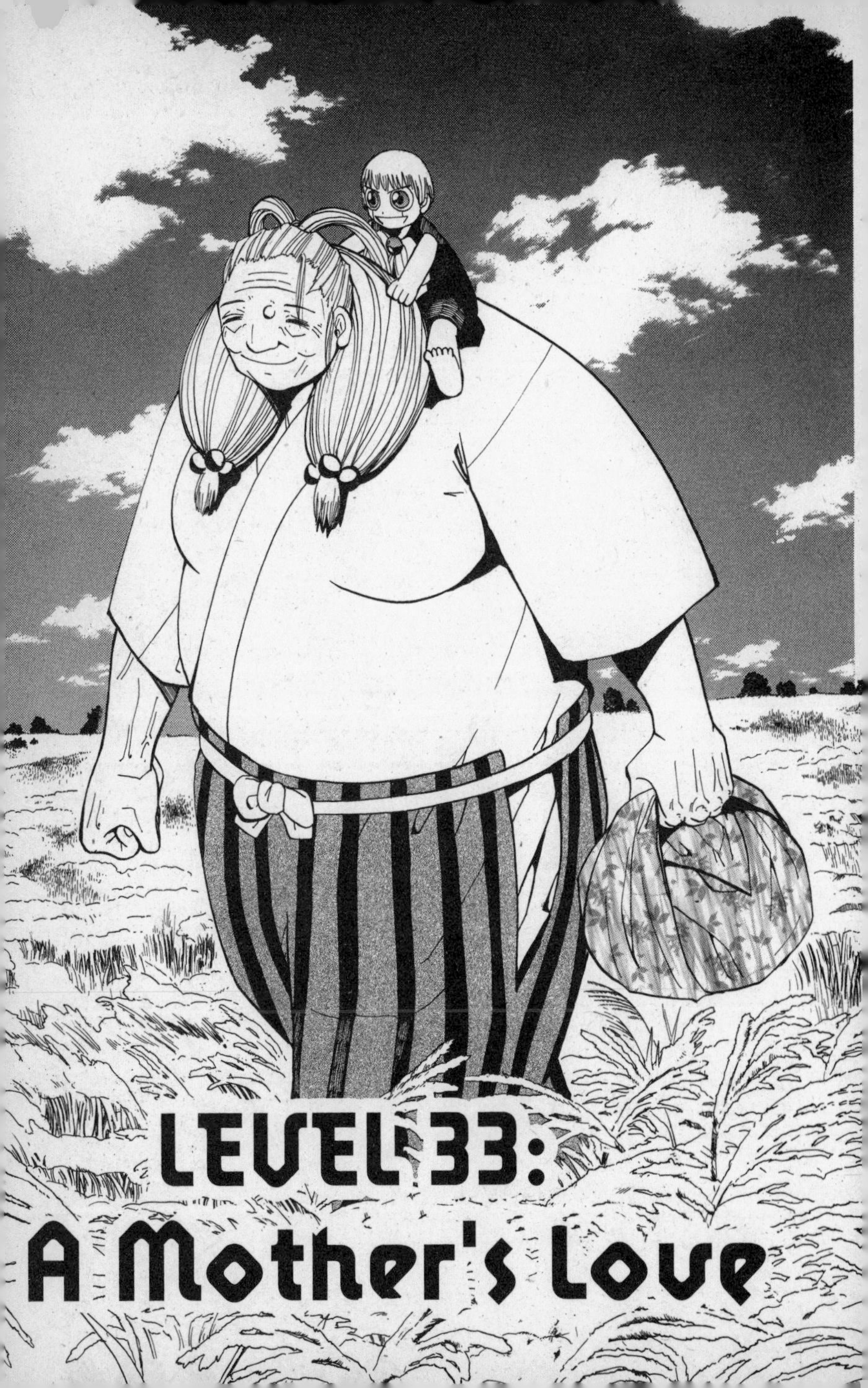

LEVEL 33: A Mother's Love

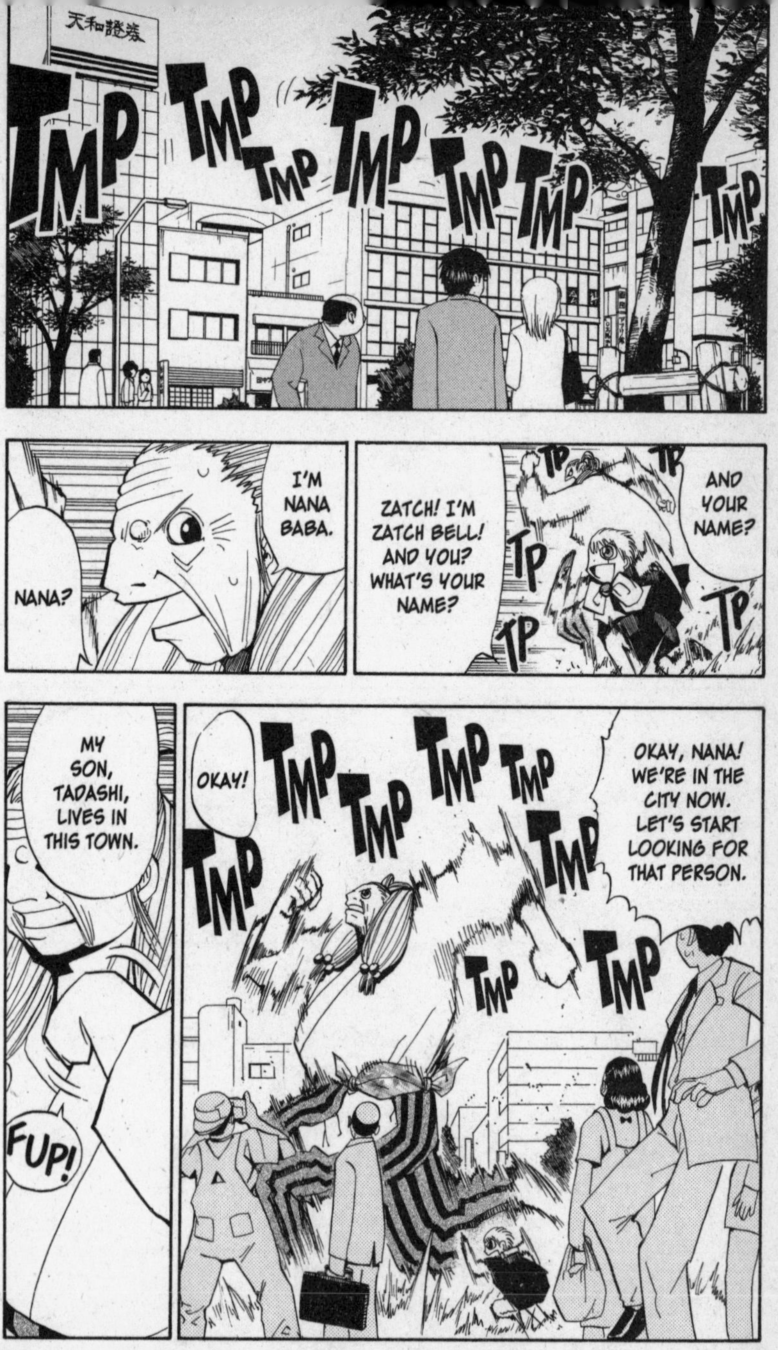
TMP TMP TMP TMP TMP TMP TMP
AND YOUR NAME?
TP TP TP TP TP
ZATCH! I'M ZATCH BELL! AND YOU? WHAT'S YOUR NAME?
I'M NANA BABA.
NANA?
OKAY, NANA! WE'RE IN THE CITY NOW. LET'S START LOOKING FOR THAT PERSON.
TMP TMP TMP TMP TMP TMP TMP
OKAY!
MY SON, TADASHI, LIVES IN THIS TOWN.
FUP!

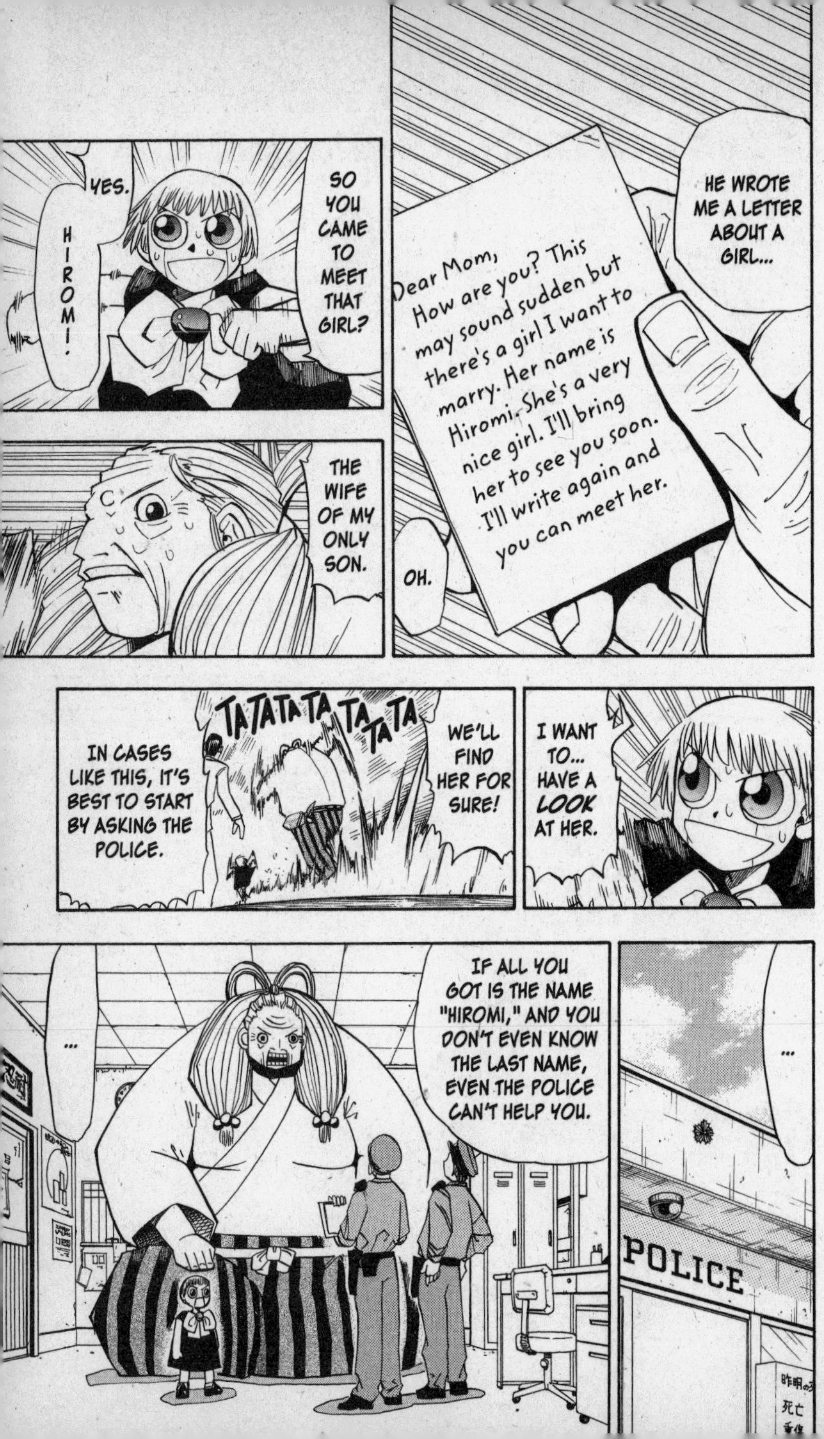
HE WROTE ME A LETTER ABOUT A GIRL...
Dear Mom, How are you? This may sound sudden but there's a girl I want to marry. Her name is Hiromi. She's a very nice girl. I'll bring her to see you soon. I'll write again and you can meet her.
OH.
SO YOU CAME TO MEET THAT GIRL?
YES.
HIROMI!
THE WIFE OF MY ONLY SON.
I WANT TO... HAVE A LOOK AT HER.
WE'LL FIND HER FOR SURE!
TATATATA TATATA
IN CASES LIKE THIS, IT'S BEST TO START BY ASKING THE POLICE.
...
POLICE
IF ALL YOU GOT IS THE NAME "HIROMI," AND YOU DON'T EVEN KNOW THE LAST NAME, EVEN THE POLICE CAN'T HELP YOU.
...

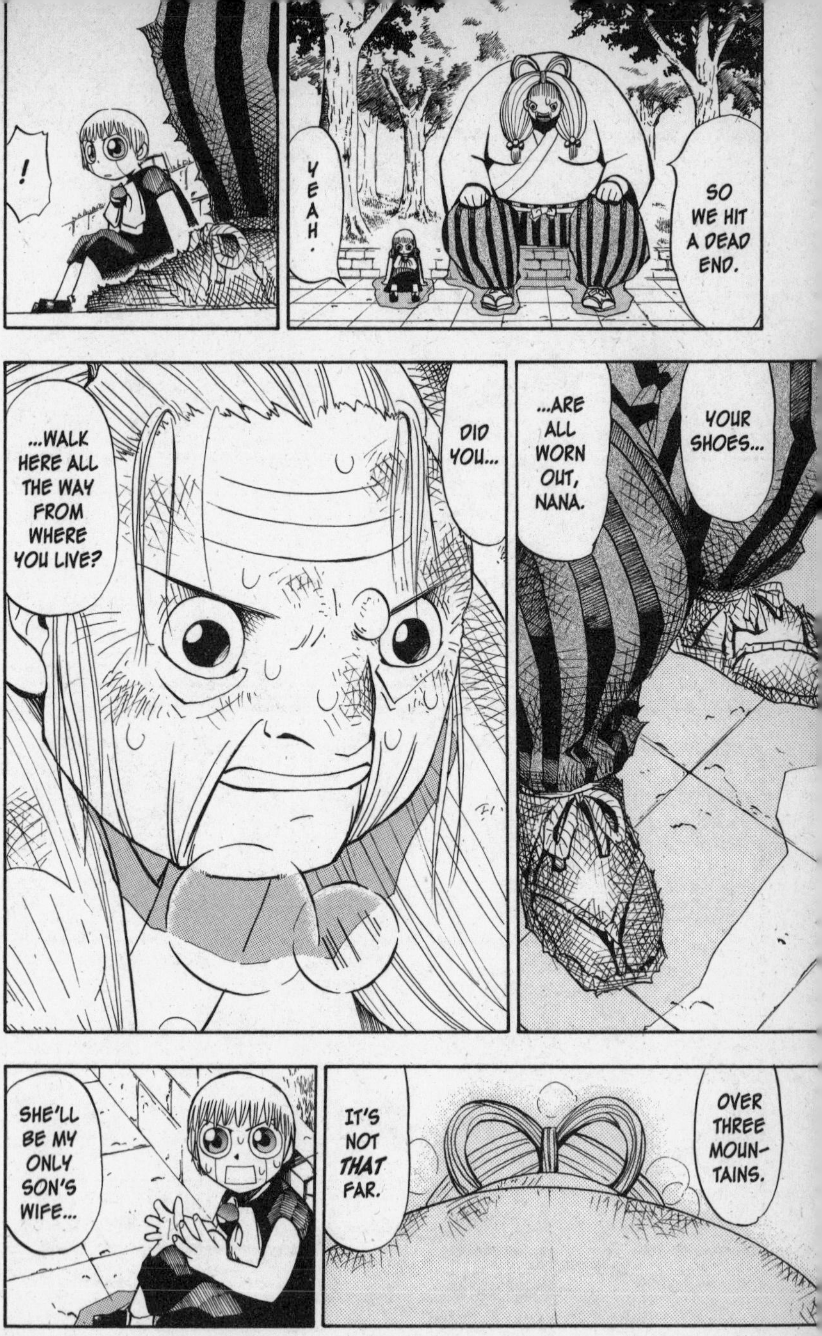
SO WE HIT A DEAD END.
YEAH.
!
YOUR SHOES...
...ARE ALL WORN OUT, NANA.
DID YOU...
...WALK HERE ALL THE WAY FROM WHERE YOU LIVE?
OVER THREE MOUN-TAINS.
IT'S NOT *THAT* FAR.
SHE'LL BE MY ONLY SON'S WIFE...

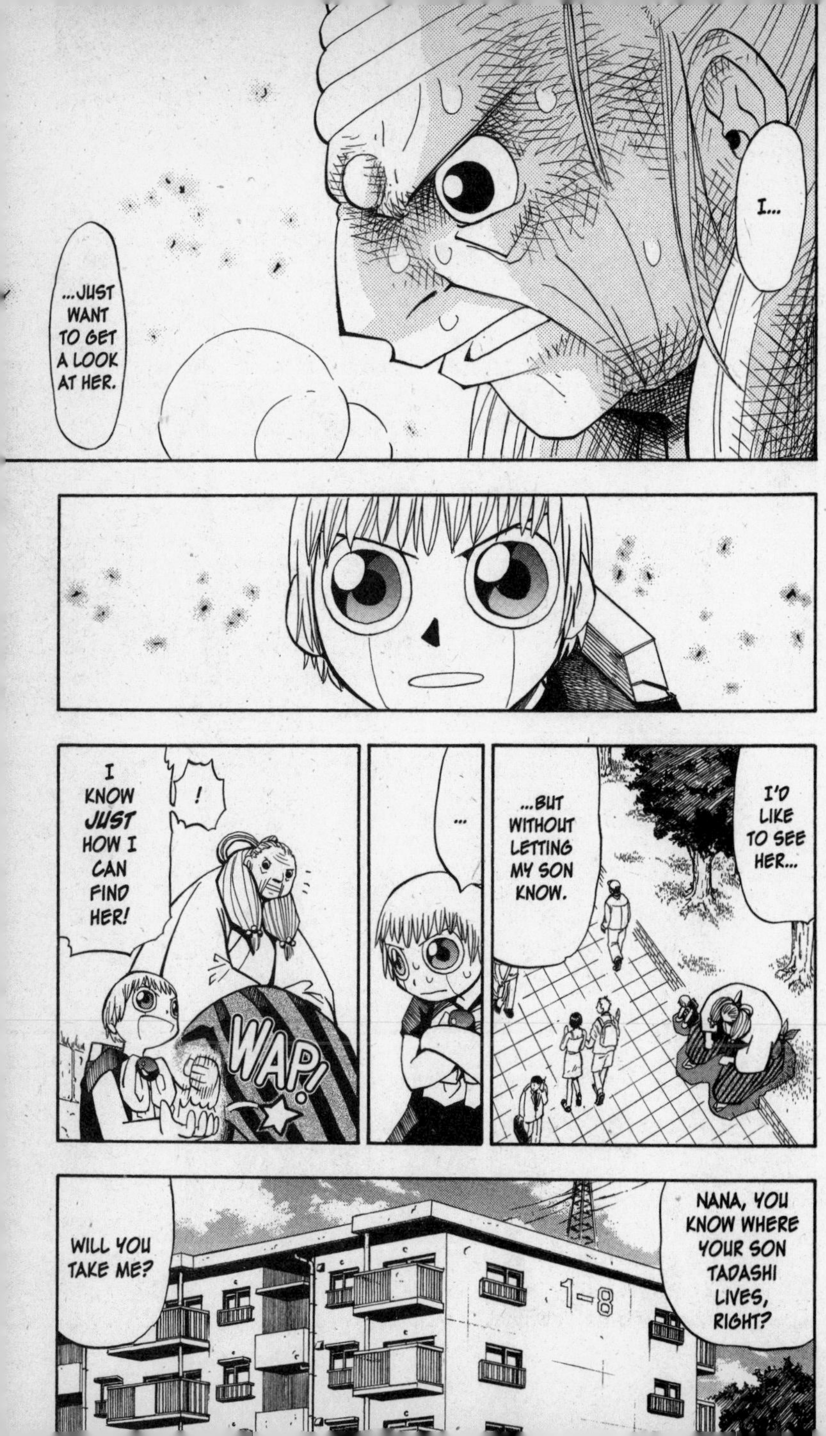
I...
...JUST WANT TO GET A LOOK AT HER.
I'D LIKE TO SEE HER...
...BUT WITHOUT LETTING MY SON KNOW.
...
!
I KNOW JUST HOW I CAN FIND HER!
WAP!
NANA, YOU KNOW WHERE YOUR SON TADASHI LIVES, RIGHT?
1-8
WILL YOU TAKE ME?

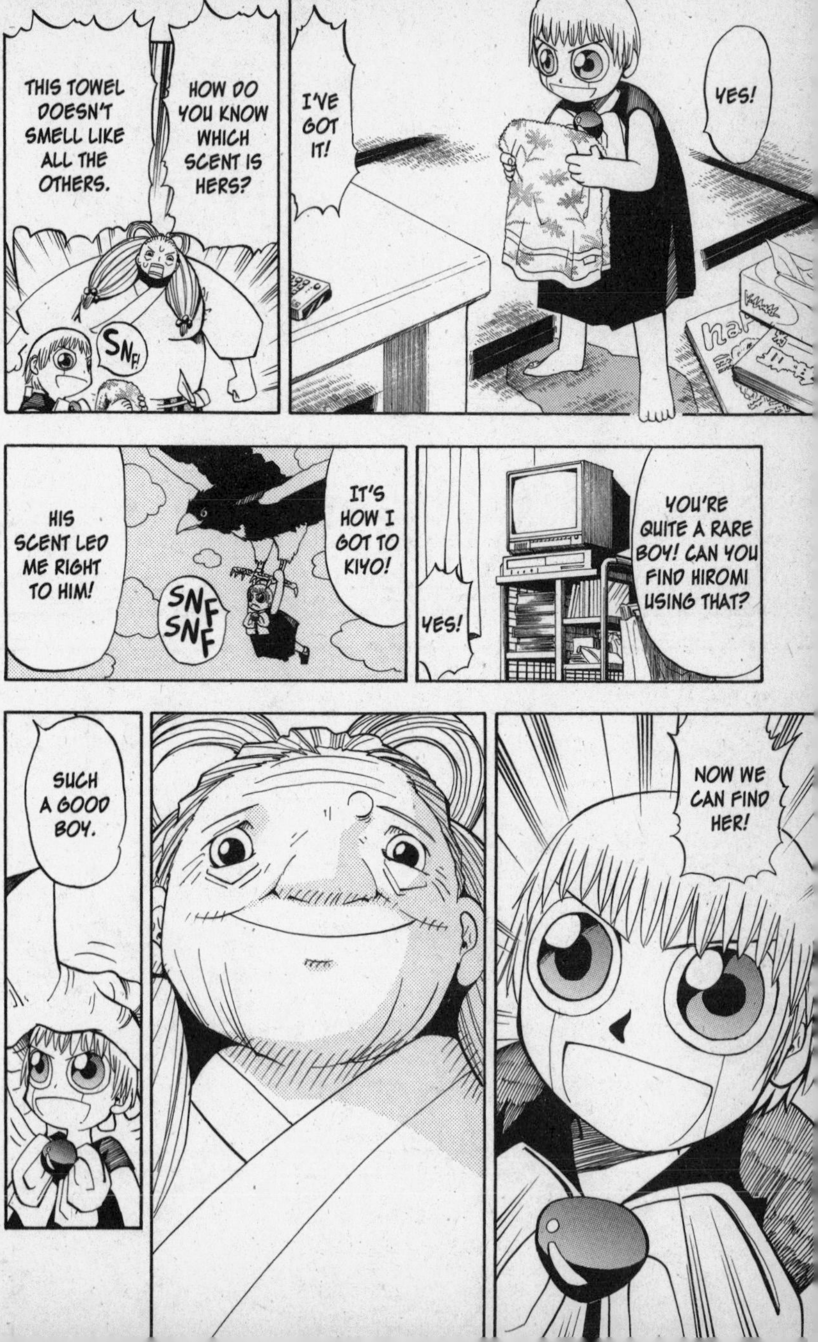
YES!
I'VE GOT IT!
HOW DO YOU KNOW WHICH SCENT IS HERS?
THIS TOWEL DOESN'T SMELL LIKE ALL THE OTHERS.
SNF!
YOU'RE QUITE A RARE BOY! CAN YOU FIND HIROMI USING THAT?
YES!
IT'S HOW I GOT TO KIYO!
HIS SCENT LED ME RIGHT TO HIM!
SNF SNF
NOW WE CAN FIND HER!
SUCH A GOOD BOY.

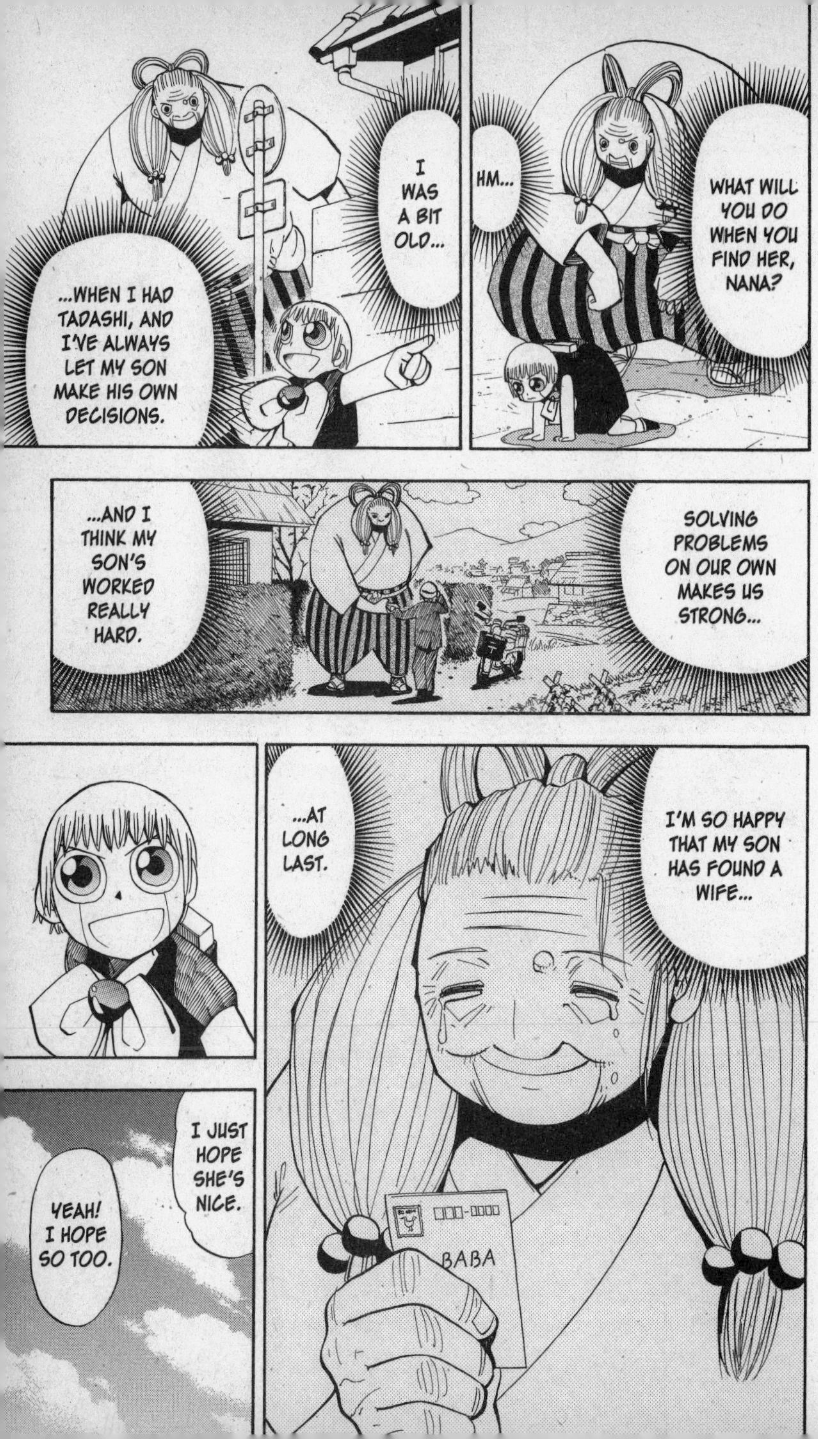
WHAT WILL YOU DO WHEN YOU FIND HER, NANA?
HM...
I WAS A BIT OLD...
...WHEN I HAD TADASHI, AND I'VE ALWAYS LET MY SON MAKE HIS OWN DECISIONS.
SOLVING PROBLEMS ON OUR OWN MAKES US STRONG...
...AND I THINK MY SON'S WORKED REALLY HARD.
I'M SO HAPPY THAT MY SON HAS FOUND A WIFE...
...AT LONG LAST.
BABA
I JUST HOPE SHE'S NICE.
YEAH! I HOPE SO TOO.

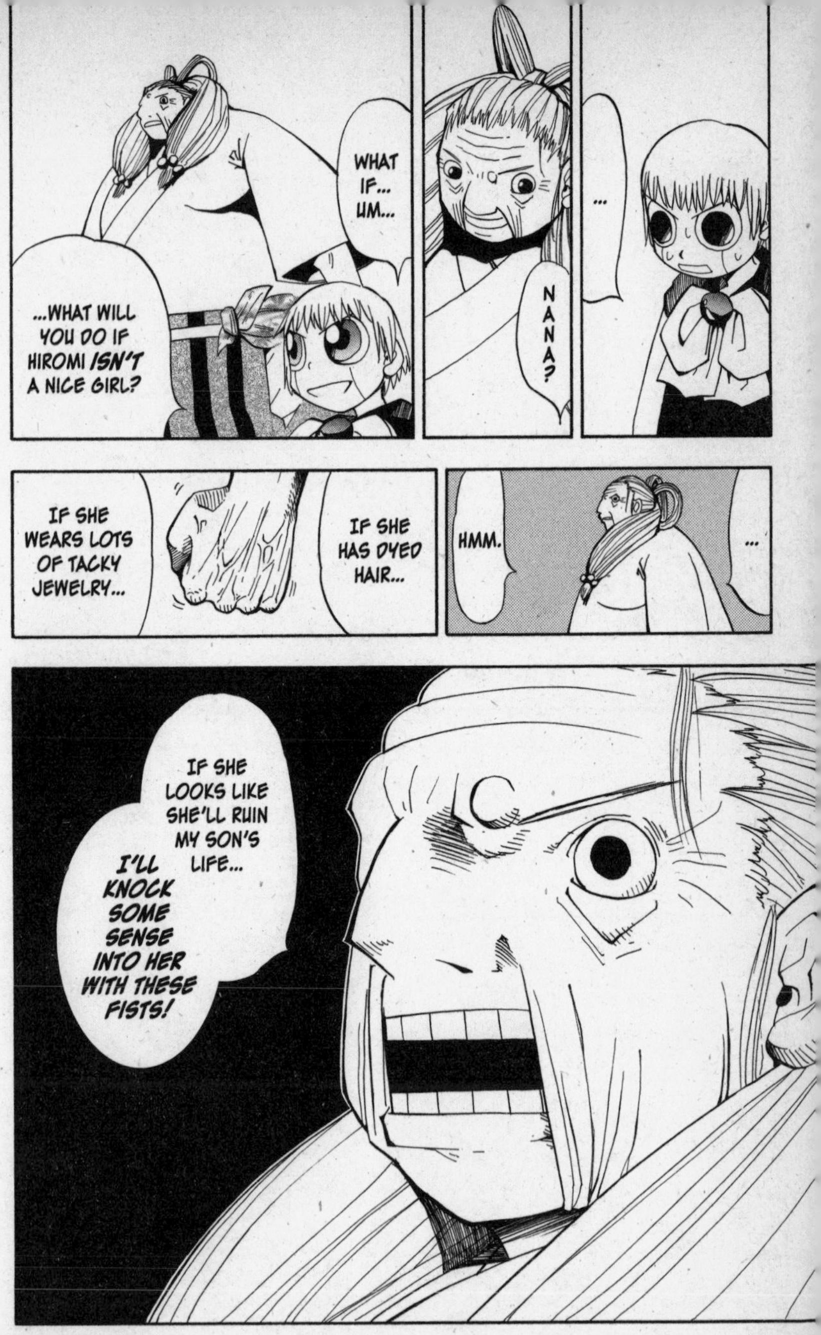
...
NANA?
WHAT IF... UM...
...WHAT WILL YOU DO IF HIROMI ISN'T A NICE GIRL?
...
HMM.
IF SHE HAS DYED HAIR...
IF SHE WEARS LOTS OF TACKY JEWELRY...
IF SHE LOOKS LIKE SHE'LL RUIN MY SON'S LIFE...
I'LL KNOCK SOME SENSE INTO HER WITH THESE FISTS!

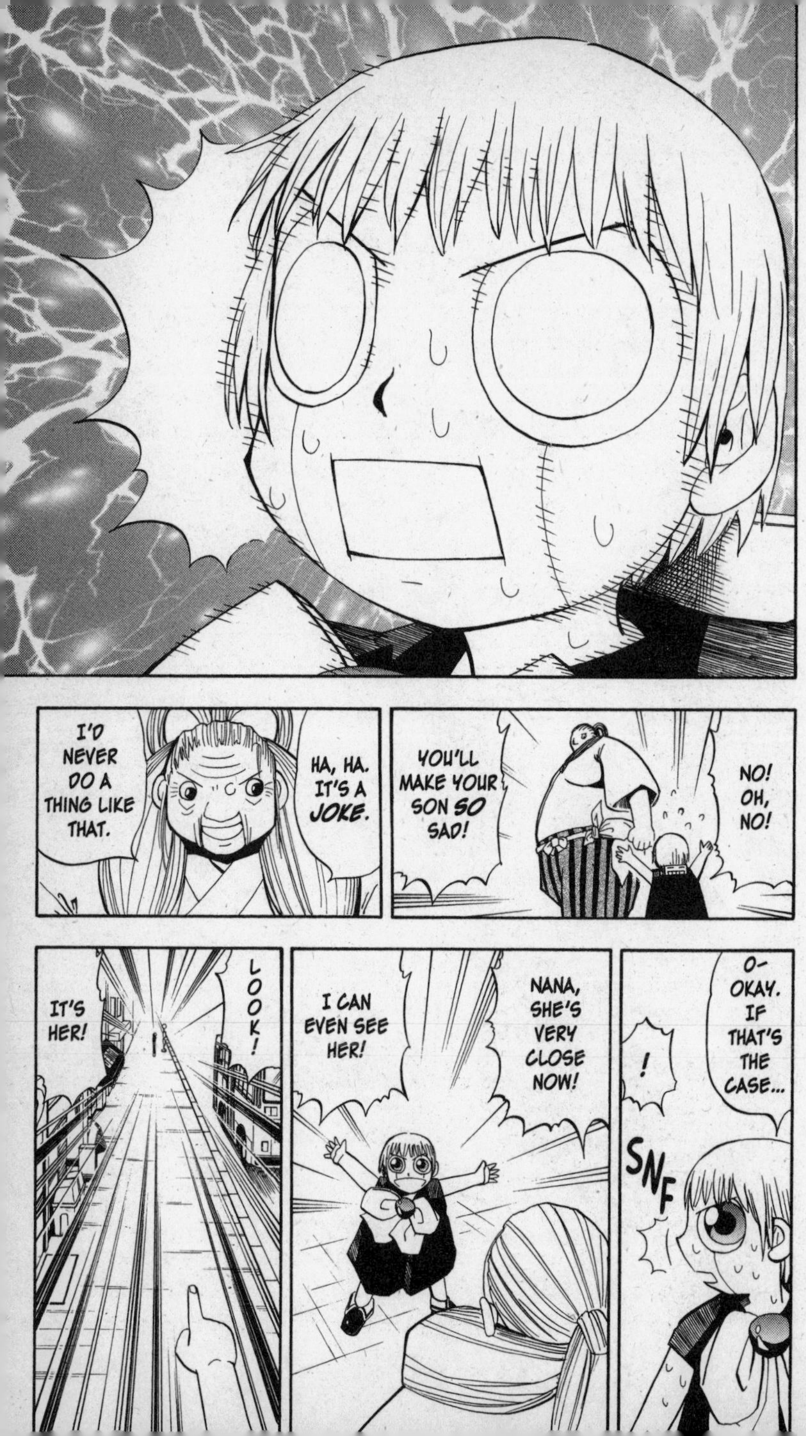
NO! OH, NO!
YOU'LL MAKE YOUR SON SO SAD!
HA, HA. IT'S A JOKE.
I'D NEVER DO A THING LIKE THAT.
O-OKAY. IF THAT'S THE CASE...
!
SNF
NANA, SHE'S VERY CLOSE NOW!
I CAN EVEN SEE HER!
LOOK!
IT'S HER!

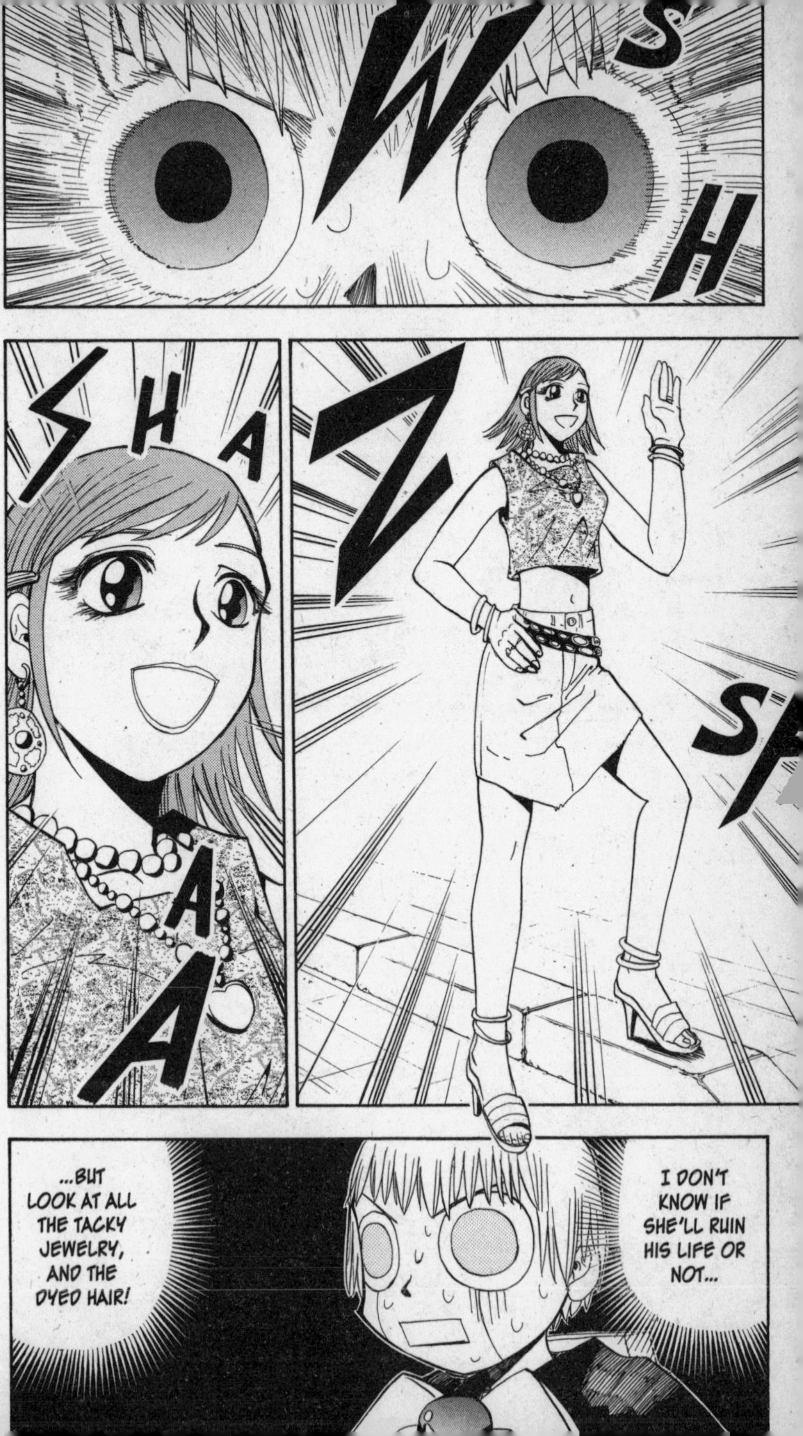
WHOOSH
SHAAA
I DON'T KNOW IF SHE'LL RUIN HIS LIFE OR NOT...
...BUT LOOK AT ALL THE TACKY JEWELRY, AND THE DYED HAIR!

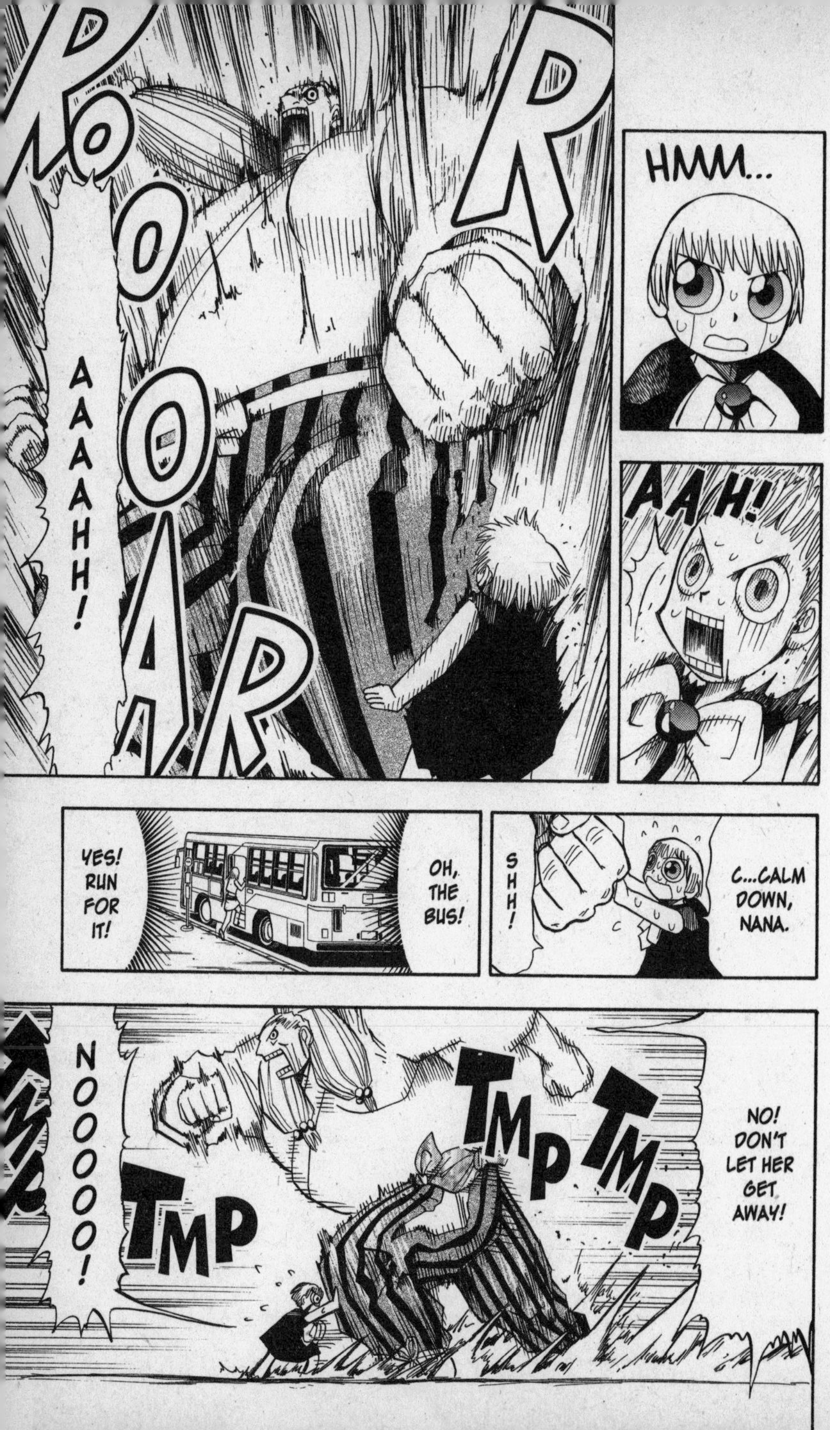
HMMM...
AAH!
ROOOOAR
AAAAAHH!
C...CALM DOWN, NANA.
SHH!
OH, THE BUS!
YES! RUN FOR IT!
NO! DON'T LET HER GET AWAY!
TMP
TMP
TMP
NOOOOOO!

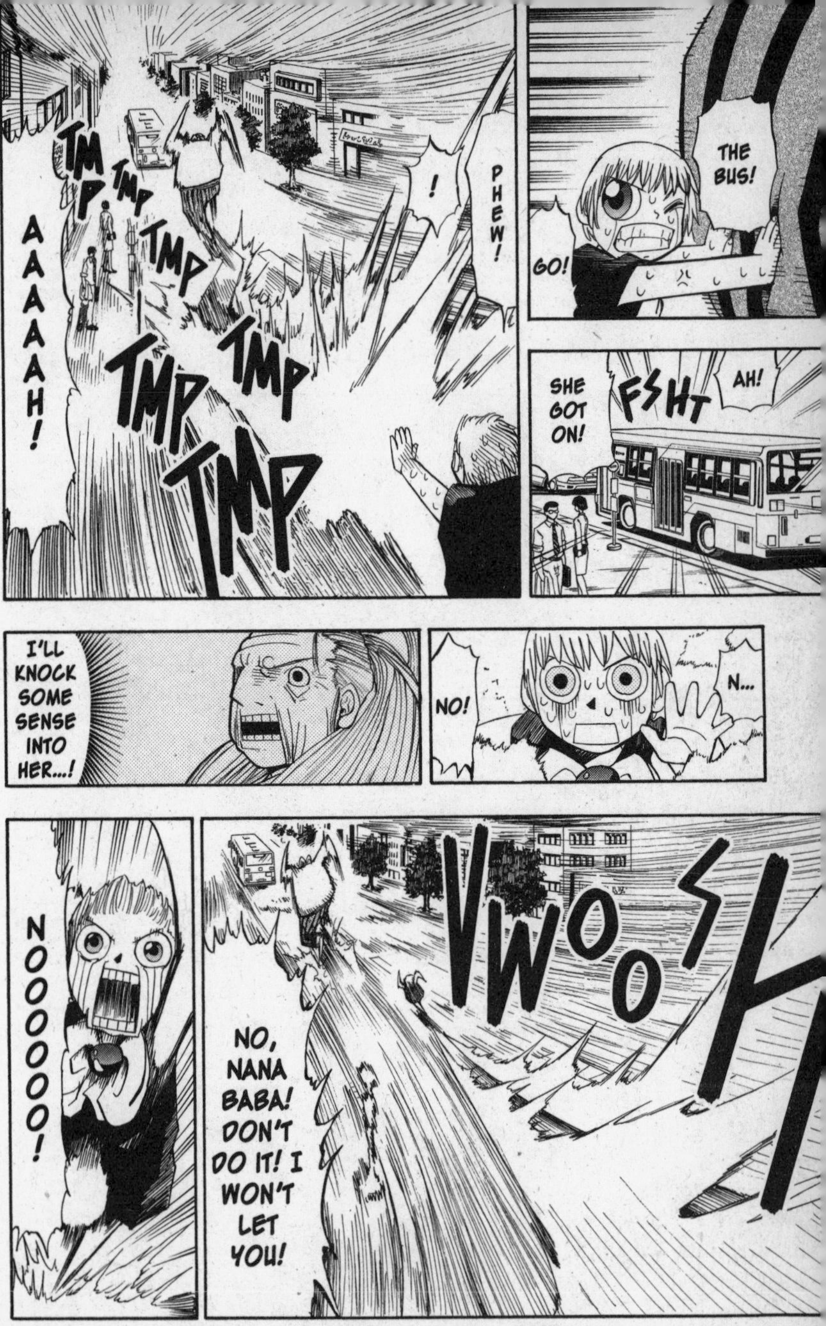
THE BUS!
GO!
AH!
FSHT
SHE GOT ON!
PHEW!
!
TMP
TMP
TMP
TMP
TMP
TMP
AAAAAAH!
N...
NO!
I'LL KNOCK SOME SENSE INTO HER...!
VWOOSH
NO, NANA BABA! DON'T DO IT! I WON'T LET YOU!
NOOOOOOOO!

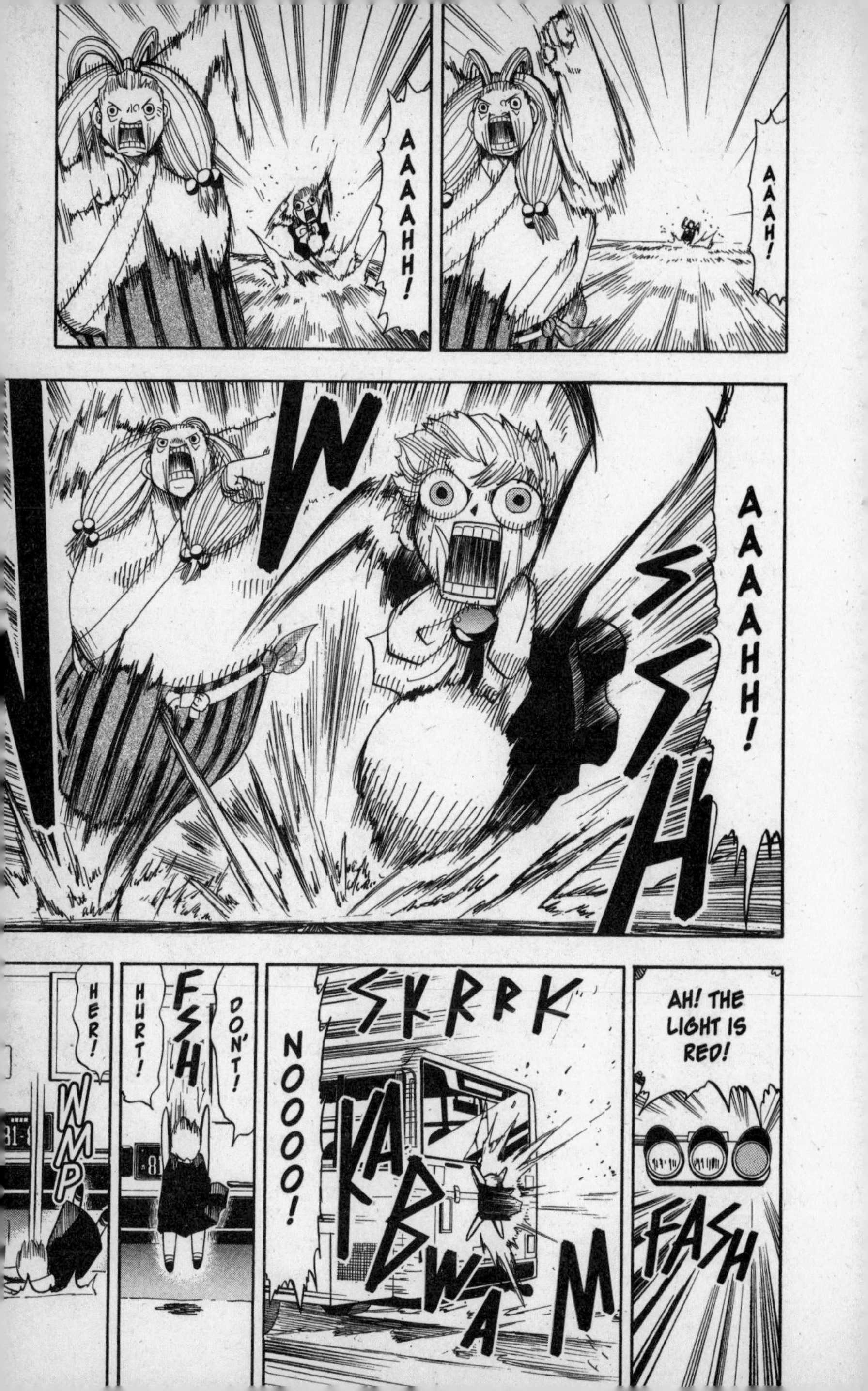
AAAAH!
AAAAAHH!
WSSH
AAAAAHH!
AH! THE LIGHT IS RED!
FASH
SKRRK
NOOOOO!
KABWAM
DON'T!
HURT!
FSH
HER!
WMP

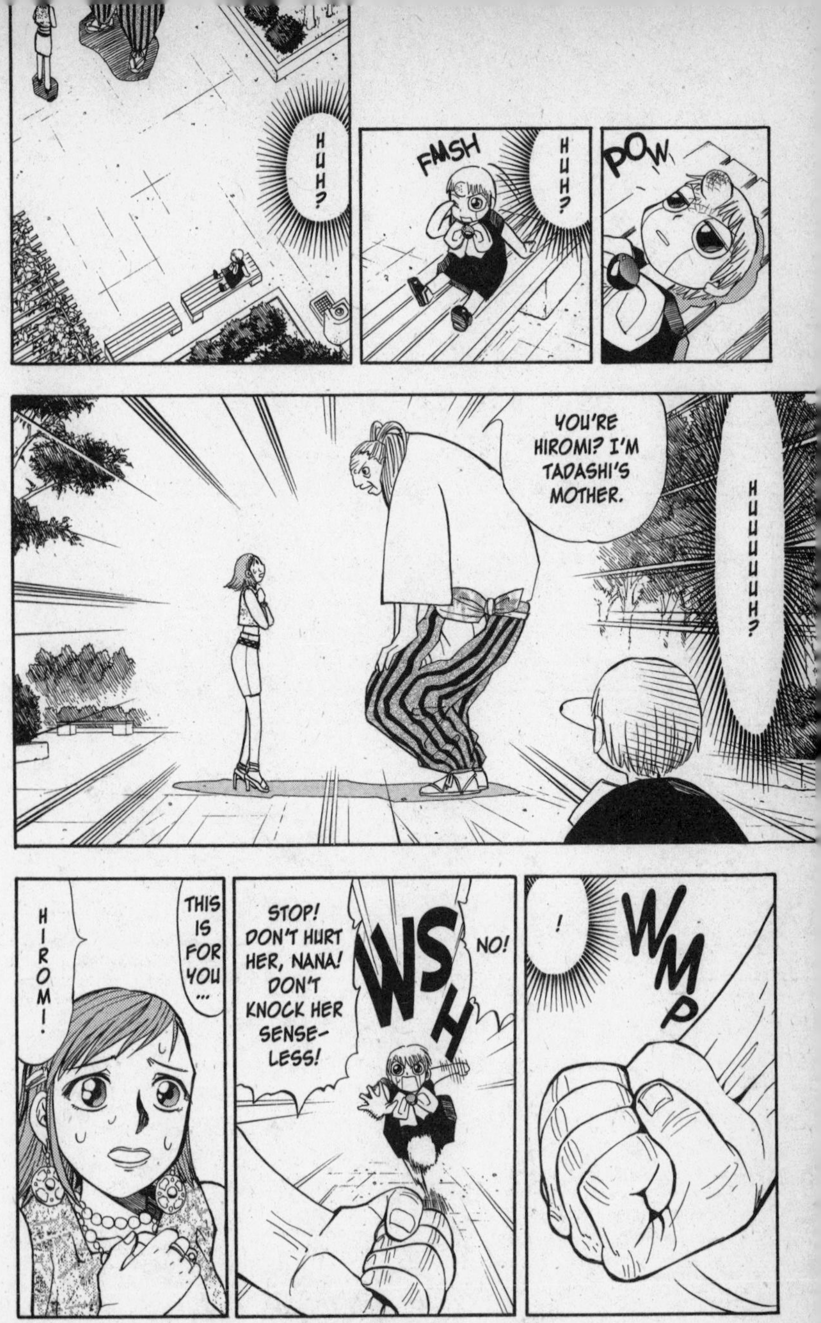
POW
FMSH
HUH?
HUH?
HUUUUUH?
YOU'RE HIROMI? I'M TADASHI'S MOTHER.
!
WMP
NO!
WSH
STOP! DON'T HURT HER, NANA! DON'T KNOCK HER SENSE-LESS!
THIS IS FOR YOU...
HIROMI!

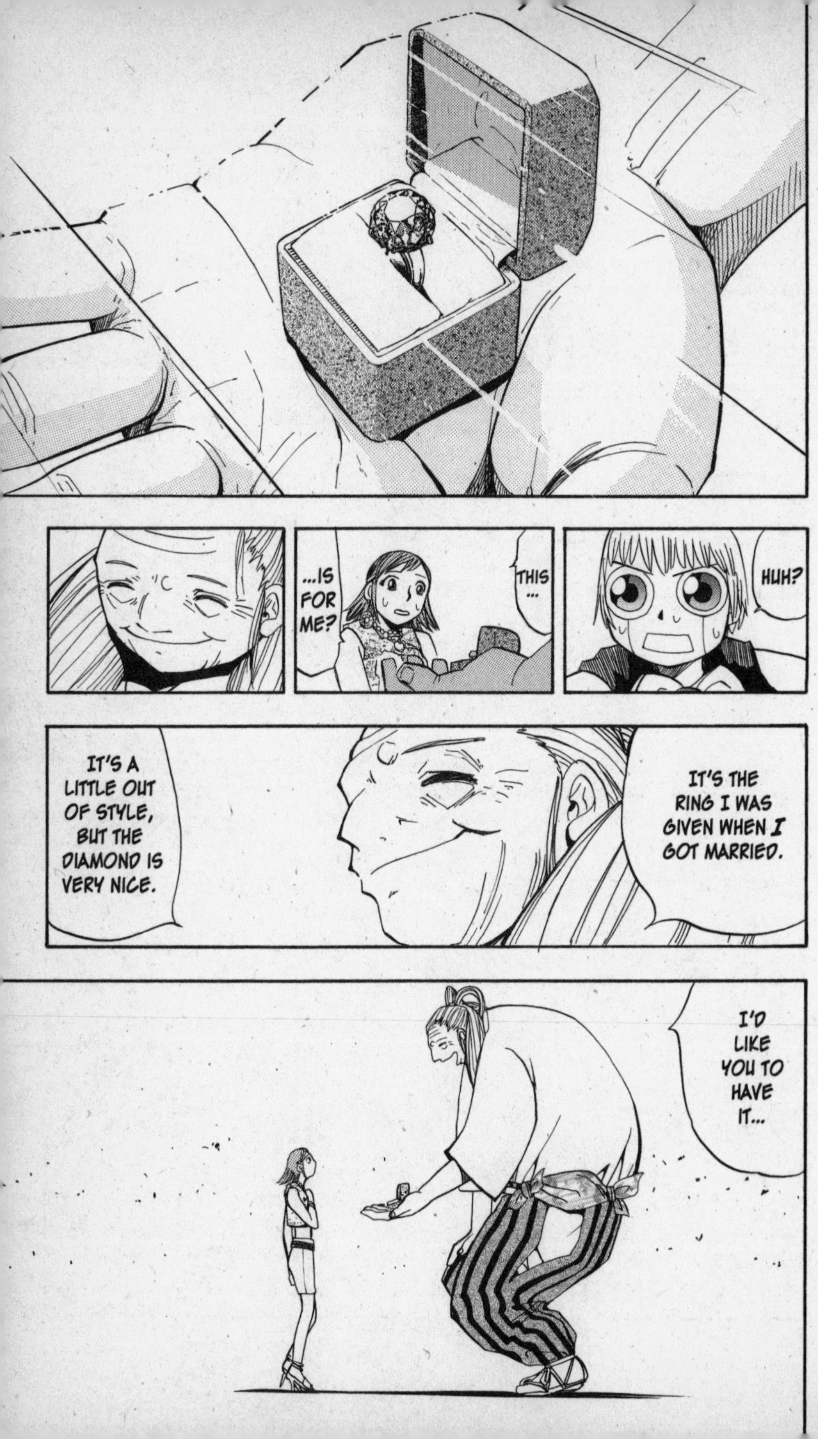
HUH?
THIS ...
...IS FOR ME?
IT'S THE RING I WAS GIVEN WHEN *I* GOT MARRIED.
IT'S A LITTLE OUT OF STYLE, BUT THE DIAMOND IS VERY NICE.
I'D LIKE YOU TO HAVE IT...

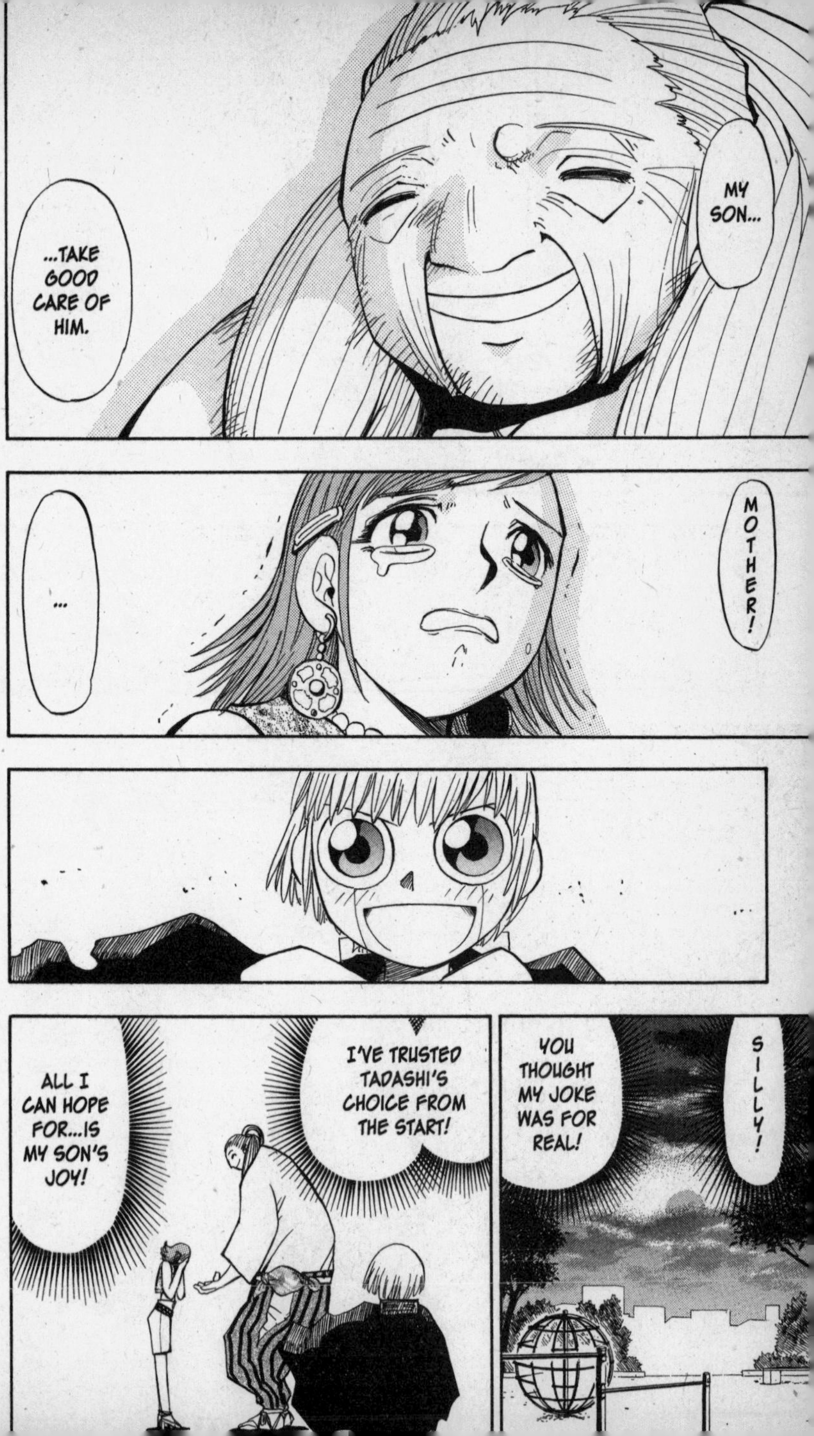
MY SON...
...TAKE GOOD CARE OF HIM.
MOTHER!
...
SILLY!
YOU THOUGHT MY JOKE WAS FOR REAL!
I'VE TRUSTED TADASHI'S CHOICE FROM THE START!
ALL I CAN HOPE FOR...IS MY SON'S JOY!

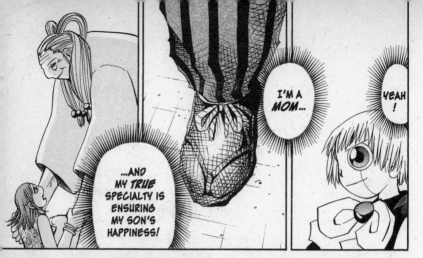

I'M A *MOM*...

YEAH!

...AND MY *TRUE* SPECIALTY IS ENSURING MY SON'S HAPPINESS!

YES, IT IS...

YES!

I HOPE I'VE GOT A MOTHER LIKE THAT SOME-WHERE!

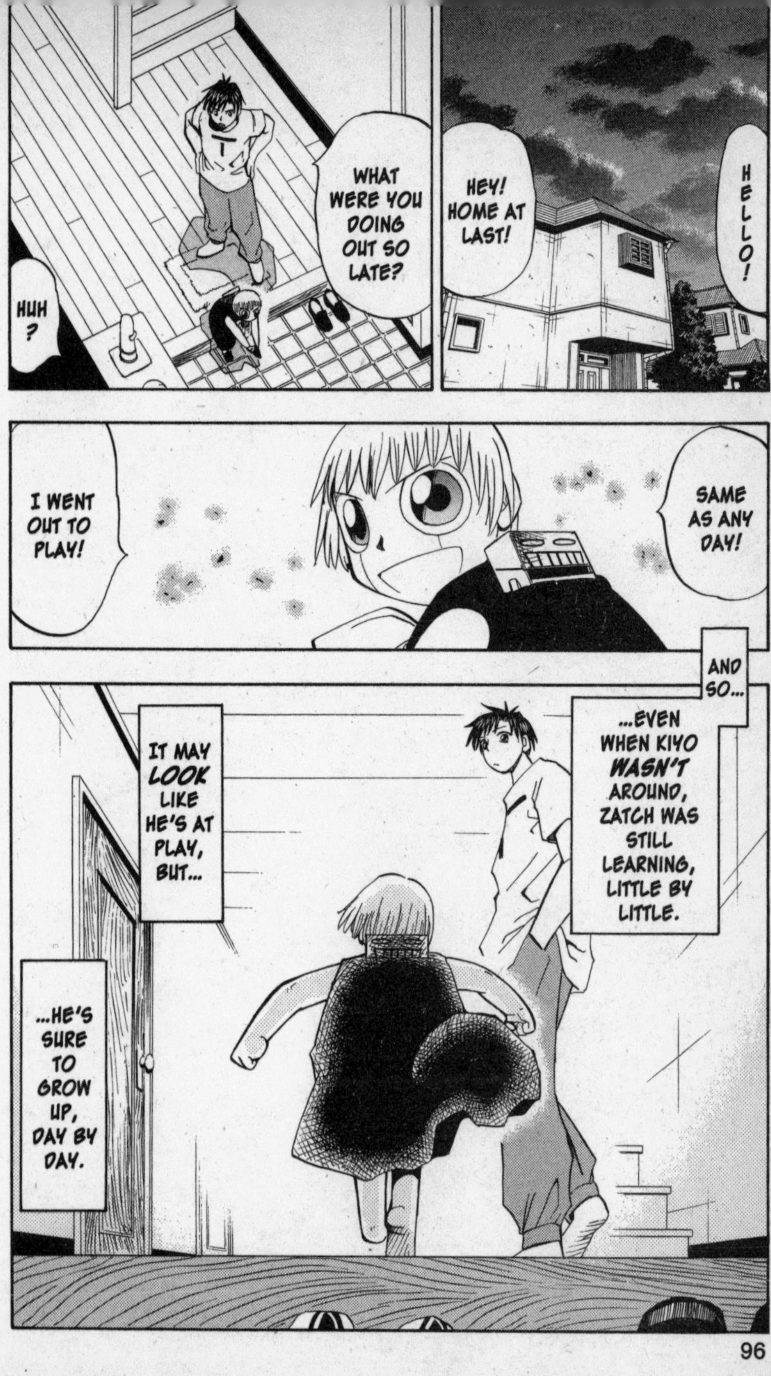
HELLO!
HEY! HOME AT LAST!
WHAT WERE YOU DOING OUT SO LATE?
HUH?
SAME AS ANY DAY!
I WENT OUT TO PLAY!
AND SO...
...EVEN WHEN KIYO WASN'T AROUND, ZATCH WAS STILL LEARNING, LITTLE BY LITTLE.
IT MAY LOOK LIKE HE'S AT PLAY, BUT...
...HE'S SURE TO GROW UP, DAY BY DAY.

LEVEL 34:
The Worst Teacher

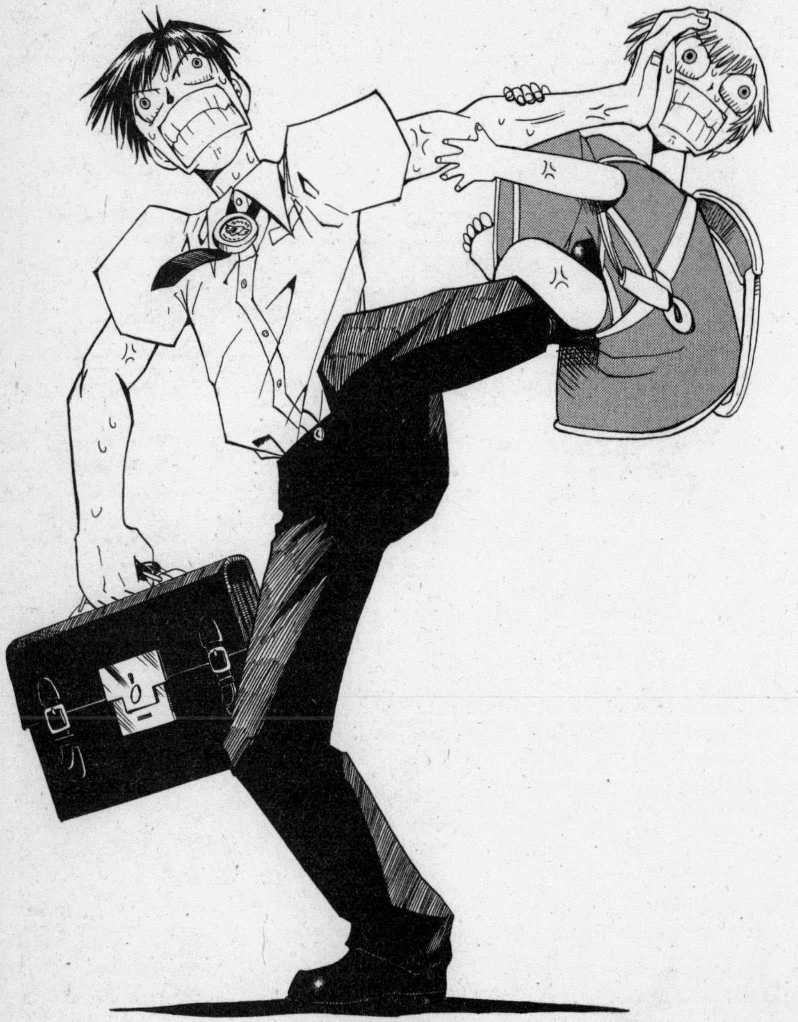

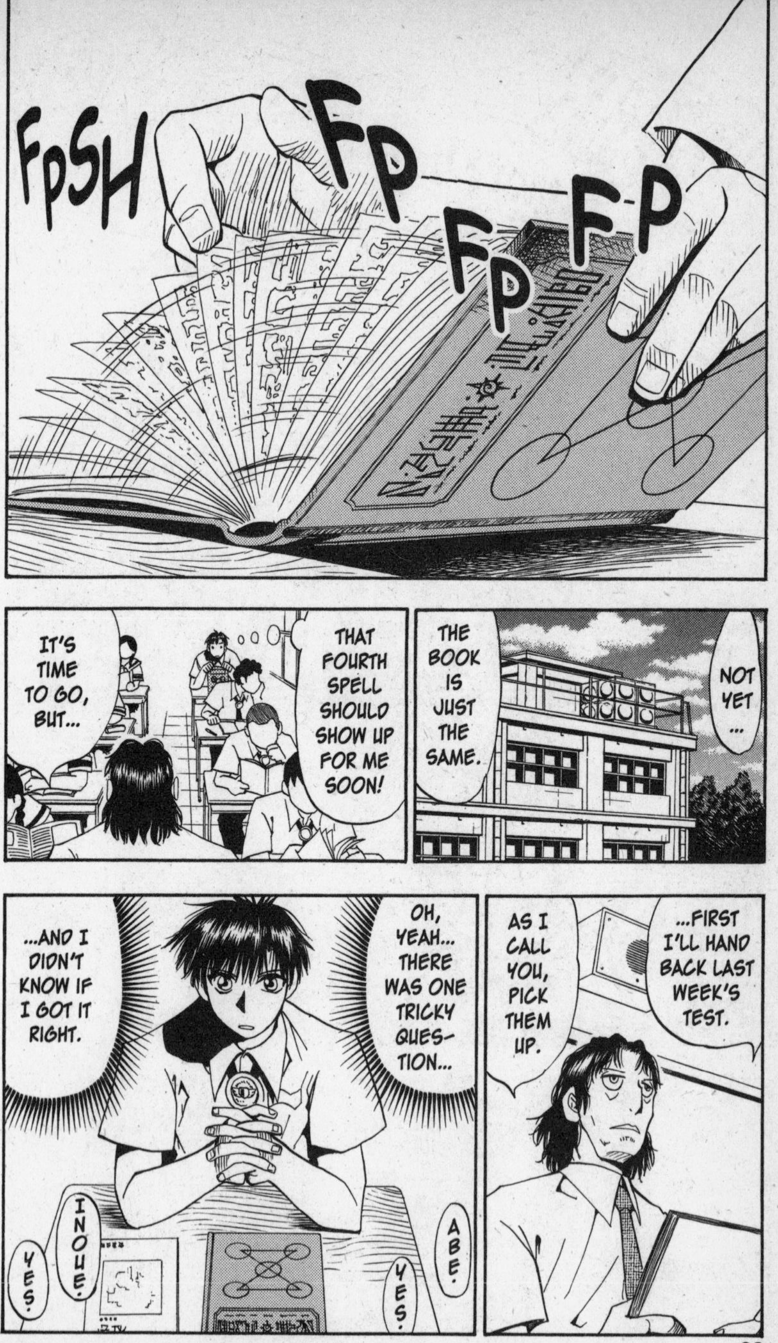
F-P
FP
FP
FPSH
NOT YET...
THE BOOK IS JUST THE SAME.
THAT FOURTH SPELL SHOULD SHOW UP FOR ME SOON!
IT'S TIME TO GO, BUT...
...FIRST I'LL HAND BACK LAST WEEK'S TEST.
AS I CALL YOU, PICK THEM UP.
OH, YEAH... THERE WAS ONE TRICKY QUES-TION...
...AND I DIDN'T KNOW IF I GOT IT RIGHT.
ABE.
YES.
INOUE.
YES.

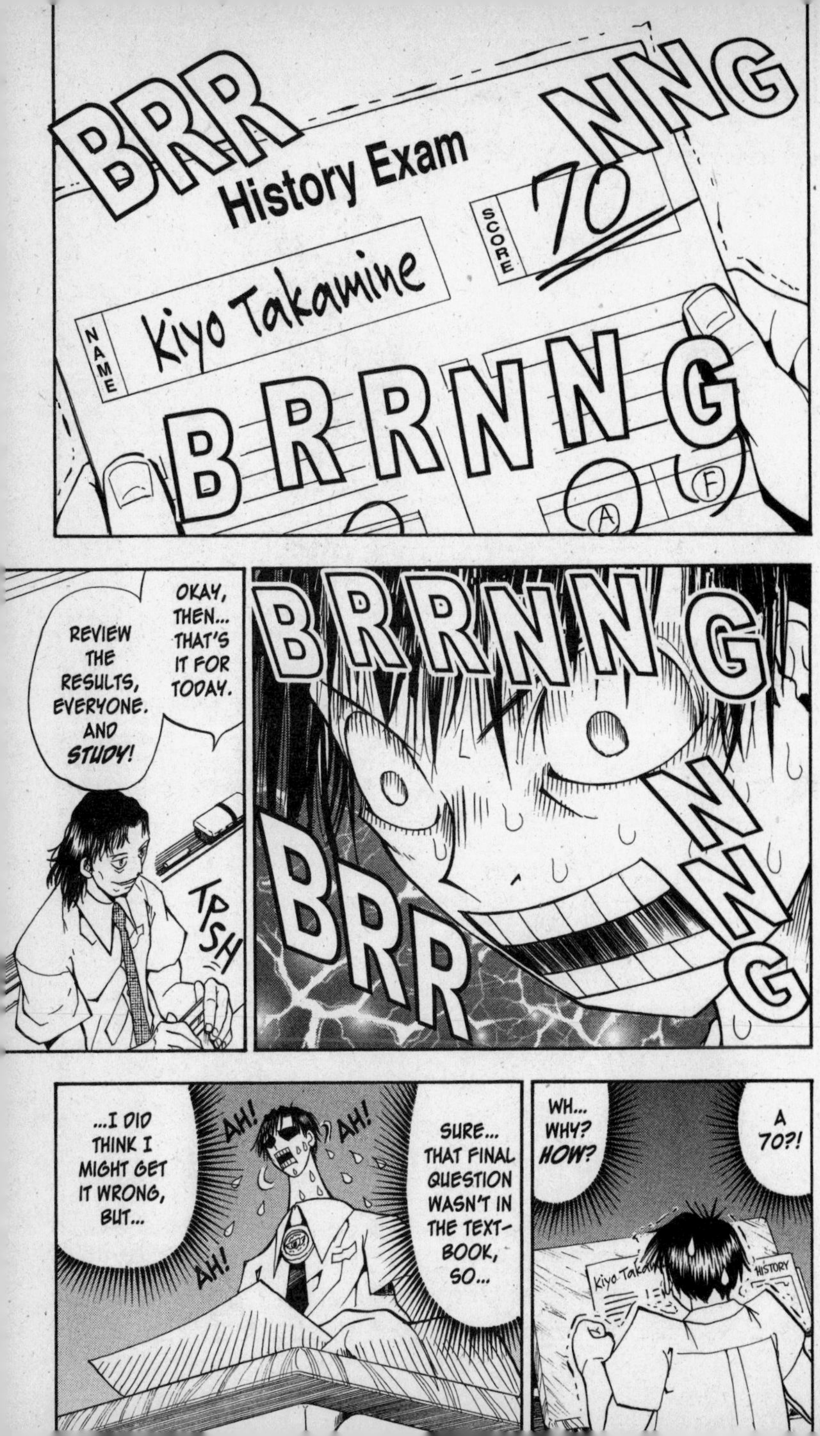
BRR NNG
History Exam
SCORE 70
NAME Kiyo Takamine
BRRNNG
BRRNNG
BRR NNG
OKAY, THEN... THAT'S IT FOR TODAY.
REVIEW THE RESULTS, EVERYONE. AND *STUDY!*
TPSH
A 70?!
WH... WHY? *HOW?*
HISTORY
Kiyo Taka
SURE... THAT FINAL QUESTION WASN'T IN THE TEXT-BOOK, SO...
...I DID THINK I MIGHT GET IT WRONG, BUT...
AH!
AH!
AH!

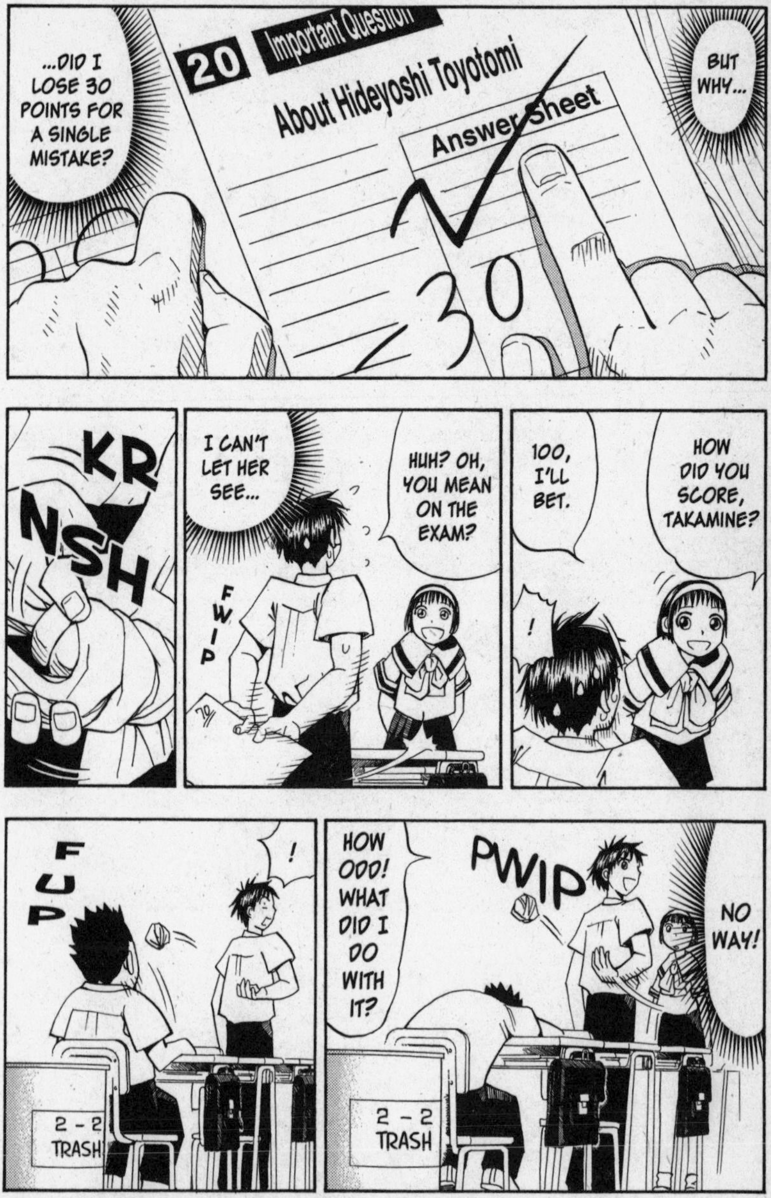
BUT WHY...
20
Important Question
About Hideyoshi Toyotomi
Answer Sheet
...DID I LOSE 30 POINTS FOR A SINGLE MISTAKE?
30
HOW DID YOU SCORE, TAKAMINE?
100, I'LL BET.
!
HUH? OH, YOU MEAN ON THE EXAM?
I CAN'T LET HER SEE...
FWIP
KRNSH
NO WAY!
PWIP
HOW ODD! WHAT DID I DO WITH IT?
2 - 2 TRASH
!
FUP
2 - 2 TRASH

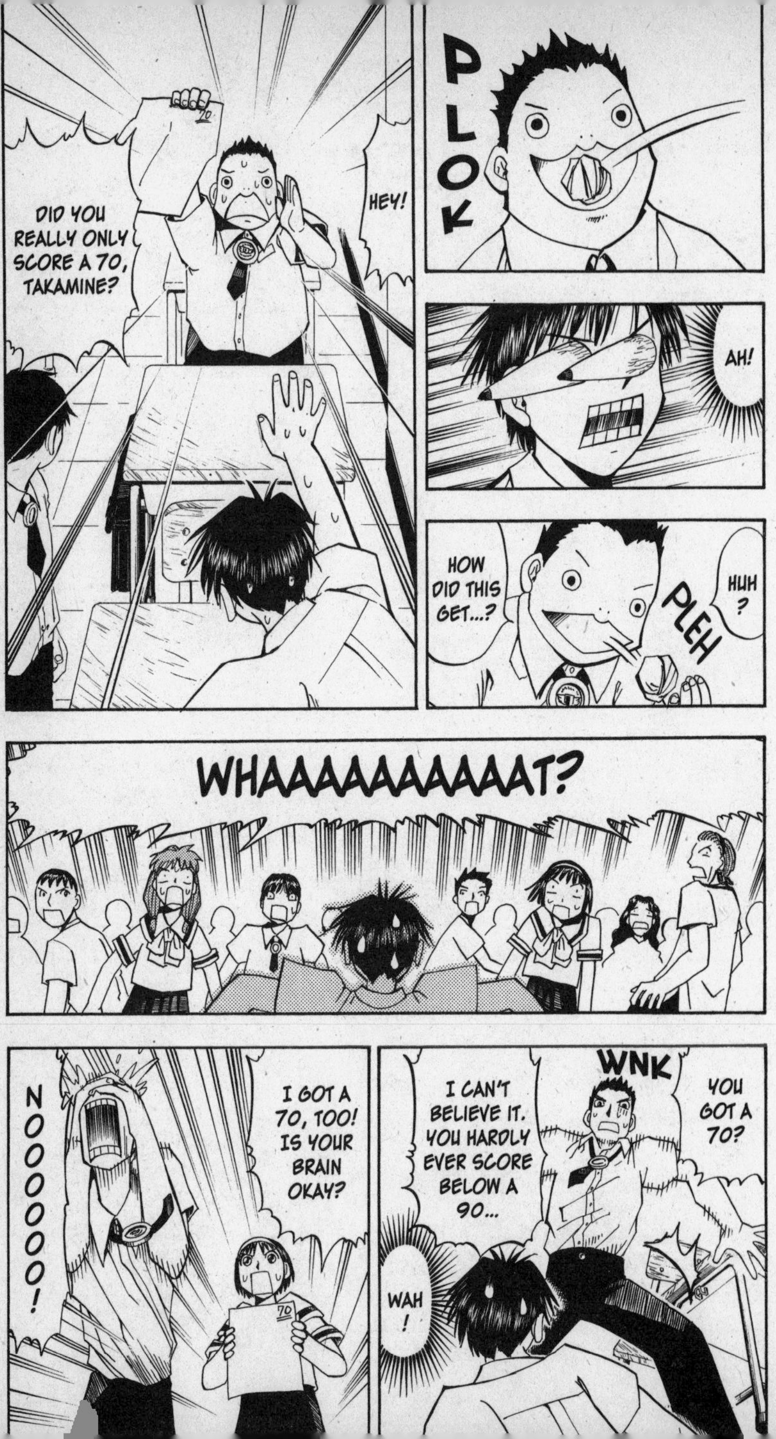
DID YOU REALLY ONLY SCORE A 70, TAKAMINE?
HEY!
PLOK
AH!
HUH?
PLEH
HOW DID THIS GET...?
WHAAAAAAAAAAT?
YOU GOT A 70?
WNK
I CAN'T BELIEVE IT. YOU HARDLY EVER SCORE BELOW A 90...
WAH!
I GOT A 70, TOO! IS YOUR BRAIN OKAY?
NOOOOOOO!

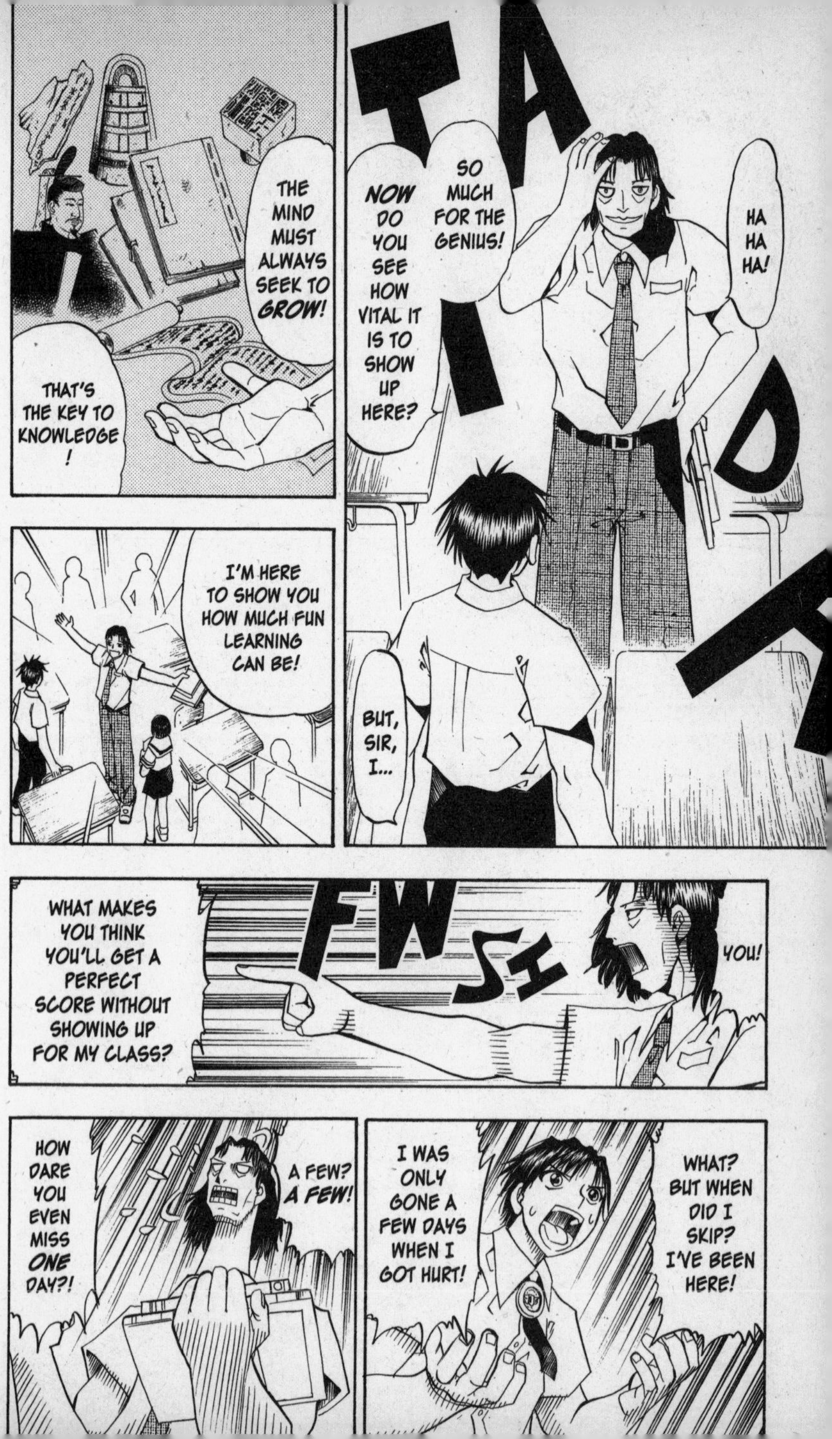
HA HA HA!
SO MUCH FOR THE GENIUS!
NOW DO YOU SEE HOW VITAL IT IS TO SHOW UP HERE?
BUT, SIR, I...
THE MIND MUST ALWAYS SEEK TO GROW!
THAT'S THE KEY TO KNOWLEDGE!
I'M HERE TO SHOW YOU HOW MUCH FUN LEARNING CAN BE!
YOU!
FWSH
WHAT MAKES YOU THINK YOU'LL GET A PERFECT SCORE WITHOUT SHOWING UP FOR MY CLASS?
WHAT? BUT WHEN DID I SKIP? I'VE BEEN HERE!
I WAS ONLY GONE A FEW DAYS WHEN I GOT HURT!
A FEW? A FEW!
HOW DARE YOU EVEN MISS ONE DAY?!

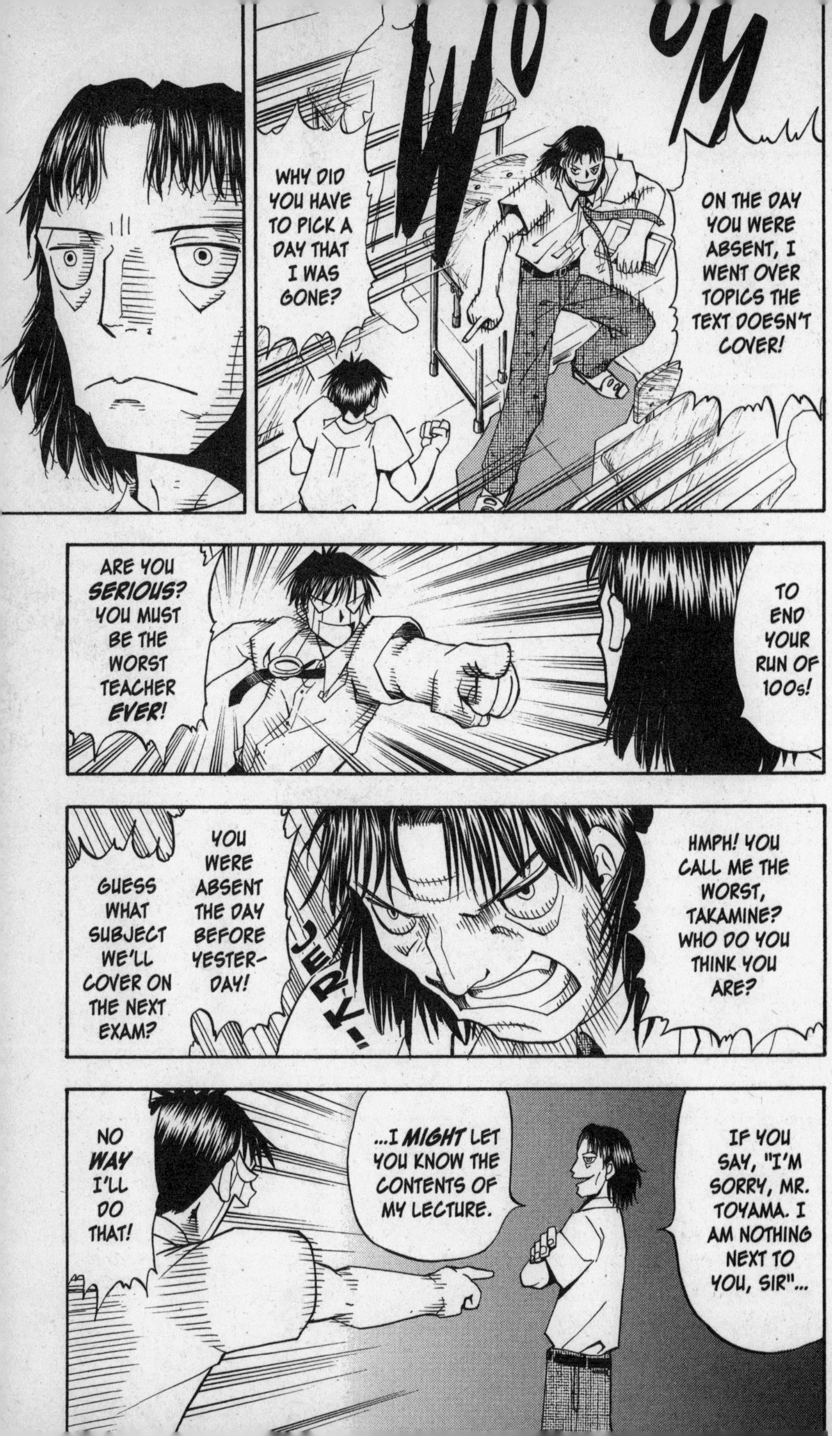
ON THE DAY YOU WERE ABSENT, I WENT OVER TOPICS THE TEXT DOESN'T COVER!
WHY DID YOU HAVE TO PICK A DAY THAT I WAS GONE?
TO END YOUR RUN OF 100s!
ARE YOU *SERIOUS?* YOU MUST BE THE WORST TEACHER *EVER!*
HMPH! YOU CALL ME THE WORST, TAKAMINE? WHO DO YOU THINK YOU ARE?
JERK!
YOU WERE ABSENT THE DAY BEFORE YESTERDAY!
GUESS WHAT SUBJECT WE'LL COVER ON THE NEXT EXAM?
IF YOU SAY, "I'M SORRY, MR. TOYAMA. I AM NOTHING NEXT TO YOU, SIR"...
...I *MIGHT* LET YOU KNOW THE CONTENTS OF MY LECTURE.
NO *WAY* I'LL DO THAT!

HA HA HA! YOU'LL REGRET THIS! HA HA!
GRRR!
TOYAMA!
HEY!
IT'S NOT WORTH APOLOGIZING TO THE CREEP.
TMSH
NO?
HE'S RIGHT, KIYO. YOU CAN BORROW OUR NOTES FROM THE LECTURE!
FAP
HISTORY
BUT I...
I'LL GIVE YOU MINE, TOO!
HUP
TOGETHER!
WOW...
I'M IN YOUR DEBT, GUYS!
HE WON'T GET AWAY WITH THIS!
THANKS TO ALL OF YOU, I CAN *WIN* THIS BATTLE!

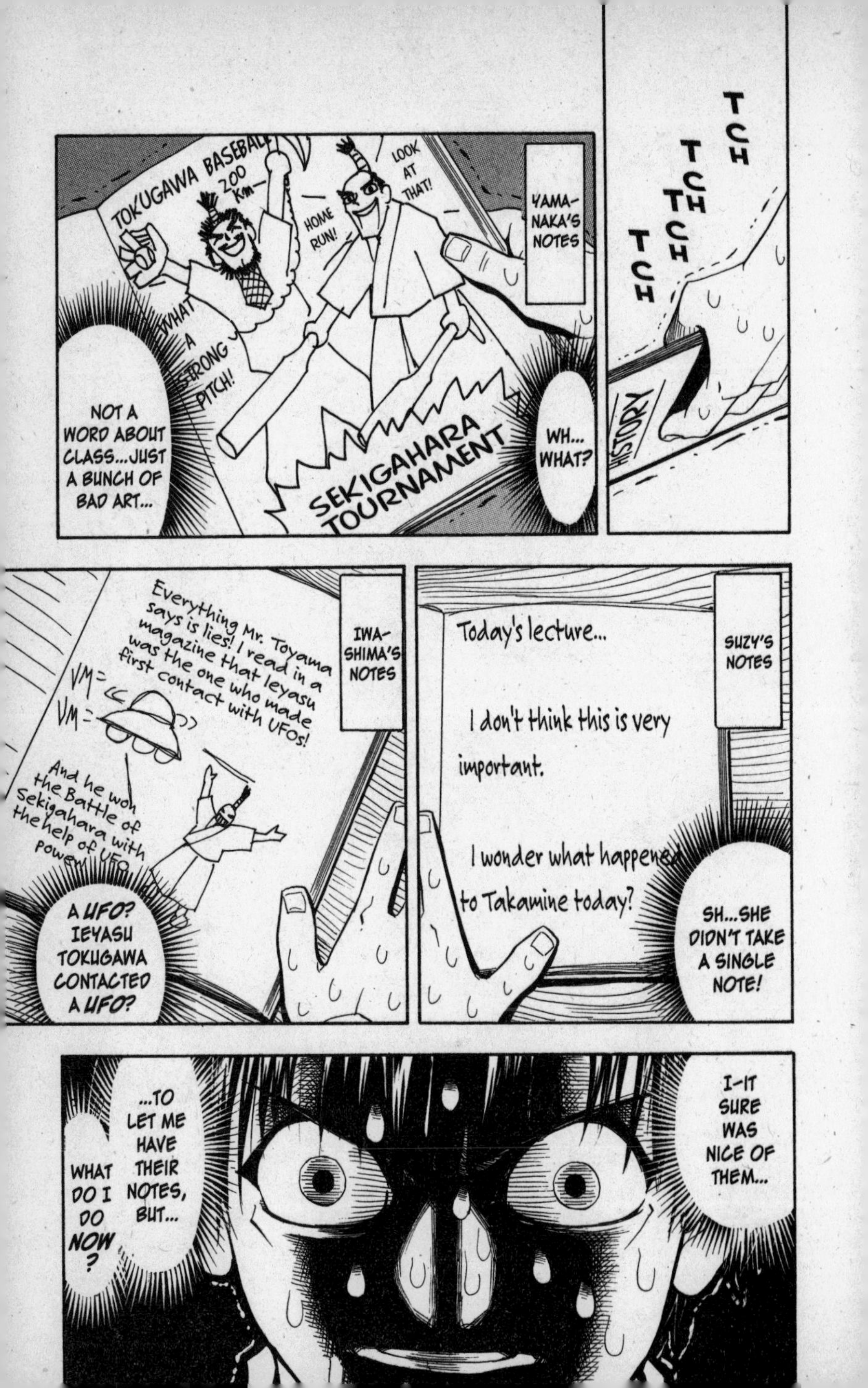
TCH TCH TCH TCH TCH
HISTORY
YAMA-NAKA'S NOTES
LOOK AT THAT!
HOME RUN!
TOKUGAWA BASEBAL
200 Km
WHAT A STRONG PITCH!
SEKIGAHARA TOURNAMENT
WH... WHAT?
NOT A WORD ABOUT CLASS...JUST A BUNCH OF BAD ART...
SUZY'S NOTES
Today's lecture...
I don't think this is very important.
I wonder what happened to Takamine today?
SH...SHE DIDN'T TAKE A SINGLE NOTE!
IWA-SHIMA'S NOTES
Everything Mr. Toyama says is lies! I read in a magazine that Ieyasu was the one who made first contact with UFOs!
And he won the Battle of Sekigahara with the help of UFO power
A UFO? IEYASU TOKUGAWA CONTACTED A UFO?
I-IT SURE WAS NICE OF THEM...
...TO LET ME HAVE THEIR NOTES, BUT...
WHAT DO I DO NOW?

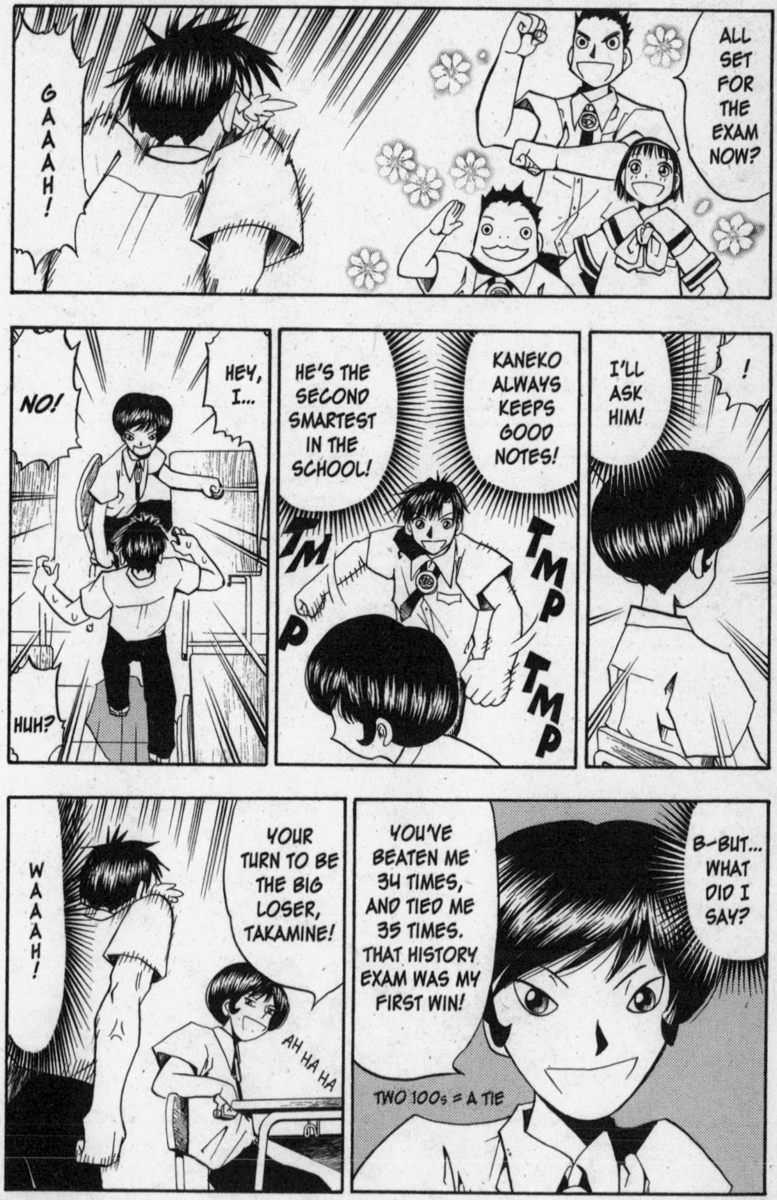
ALL SET FOR THE EXAM NOW?
GAAAAH!
!
I'LL ASK HIM!
KANEKO ALWAYS KEEPS GOOD NOTES!
HE'S THE SECOND SMARTEST IN THE SCHOOL!
TMP
TMP
TMP
TMP
HEY, I...
NO!
HUH?
B-BUT... WHAT DID I SAY?
YOU'VE BEATEN ME 34 TIMES, AND TIED ME 35 TIMES. THAT HISTORY EXAM WAS MY FIRST WIN!
TWO 100s = A TIE
YOUR TURN TO BE THE BIG LOSER, TAKAMINE!
AH HA HA
WAAAAH!

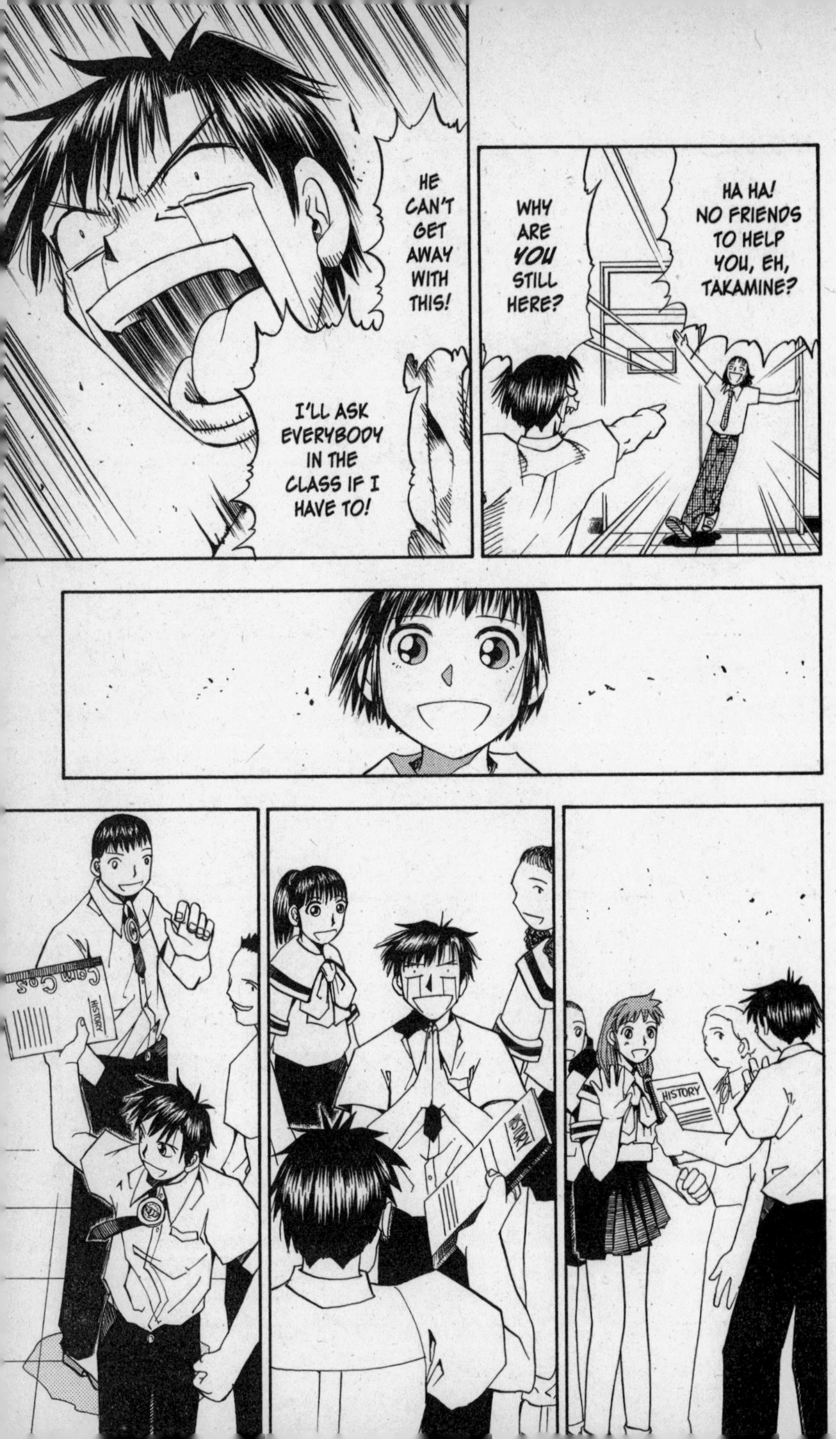
HA HA! NO FRIENDS TO HELP YOU, EH, TAKAMINE?
WHY ARE YOU STILL HERE?
HE CAN'T GET AWAY WITH THIS!
I'LL ASK EVERYBODY IN THE CLASS IF I HAVE TO!
HISTORY
HISTORY
HISTORY

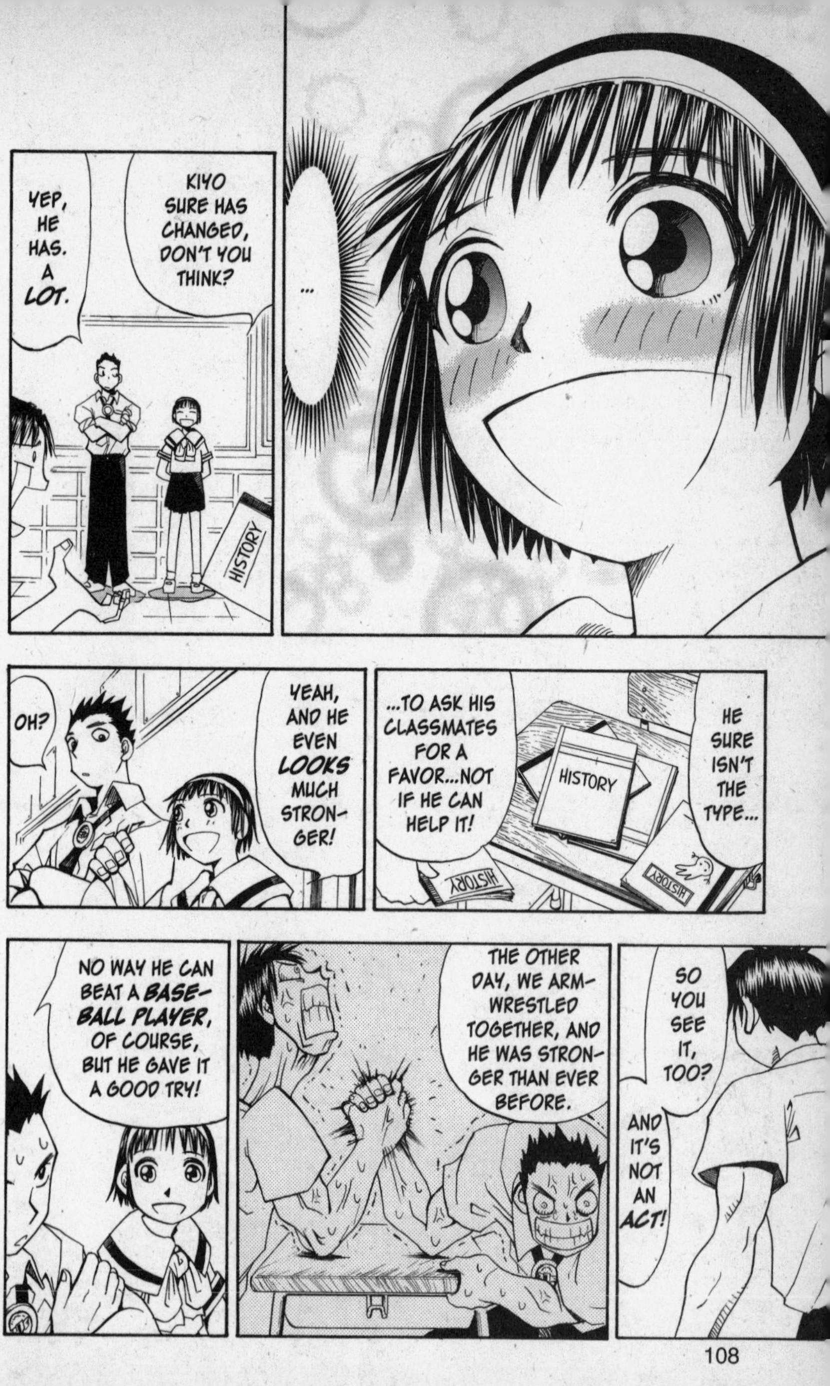
...
KIYO SURE HAS CHANGED, DON'T YOU THINK?
YEP, HE HAS. A LOT.
HE SURE ISN'T THE TYPE...
...TO ASK HIS CLASSMATES FOR A FAVOR...NOT IF HE CAN HELP IT!
HISTORY
YEAH, AND HE EVEN LOOKS MUCH STRONGER!
OH?
SO YOU SEE IT, TOO?
AND IT'S NOT AN ACT!
THE OTHER DAY, WE ARM-WRESTLED TOGETHER, AND HE WAS STRONGER THAN EVER BEFORE.
NO WAY HE CAN BEAT A BASEBALL PLAYER, OF COURSE, BUT HE GAVE IT A GOOD TRY!

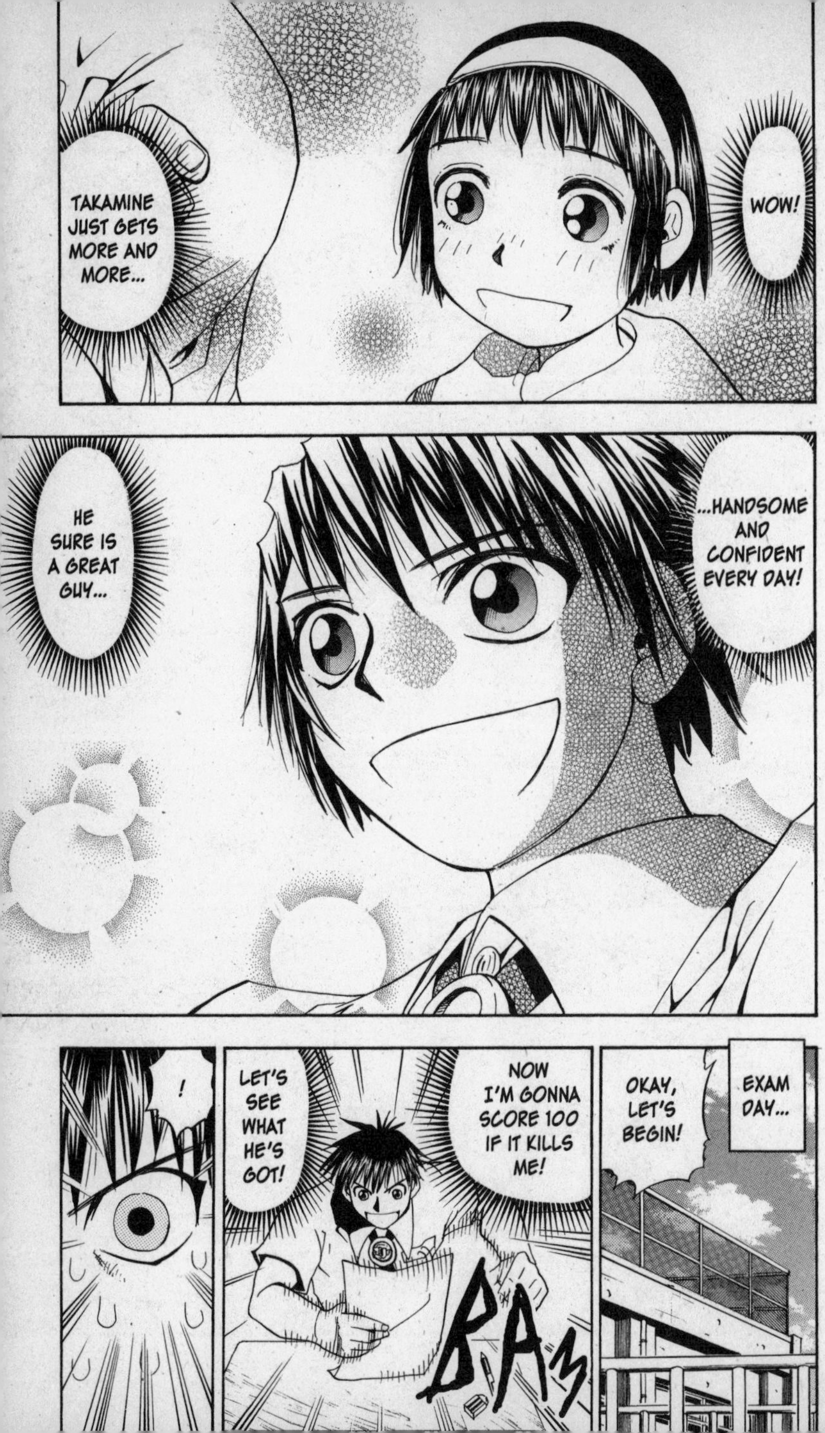
WOW!
TAKAMINE JUST GETS MORE AND MORE...
...HANDSOME AND CONFIDENT EVERY DAY!
HE SURE IS A GREAT GUY...
EXAM DAY...
OKAY, LET'S BEGIN!
NOW I'M GONNA SCORE 100 IF IT KILLS ME!
LET'S SEE WHAT HE'S GOT!
BAM
!

Important Question (50 points)

20 When did Mr. Toyama fall in love for the first time? And whom did he fall in love with?

When?	Whom?

HEH HEH HEH HEH HEH!

HA HA HA HA HA!

GO ON! ANSWER THAT, TAKAMINE! EVEN THE *CLASS* DOESN'T KNOW!

SHOW ME HOW SMART YOU ARE!

UH...

...AND THE VICE-PRINCIPAL MADE MR. TOYAMA PROMISE NEVER TO GIVE RIDICULOUS EXAMS AGAIN.

THE EXAM WAS CALLED OFF...

WHAT KIND OF TEST IS *THIS*?!

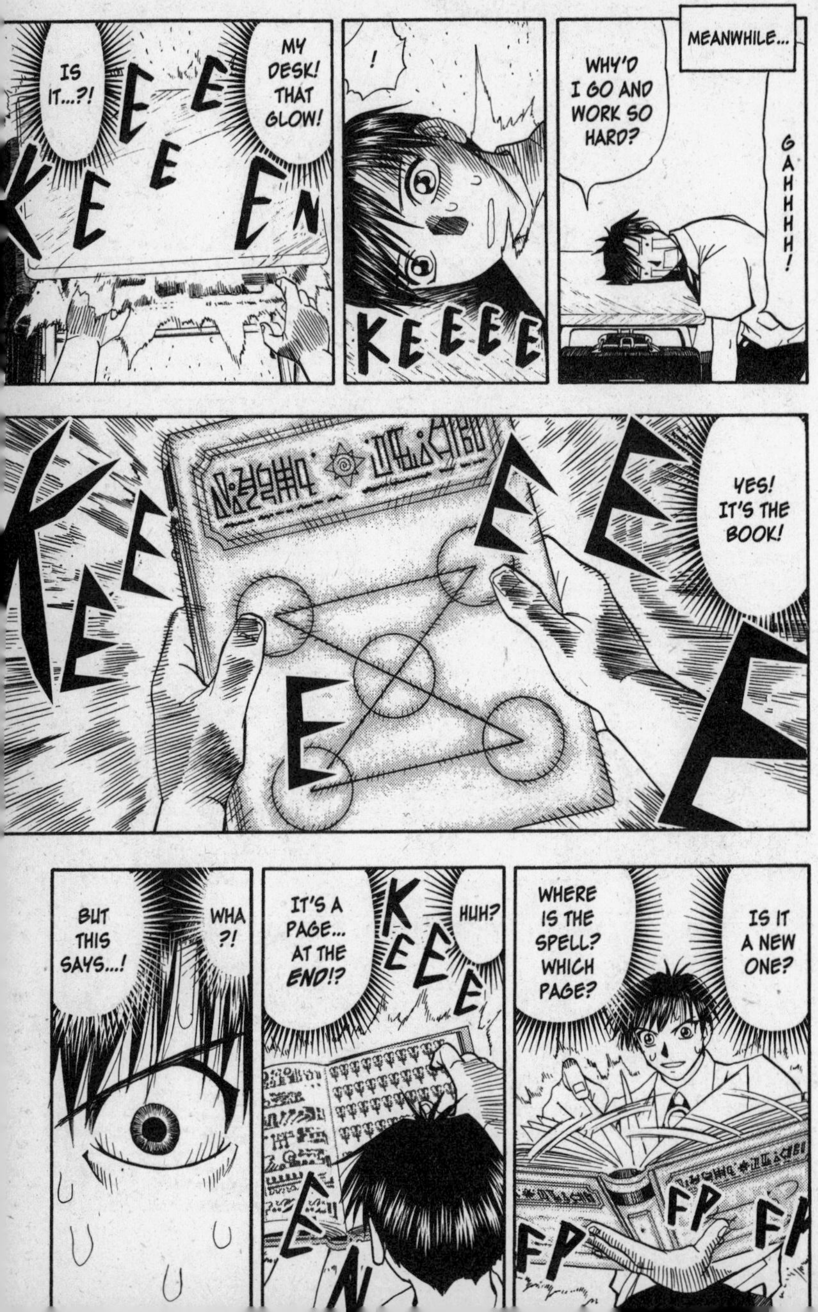
MEANWHILE...
WHY'D I GO AND WORK SO HARD?
GAHHHHH!
!
KEEEE
MY DESK! THAT GLOW!
IS IT...?!
KEEEEEN
YES! IT'S THE BOOK!
KEEEEEE
IS IT A NEW ONE?
WHERE IS THE SPELL? WHICH PAGE?
FP FP FP
HUH?
IT'S A PAGE... AT THE END!?
KEEEEN
WHA ?!
BUT THIS SAYS...!

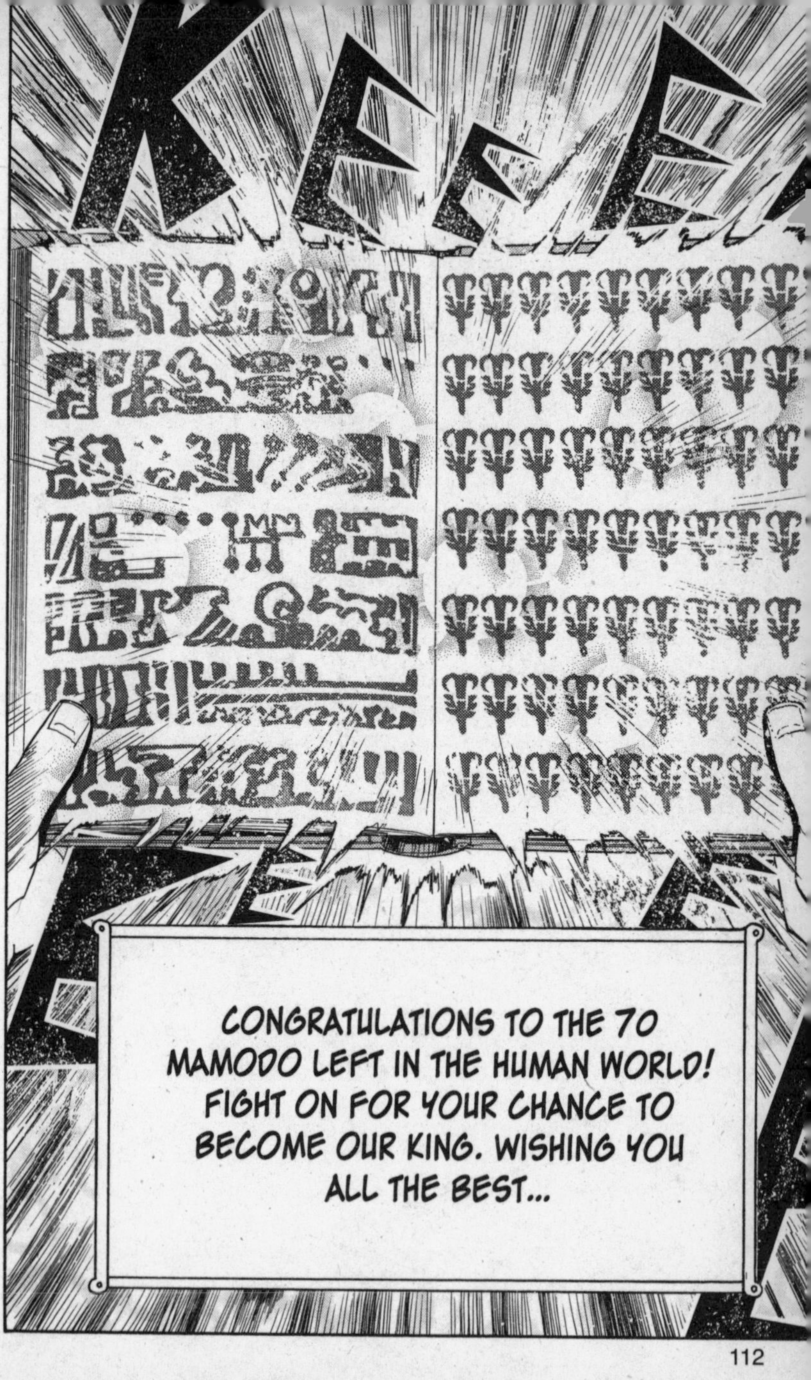
CONGRATULATIONS TO THE 70 MAMODO LEFT IN THE HUMAN WORLD! FIGHT ON FOR YOUR CHANCE TO BECOME OUR KING. WISHING YOU ALL THE BEST...

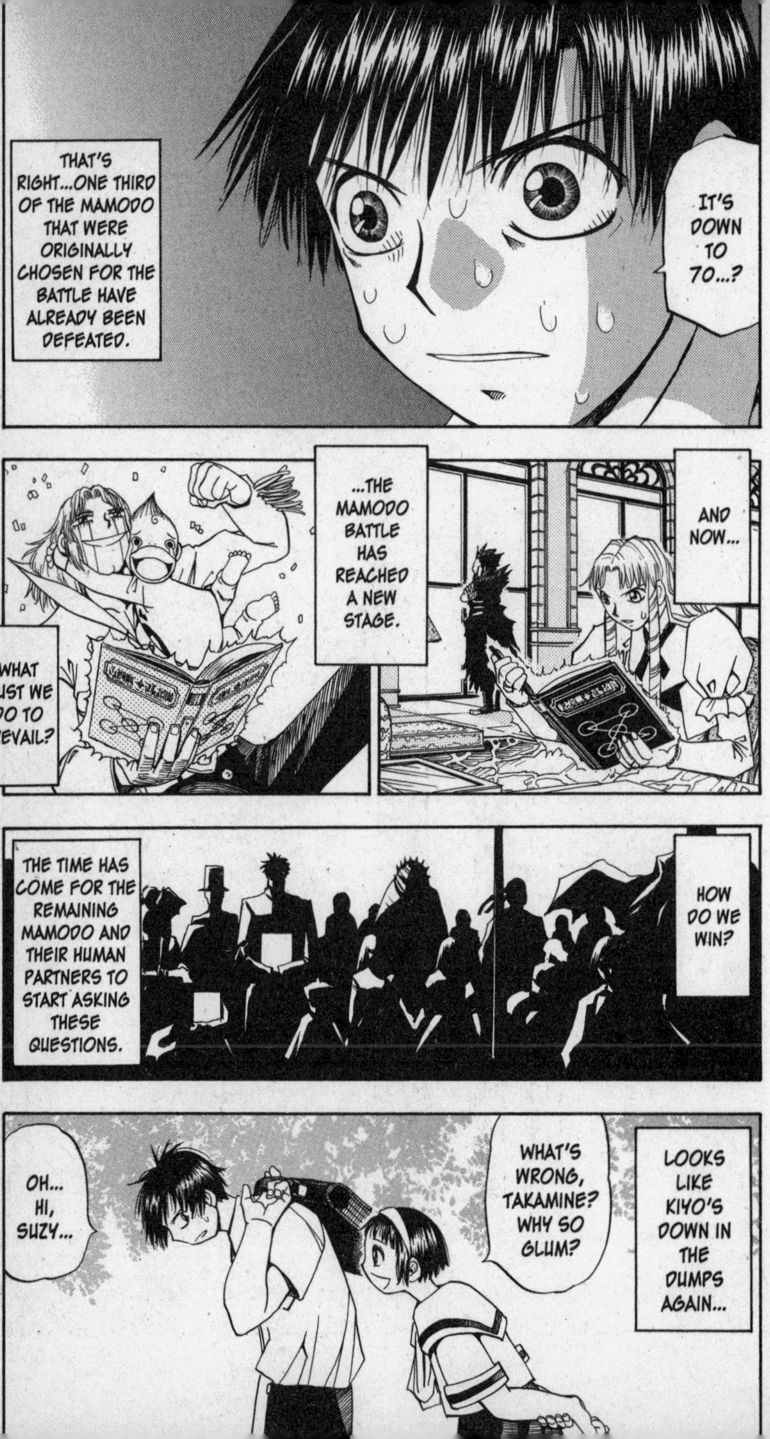
IT'S DOWN TO 70...?
THAT'S RIGHT...ONE THIRD OF THE MAMODO THAT WERE ORIGINALLY CHOSEN FOR THE BATTLE HAVE ALREADY BEEN DEFEATED.
AND NOW...
...THE MAMODO BATTLE HAS REACHED A NEW STAGE.
WHAT MUST WE DO TO PREVAIL?
HOW DO WE WIN?
THE TIME HAS COME FOR THE REMAINING MAMODO AND THEIR HUMAN PARTNERS TO START ASKING THESE QUESTIONS.
LOOKS LIKE KIYO'S DOWN IN THE DUMPS AGAIN...
WHAT'S WRONG, TAKAMINE? WHY SO GLUM?
OH... HI, SUZY...

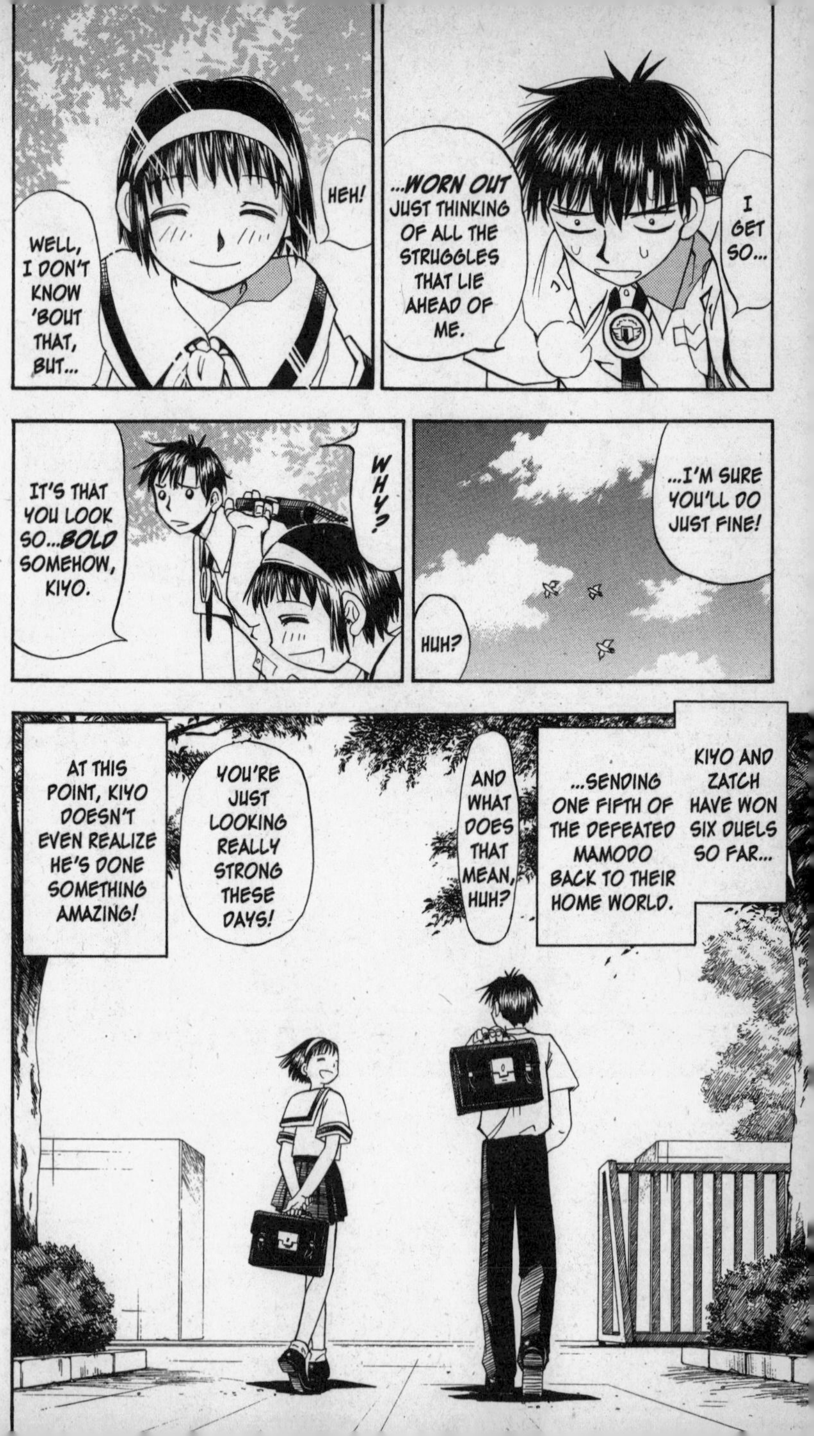
I GET SO...
...WORN OUT JUST THINKING OF ALL THE STRUGGLES THAT LIE AHEAD OF ME.
HEH!
WELL, I DON'T KNOW 'BOUT THAT, BUT...
...I'M SURE YOU'LL DO JUST FINE!
HUH?
WHY?
IT'S THAT YOU LOOK SO...BOLD SOMEHOW, KIYO.
KIYO AND ZATCH HAVE WON SIX DUELS SO FAR...
...SENDING ONE FIFTH OF THE DEFEATED MAMODO BACK TO THEIR HOME WORLD.
AND WHAT DOES THAT MEAN, HUH?
YOU'RE JUST LOOKING REALLY STRONG THESE DAYS!
AT THIS POINT, KIYO DOESN'T EVEN REALIZE HE'S DONE SOMETHING AMAZING!

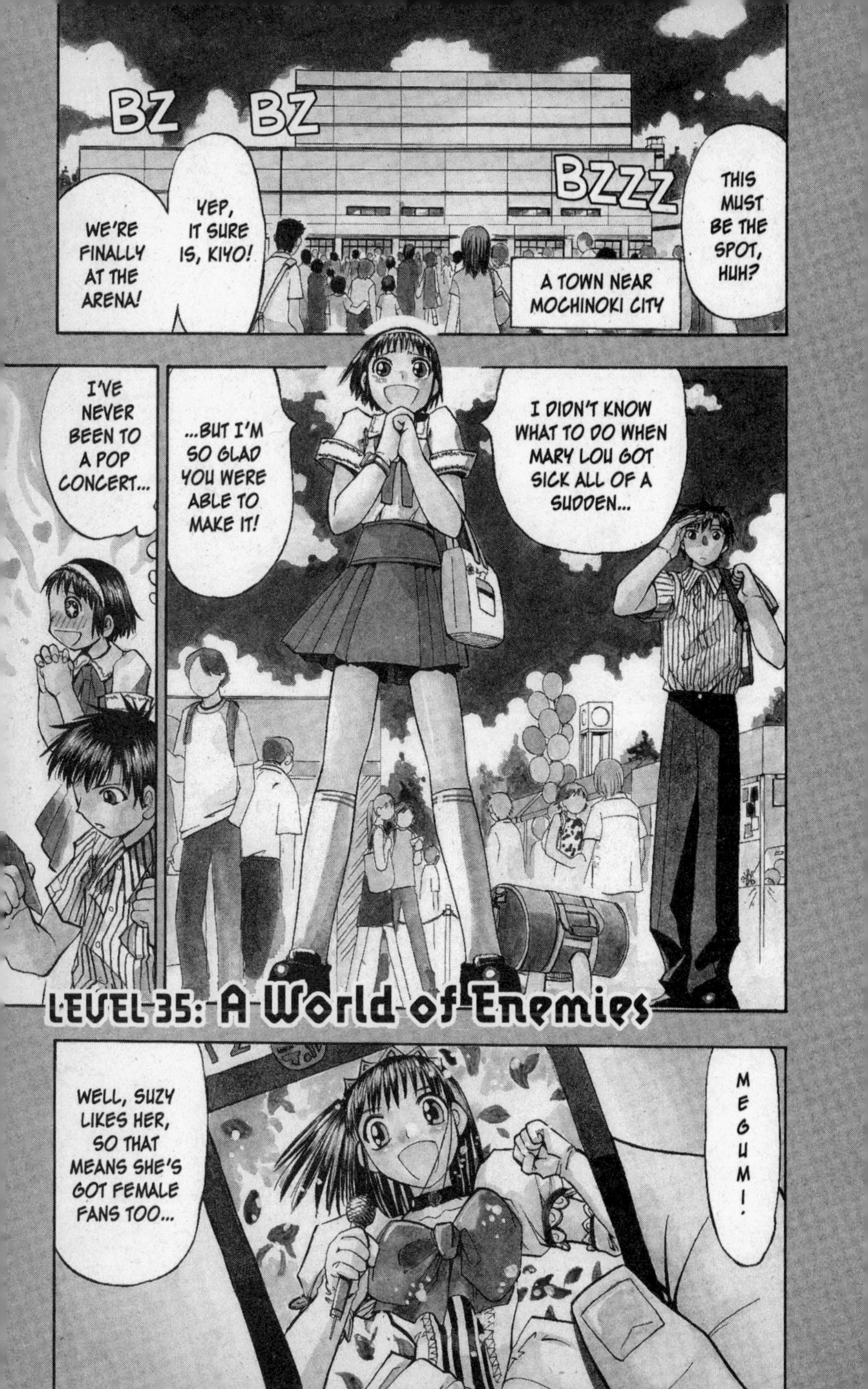
THIS MUST BE THE SPOT, HUH?
BZZZ
BZ
BZ
A TOWN NEAR MOCHINOKI CITY
YEP, IT SURE IS, KIYO!
WE'RE FINALLY AT THE ARENA!
I DIDN'T KNOW WHAT TO DO WHEN MARY LOU GOT SICK ALL OF A SUDDEN...
...BUT I'M SO GLAD YOU WERE ABLE TO MAKE IT!
I'VE NEVER BEEN TO A POP CONCERT...
LEVEL 35: A World of Enemies
MEGUMI!
WELL, SUZY LIKES HER, SO THAT MEANS SHE'S GOT FEMALE FANS TOO...

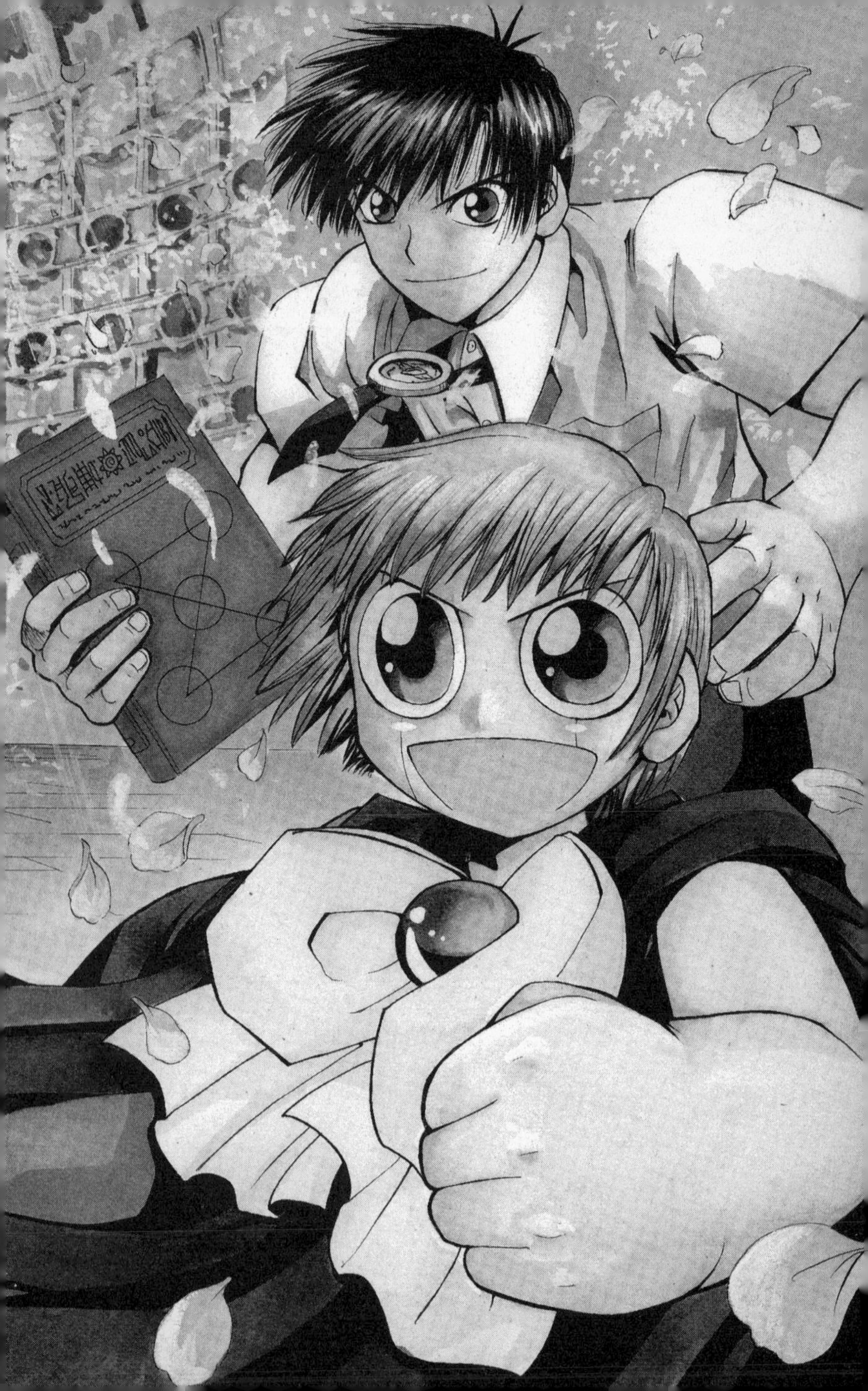

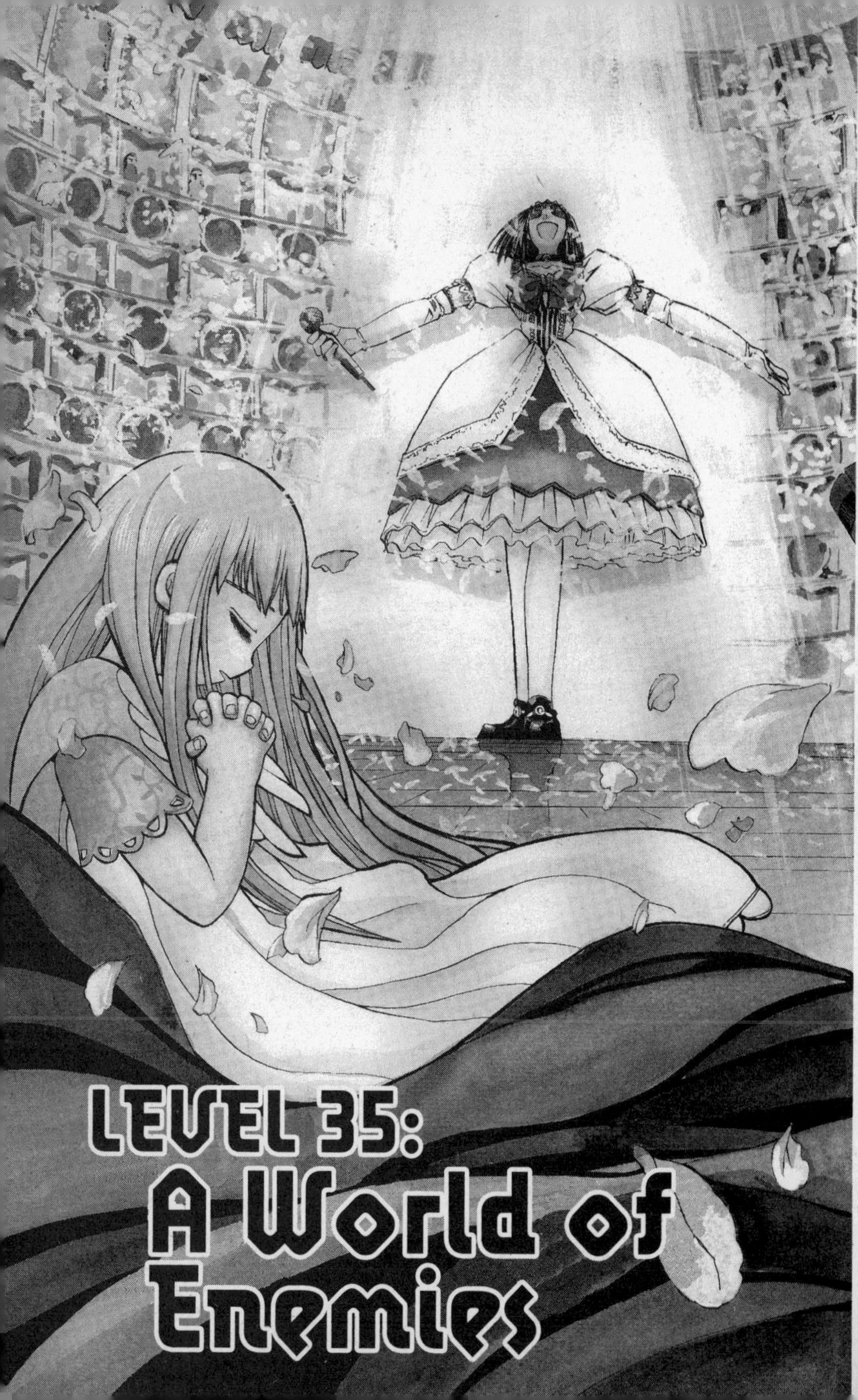
LEVEL 35:
A World of Enemies

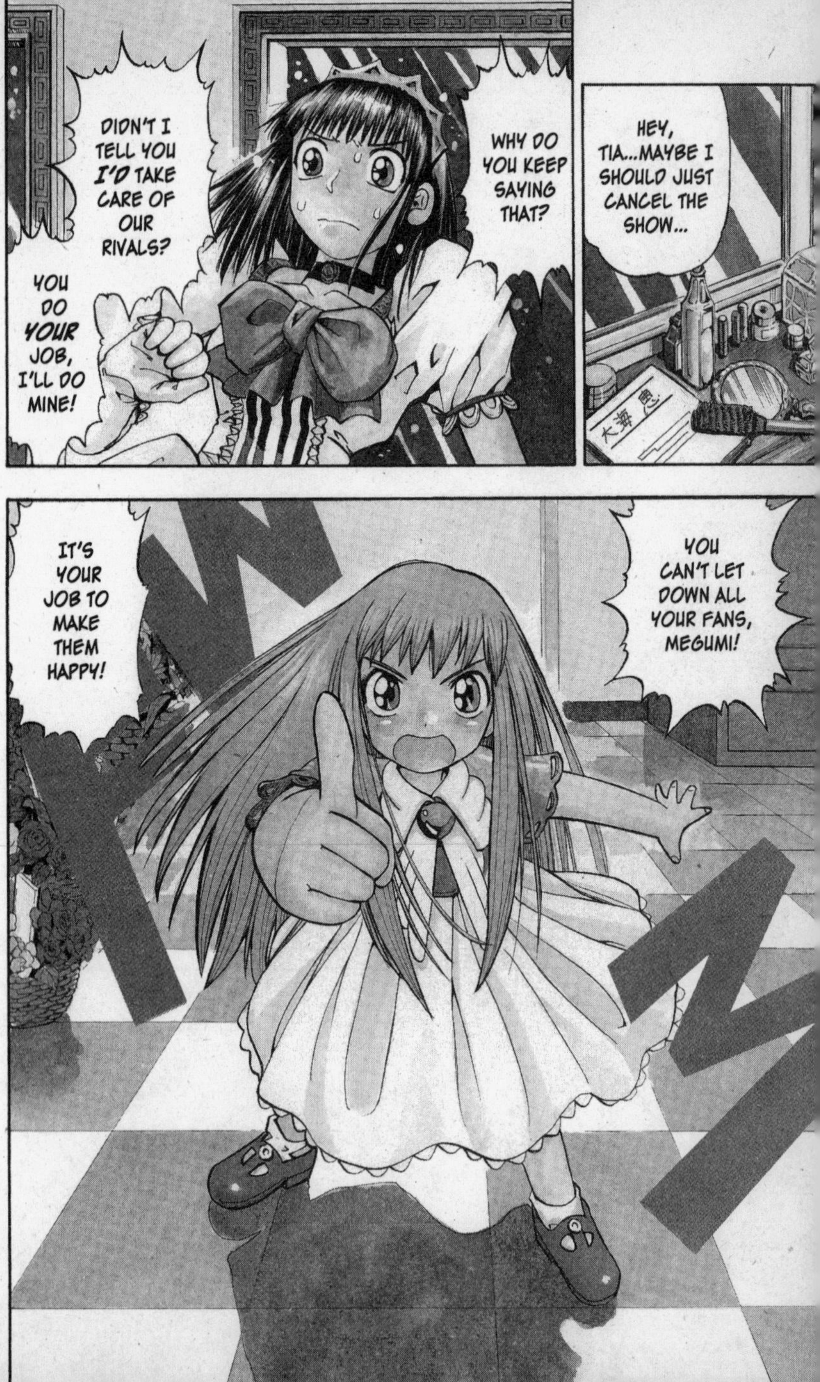
HEY, TIA...MAYBE I SHOULD JUST CANCEL THE SHOW...
WHY DO YOU KEEP SAYING THAT?
DIDN'T I TELL YOU I'D TAKE CARE OF OUR RIVALS?
YOU DO YOUR JOB, I'LL DO MINE!
YOU CAN'T LET DOWN ALL YOUR FANS, MEGUMI!
IT'S YOUR JOB TO MAKE THEM HAPPY!

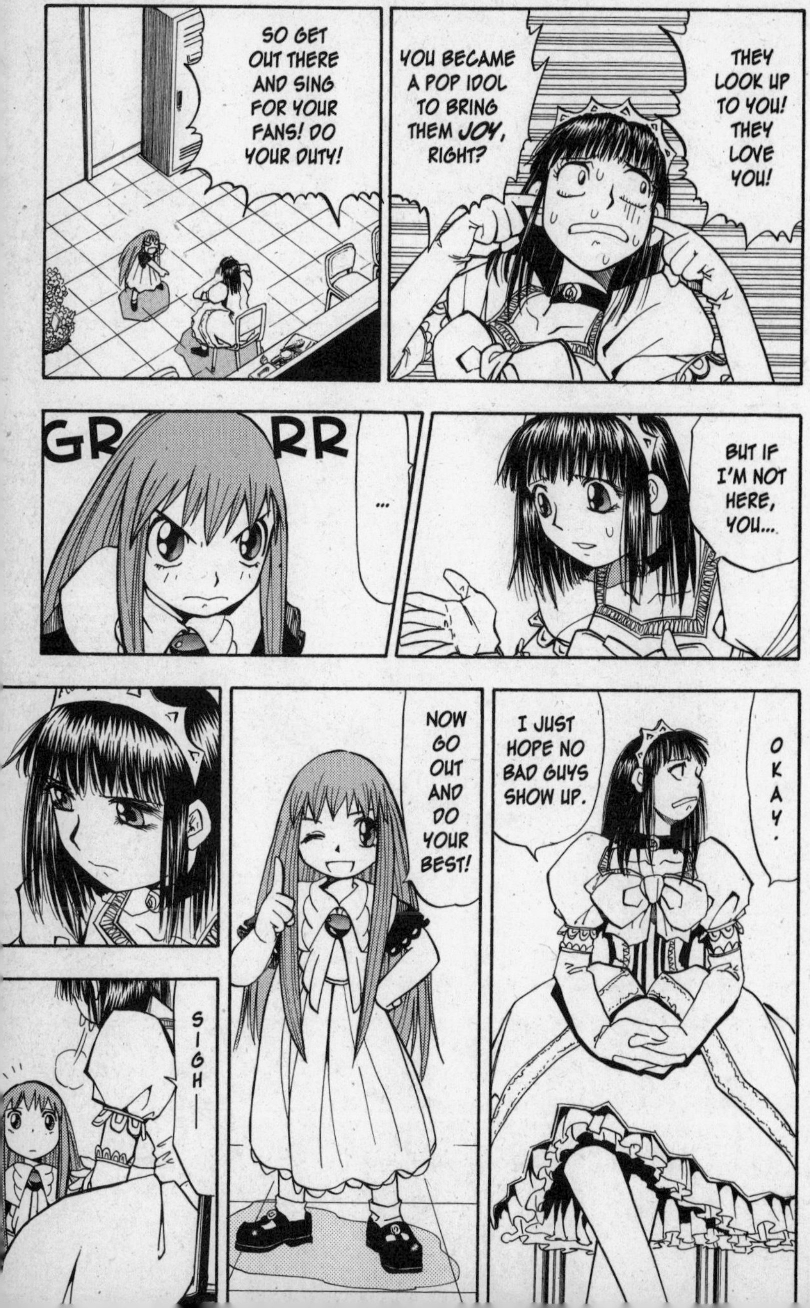
THEY LOOK UP TO YOU! THEY LOVE YOU!
YOU BECAME A POP IDOL TO BRING THEM *JOY*, RIGHT?
SO GET OUT THERE AND SING FOR YOUR FANS! DO YOUR DUTY!
BUT IF I'M NOT HERE, YOU...
...
GRRR
OKAY.
I JUST HOPE NO BAD GUYS SHOW UP.
NOW GO OUT AND DO YOUR BEST!
SIGH—

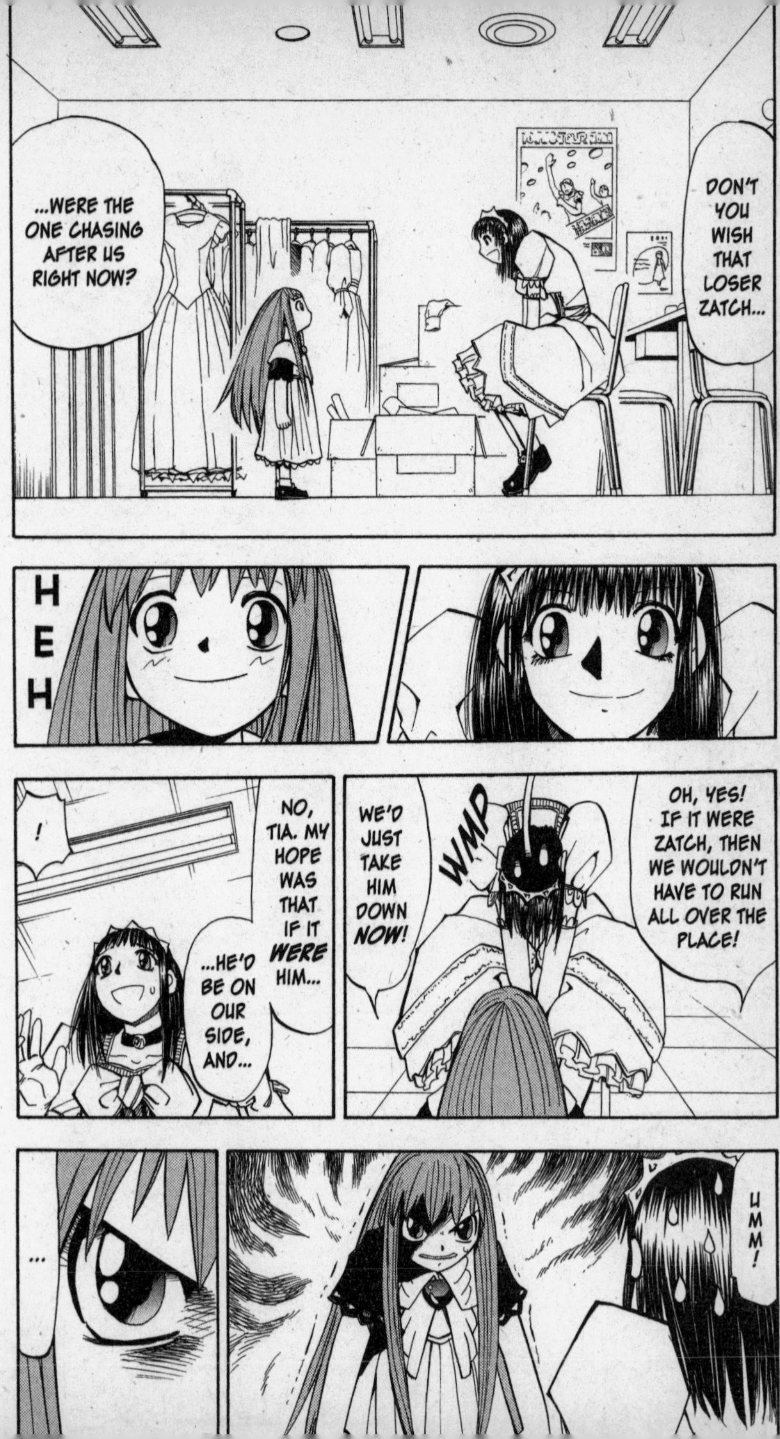
DON'T YOU WISH THAT LOSER ZATCH...
...WERE THE ONE CHASING AFTER US RIGHT NOW?
HEH
OH, YES! IF IT WERE ZATCH, THEN WE WOULDN'T HAVE TO RUN ALL OVER THE PLACE!
WMP
WE'D JUST TAKE HIM DOWN NOW!
NO, TIA. MY HOPE WAS THAT IF IT WERE HIM...
...HE'D BE ON OUR SIDE, AND...
!
UMM!
...

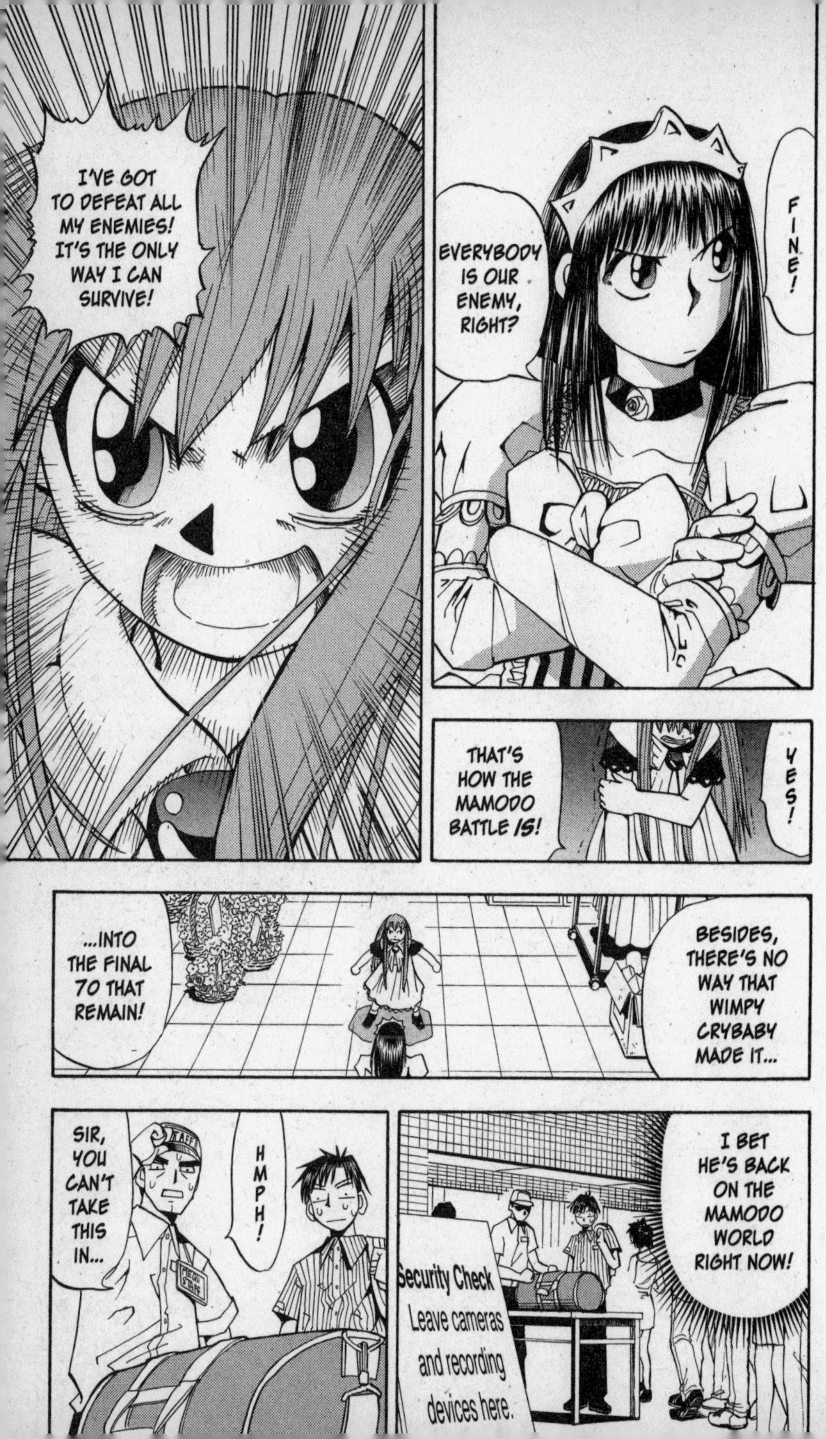
FINE!
EVERYBODY IS OUR ENEMY, RIGHT?
YES!
THAT'S HOW THE MAMODO BATTLE IS!
I'VE GOT TO DEFEAT ALL MY ENEMIES! IT'S THE ONLY WAY I CAN SURVIVE!
BESIDES, THERE'S NO WAY THAT WIMPY CRYBABY MADE IT...
...INTO THE FINAL 70 THAT REMAIN!
I BET HE'S BACK ON THE MAMODO WORLD RIGHT NOW!
Security Check
Leave cameras and recording devices here.
HMPH!
SIR, YOU CAN'T TAKE THIS IN...

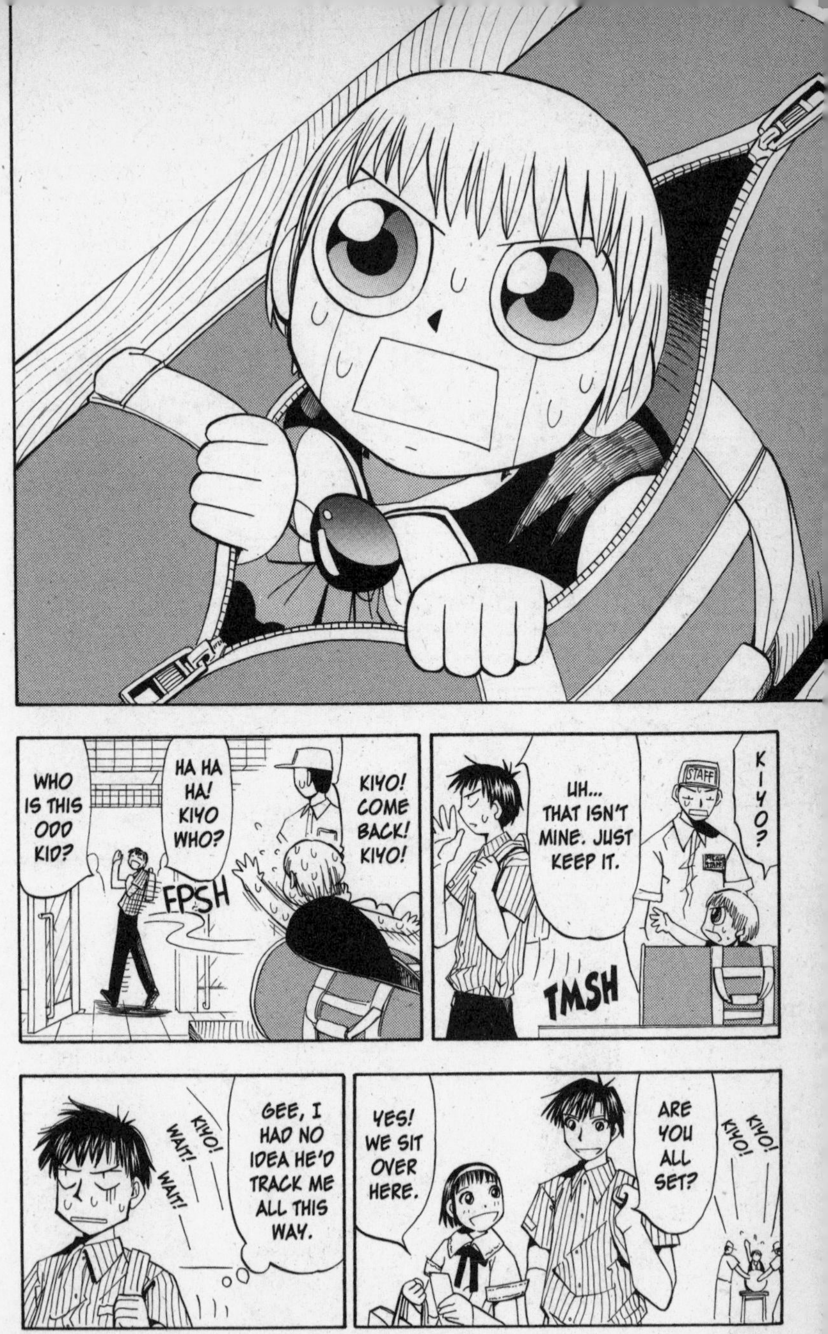
KIYO?
UH... THAT ISN'T MINE. JUST KEEP IT.
TMSH
KIYO! COME BACK! KIYO!
HA HA HA! KIYO WHO?
WHO IS THIS ODD KID?
FPSH
KIYO! KIYO!
ARE YOU ALL SET?
YES! WE SIT OVER HERE.
GEE, I HAD NO IDEA HE'D TRACK ME ALL THIS WAY.
KIYO! WAIT!
WAIT!

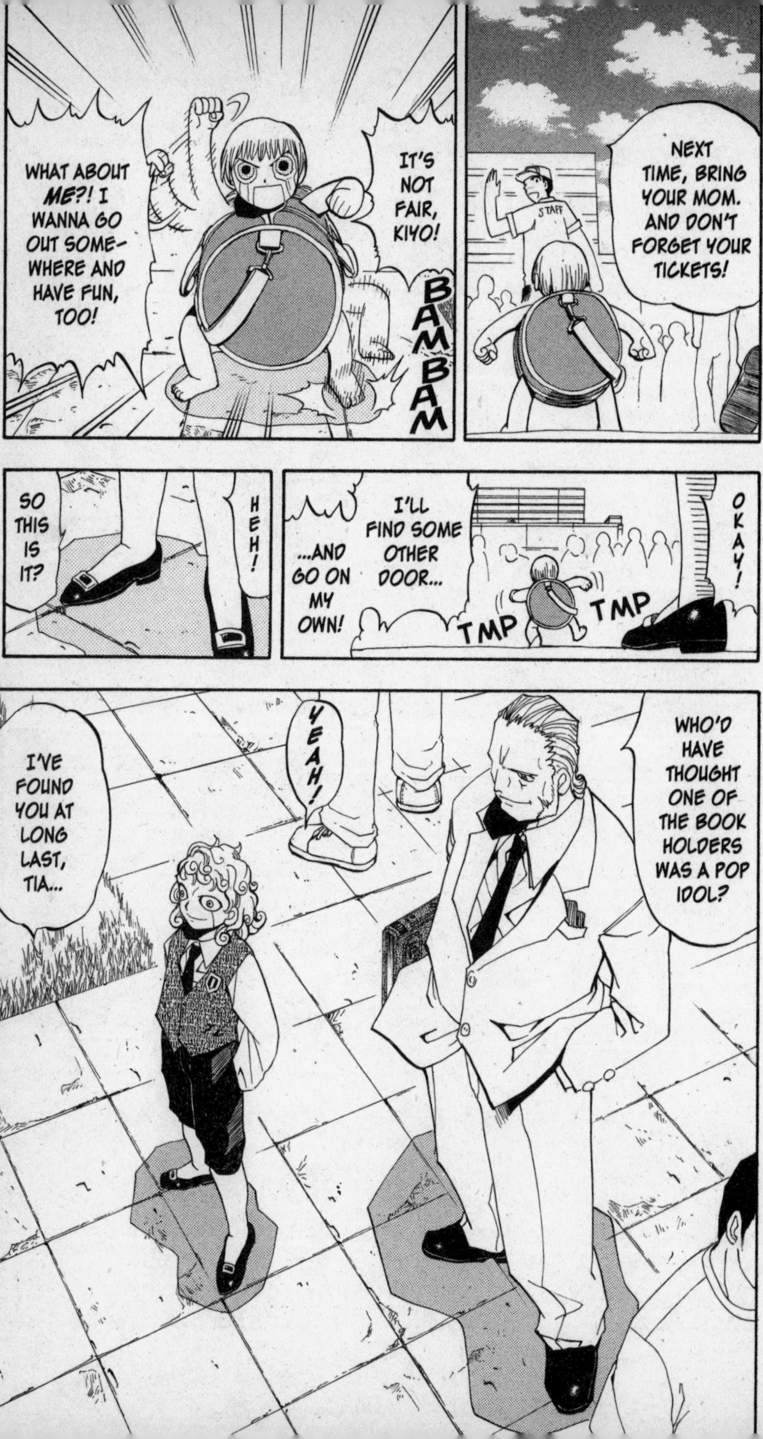
NEXT TIME, BRING YOUR MOM. AND DON'T FORGET YOUR TICKETS!
STAFF
IT'S NOT FAIR, KIYO!
BAM BAM
WHAT ABOUT *ME?!* I WANNA GO OUT SOME-WHERE AND HAVE FUN, TOO!
OKAY!
I'LL FIND SOME OTHER DOOR...
...AND GO ON MY OWN!
TMP TMP
HEH!
SO THIS IS IT?
WHO'D HAVE THOUGHT ONE OF THE BOOK HOLDERS WAS A POP IDOL?
YEAH!
I'VE FOUND YOU AT LONG LAST, TIA...

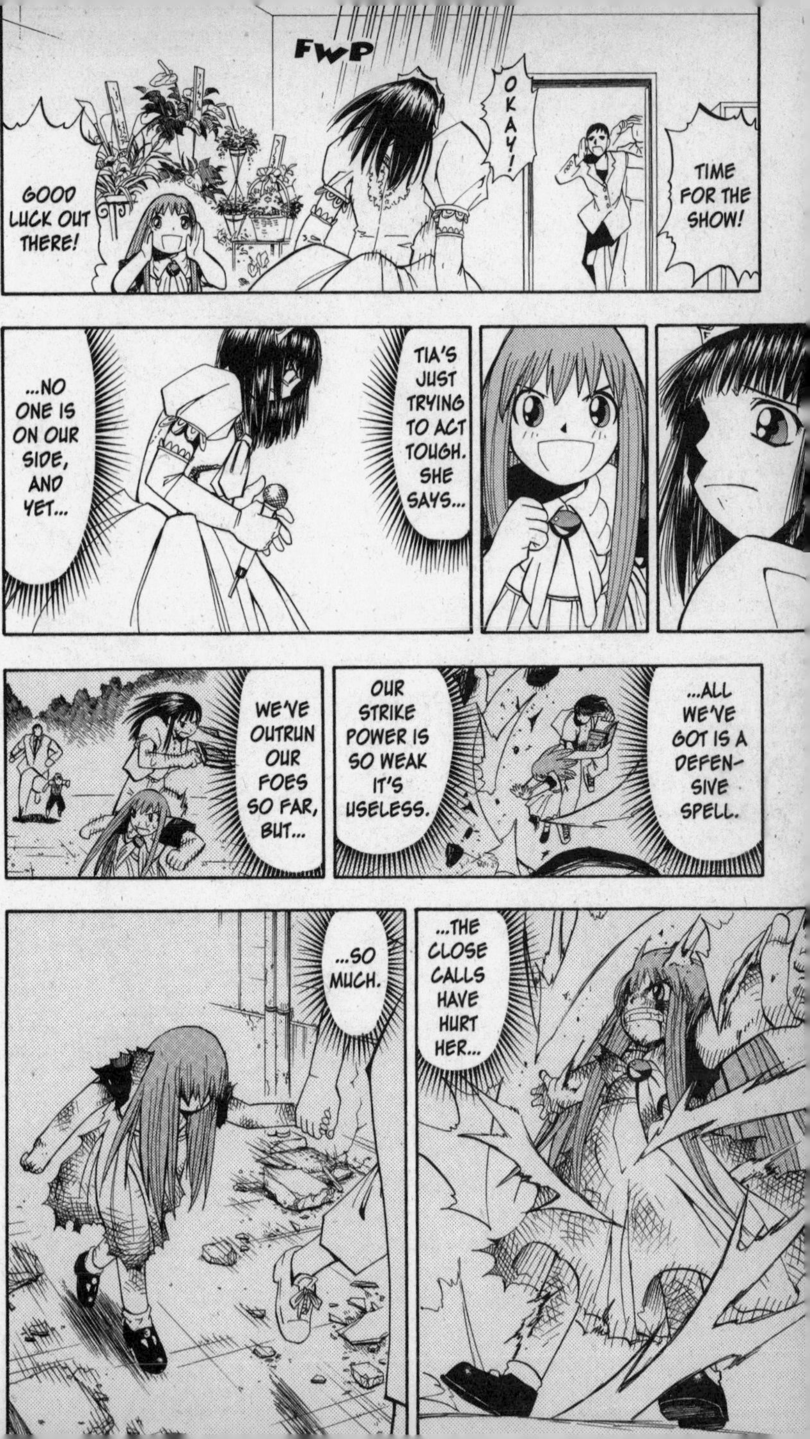
TIME FOR THE SHOW!
OKAY!
FWP
GOOD LUCK OUT THERE!
TIA'S JUST TRYING TO ACT TOUGH. SHE SAYS...
...NO ONE IS ON OUR SIDE, AND YET...
...ALL WE'VE GOT IS A DEFEN-SIVE SPELL.
OUR STRIKE POWER IS SO WEAK IT'S USELESS.
WE'VE OUTRUN OUR FOES SO FAR, BUT...
...THE CLOSE CALLS HAVE HURT HER...
...SO MUCH.

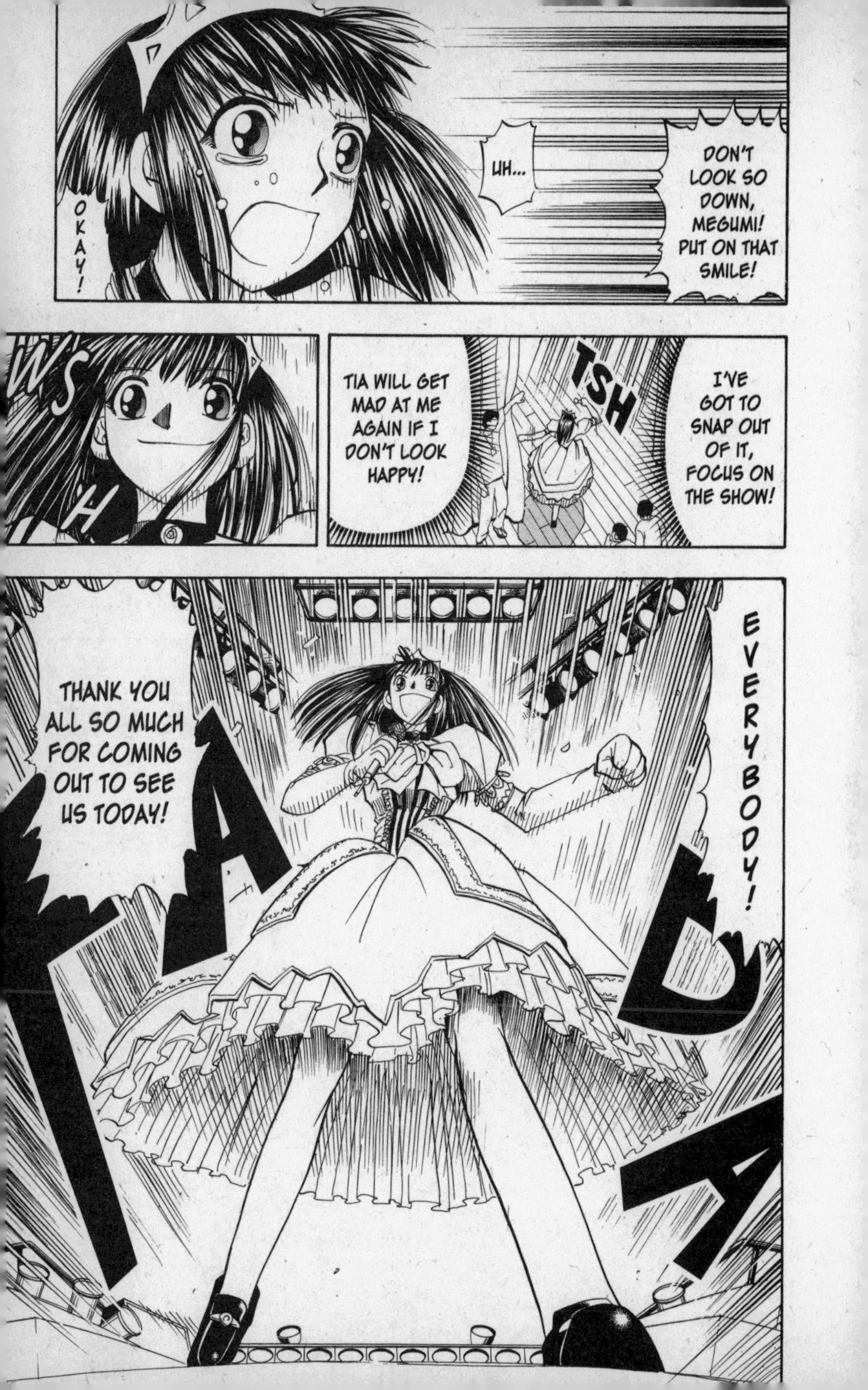
DON'T LOOK SO DOWN, MEGUMI! PUT ON THAT SMILE!
UH...
OKAY!
I'VE GOT TO SNAP OUT OF IT, FOCUS ON THE SHOW!
TSH
TIA WILL GET MAD AT ME AGAIN IF I DON'T LOOK HAPPY!
EVERYBODY!
THANK YOU ALL SO MUCH FOR COMING OUT TO SEE US TODAY!

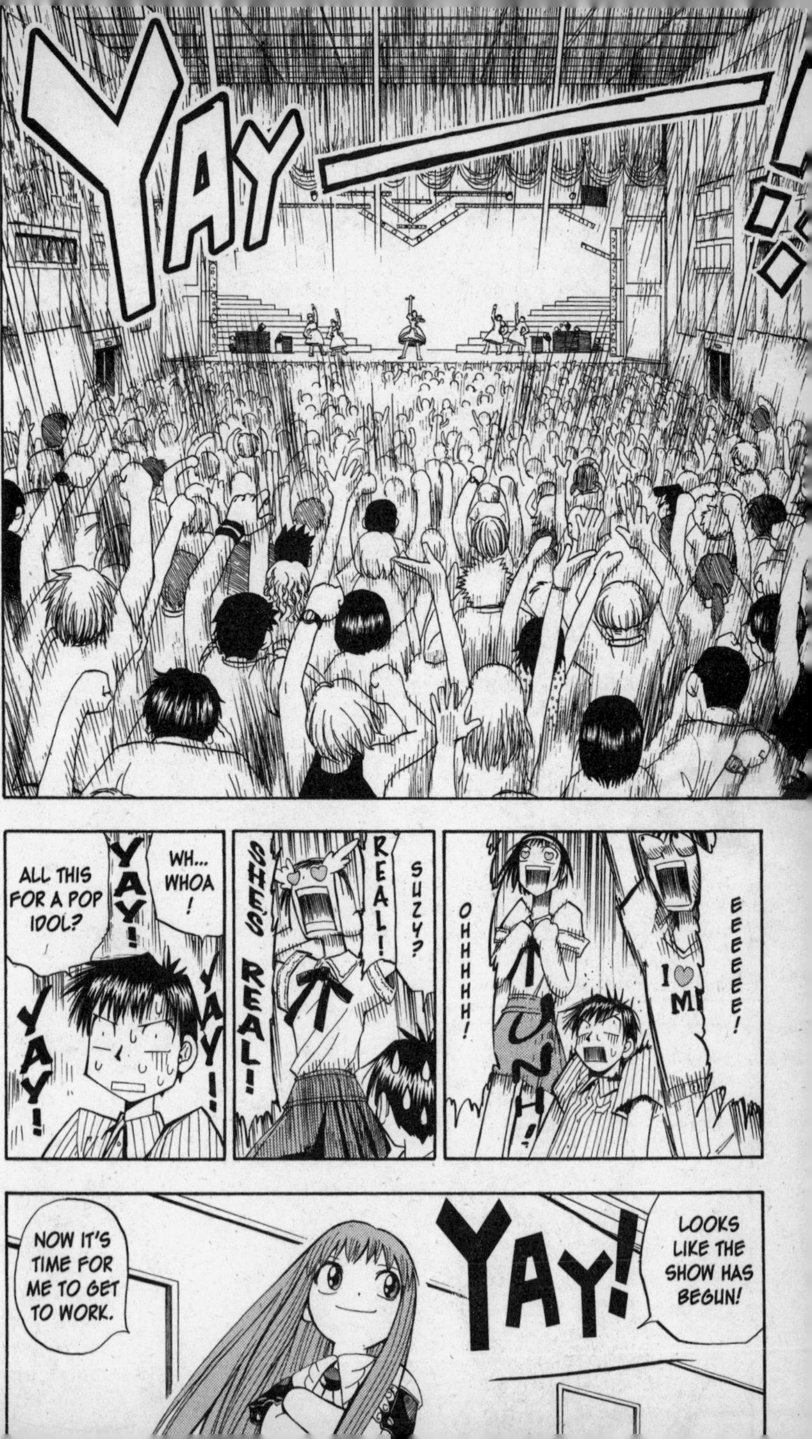
YAY——!!
EEEEEEE!
OHHHHHH!
SUZY?
REAL!
SHE'S REAL!
WH... WHOA!
YAY!
ALL THIS FOR A POP IDOL?
YAY!
YAY!
LOOKS LIKE THE SHOW HAS BEGUN!
YAY!
NOW IT'S TIME FOR ME TO GET TO WORK.

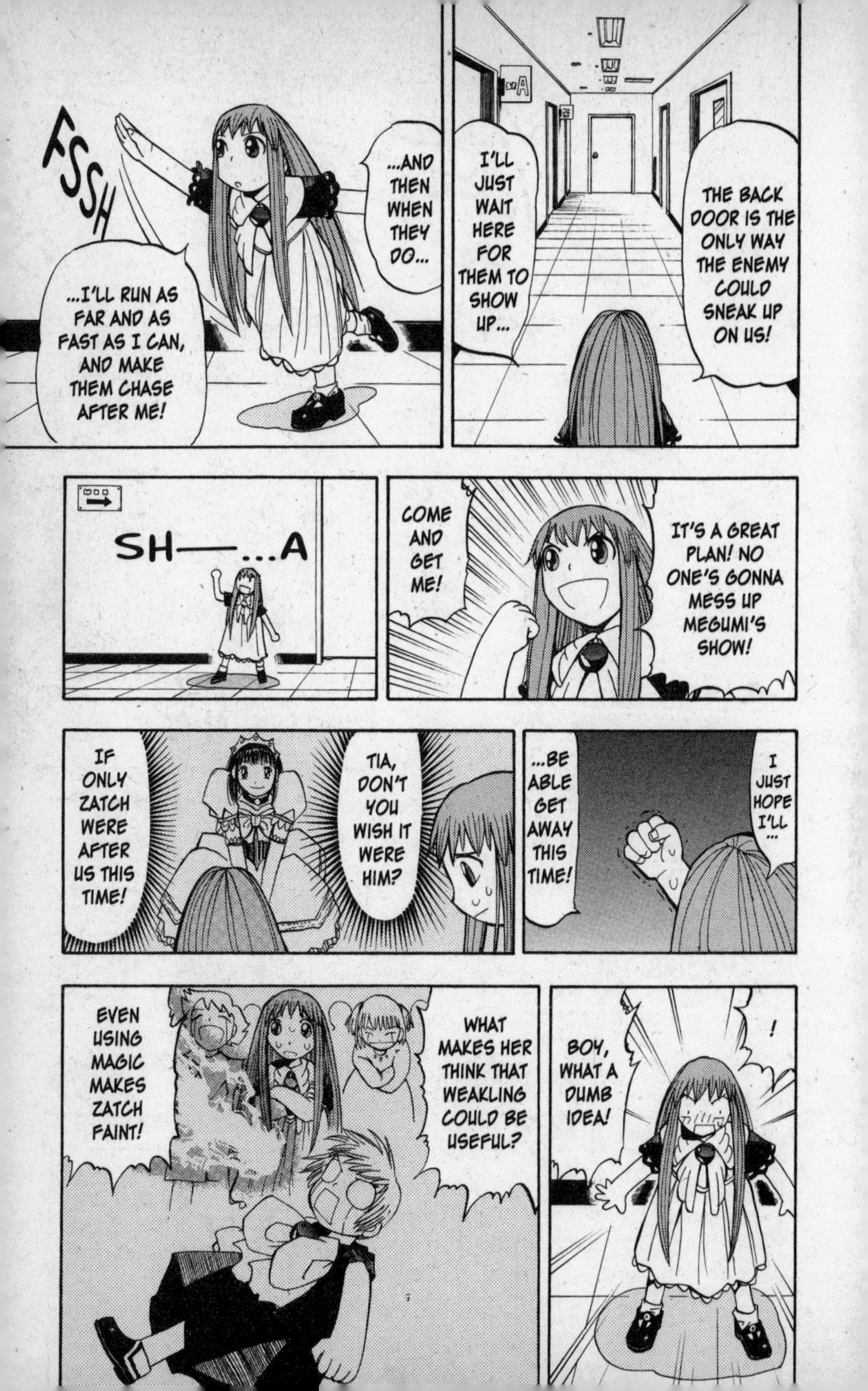
THE BACK DOOR IS THE ONLY WAY THE ENEMY COULD SNEAK UP ON US!
I'LL JUST WAIT HERE FOR THEM TO SHOW UP...
...AND THEN WHEN THEY DO...
FSSH
...I'LL RUN AS FAR AND AS FAST AS I CAN, AND MAKE THEM CHASE AFTER ME!
IT'S A GREAT PLAN! NO ONE'S GONNA MESS UP MEGUMI'S SHOW!
COME AND GET ME!
SH—...A
I JUST HOPE I'LL...
...BE ABLE GET AWAY THIS TIME!
TIA, DON'T YOU WISH IT WERE HIM?
IF ONLY ZATCH WERE AFTER US THIS TIME!
!
BOY, WHAT A DUMB IDEA!
WHAT MAKES HER THINK THAT WEAKLING COULD BE USEFUL?
EVEN USING MAGIC MAKES ZATCH FAINT!

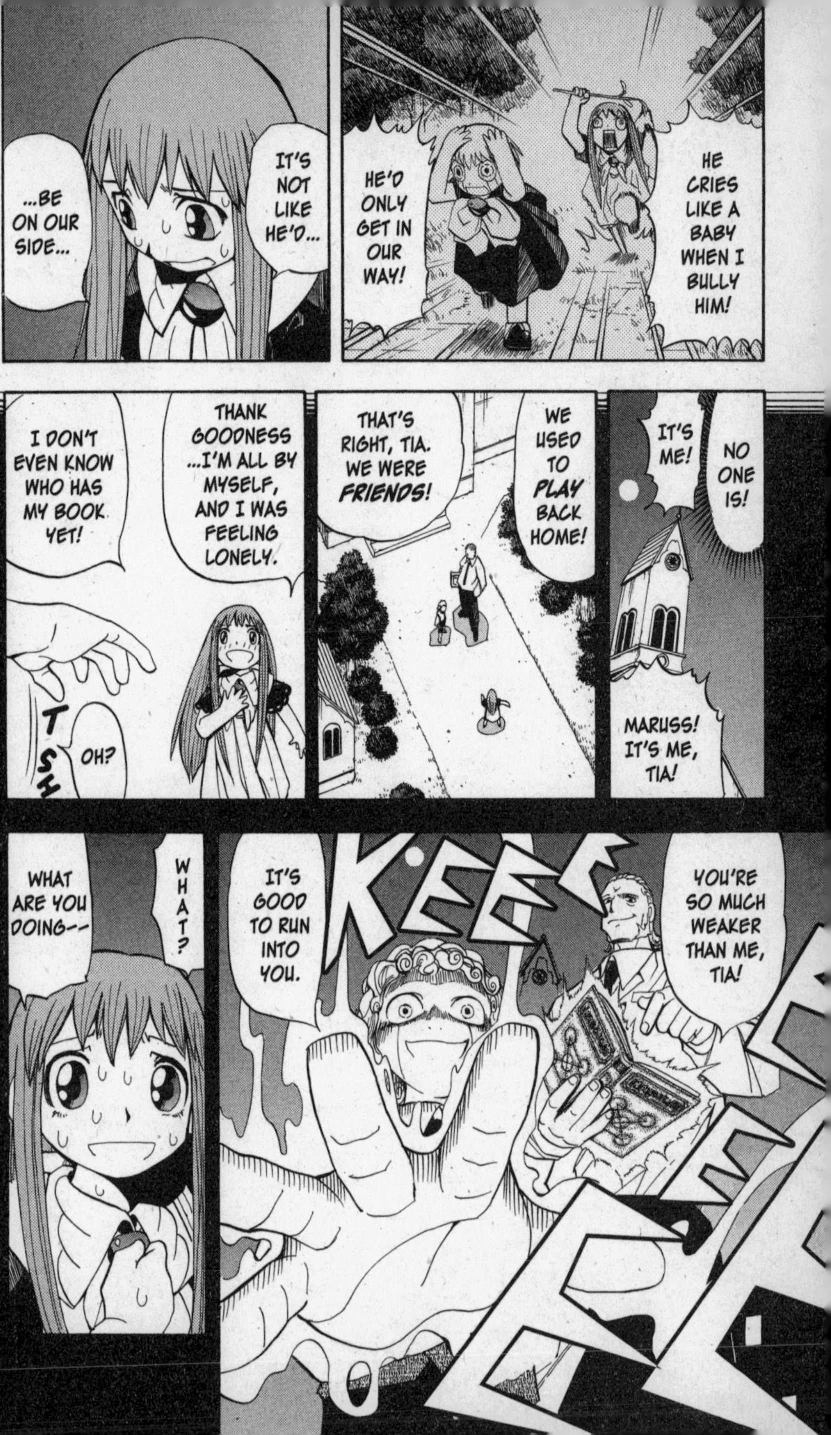
HE CRIES LIKE A BABY WHEN I BULLY HIM!
HE'D ONLY GET IN OUR WAY!
IT'S NOT LIKE HE'D...
...BE ON OUR SIDE...
NO ONE IS!
IT'S ME!
MARUSS! IT'S ME, TIA!
WE USED TO PLAY BACK HOME!
THAT'S RIGHT, TIA. WE WERE FRIENDS!
THANK GOODNESS ...I'M ALL BY MYSELF, AND I WAS FEELING LONELY.
I DON'T EVEN KNOW WHO HAS MY BOOK YET!
TSH
OH?
YOU'RE SO MUCH WEAKER THAN ME, TIA!
KEEEEE
IT'S GOOD TO RUN INTO YOU.
WHAT?
WHAT ARE YOU DOING--

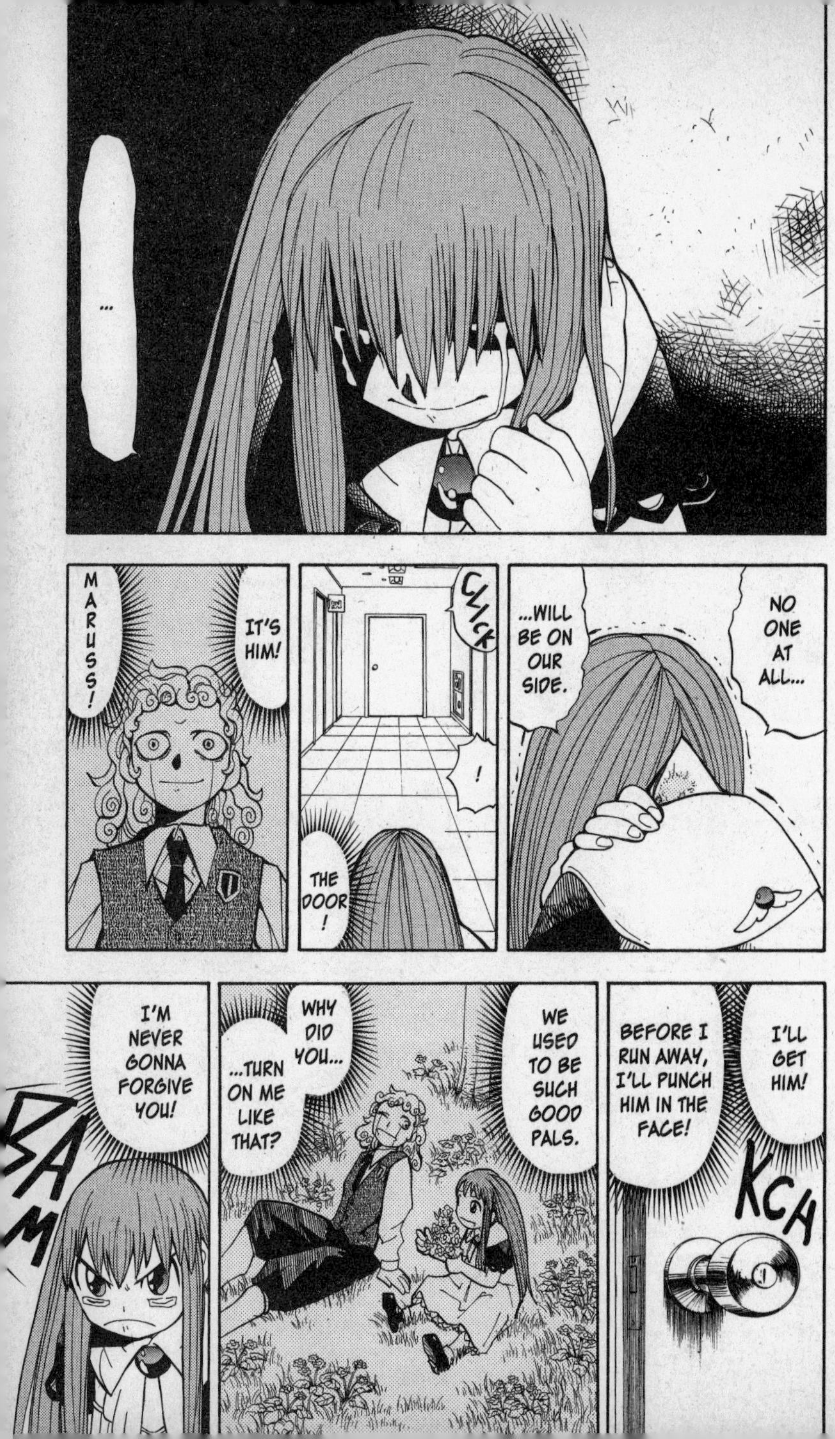
...
NO ONE AT ALL...
...WILL BE ON OUR SIDE.
CLICK
!
THE DOOR!
IT'S HIM!
MARUSS!
I'LL GET HIM!
BEFORE I RUN AWAY, I'LL PUNCH HIM IN THE FACE!
KCH
WE USED TO BE SUCH GOOD PALS.
WHY DID YOU...
...TURN ON ME LIKE THAT?
I'M NEVER GONNA FORGIVE YOU!
BAM

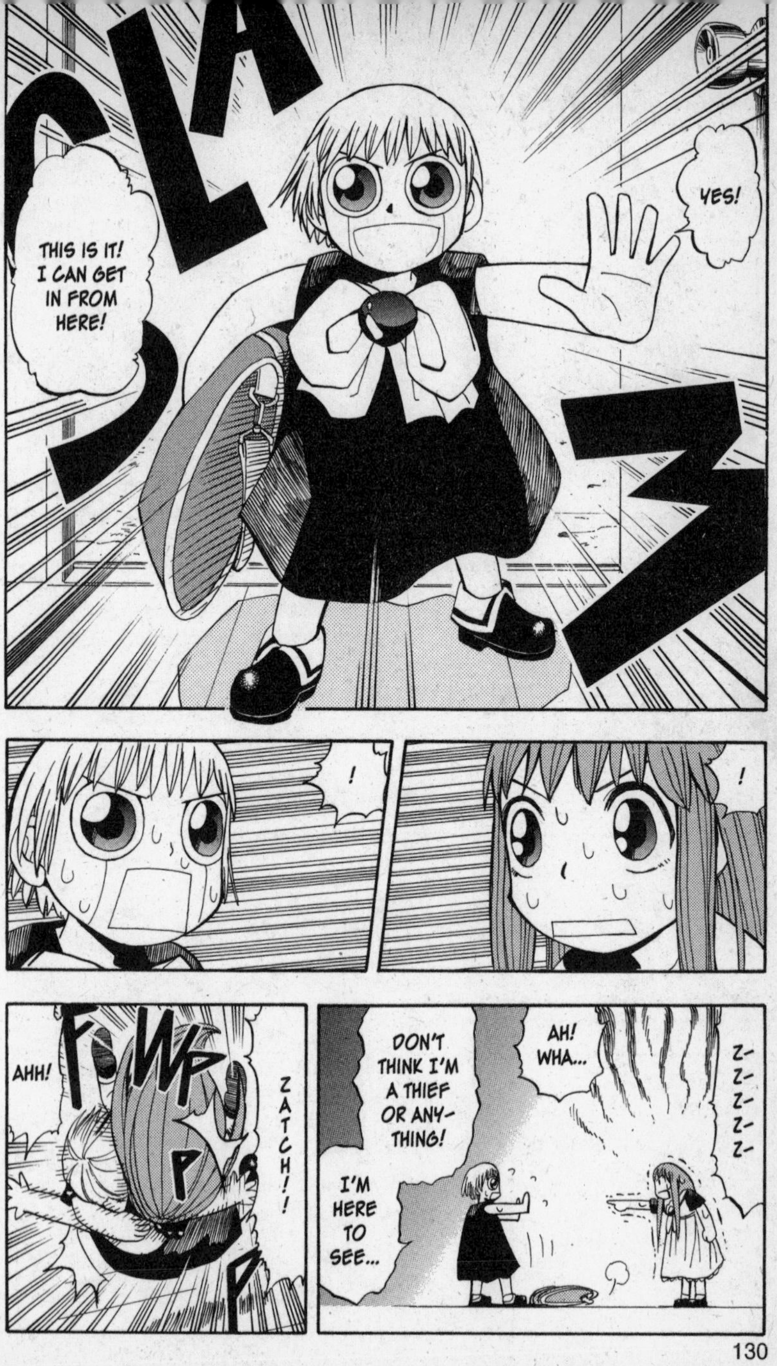
YES!
THIS IS IT! I CAN GET IN FROM HERE!
!
!
Z-Z-Z-Z-Z-
AH! WHA...
DON'T THINK I'M A THIEF OR ANY-THING!
I'M HERE TO SEE...
ZATCH!!
AHH!

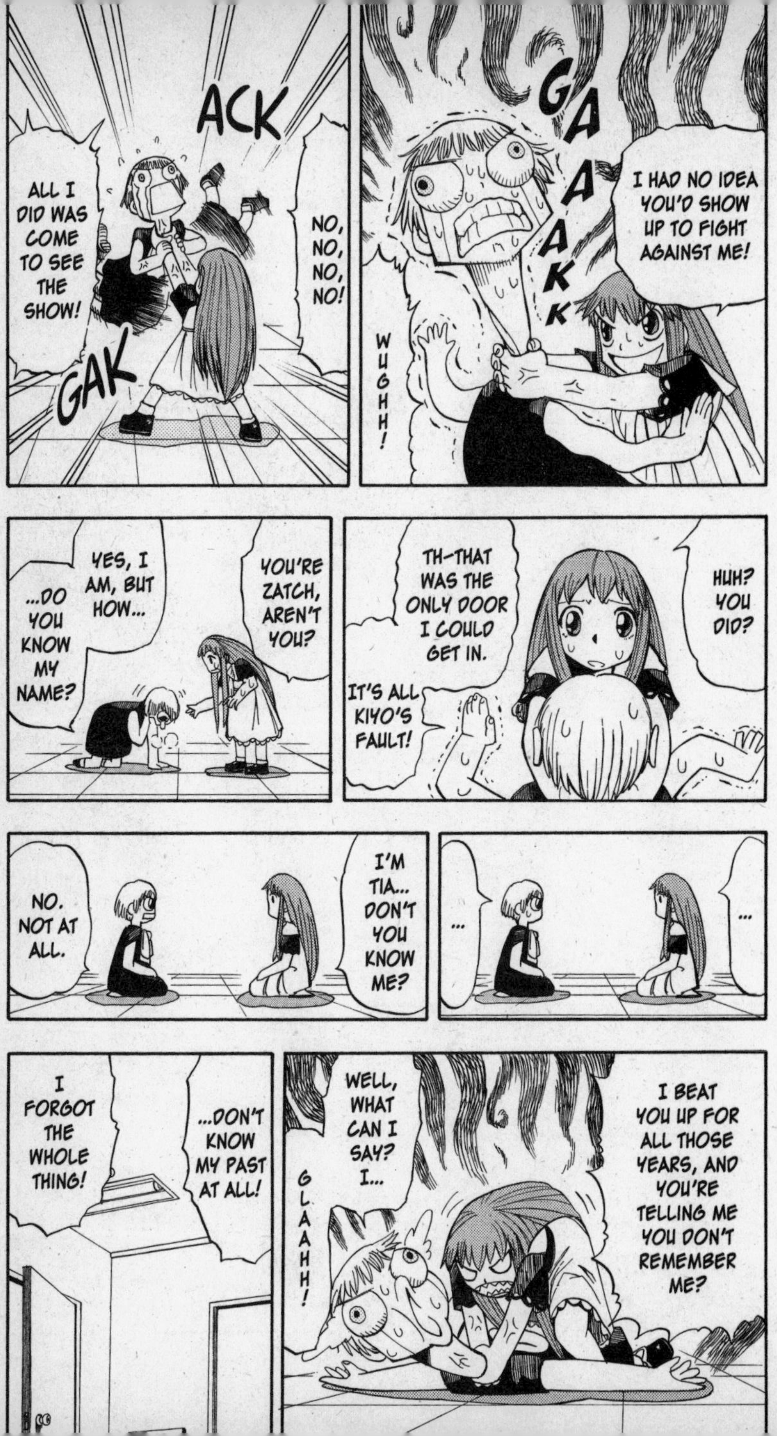
GAAAKK
I HAD NO IDEA YOU'D SHOW UP TO FIGHT AGAINST ME!
WUGHH!
NO, NO, NO, NO!
ACK
ALL I DID WAS COME TO SEE THE SHOW!
GAK
HUH? YOU DID?
TH-THAT WAS THE ONLY DOOR I COULD GET IN.
IT'S ALL KIYO'S FAULT!
YOU'RE ZATCH, AREN'T YOU?
YES, I AM, BUT HOW...
...DO YOU KNOW MY NAME?
...
...
I'M TIA... DON'T YOU KNOW ME?
NO. NOT AT ALL.
I BEAT YOU UP FOR ALL THOSE YEARS, AND YOU'RE TELLING ME YOU DON'T REMEMBER ME?
WELL, WHAT CAN I SAY? I...
GLAAHH!
...DON'T KNOW MY PAST AT ALL!
I FORGOT THE WHOLE THING!

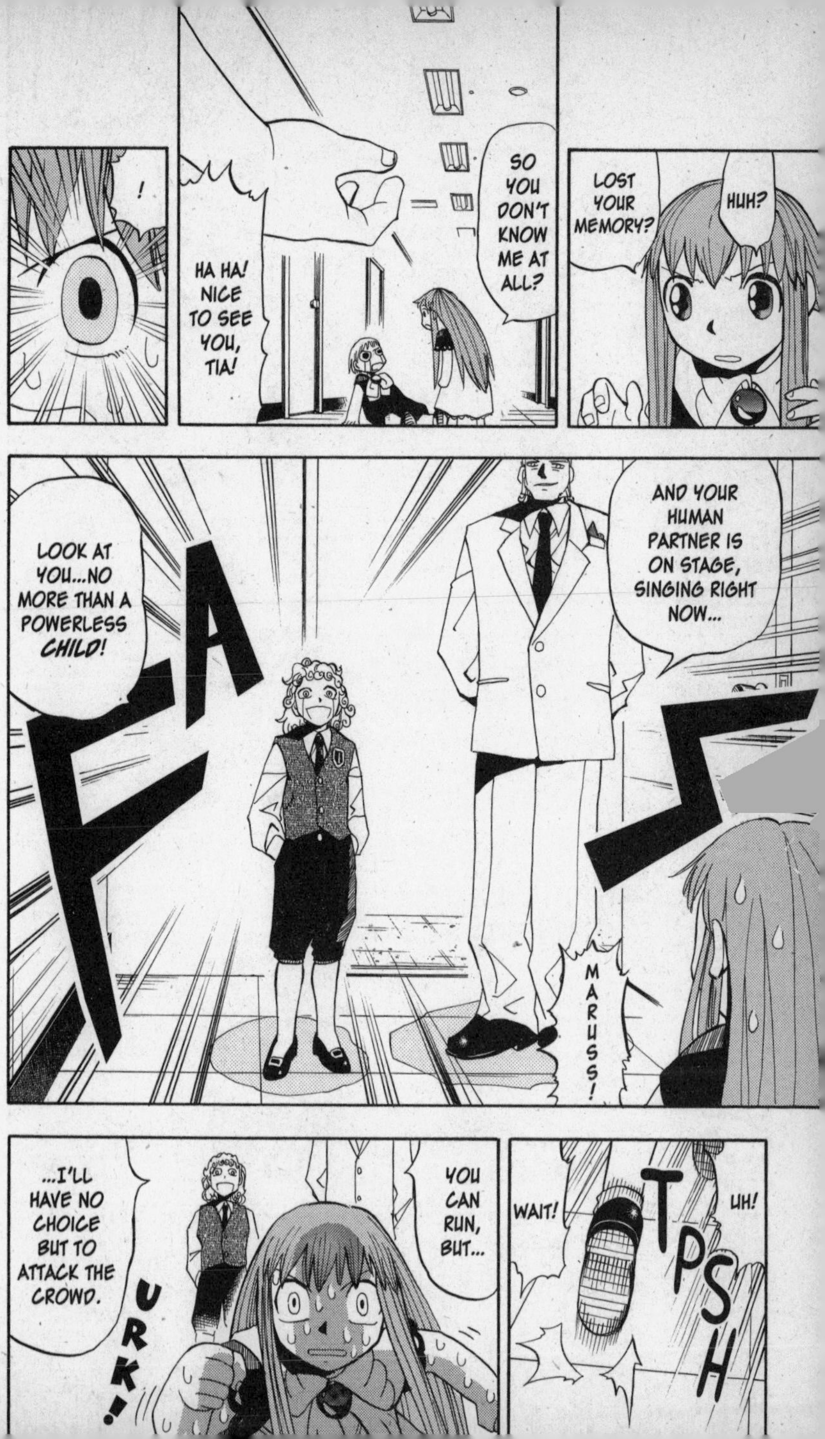

HUH?
LOST YOUR MEMORY?
SO YOU DON'T KNOW ME AT ALL?
HA HA! NICE TO SEE YOU, TIA!
!
AND YOUR HUMAN PARTNER IS ON STAGE, SINGING RIGHT NOW...
MARUSS!
LOOK AT YOU...NO MORE THAN A POWERLESS CHILD!
UH!
TPSH
WAIT!
YOU CAN RUN, BUT...
...I'LL HAVE NO CHOICE BUT TO ATTACK THE CROWD.
URK!

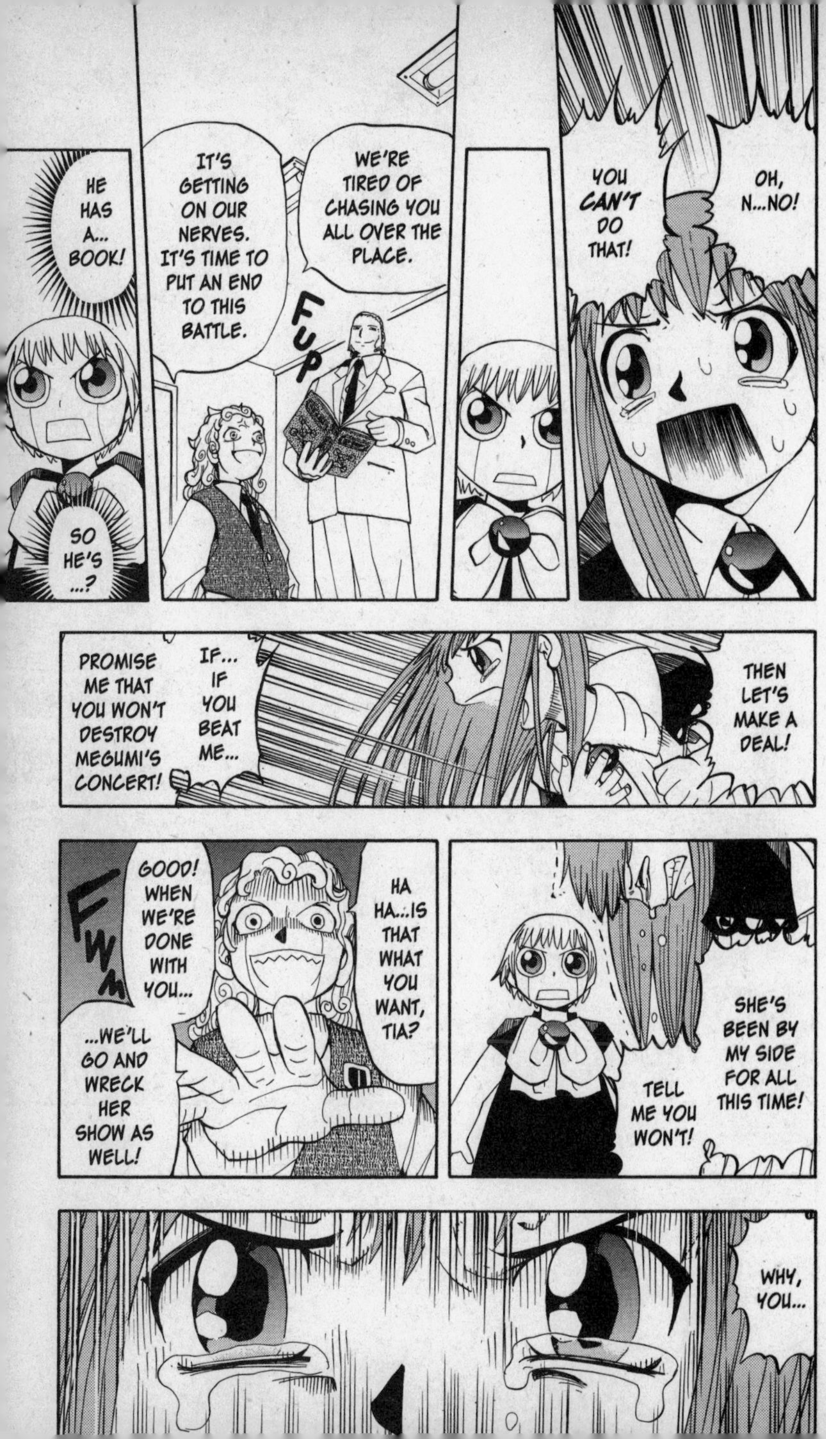
OH, N...NO!
YOU CAN'T DO THAT!
WE'RE TIRED OF CHASING YOU ALL OVER THE PLACE.
FUP
IT'S GETTING ON OUR NERVES. IT'S TIME TO PUT AN END TO THIS BATTLE.
HE HAS A... BOOK!
SO HE'S ...?
THEN LET'S MAKE A DEAL!
IF... IF YOU BEAT ME...
PROMISE ME THAT YOU WON'T DESTROY MEGUMI'S CONCERT!
SHE'S BEEN BY MY SIDE FOR ALL THIS TIME!
TELL ME YOU WON'T!
HA HA...IS THAT WHAT YOU WANT, TIA?
FWM
GOOD! WHEN WE'RE DONE WITH YOU...
...WE'LL GO AND WRECK HER SHOW AS WELL!
WHY, YOU...

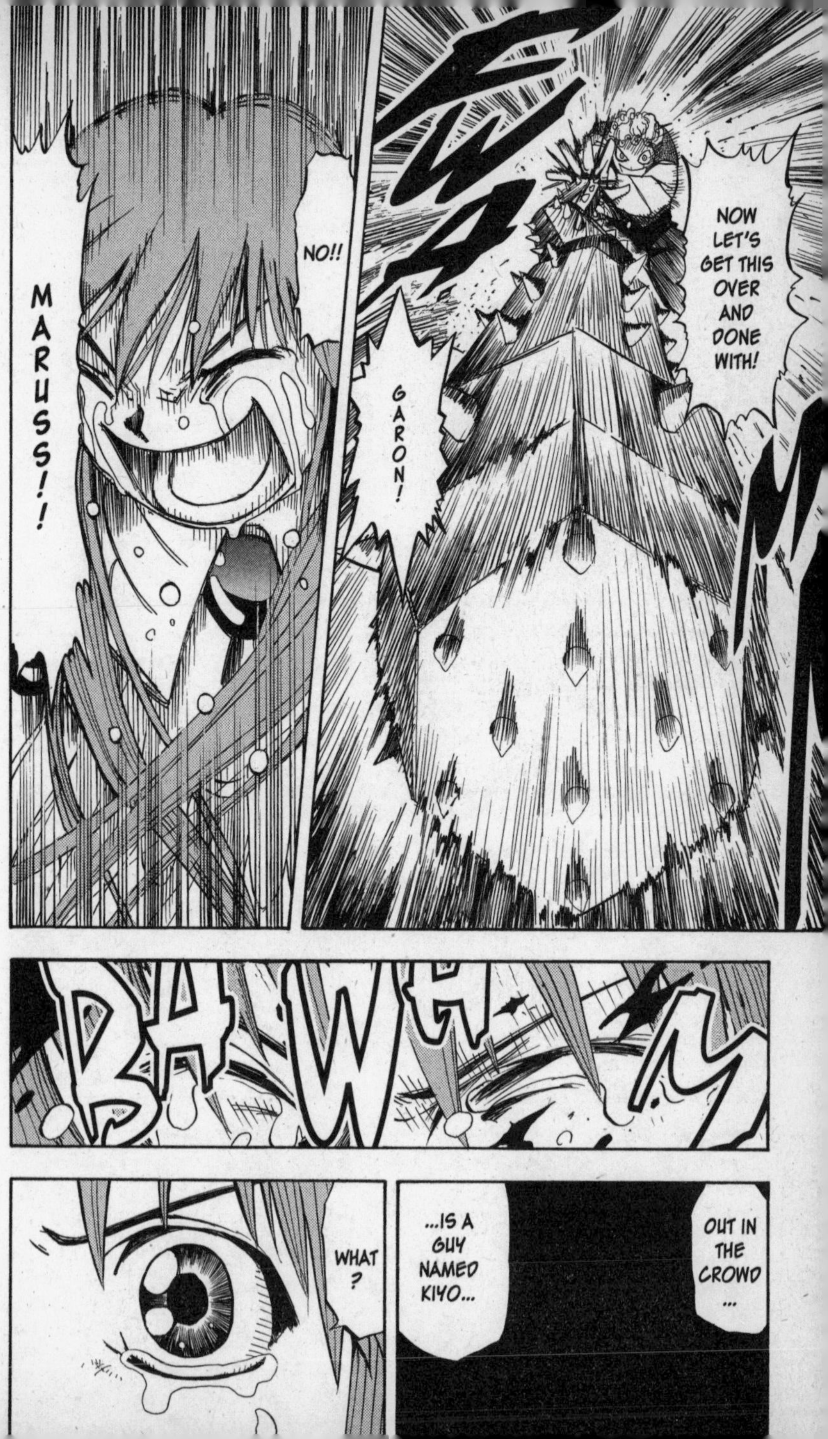
NOW LET'S GET THIS OVER AND DONE WITH!
GARON!
NO!!
MARUSS!!
OUT IN THE CROWD...
...IS A GUY NAMED KIYO...
WHAT?

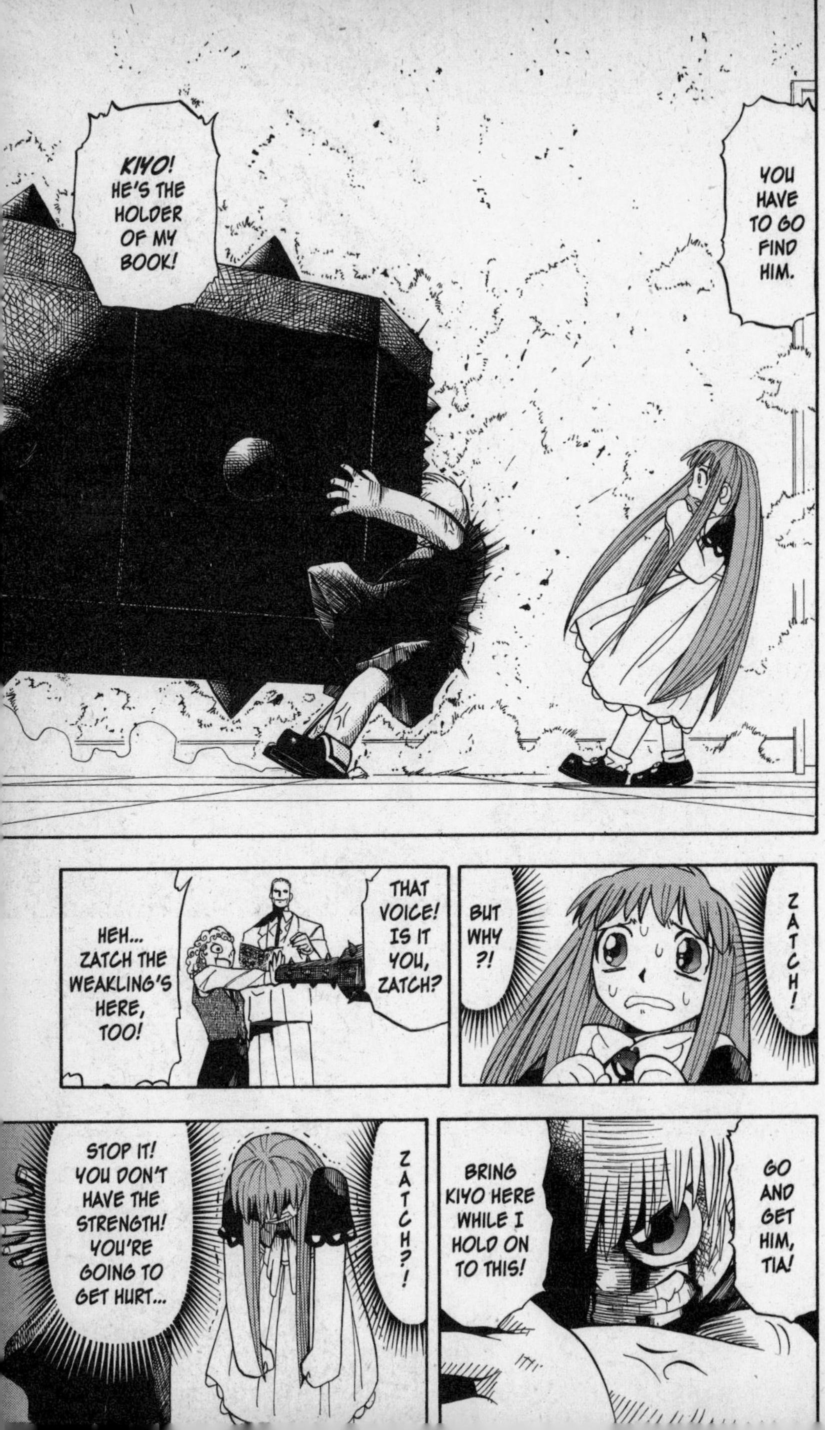
YOU HAVE TO GO FIND HIM.
KIYO! HE'S THE HOLDER OF MY BOOK!
ZATCH!
BUT WHY?!
THAT VOICE! IS IT YOU, ZATCH?
HEH... ZATCH THE WEAKLING'S HERE, TOO!
GO AND GET HIM, TIA!
BRING KIYO HERE WHILE I HOLD ON TO THIS!
ZATCH?!
STOP IT! YOU DON'T HAVE THE STRENGTH! YOU'RE GOING TO GET HURT...

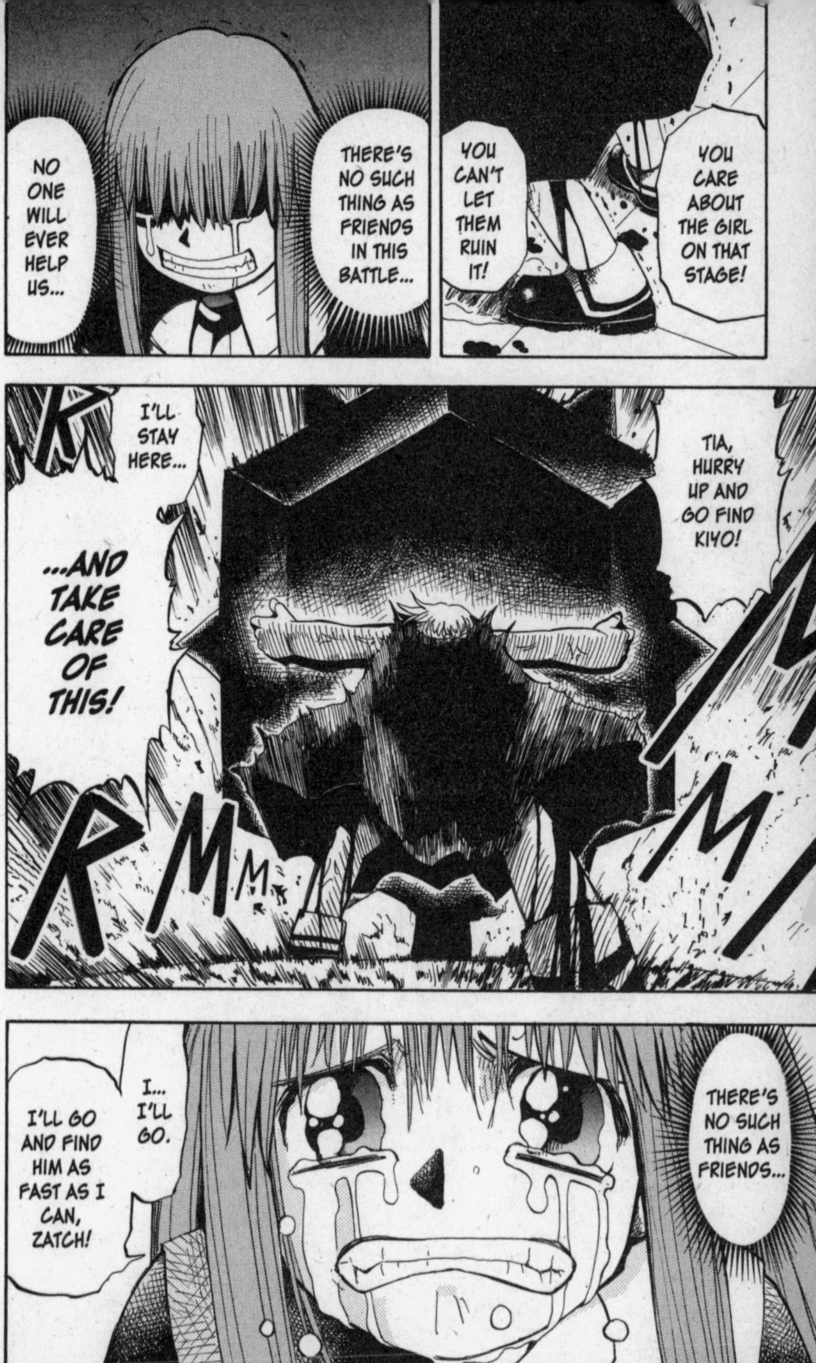
YOU CARE ABOUT THE GIRL ON THAT STAGE!
YOU CAN'T LET THEM RUIN IT!
THERE'S NO SUCH THING AS FRIENDS IN THIS BATTLE...
NO ONE WILL EVER HELP US...
TIA, HURRY UP AND GO FIND KIYO!
I'LL STAY HERE...
...AND TAKE CARE OF THIS!
THERE'S NO SUCH THING AS FRIENDS...
I... I'LL GO.
I'LL GO AND FIND HIM AS FAST AS I CAN, ZATCH!

LEVEL 36: A Solitary Soldier

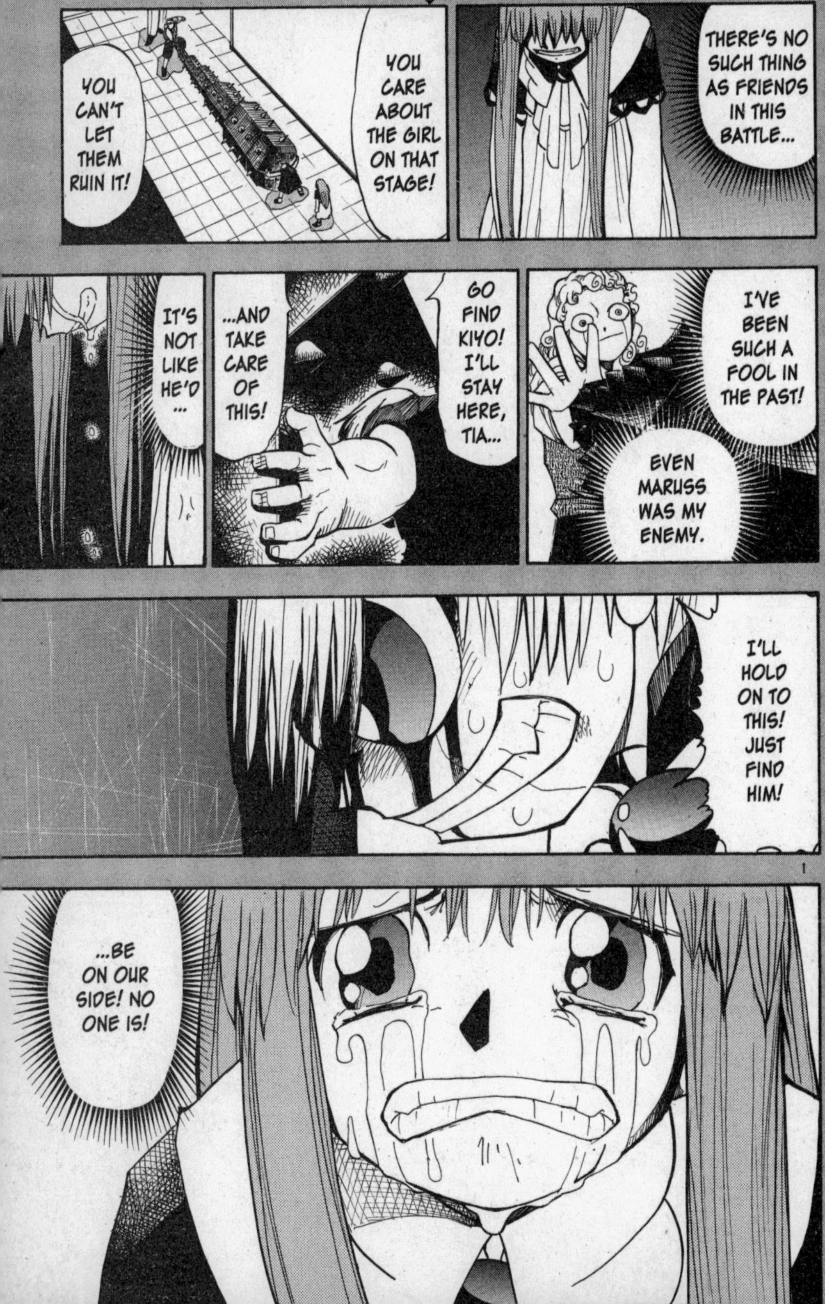
THERE'S NO SUCH THING AS FRIENDS IN THIS BATTLE...
YOU CARE ABOUT THE GIRL ON THAT STAGE!
YOU CAN'T LET THEM RUIN IT!
I'VE BEEN SUCH A FOOL IN THE PAST!
EVEN MARUSS WAS MY ENEMY.
GO FIND KIYO! I'LL STAY HERE, TIA...
...AND TAKE CARE OF THIS!
IT'S NOT LIKE HE'D ...
I'LL HOLD ON TO THIS! JUST FIND HIM!
...BE ON OUR SIDE! NO ONE IS!

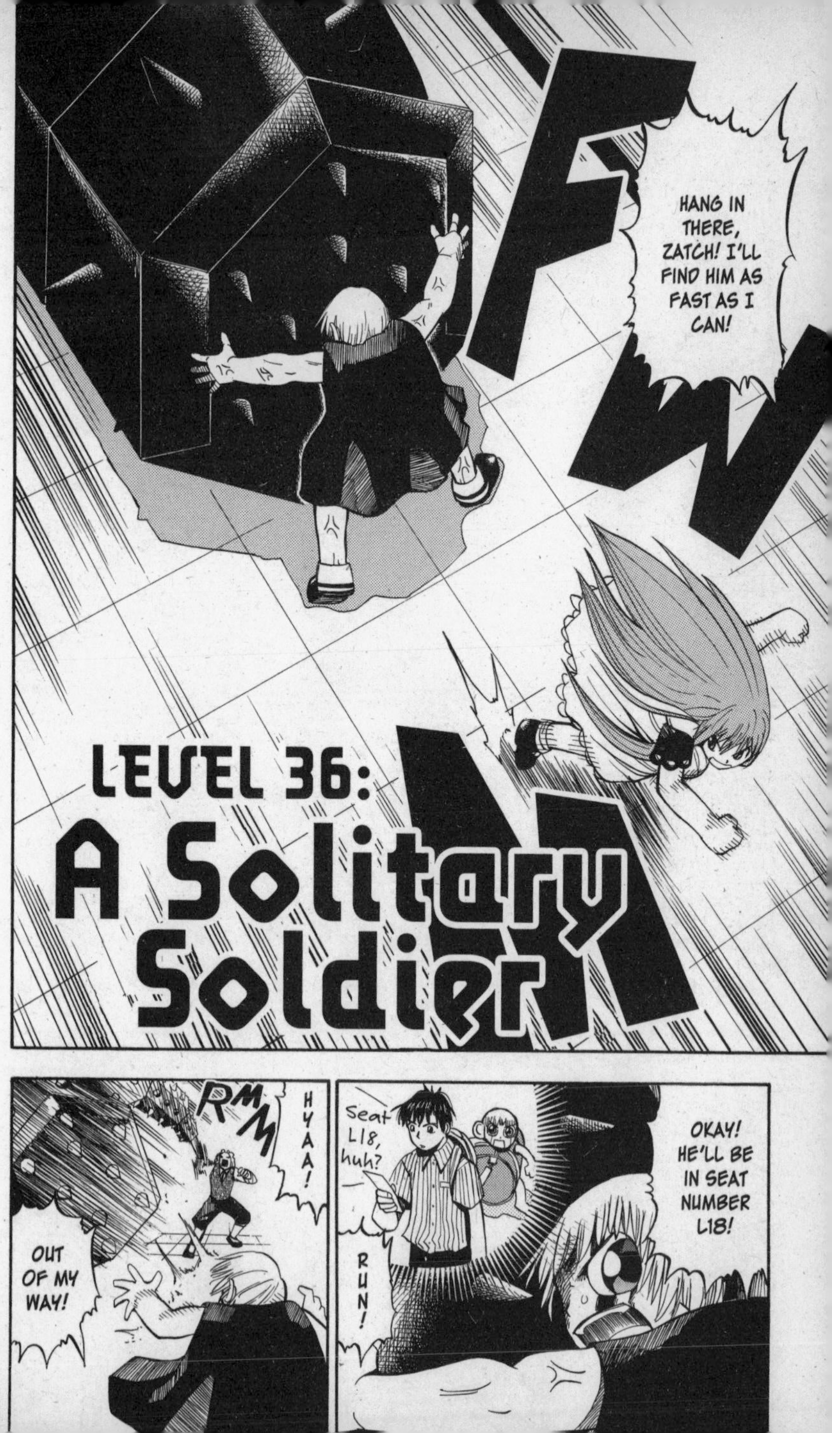
HANG IN THERE, ZATCH! I'LL FIND HIM AS FAST AS I CAN!
FWW
LEVEL 36:
A Solitary Soldier
OKAY! HE'LL BE IN SEAT NUMBER L18!
Seat L18, huh?
RUN!
HYAA!
RMM
OUT OF MY WAY!

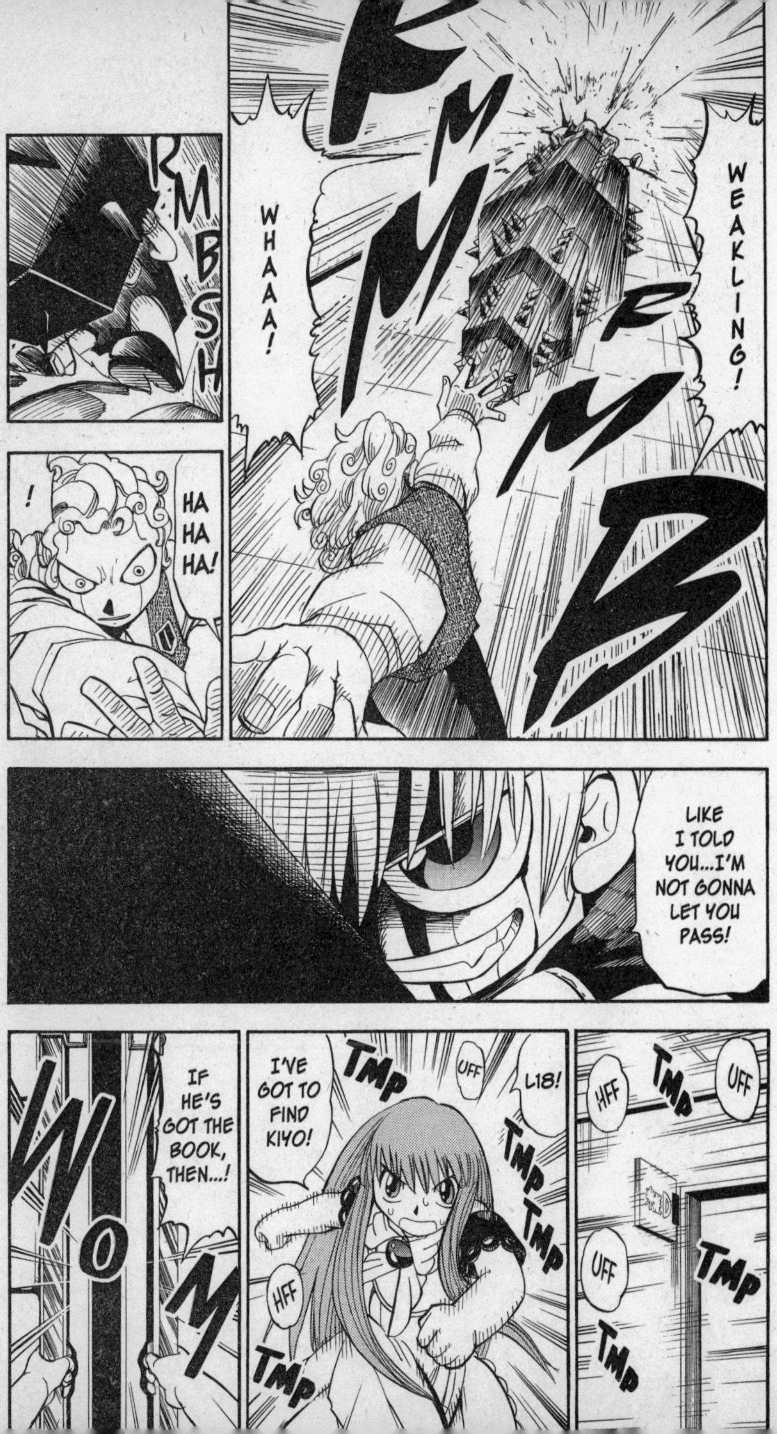
WEAKLING!
WHAAAA!
RMBSH
HA HA HA!
!
LIKE I TOLD YOU...I'M NOT GONNA LET YOU PASS!
TMp
UFF
HFF
TMp
UFF
TMp
L18!
UFF
TMp
I'VE GOT TO FIND KIYO!
TMp
TMp
HFF
TMp
IF HE'S GOT THE BOOK, THEN...!
WOM

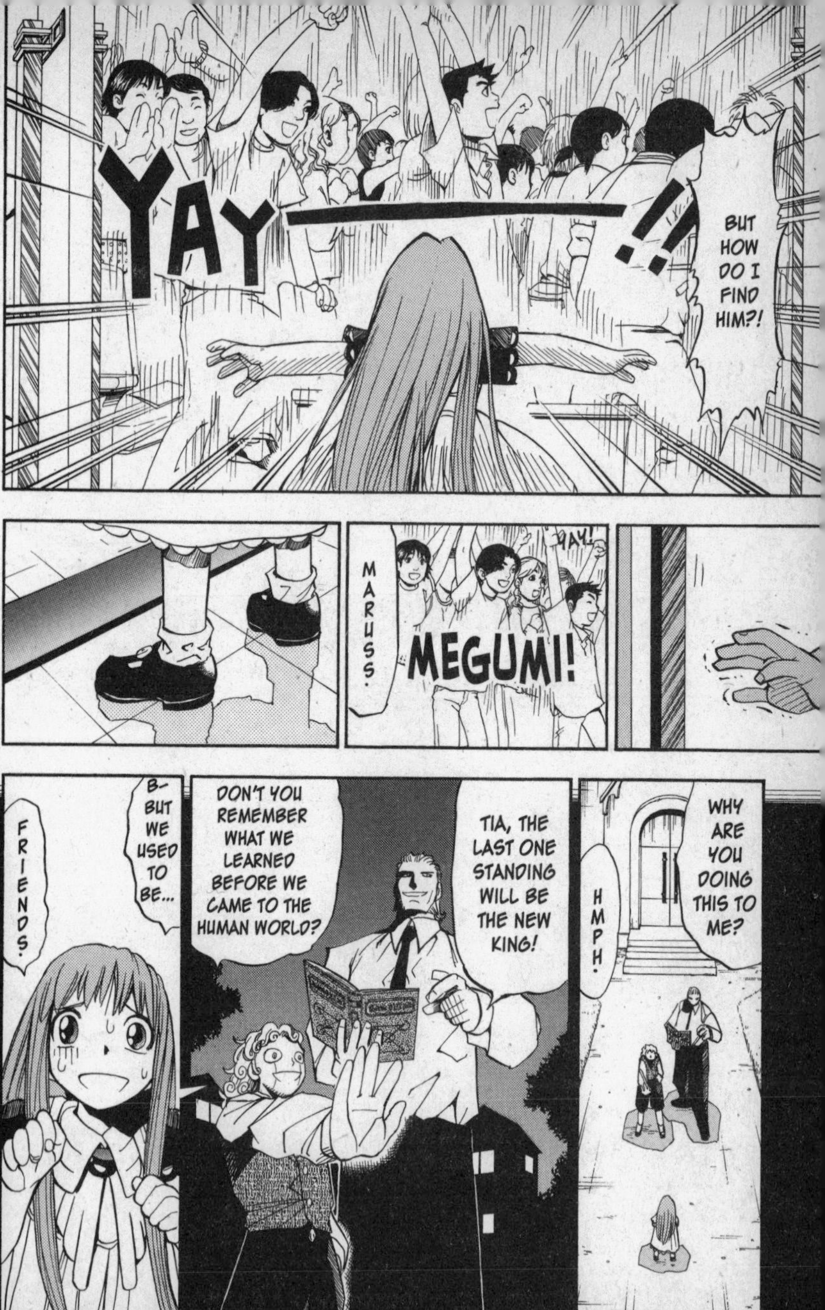
BUT HOW DO I FIND HIM?!
YAY—!!
YAY!
MARUSS.
MEGUMI!
WHY ARE YOU DOING THIS TO ME?
HMPH.
TIA, THE LAST ONE STANDING WILL BE THE NEW KING!
DON'T YOU REMEMBER WHAT WE LEARNED BEFORE WE CAME TO THE HUMAN WORLD?
B-BUT WE USED TO BE...
FRIENDS.

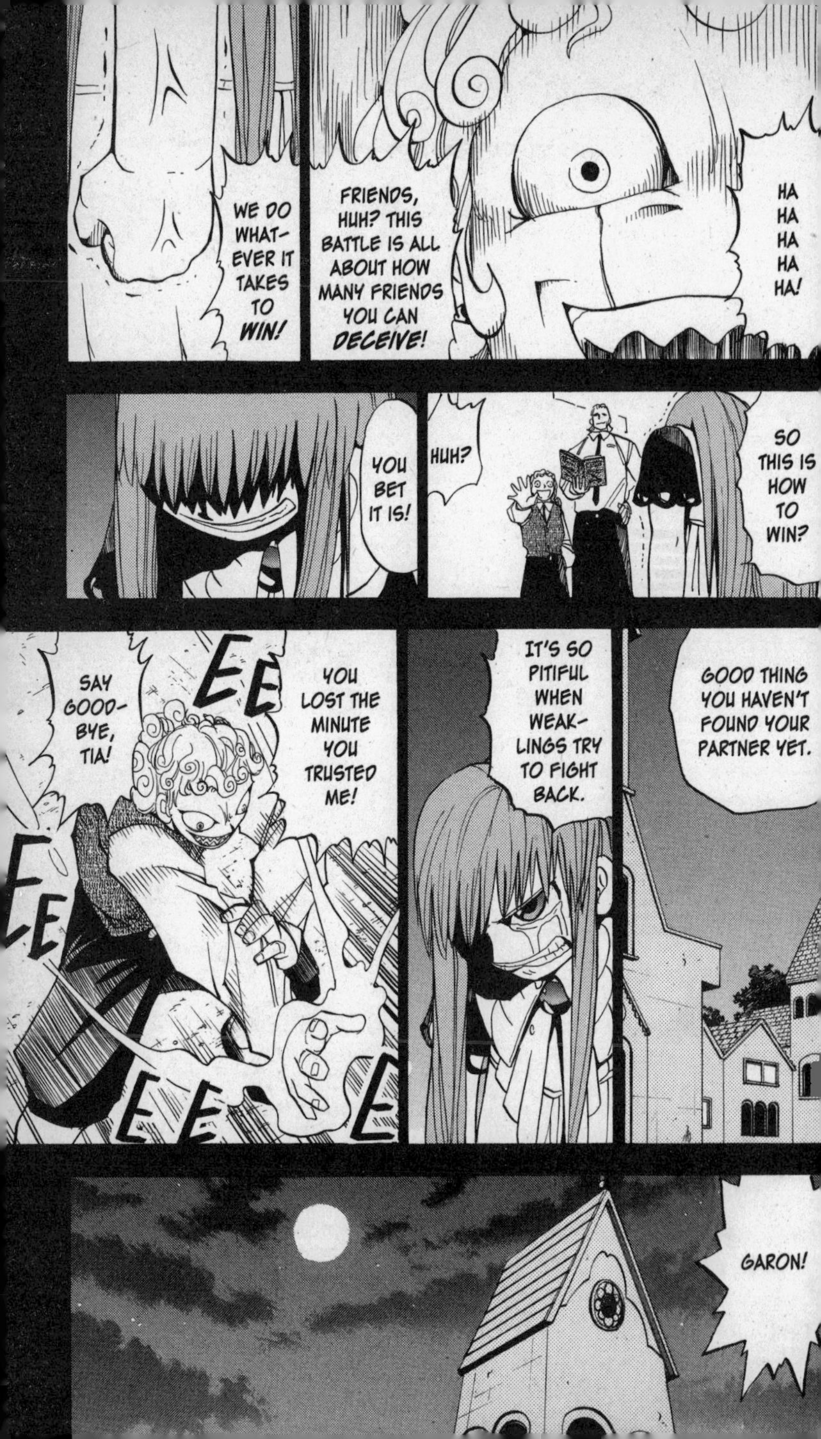
HA HA HA HA HA!
FRIENDS, HUH? THIS BATTLE IS ALL ABOUT HOW MANY FRIENDS YOU CAN DECEIVE!
WE DO WHATEVER IT TAKES TO WIN!
SO THIS IS HOW TO WIN?
HUH?
YOU BET IT IS!
GOOD THING YOU HAVEN'T FOUND YOUR PARTNER YET.
IT'S SO PITIFUL WHEN WEAKLINGS TRY TO FIGHT BACK.
YOU LOST THE MINUTE YOU TRUSTED ME!
SAY GOOD-BYE, TIA!
EE
EEE
EEE
GARON!

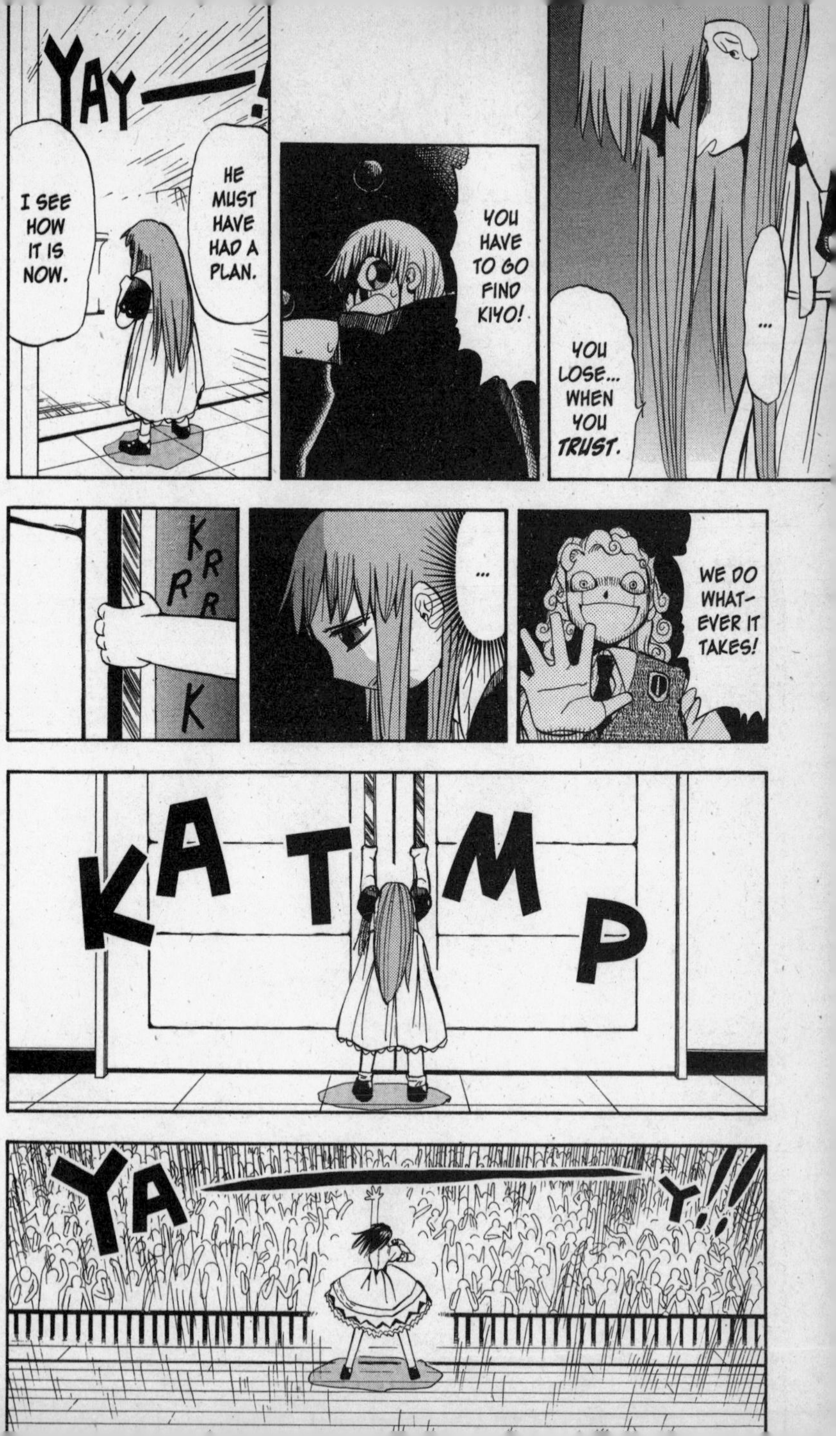
...
YOU LOSE... WHEN YOU TRUST.
YOU HAVE TO GO FIND KIYO!
YAY—!
HE MUST HAVE HAD A PLAN.
I SEE HOW IT IS NOW.
WE DO WHAT-EVER IT TAKES!
...
KRRRK
KATMP
YA——Y!!

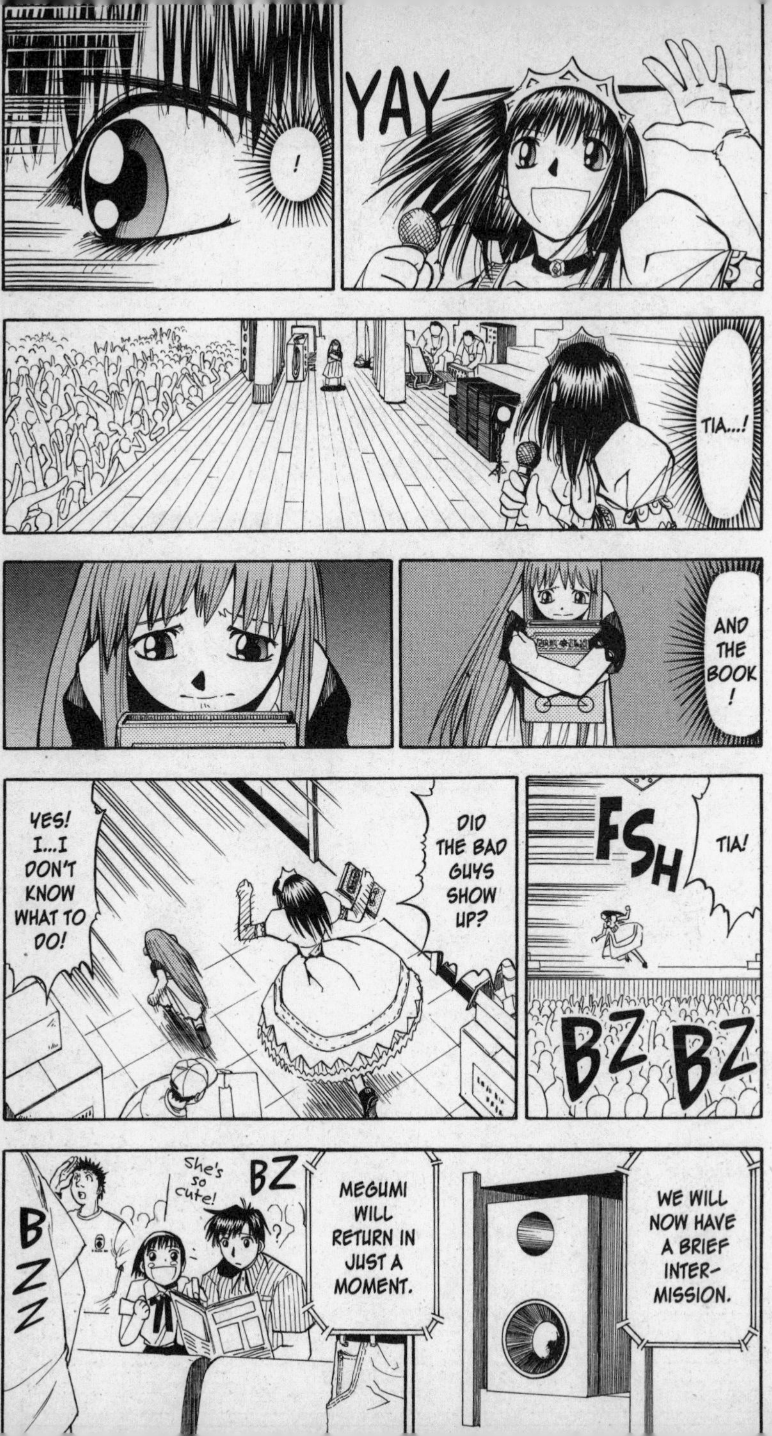
YAY
!
TIA...!
AND THE BOOK!
FSH
TIA!
BZ BZ
DID THE BAD GUYS SHOW UP?
YES! I...I DON'T KNOW WHAT TO DO!
WE WILL NOW HAVE A BRIEF INTER-MISSION.
MEGUMI WILL RETURN IN JUST A MOMENT.
BZ
She's so cute!
?
BZZ

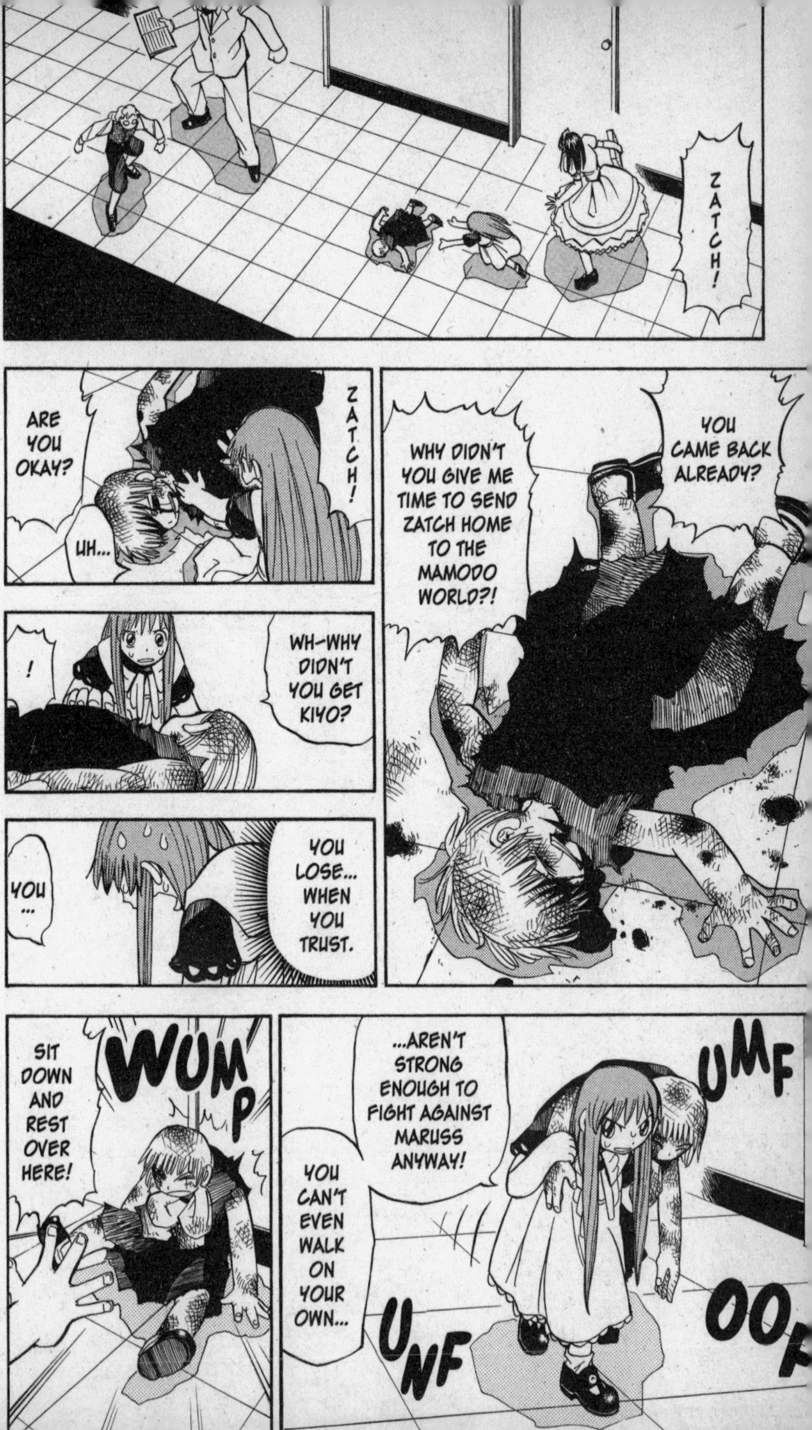
ZATCH!
YOU CAME BACK ALREADY?
WHY DIDN'T YOU GIVE ME TIME TO SEND ZATCH HOME TO THE MAMODO WORLD?!
ZATCH!
ARE YOU OKAY?
UH...
WH-WHY DIDN'T YOU GET KIYO?
!
YOU LOSE... WHEN YOU TRUST.
YOU...
UMF
OOF
YOU CAN'T EVEN WALK ON YOUR OWN...
...AREN'T STRONG ENOUGH TO FIGHT AGAINST MARUSS ANYWAY!
UNF
WUMP
SIT DOWN AND REST OVER HERE!

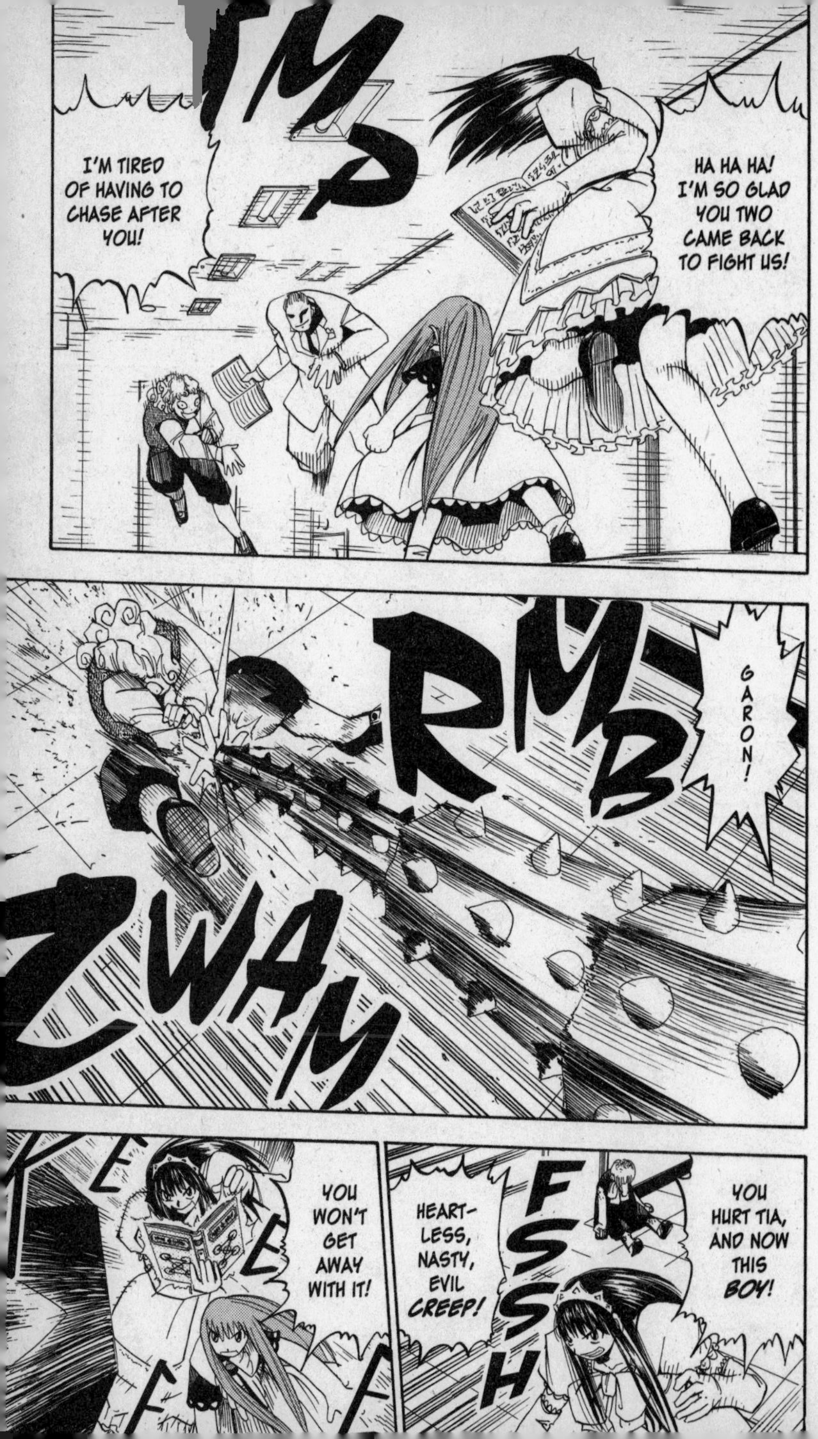

HA HA HA! I'M SO GLAD YOU TWO CAME BACK TO FIGHT US!
I'M TIRED OF HAVING TO CHASE AFTER YOU!
GARON!
RMB
ZWAM
YOU HURT TIA, AND NOW THIS BOY!
FSSH
HEART-LESS, NASTY, EVIL CREEP!
YOU WON'T GET AWAY WITH IT!

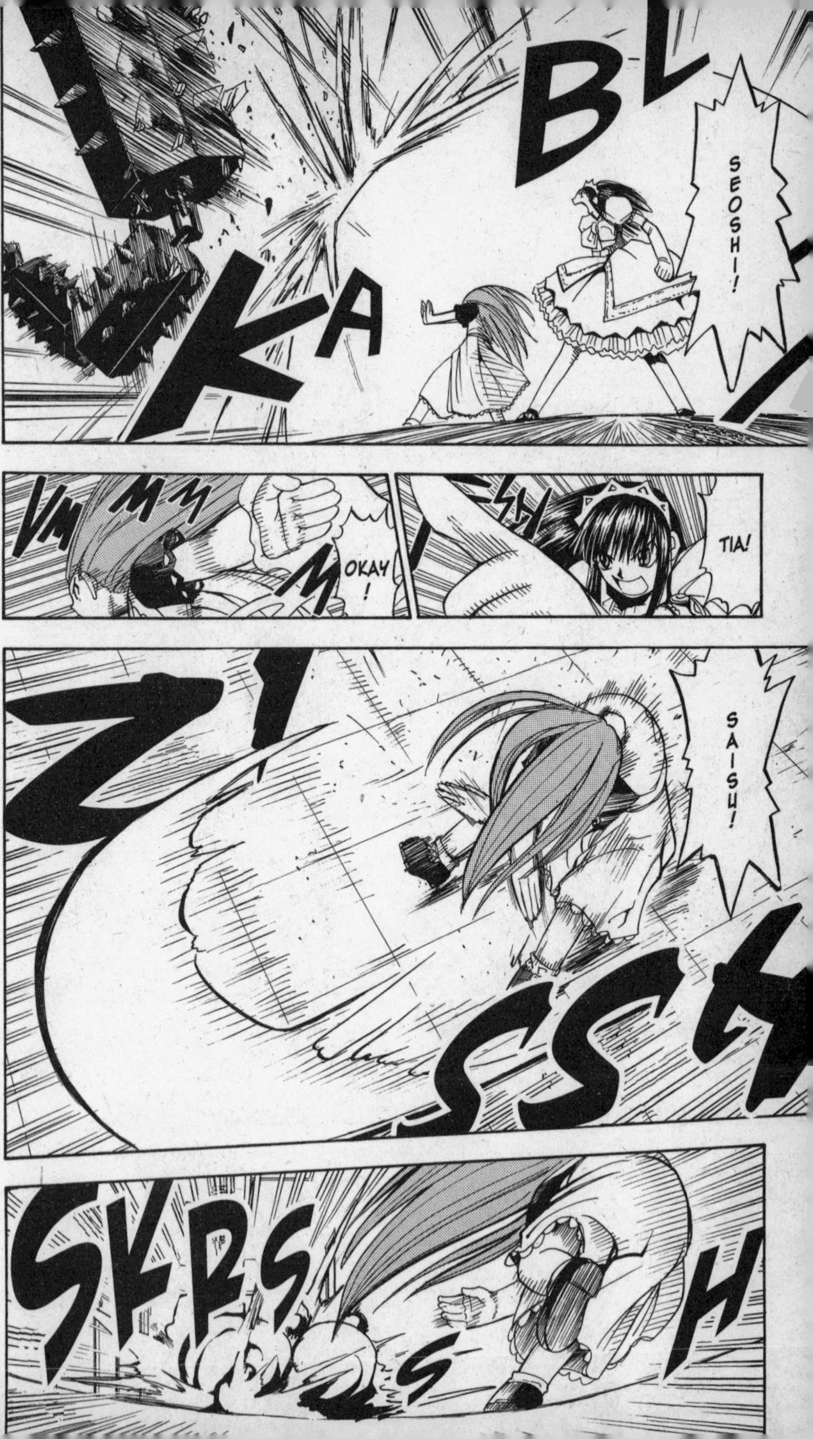
SEOSHI!
BL
KA
TIA!
OKAY!
VMMMM
SAISU!

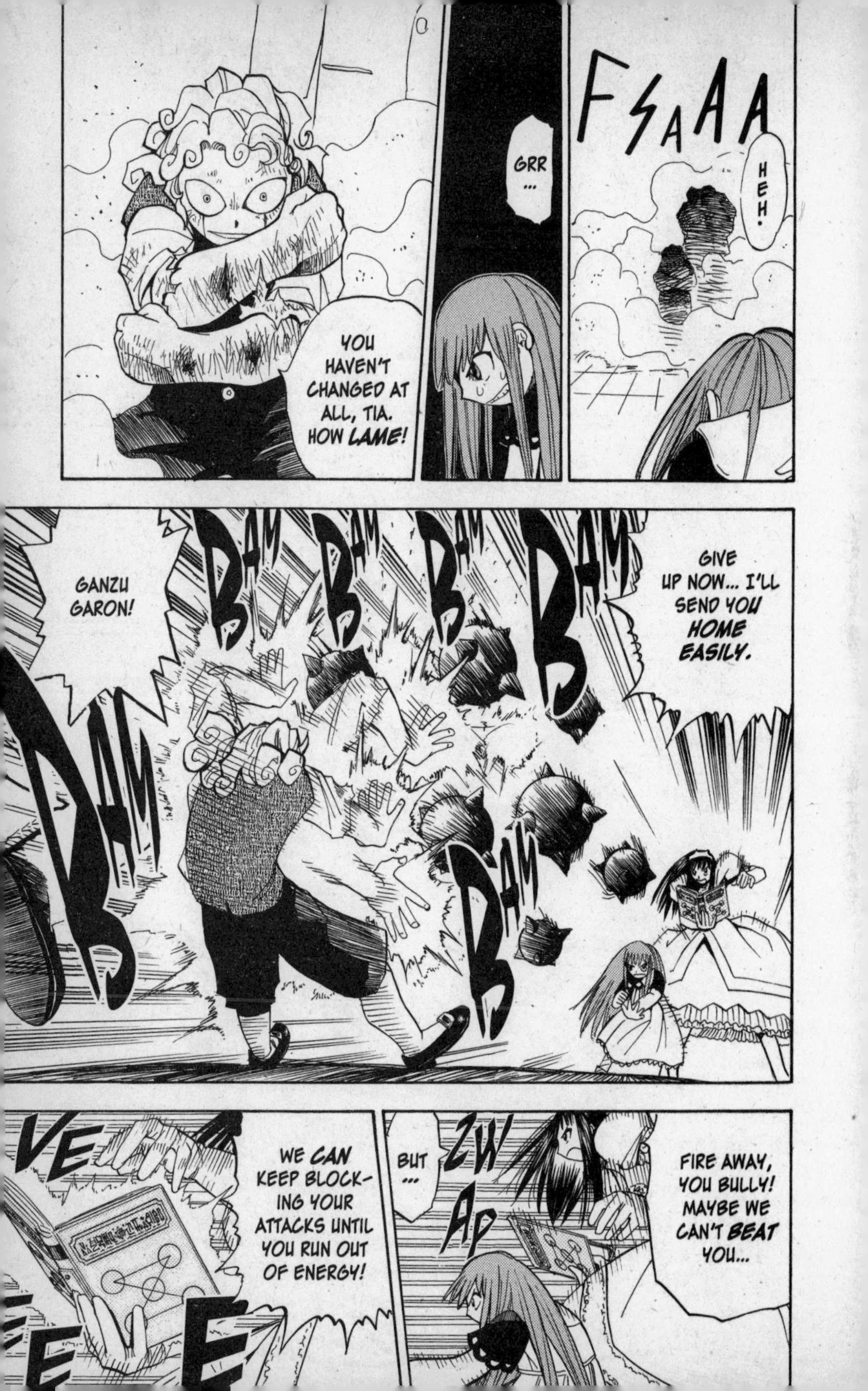
FSAAA
HEH.
GRR...
...
YOU HAVEN'T CHANGED AT ALL, TIA. HOW LAME!
GIVE UP NOW... I'LL SEND YOU HOME EASILY.
BAM
BAM
BAM
BAM
BAM
BAM
GANZU GARON!
FIRE AWAY, YOU BULLY! MAYBE WE CAN'T BEAT YOU...
ZWAP
BUT ...
WE CAN KEEP BLOCKING YOUR ATTACKS UNTIL YOU RUN OUT OF ENERGY!

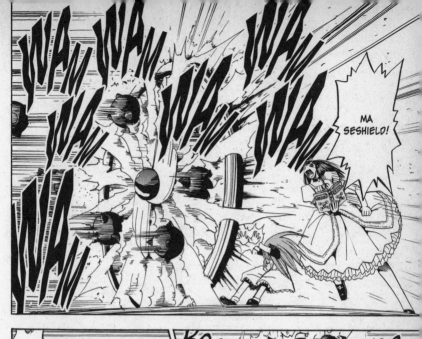

MA SESHIELD!
WAM WAM WAM
WAM WAM WAM WAM WAM
BOOM BOOM BOOM
BOOM BOOM
GRRRRR!
GO ON! SHOUT EVERY SPELL YOU'VE GOT!
WE CAN DO THIS ALL DAY!
EVERY SPELL WE'VE GOT, EH?
IF YOU SAY SO!
THE BIG ONE! LET 'EM HAVE IT!

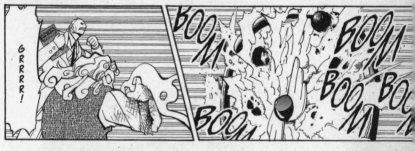

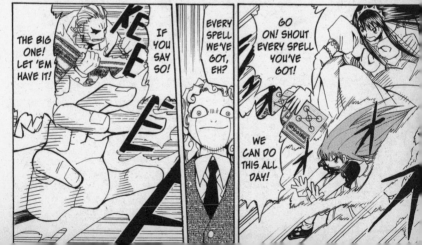

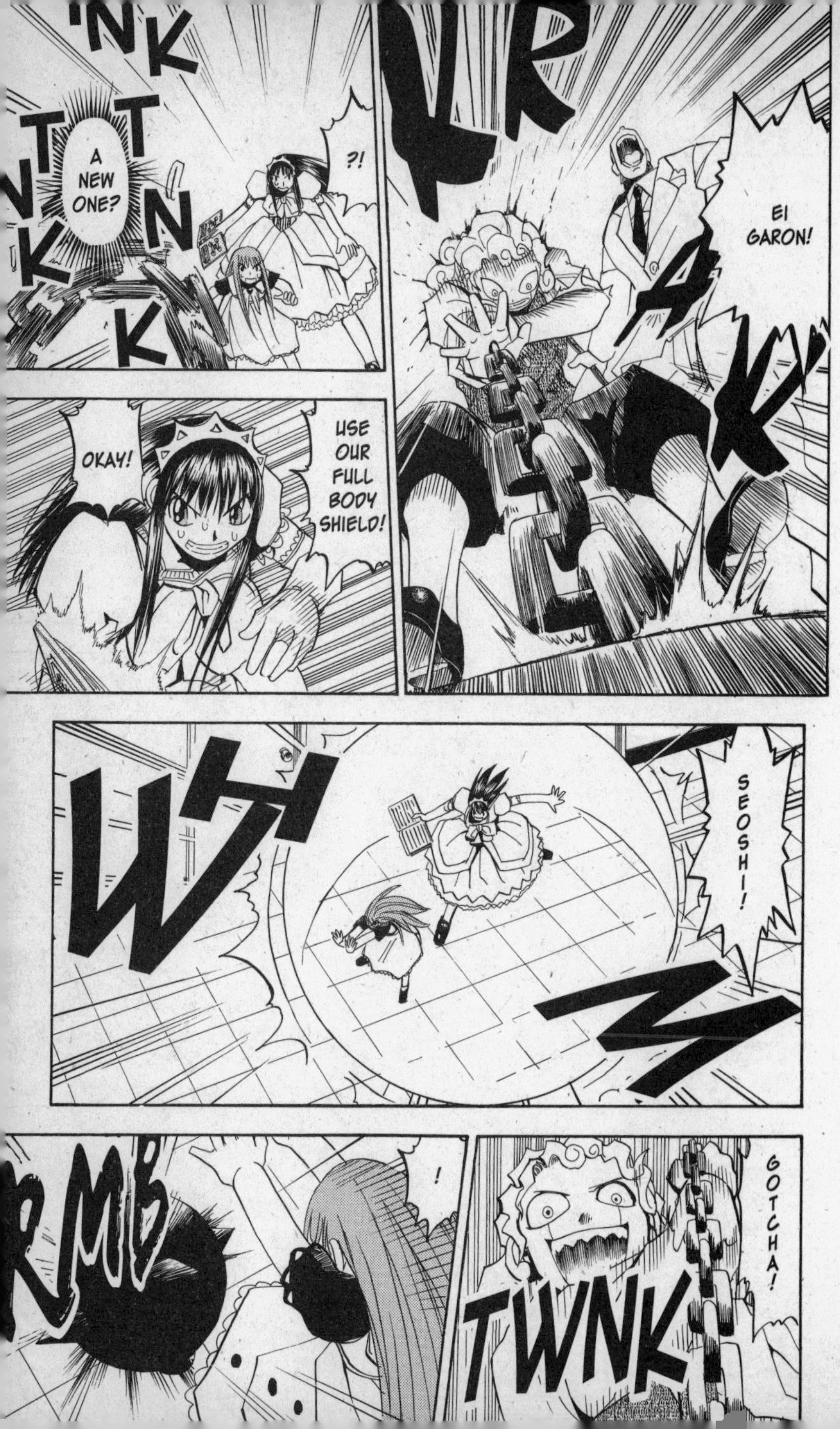
VR
EI GARON!
'NK
?!
A NEW ONE?
USE OUR FULL BODY SHIELD!
OKAY!
SEOSHI!
GOTCHA!
TWNK
!
RMB
...

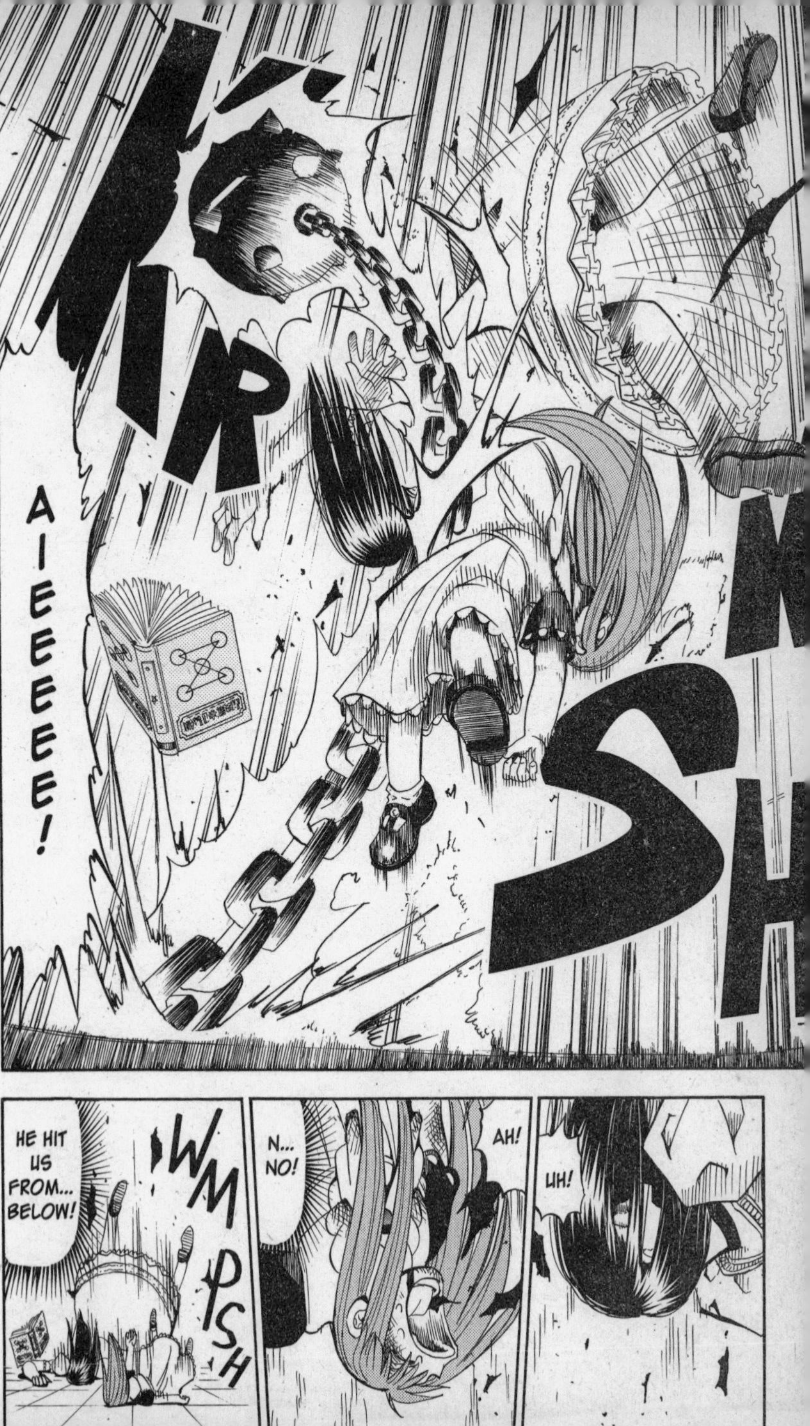
AIEEEEE!
AH!
UH!
N... NO!
WMPSH
HE HIT US FROM... BELOW!

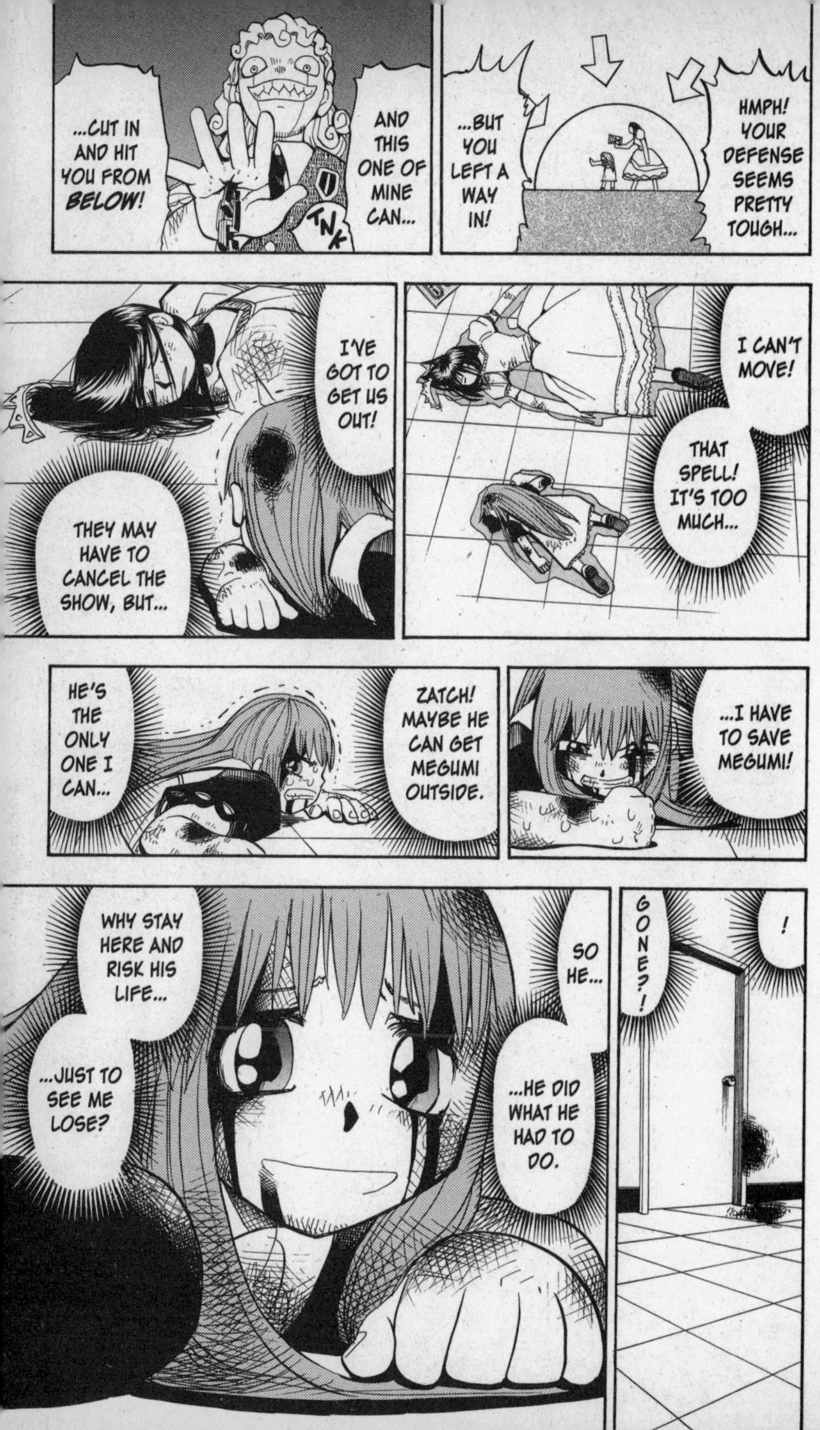
HMPH! YOUR DEFENSE SEEMS PRETTY TOUGH...
...BUT YOU LEFT A WAY IN!
AND THIS ONE OF MINE CAN...
...CUT IN AND HIT YOU FROM BELOW!
TNK
I CAN'T MOVE!
THAT SPELL! IT'S TOO MUCH...
I'VE GOT TO GET US OUT!
THEY MAY HAVE TO CANCEL THE SHOW, BUT...
...I HAVE TO SAVE MEGUMI!
ZATCH! MAYBE HE CAN GET MEGUMI OUTSIDE.
HE'S THE ONLY ONE I CAN...
!
GONE?!
SO HE...
...HE DID WHAT HE HAD TO DO.
WHY STAY HERE AND RISK HIS LIFE...
...JUST TO SEE ME LOSE?

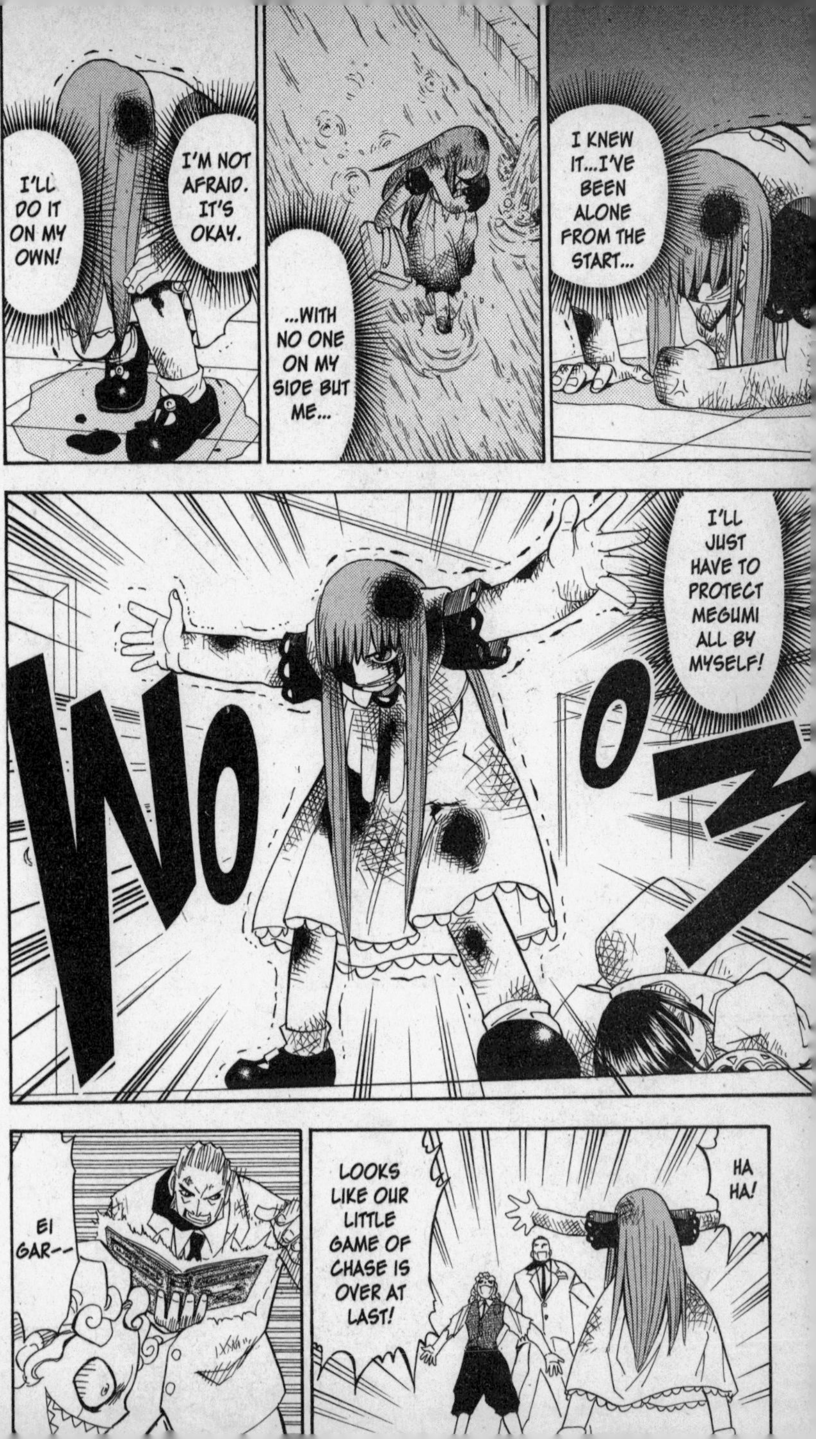
I KNEW IT...I'VE BEEN ALONE FROM THE START...
...WITH NO ONE ON MY SIDE BUT ME...
I'M NOT AFRAID. IT'S OKAY.
I'LL DO IT ON MY OWN!
I'LL JUST HAVE TO PROTECT MEGUMI ALL BY MYSELF!
NOOM
HA HA!
LOOKS LIKE OUR LITTLE GAME OF CHASE IS OVER AT LAST!
EI GAR--

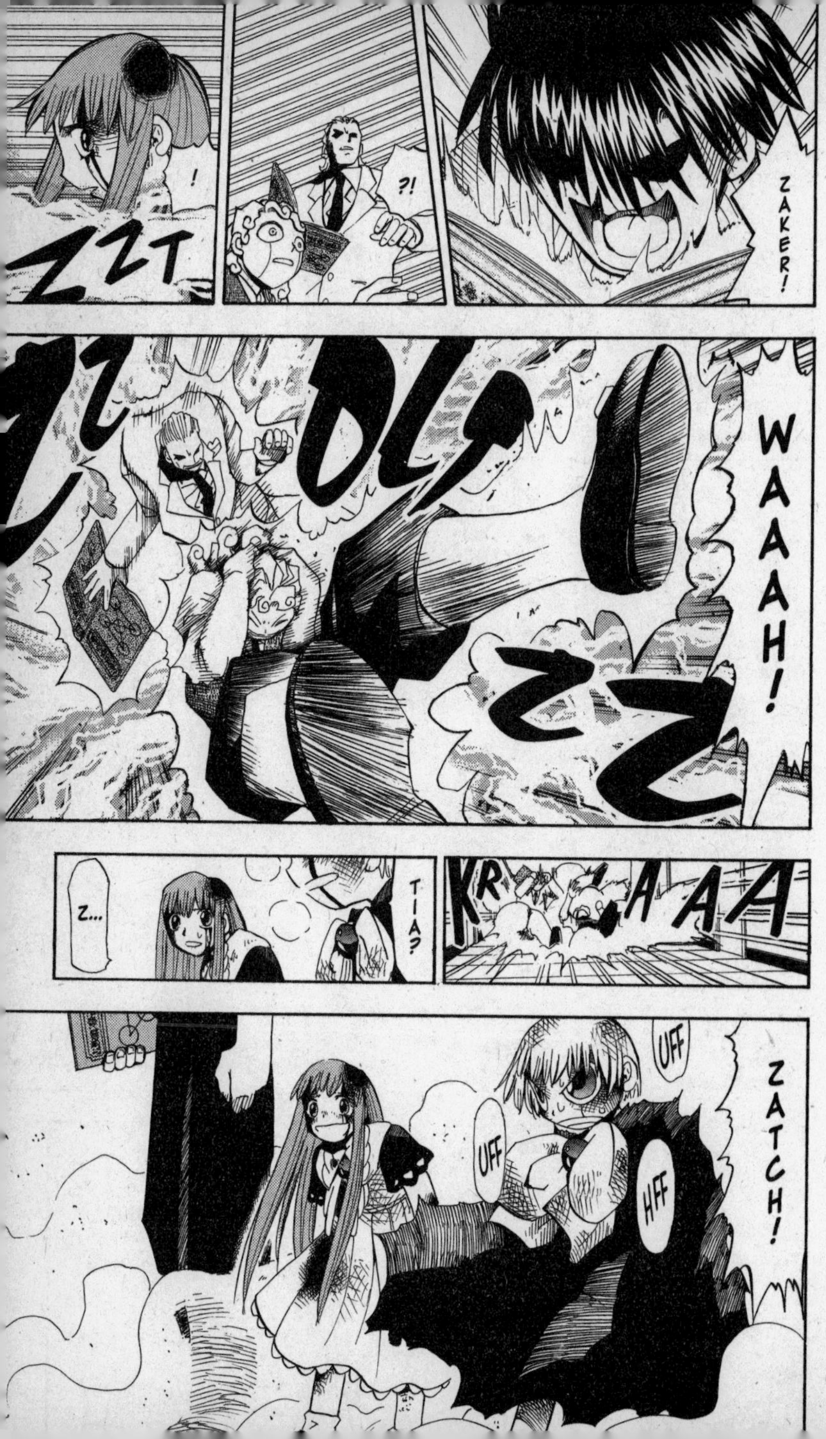
ZAKER!
?!
!
ZZT
WAAAH!
KRAAA
TIA?
Z...
ZATCH!
UFF
UFF
HFF

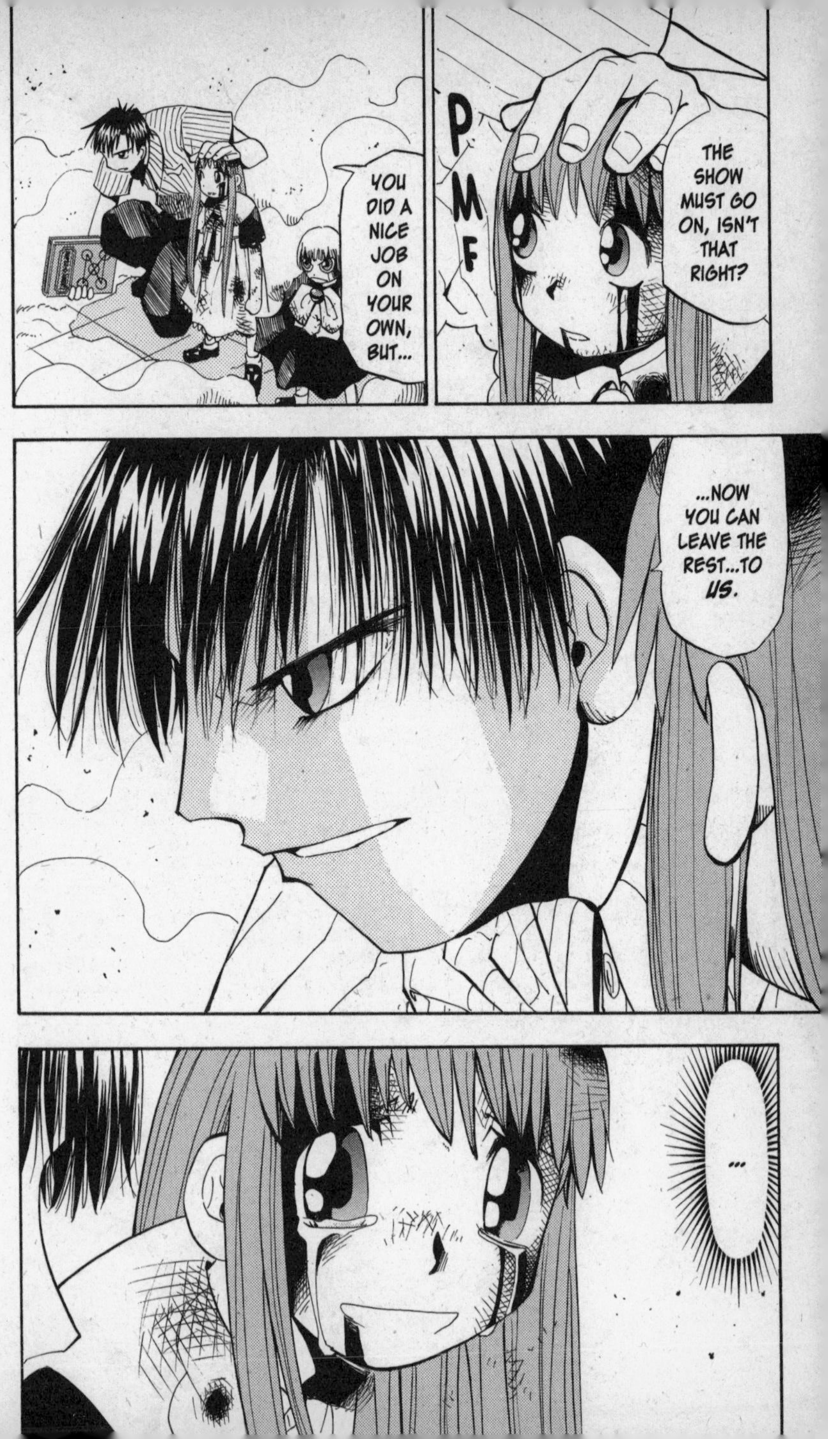
PMF
THE SHOW MUST GO ON, ISN'T THAT RIGHT?
YOU DID A NICE JOB ON YOUR OWN, BUT...
...NOW YOU CAN LEAVE THE REST...TO US.
...

LEVEL 37: The Culmination of Battle

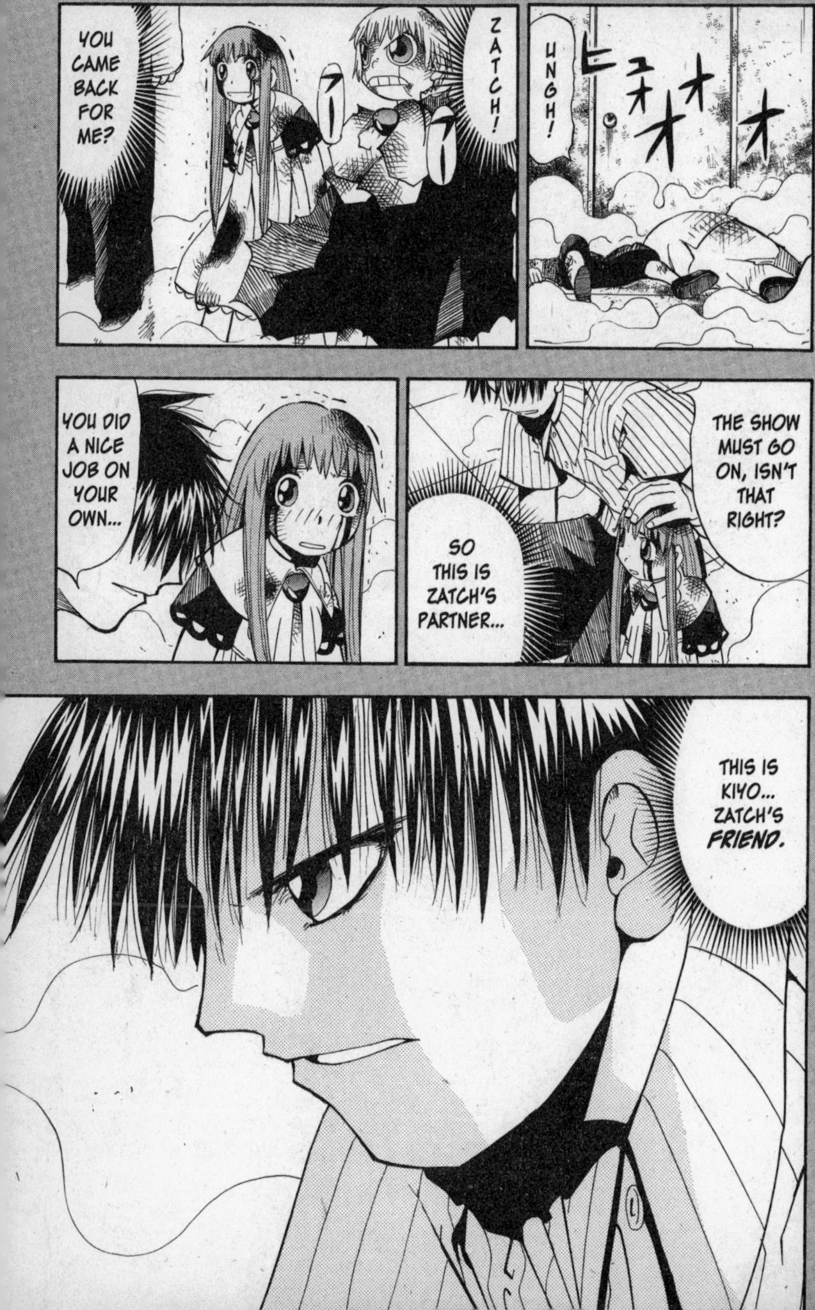
UNGH!
ヒュオオオオ
ZATCH!
YOU CAME BACK FOR ME?
THE SHOW MUST GO ON, ISN'T THAT RIGHT?
SO THIS IS ZATCH'S PARTNER...
YOU DID A NICE JOB ON YOUR OWN...
THIS IS KIYO... ZATCH'S ***FRIEND***.

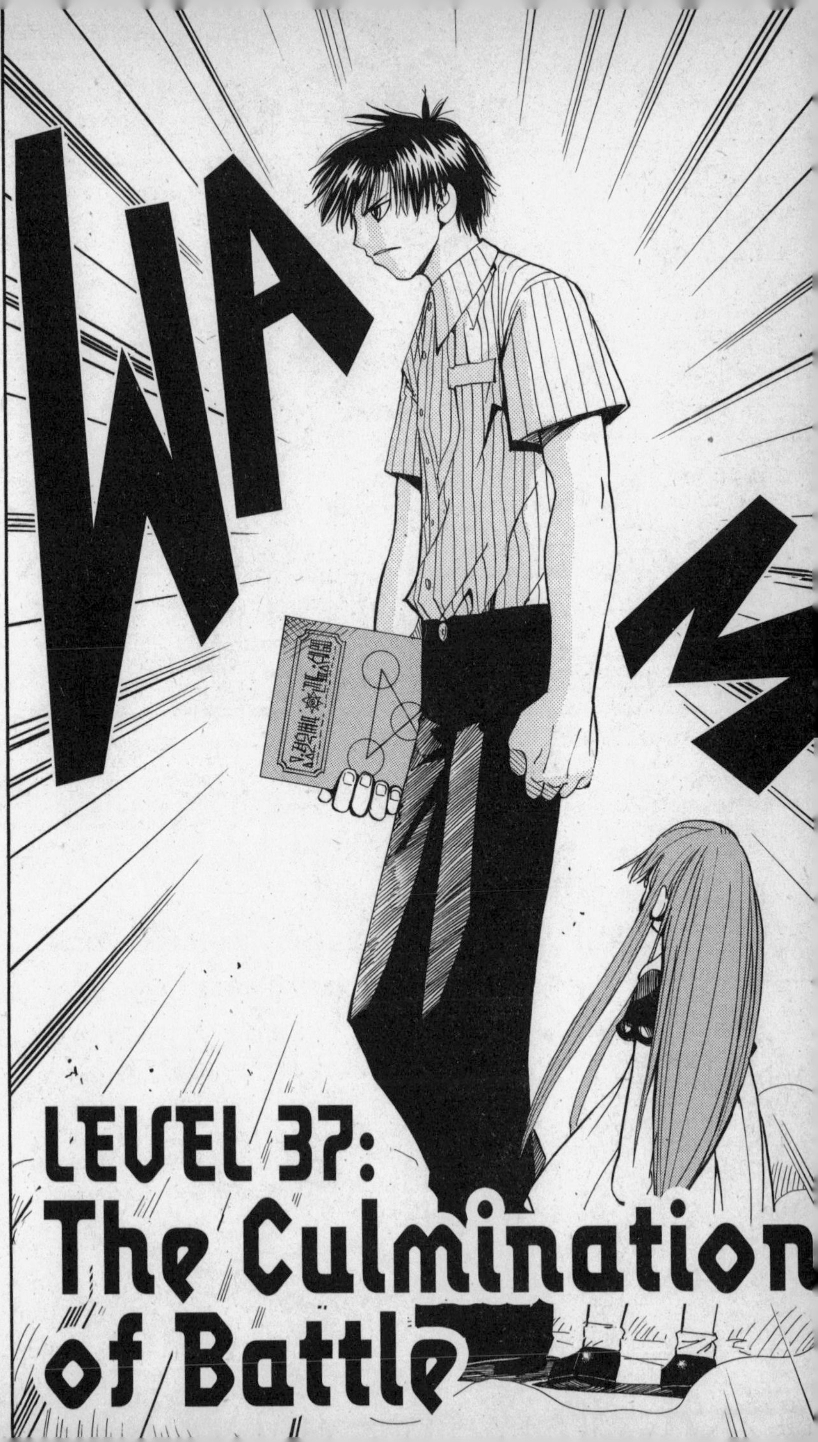
WAM

LEVEL 37: The Culmination of Battle

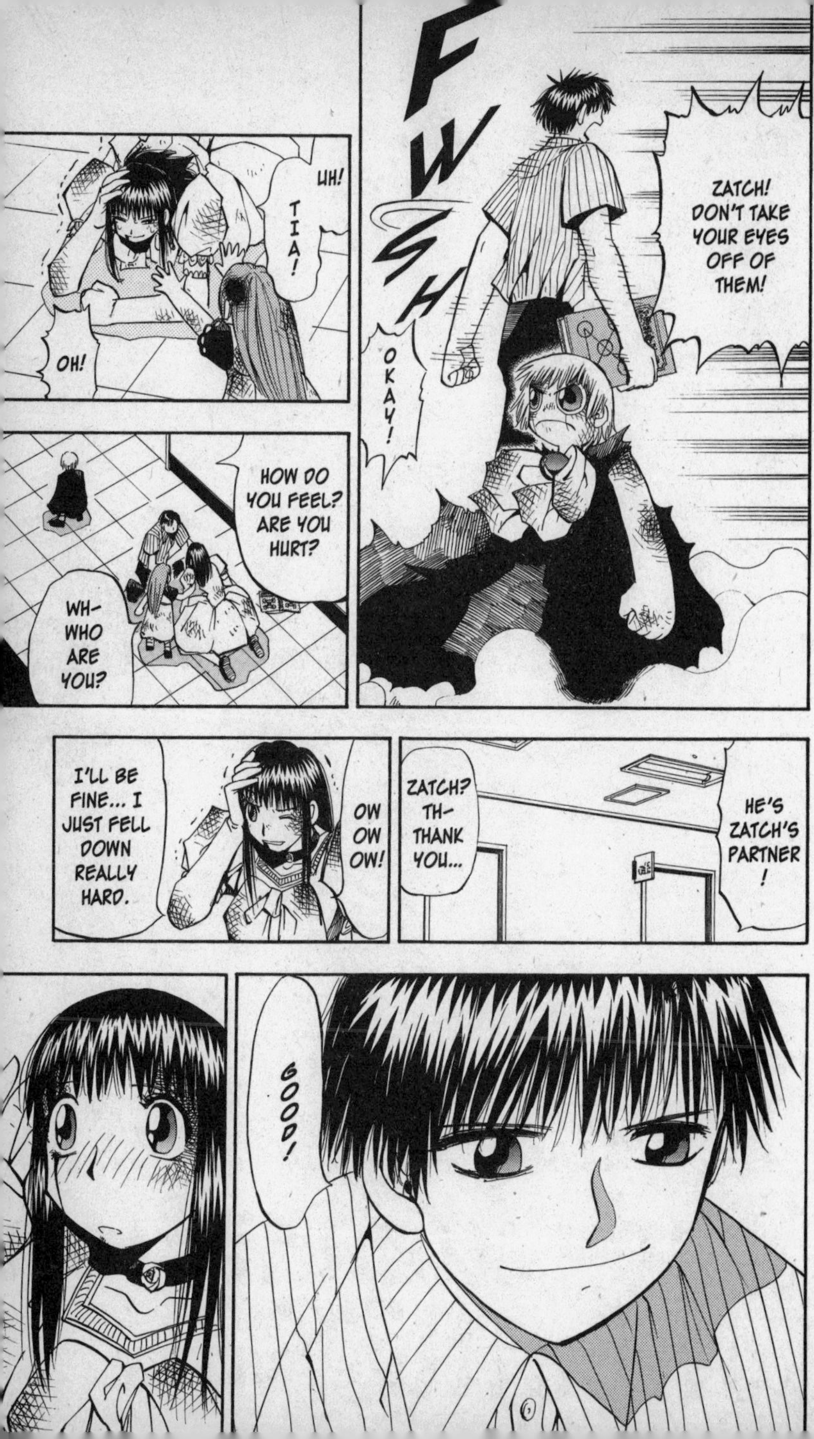
FWSH
ZATCH! DON'T TAKE YOUR EYES OFF OF THEM!
OKAY!
UH!
TIA!
OH!
HOW DO YOU FEEL? ARE YOU HURT?
WH- WHO ARE YOU?
HE'S ZATCH'S PARTNER!
ZATCH? TH- THANK YOU...
OW OW OW!
I'LL BE FINE... I JUST FELL DOWN REALLY HARD.
GOOD!

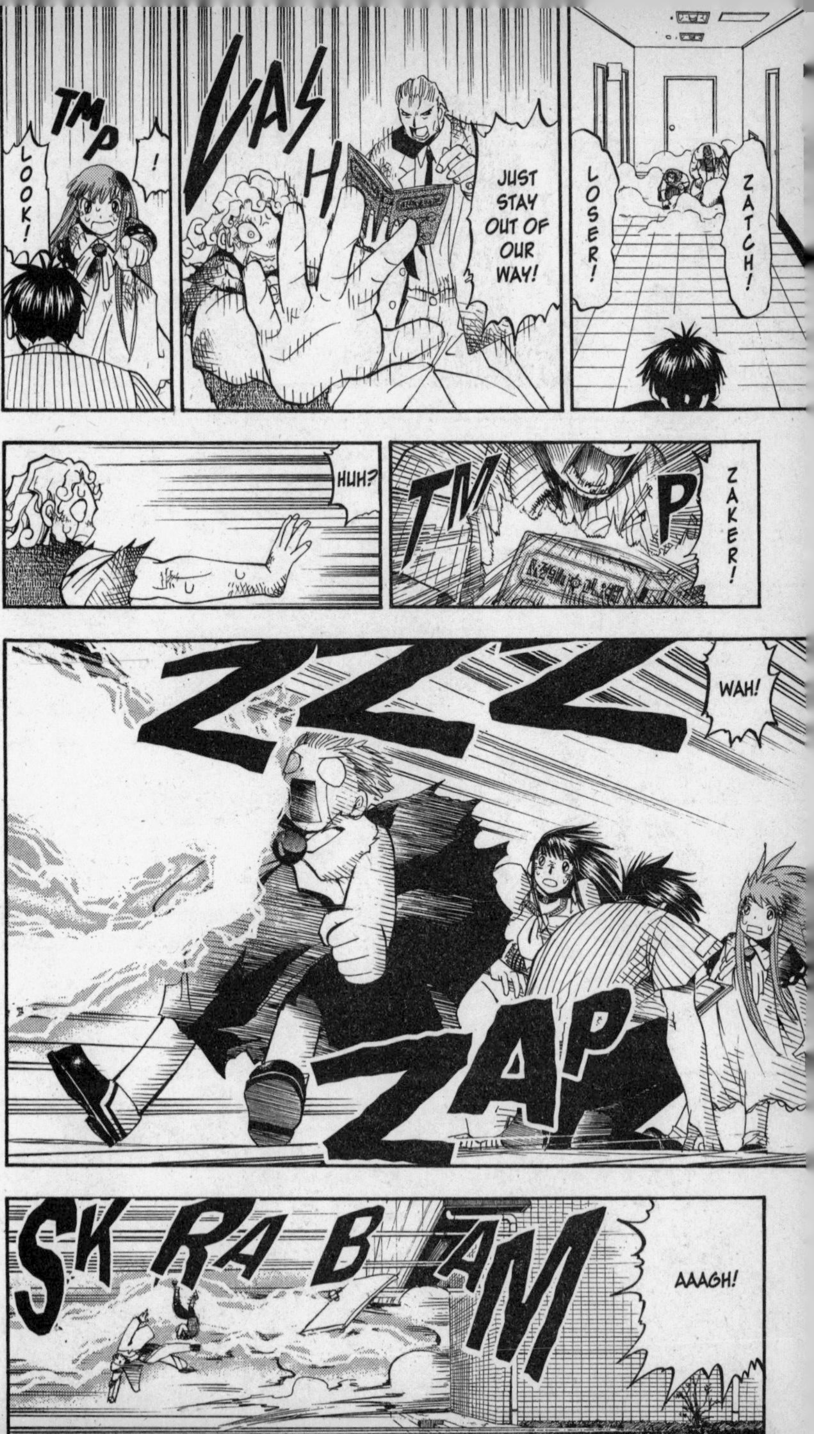
ZATCH!
LOSER!
VASH
JUST STAY OUT OF OUR WAY!
TMP
!
LOOK!
ZAKER!
TMP
HUH?
WAH!
ZZZ
ZAP
SKRABLAM
AAAGH!

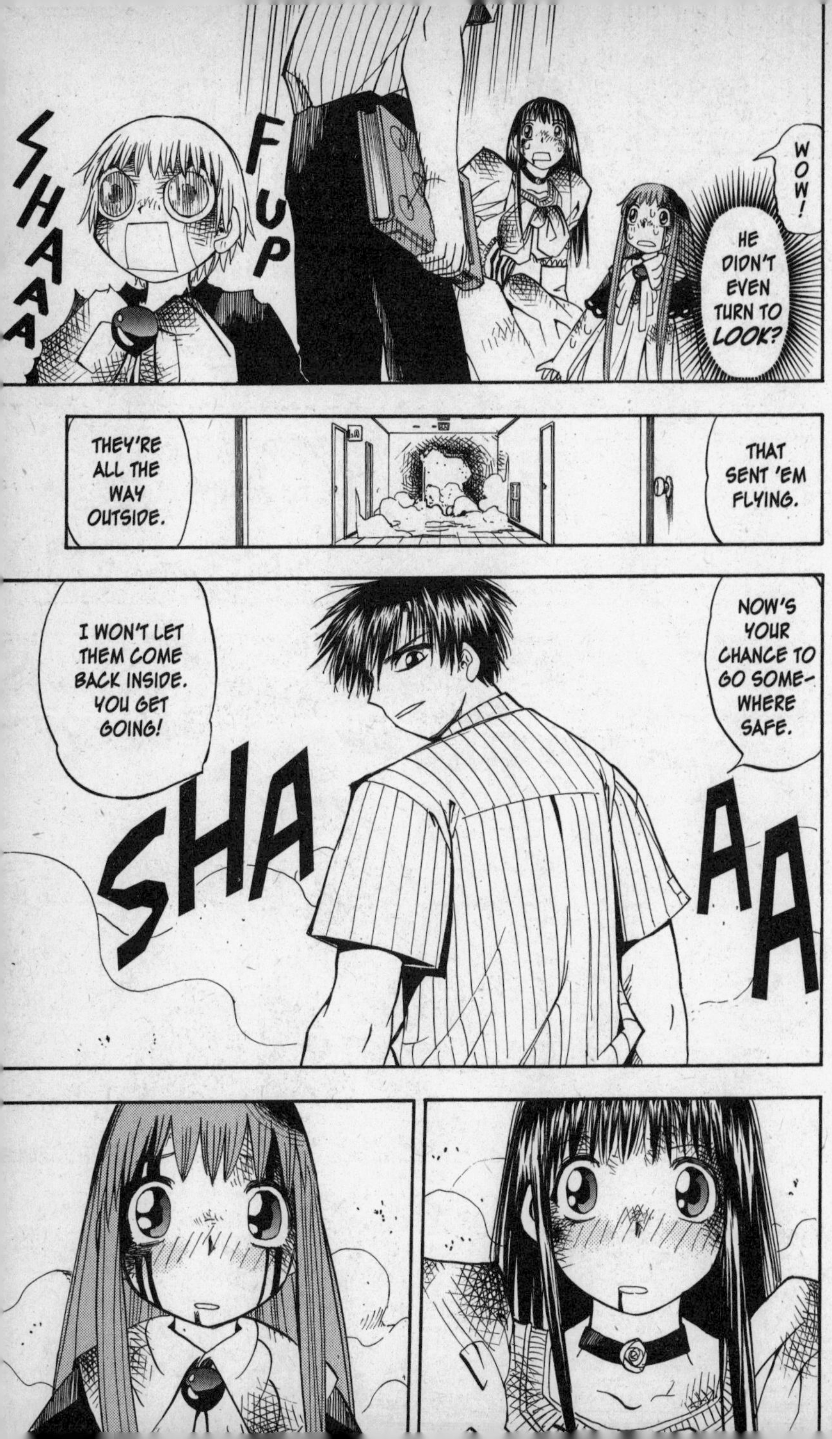
WOW!
HE DIDN'T EVEN TURN TO LOOK?
FUP
SHAAAA
THAT SENT 'EM FLYING.
THEY'RE ALL THE WAY OUTSIDE.
NOW'S YOUR CHANCE TO GO SOME-WHERE SAFE.
I WON'T LET THEM COME BACK INSIDE. YOU GET GOING!
SHAAA

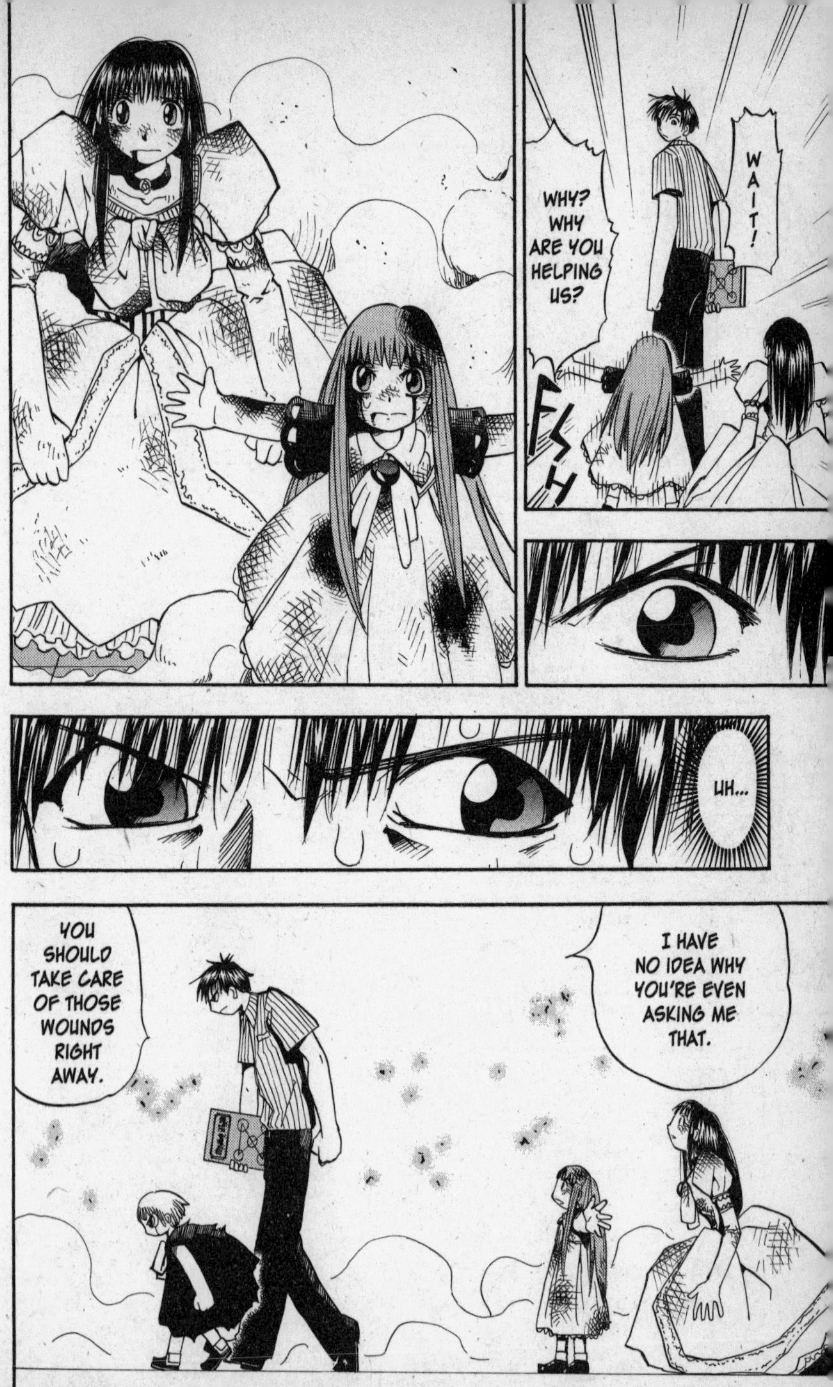
WAIT!
WHY? WHY ARE YOU HELPING US?
FSH
UH...
I HAVE NO IDEA WHY YOU'RE EVEN ASKING ME THAT.
YOU SHOULD TAKE CARE OF THOSE WOUNDS RIGHT AWAY.

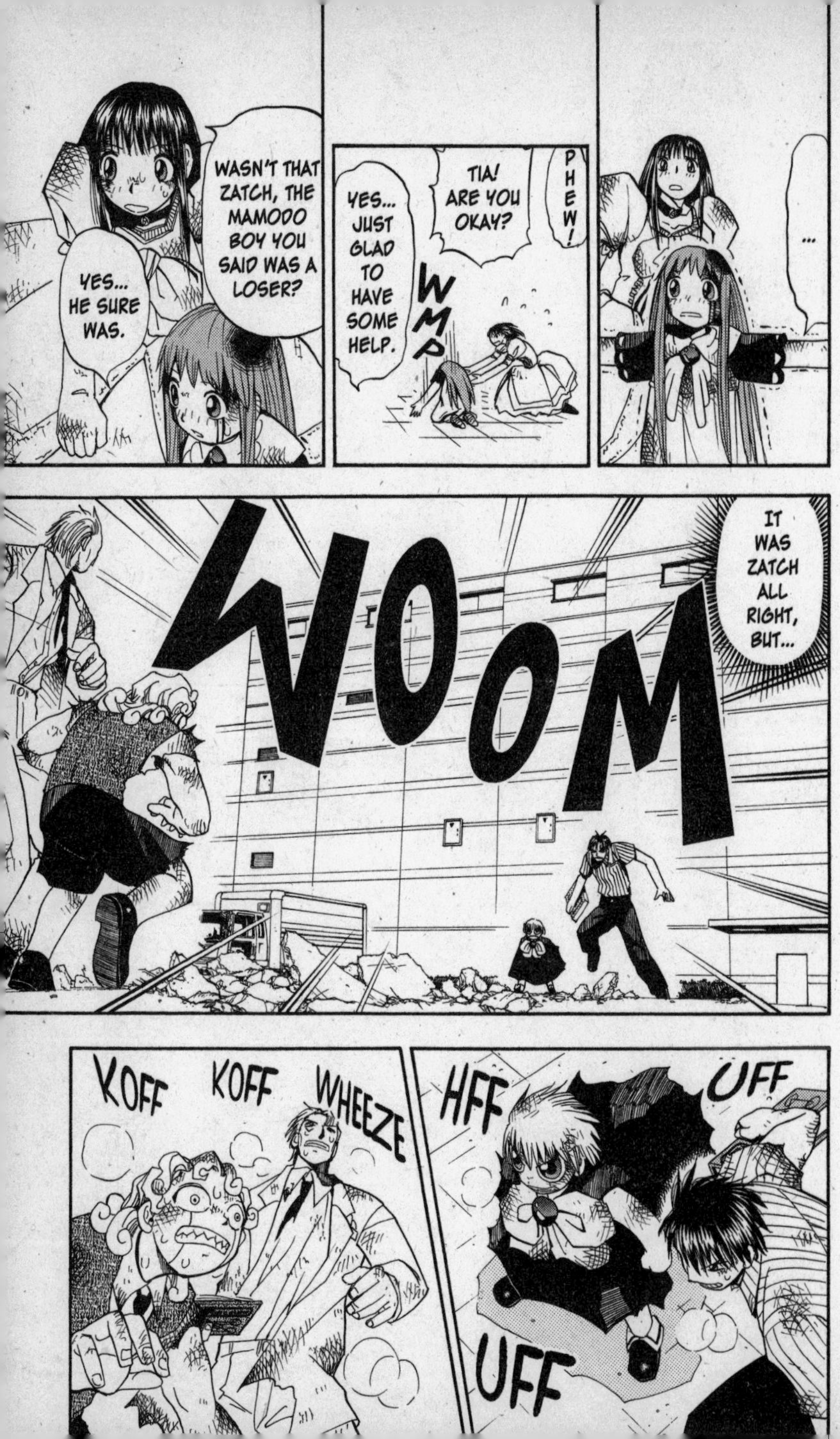
...
PHEW!
TIA! ARE YOU OKAY?
YES... JUST GLAD TO HAVE SOME HELP.
WMP
WASN'T THAT ZATCH, THE MAMODO BOY YOU SAID WAS A LOSER?
YES... HE SURE WAS.
IT WAS ZATCH ALL RIGHT, BUT...
WOOM
UFF
HFF
UFF
WHEEZE
KOFF
KOFF

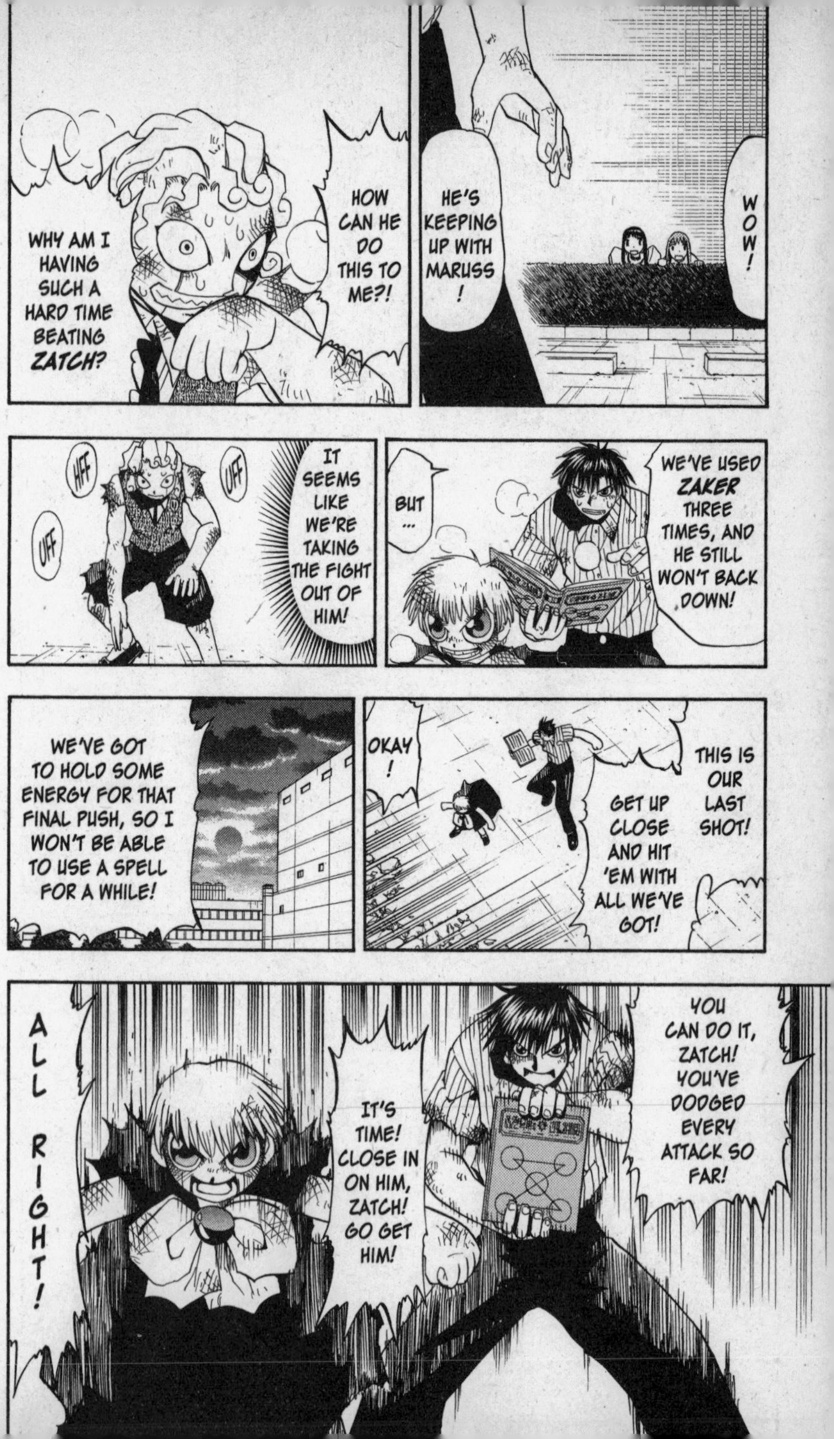
WOW!
HE'S KEEPING UP WITH MARUSS!
HOW CAN HE DO THIS TO ME?!
WHY AM I HAVING SUCH A HARD TIME BEATING ZATCH?
WE'VE USED ZAKER THREE TIMES, AND HE STILL WON'T BACK DOWN!
BUT ...
IT SEEMS LIKE WE'RE TAKING THE FIGHT OUT OF HIM!
HFF
UFF
UFF
THIS IS OUR LAST SHOT!
GET UP CLOSE AND HIT 'EM WITH ALL WE'VE GOT!
OKAY!
WE'VE GOT TO HOLD SOME ENERGY FOR THAT FINAL PUSH, SO I WON'T BE ABLE TO USE A SPELL FOR A WHILE!
YOU CAN DO IT, ZATCH! YOU'VE DODGED EVERY ATTACK SO FAR!
IT'S TIME! CLOSE IN ON HIM, ZATCH! GO GET HIM!
ALL RIGHT!

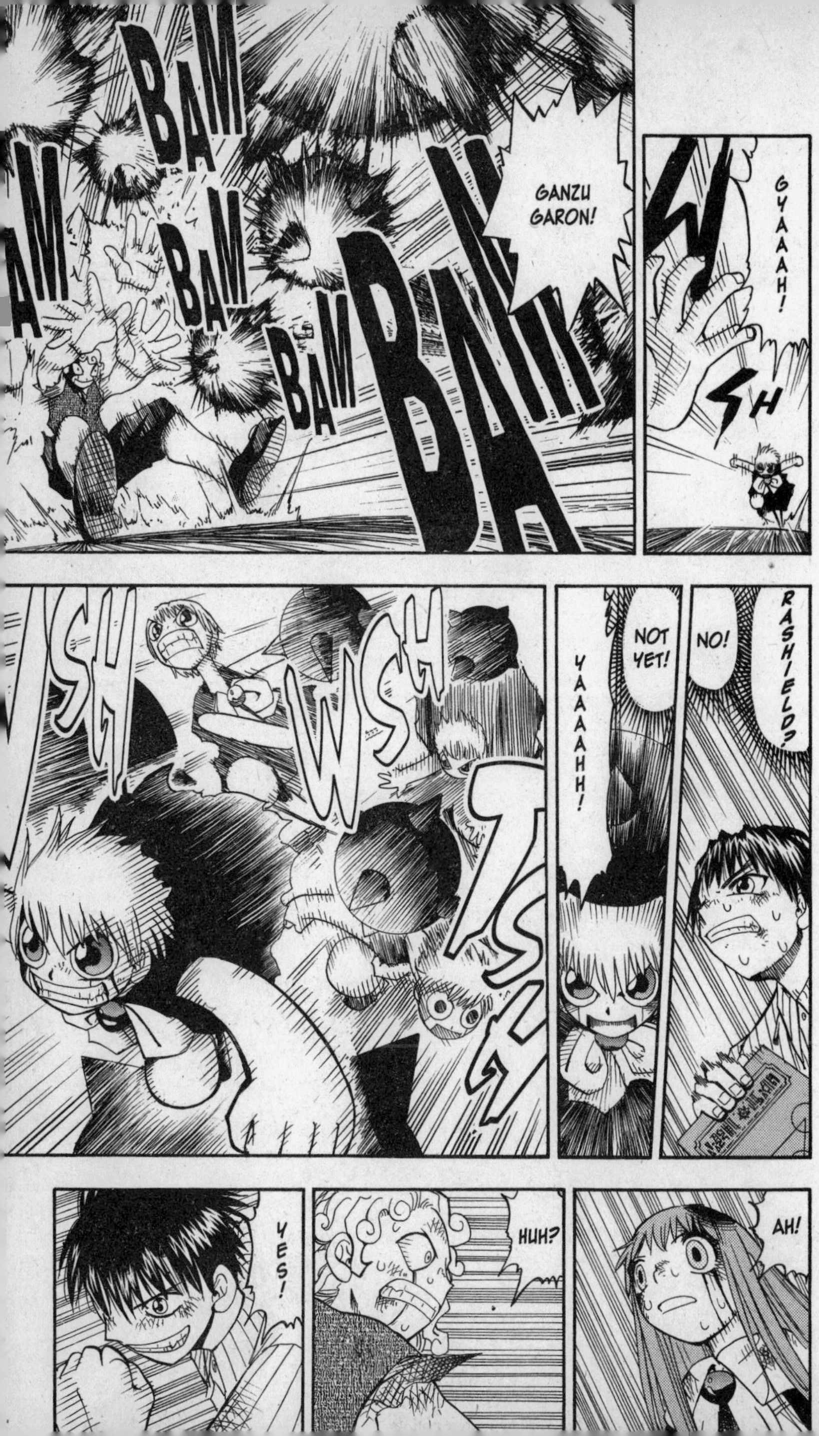
GYAAAAH!
SH
GANZU GARON!
BAM
BAM
BAM
BAM
RASHIELD?
NO!
NOT YET!
YAAAAAHH!
WSH
SH
AH!
HUH?
YES!

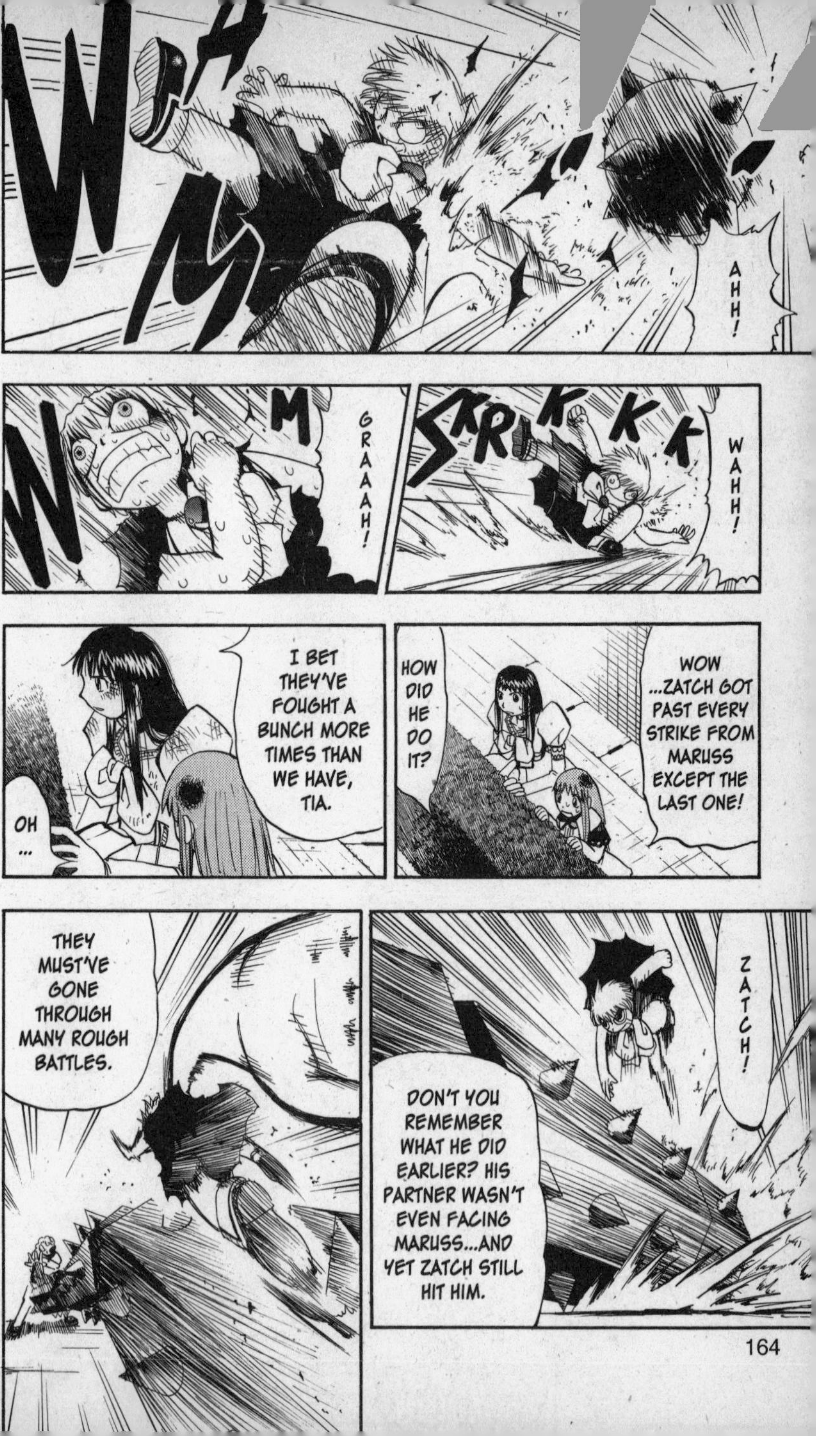
AHH!
SKRIKKK
WAHH!
GRAAAAH!
WOW ...ZATCH GOT PAST EVERY STRIKE FROM MARUSS EXCEPT THE LAST ONE!
HOW DID HE DO IT?
I BET THEY'VE FOUGHT A BUNCH MORE TIMES THAN WE HAVE, TIA.
OH ...
ZATCH!
DON'T YOU REMEMBER WHAT HE DID EARLIER? HIS PARTNER WASN'T EVEN FACING MARUSS...AND YET ZATCH STILL HIT HIM.
THEY MUST'VE GONE THROUGH MANY ROUGH BATTLES.

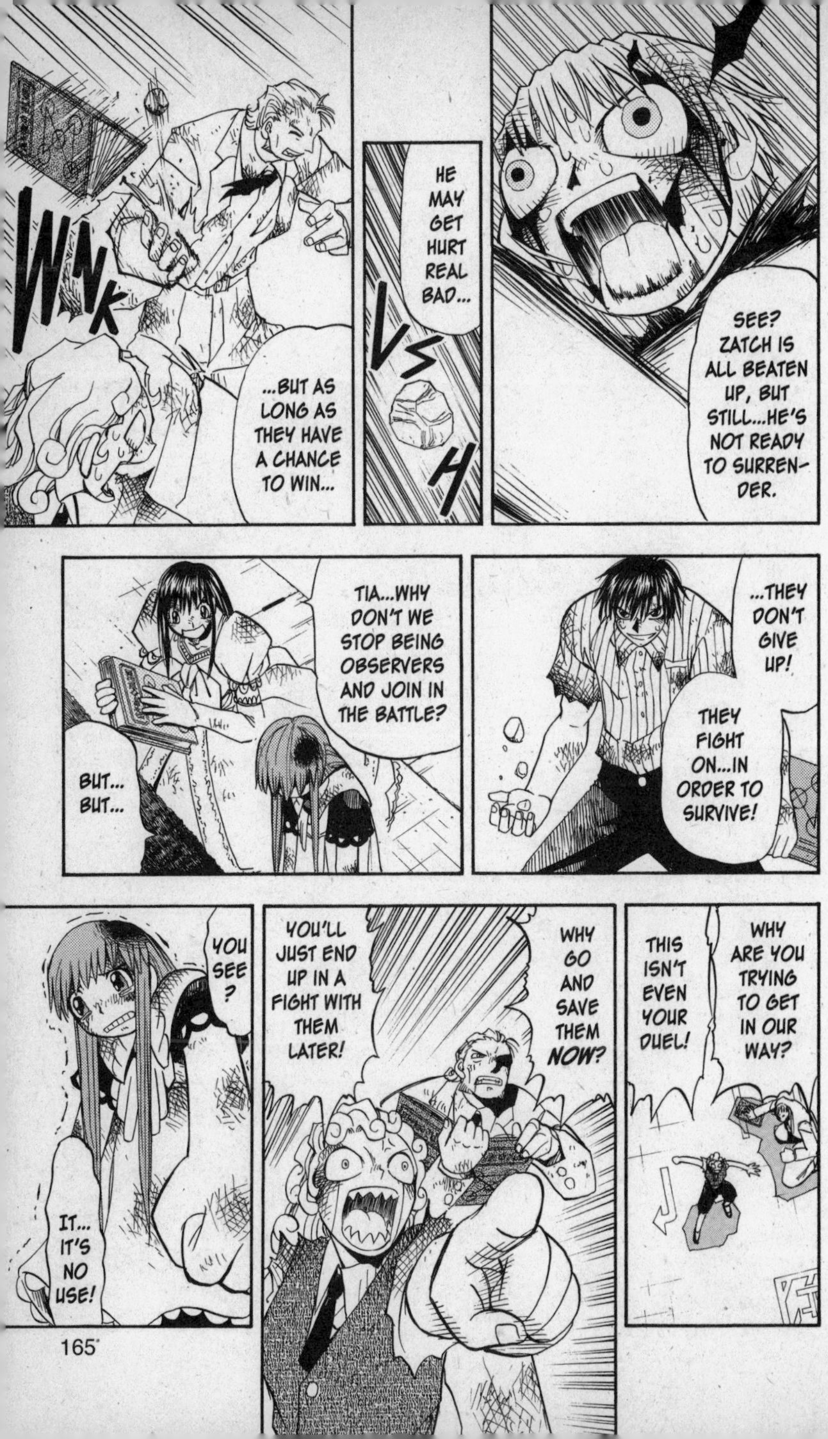
SEE? ZATCH IS ALL BEATEN UP, BUT STILL...HE'S NOT READY TO SURREN-DER.
HE MAY GET HURT REAL BAD...
VSH
...BUT AS LONG AS THEY HAVE A CHANCE TO WIN...
WINK
...THEY DON'T GIVE UP!
THEY FIGHT ON...IN ORDER TO SURVIVE!
TIA...WHY DON'T WE STOP BEING OBSERVERS AND JOIN IN THE BATTLE?
BUT... BUT...
WHY ARE YOU TRYING TO GET IN OUR WAY?
THIS ISN'T EVEN YOUR DUEL!
WHY GO AND SAVE THEM NOW?
YOU'LL JUST END UP IN A FIGHT WITH THEM LATER!
YOU SEE?
IT... IT'S NO USE!

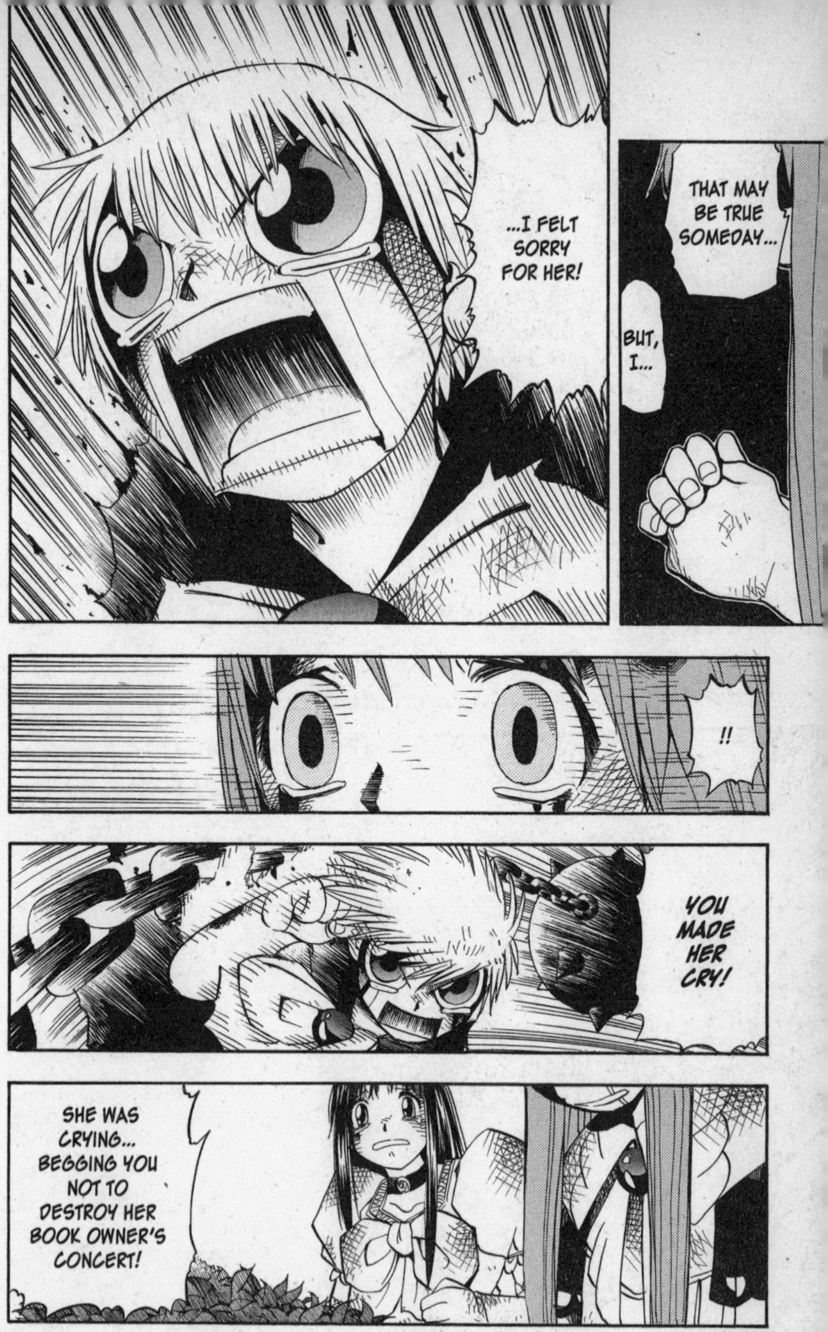
THAT MAY BE TRUE SOMEDAY...
BUT, I...
...I FELT SORRY FOR HER!
!!
YOU MADE HER CRY!
SHE WAS CRYING... BEGGING YOU NOT TO DESTROY HER BOOK OWNER'S CONCERT!

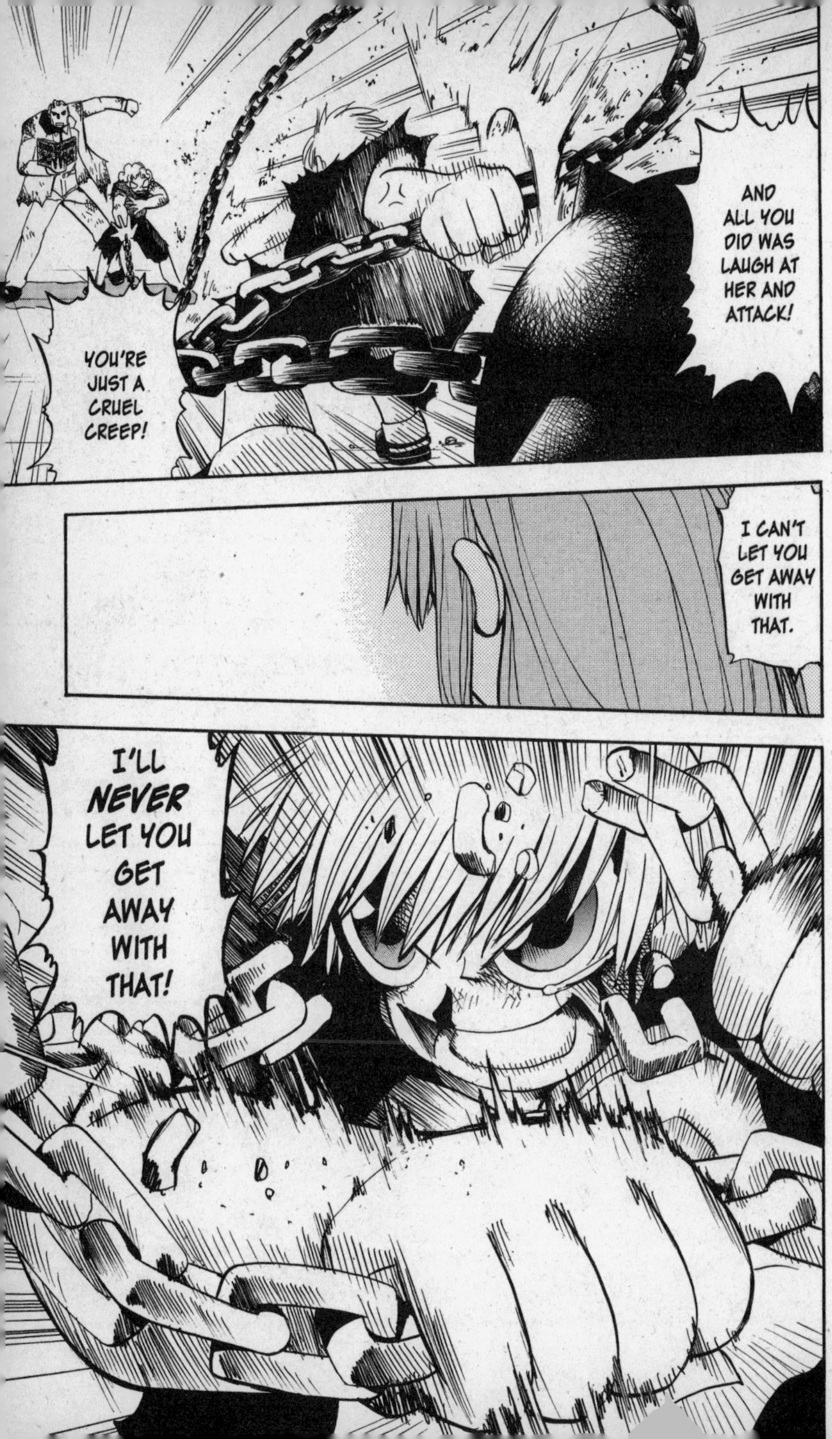
AND ALL YOU DID WAS LAUGH AT HER AND ATTACK!
YOU'RE JUST A CRUEL CREEP!
I CAN'T LET YOU GET AWAY WITH THAT.
I'LL ***NEVER*** LET YOU GET AWAY WITH THAT!

SILLY ZATCH! YOU HAVEN'T CHANGED A BIT.

YOU'RE STILL JUST THE SAME...

...AS YOU WERE BACK HOME.

ALWAYS STANDING UP FOR THE WEAK, EVEN THOUGH...

...YOU CAN'T EVER WIN.

THAT'S JUST...HOW YOU ARE.

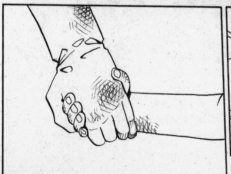

YES!

I'LL DO IT!

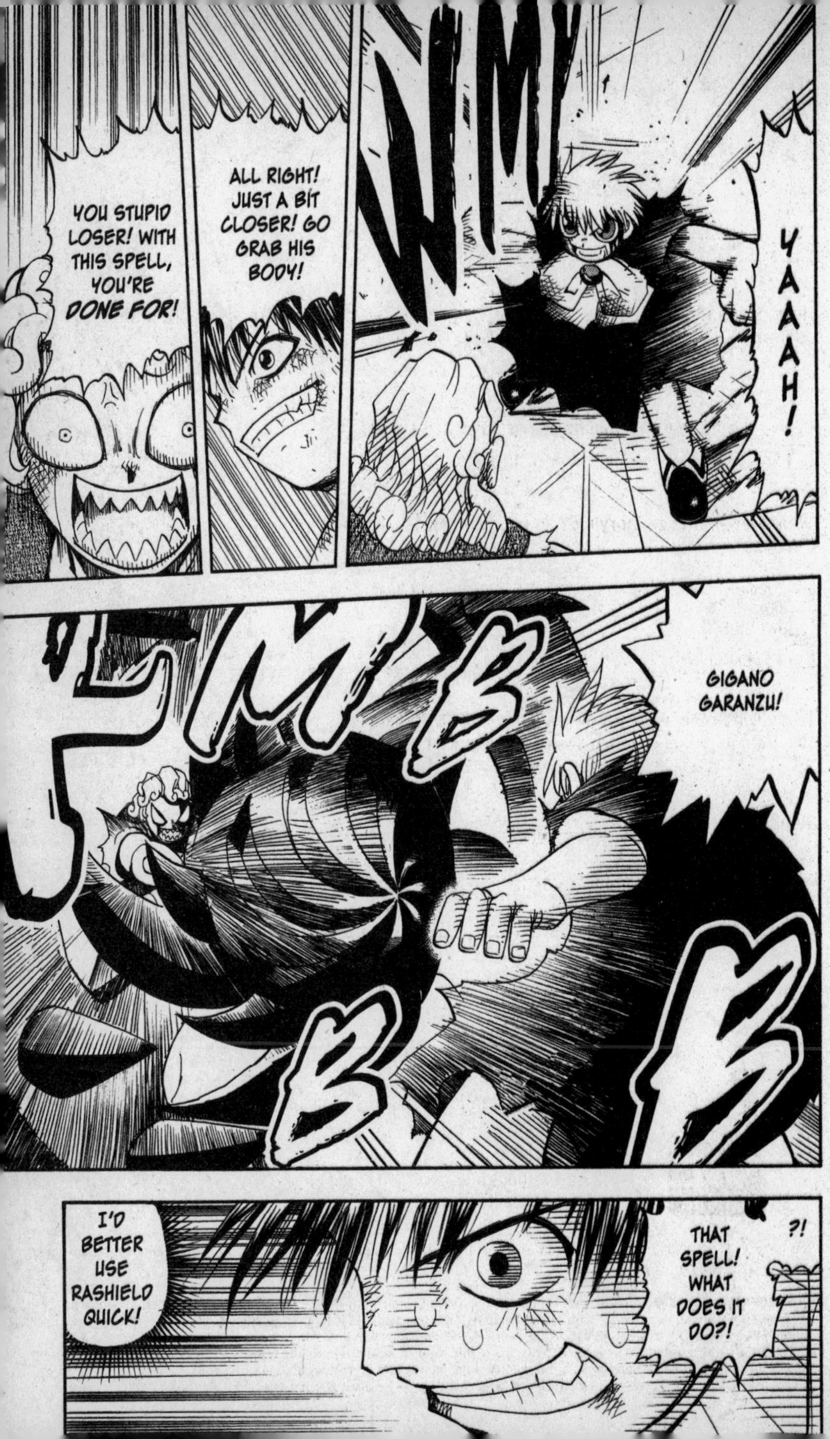
YAAAAH!
ALL RIGHT! JUST A BIT CLOSER! GO GRAB HIS BODY!
YOU STUPID LOSER! WITH THIS SPELL, YOU'RE DONE FOR!
GIGANO GARANZU!
?!
THAT SPELL! WHAT DOES IT DO?!
I'D BETTER USE RASHIELD QUICK!

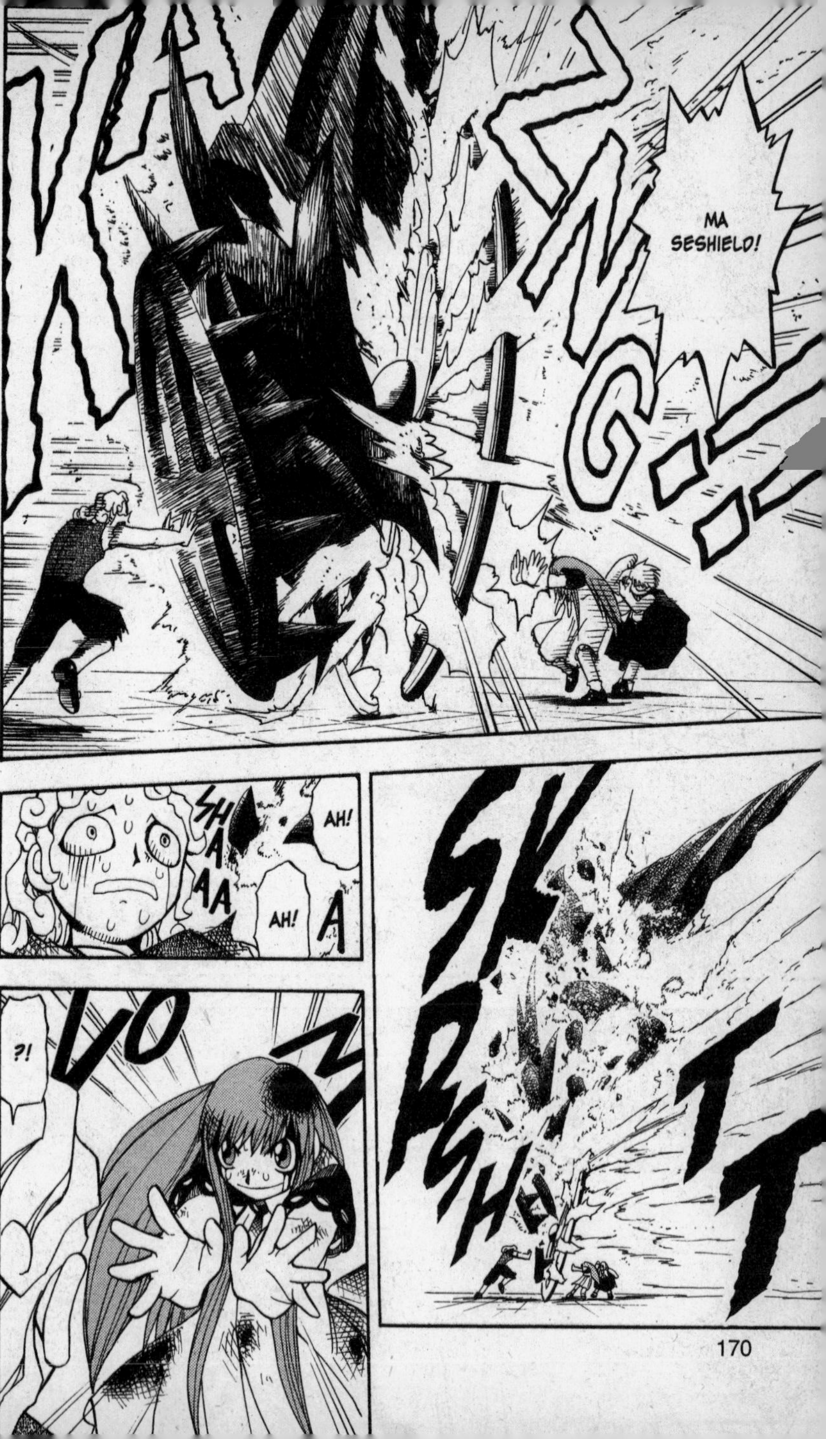
MA SESHIELD!
SHAAAA
AH!
AH!
A
?!

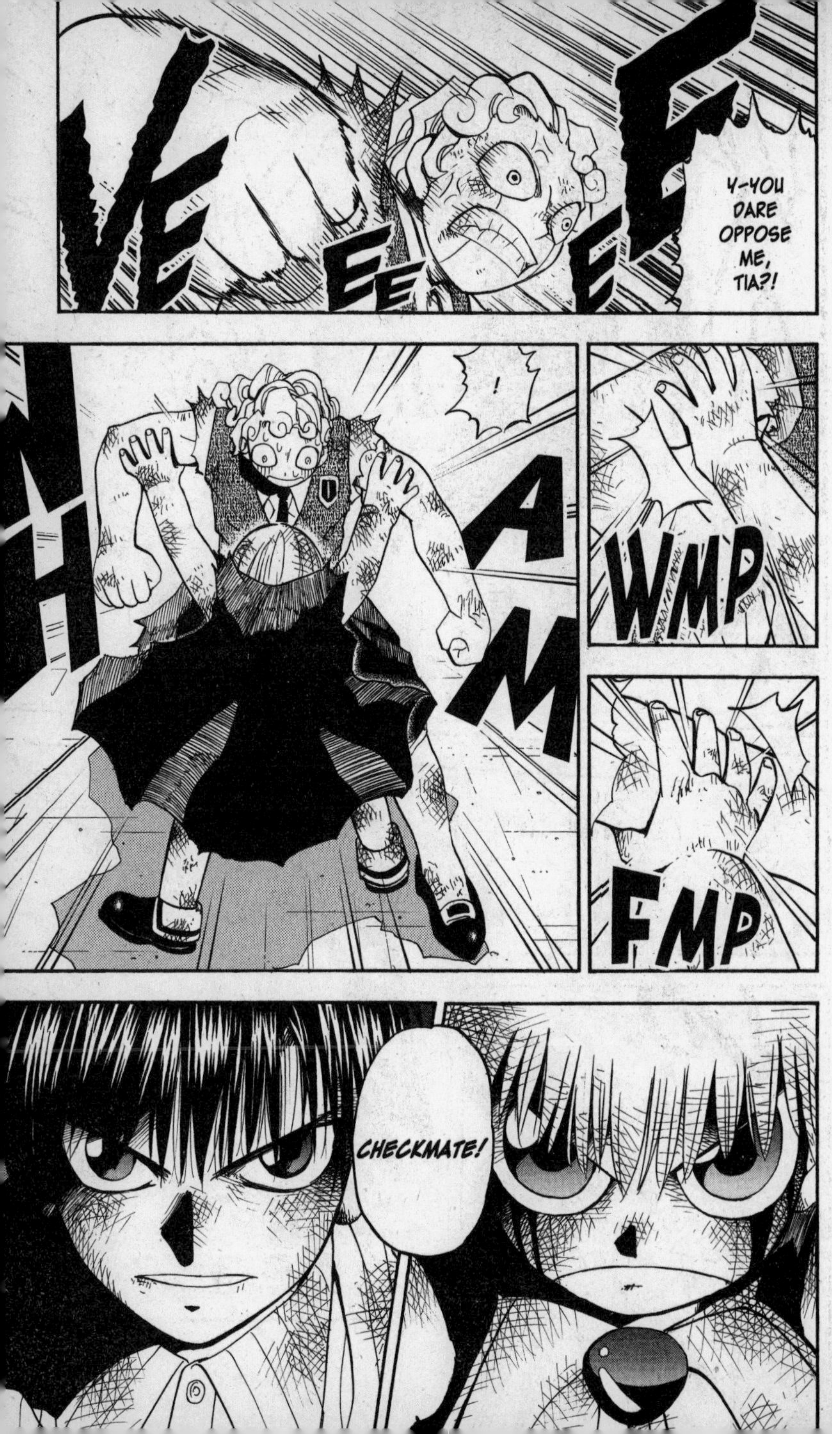
Y-YOU DARE OPPOSE ME, TIA?!
WMP
FMP
!
AM
CHECKMATE!

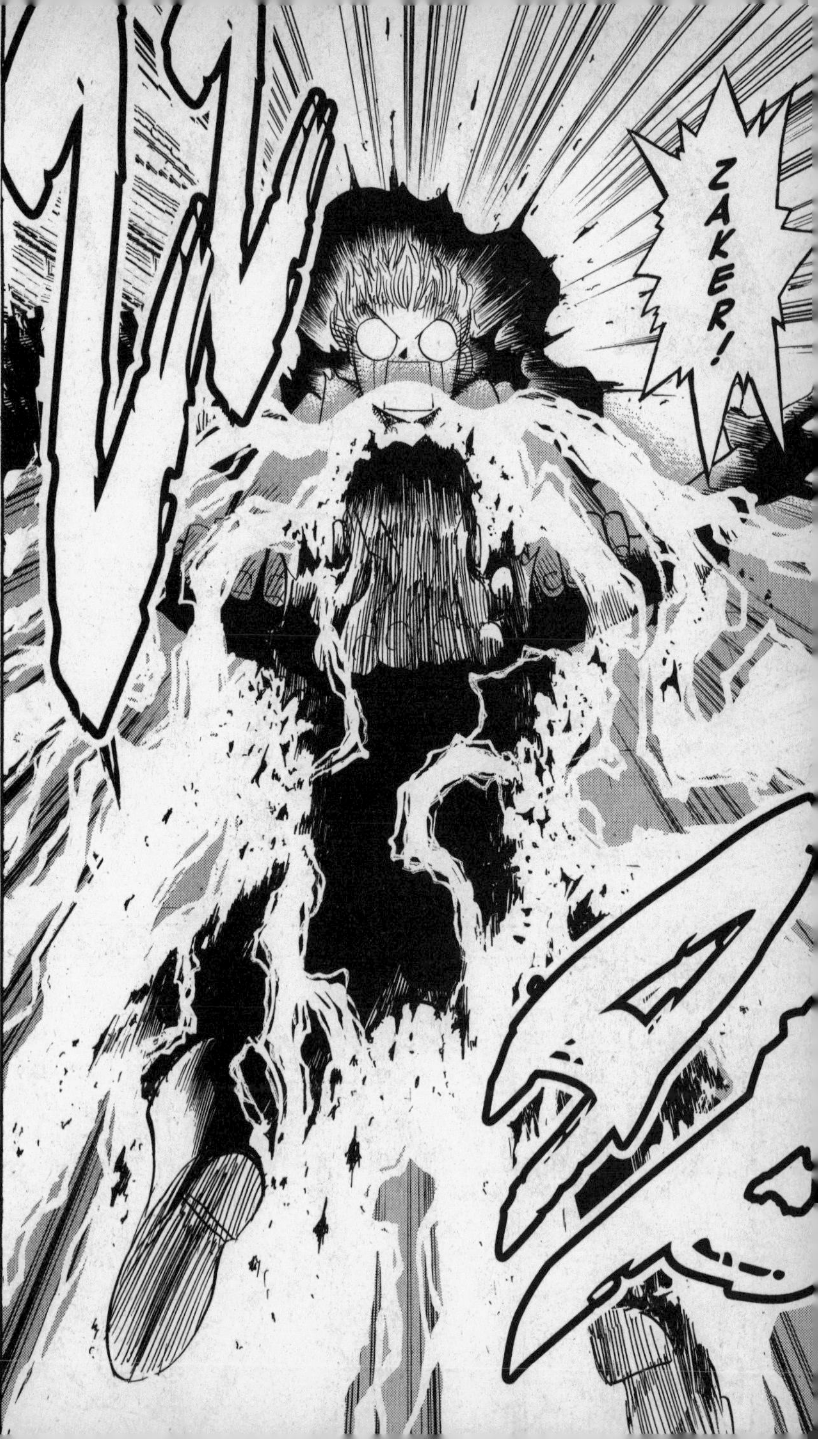
ZAKER!

LEVEL 38: A Trustworthy Friend

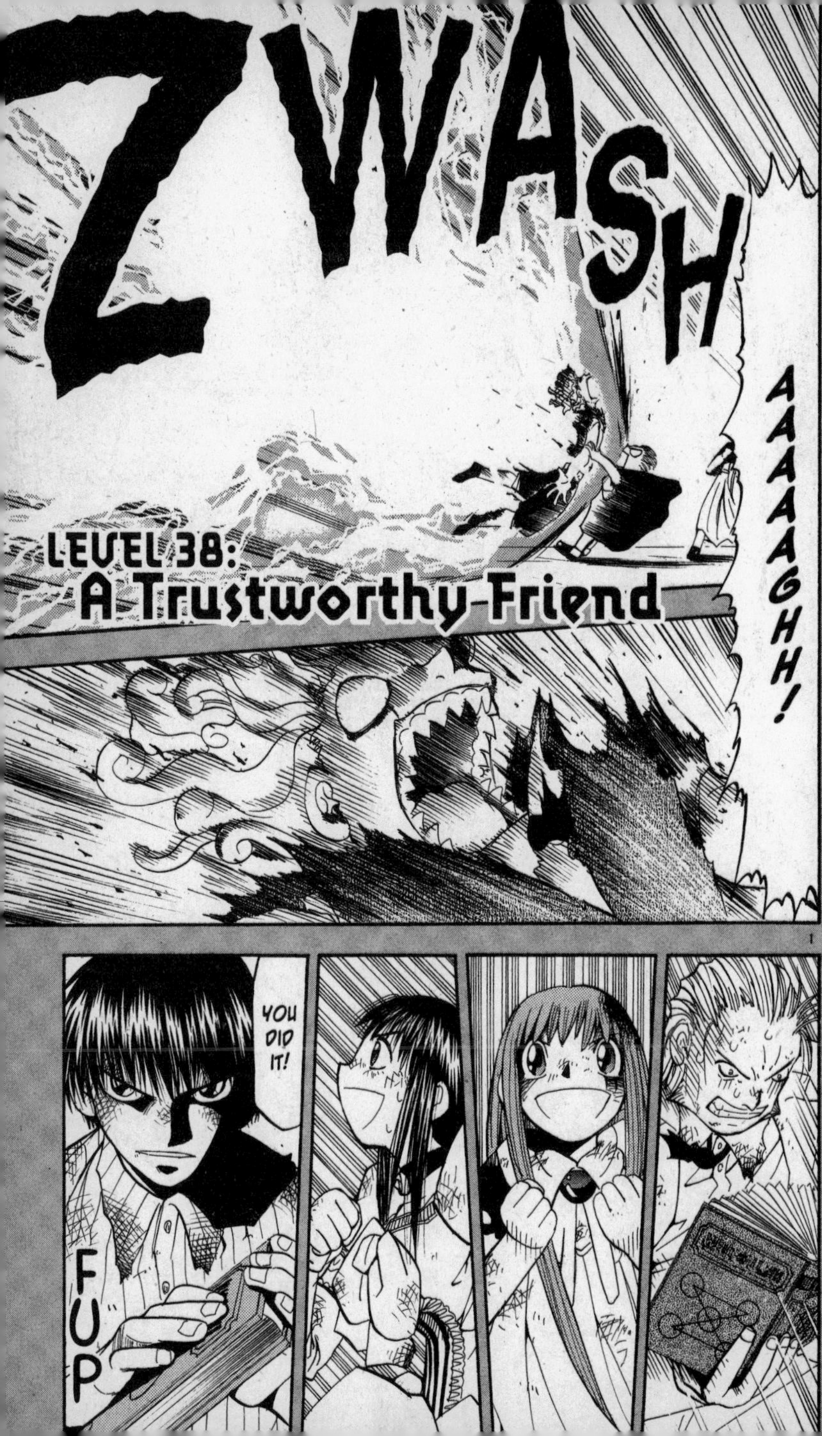
ZWASH
AAAAAGHH!
YOU DID IT!
FUP

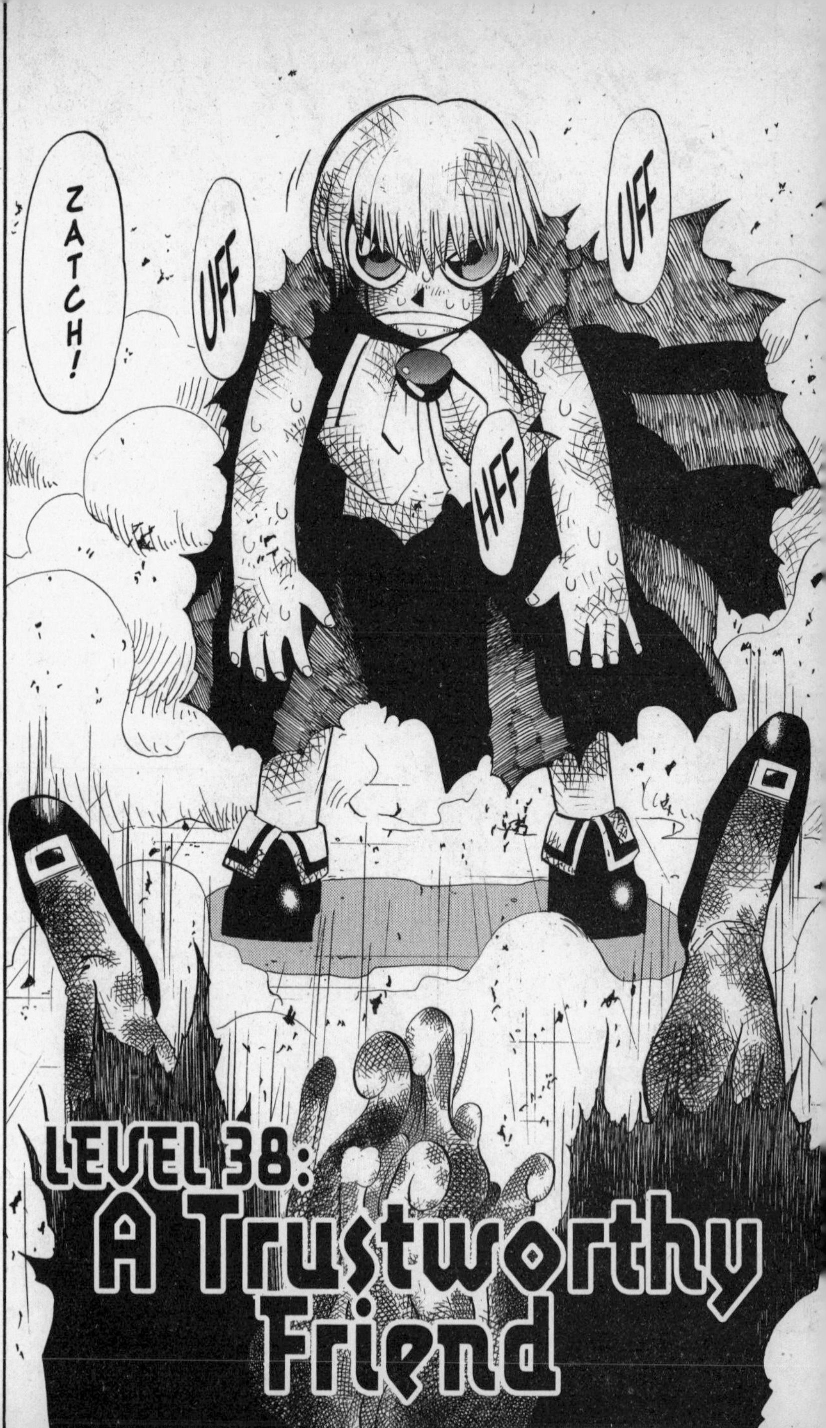
UFF
HFF
UFF
ZATCH!
LEVEL 38:
A Trustworthy Friend

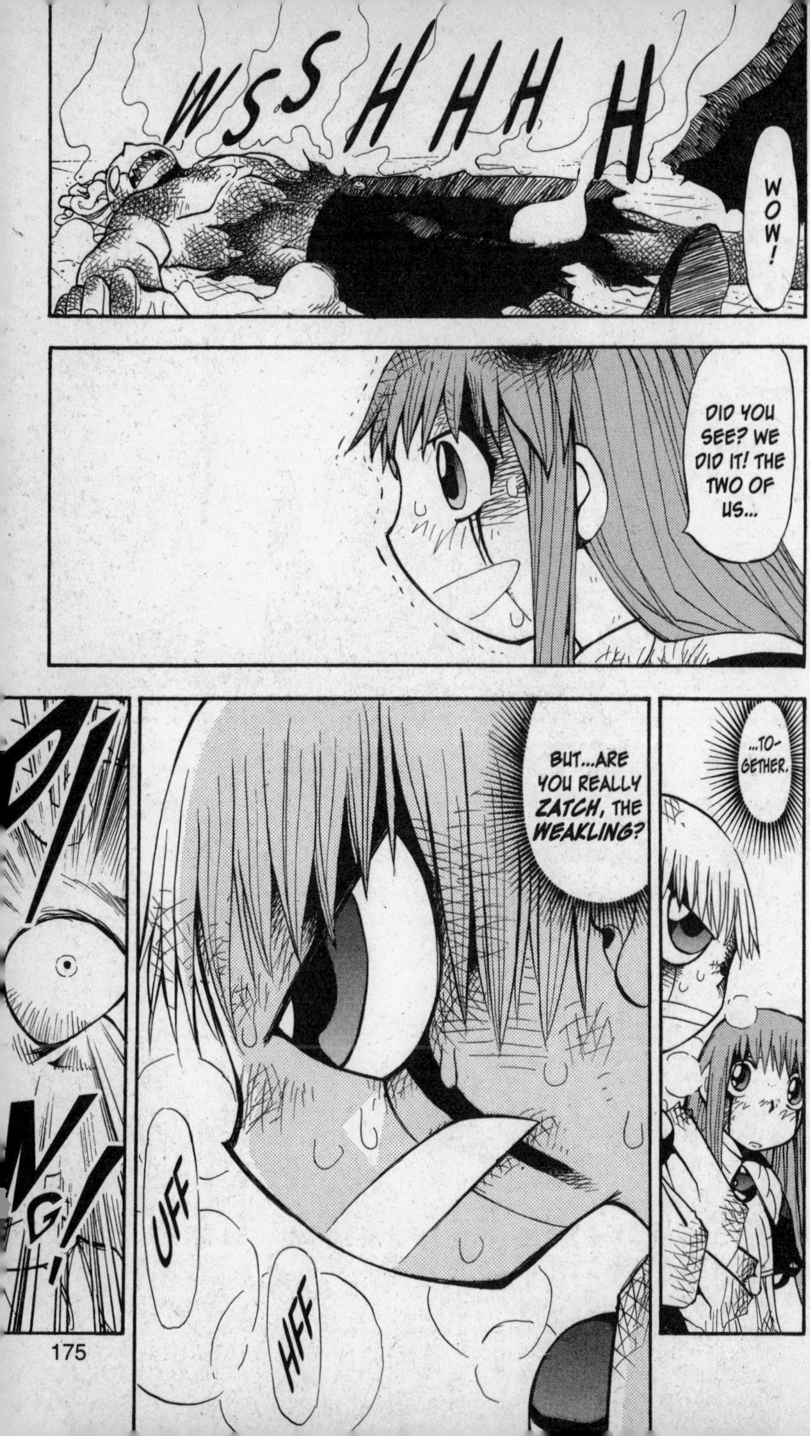
WSSHHHH
WOW!
DID YOU SEE? WE DID IT! THE TWO OF US...
...TO-GETHER.
BUT...ARE YOU REALLY ZATCH, THE WEAKLING?
UFF
HFF

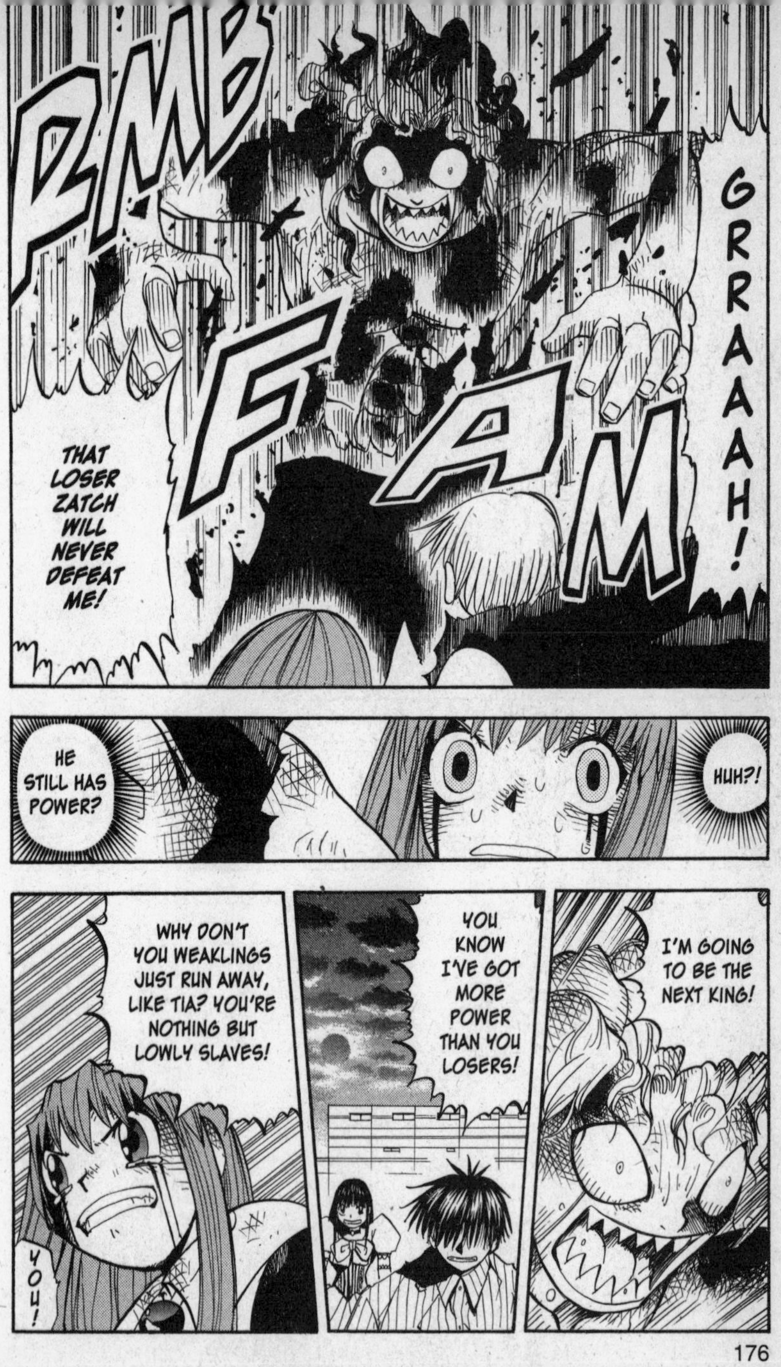
GRRAAAH!
RMB
FAM
THAT LOSER ZATCH WILL NEVER DEFEAT ME!
HUH?!
HE STILL HAS POWER?
I'M GOING TO BE THE NEXT KING!
YOU KNOW I'VE GOT MORE POWER THAN YOU LOSERS!
WHY DON'T YOU WEAKLINGS JUST RUN AWAY, LIKE TIA? YOU'RE NOTHING BUT LOWLY SLAVES!
YOU!

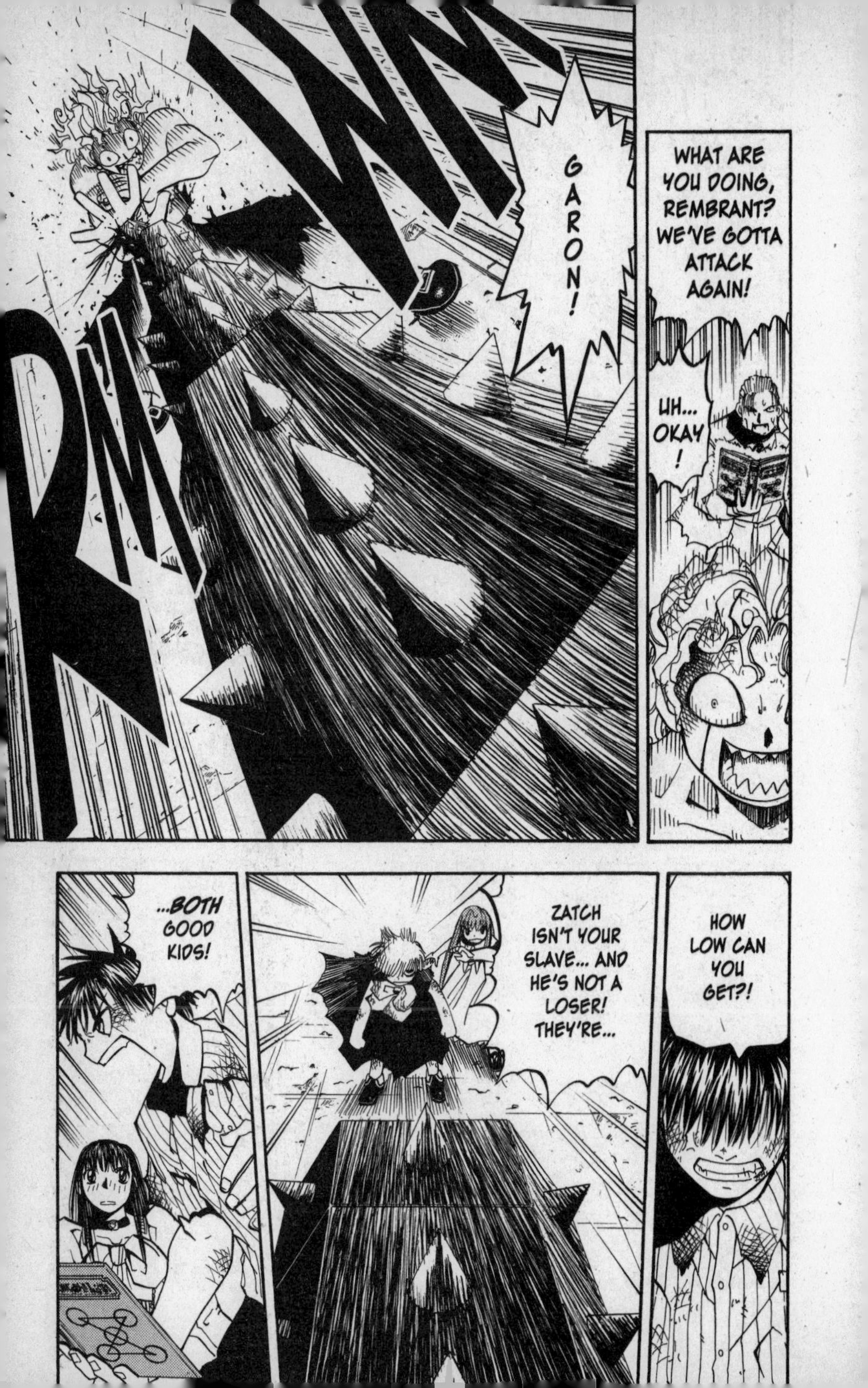
WHAT ARE YOU DOING, REMBRANT? WE'VE GOTTA ATTACK AGAIN!
UH... OKAY!
GARON!
HOW LOW CAN YOU GET?!
ZATCH ISN'T YOUR SLAVE... AND HE'S NOT A LOSER! THEY'RE...
...BOTH GOOD KIDS!

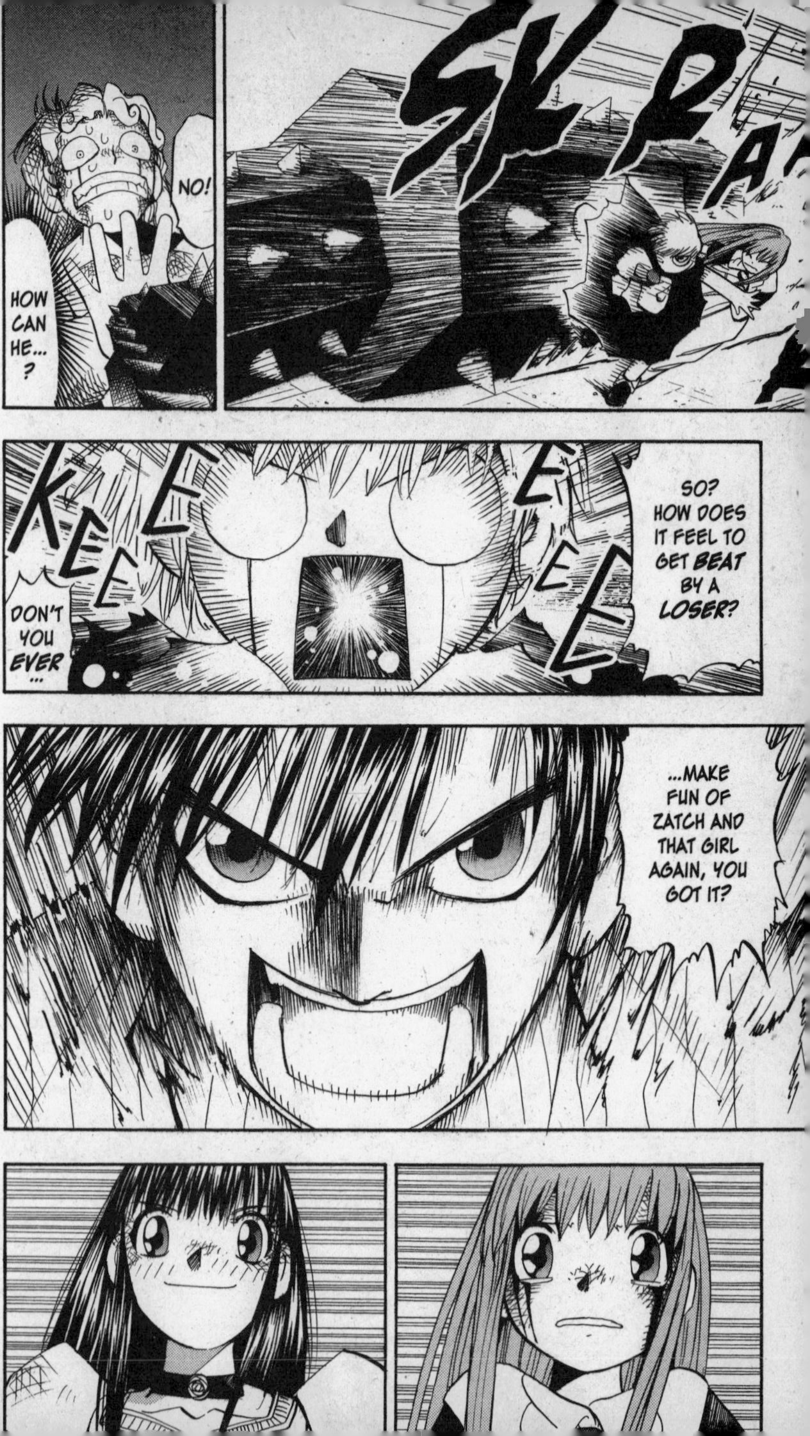
SKRA
NO!
HOW CAN HE... ?
SO? HOW DOES IT FEEL TO GET **BEAT** BY A **LOSER?**
KEEEEEEE
DON'T YOU **EVER** ...
...MAKE FUN OF ZATCH AND THAT GIRL AGAIN, YOU GOT IT?

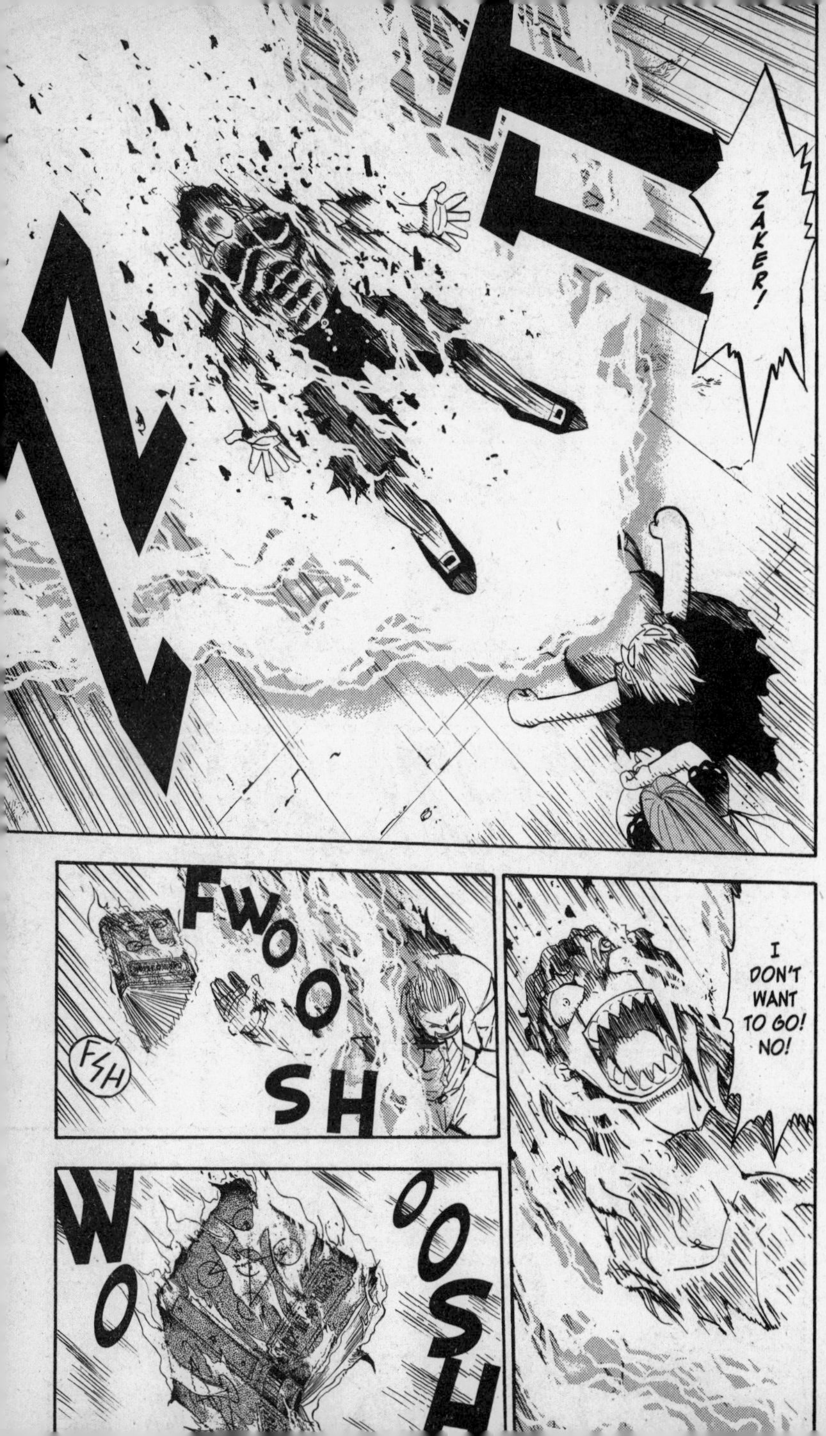
ZAKER!
I DON'T WANT TO GO! NO!
FWOOSH
FSH
WO
OOSH

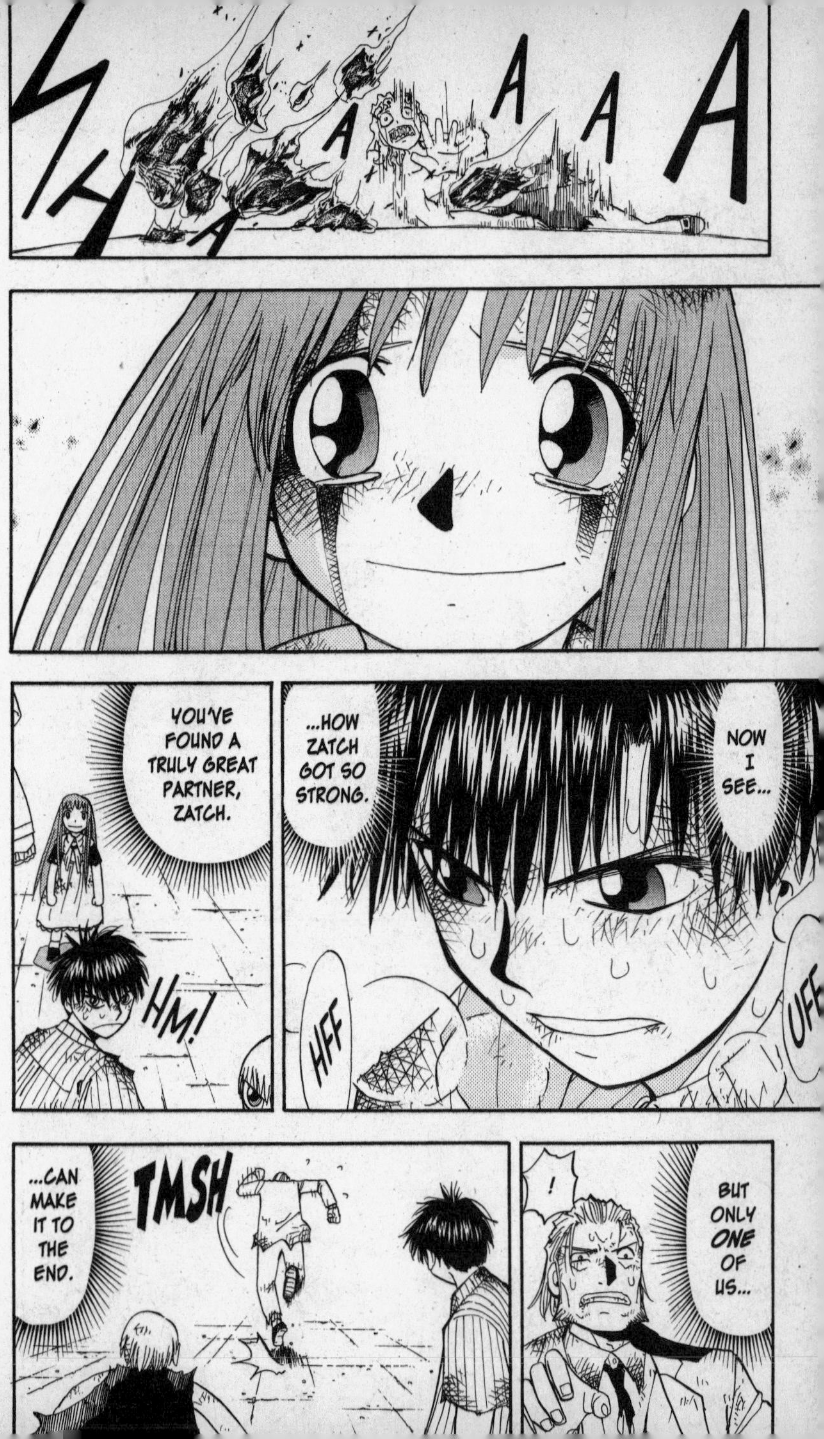
SHAAAAAA
NOW I SEE...
...HOW ZATCH GOT SO STRONG.
HFF
UFF
YOU'VE FOUND A TRULY GREAT PARTNER, ZATCH.
HM!
!
BUT ONLY ONE OF US...
...CAN MAKE IT TO THE END.
TMSH

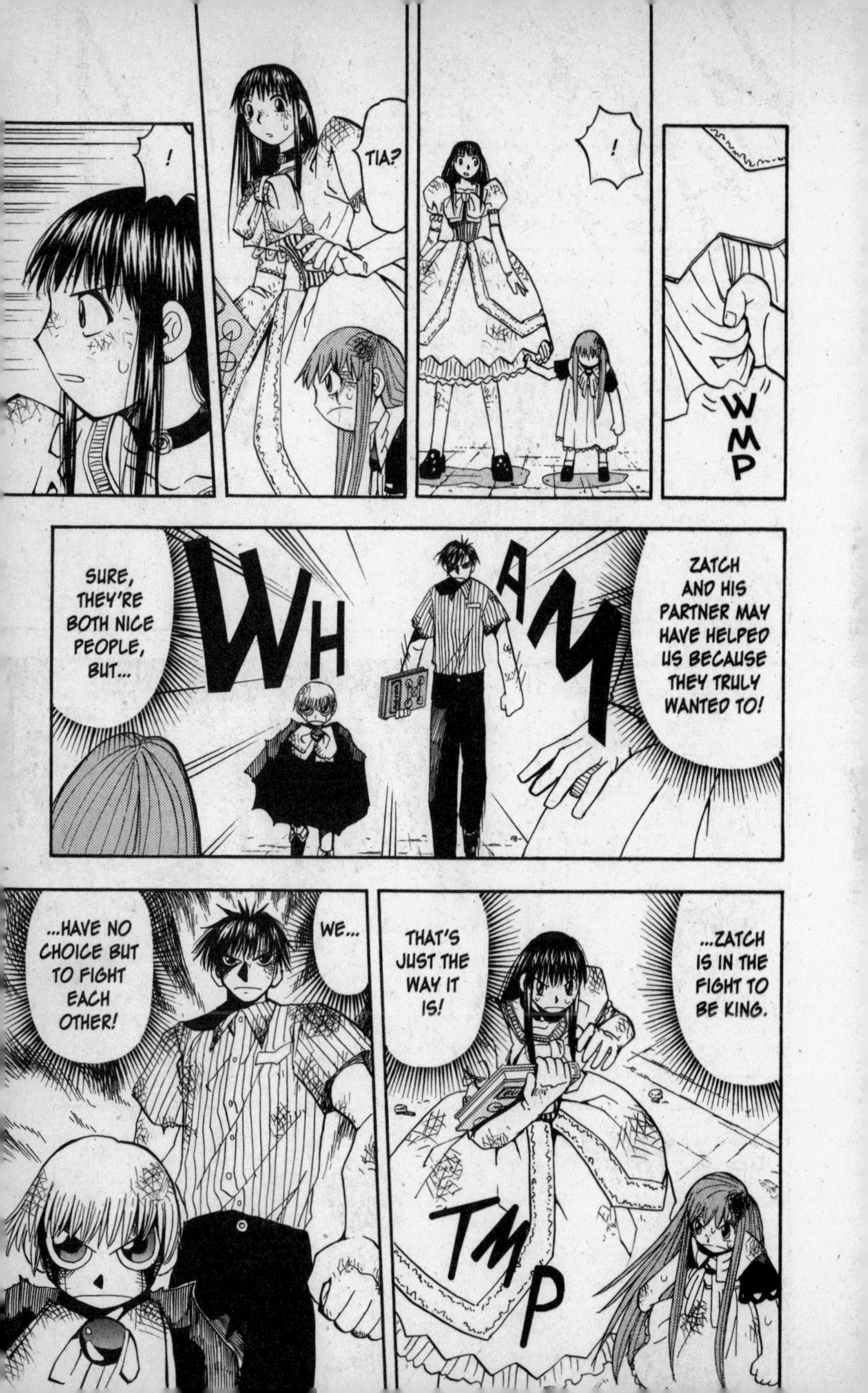
WMP
!
TIA?
!
ZATCH AND HIS PARTNER MAY HAVE HELPED US BECAUSE THEY TRULY WANTED TO!
WHAM
SURE, THEY'RE BOTH NICE PEOPLE, BUT...
...ZATCH IS IN THE FIGHT TO BE KING.
THAT'S JUST THE WAY IT IS!
TMP
WE...
...HAVE NO CHOICE BUT TO FIGHT EACH OTHER!

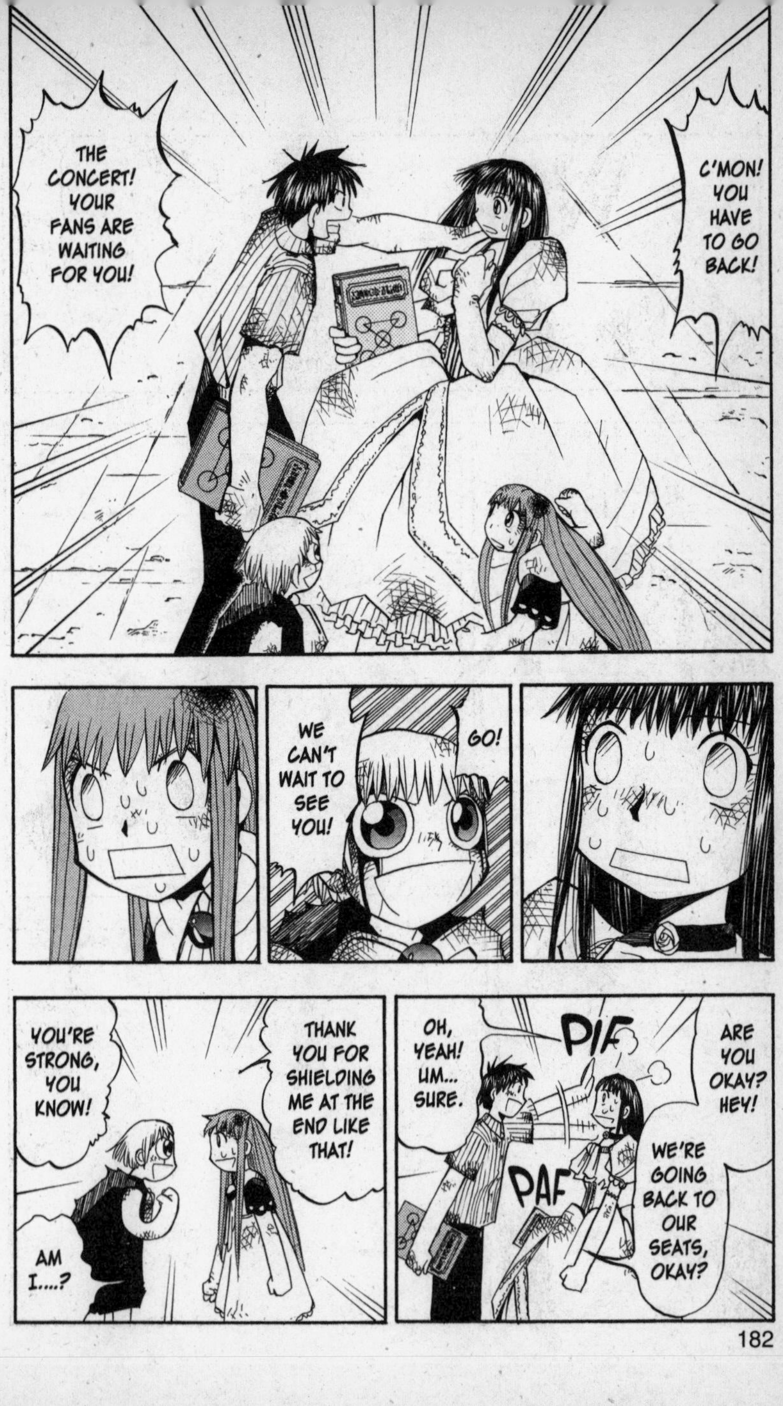

C'MON! YOU HAVE TO GO BACK!
THE CONCERT! YOUR FANS ARE WAITING FOR YOU!
GO!
WE CAN'T WAIT TO SEE YOU!
ARE YOU OKAY? HEY!
PIF
OH, YEAH! UM... SURE.
WE'RE GOING BACK TO OUR SEATS, OKAY?
PAF
THANK YOU FOR SHIELDING ME AT THE END LIKE THAT!
YOU'RE STRONG, YOU KNOW!
AM I....?

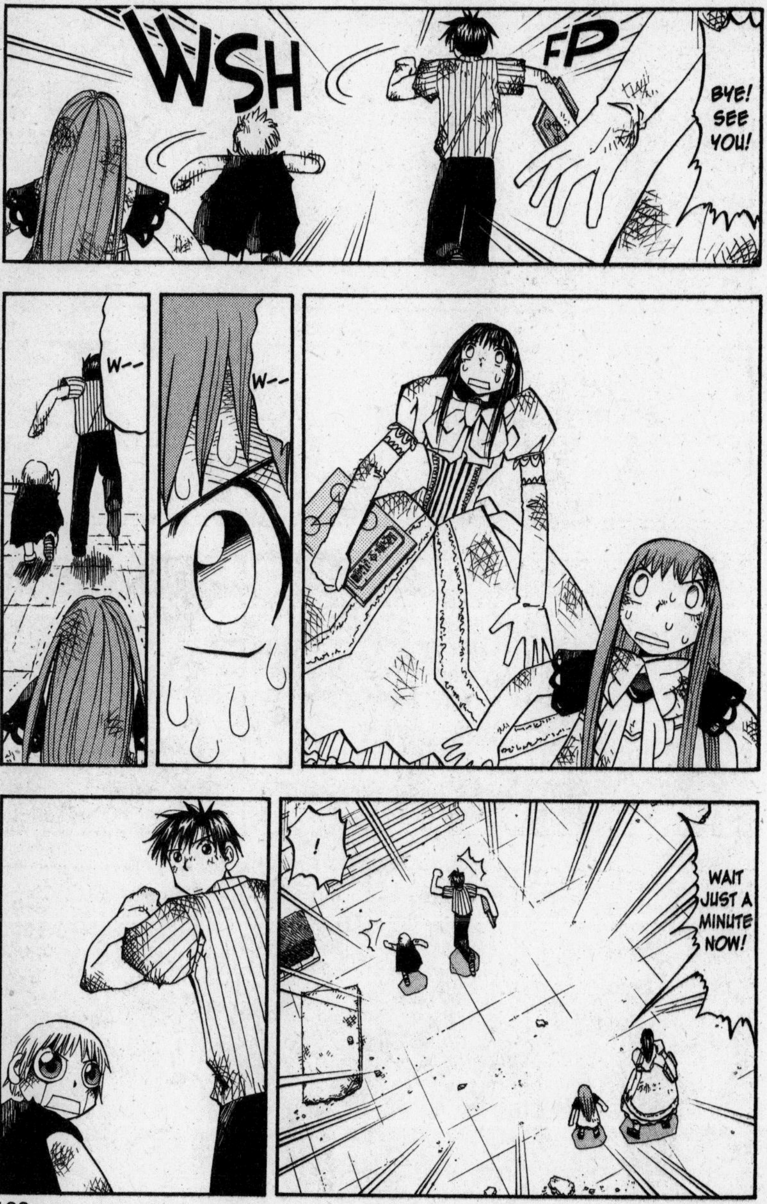
BYE! SEE YOU!
FP
WSH
W--
W--
WAIT JUST A MINUTE NOW!
!

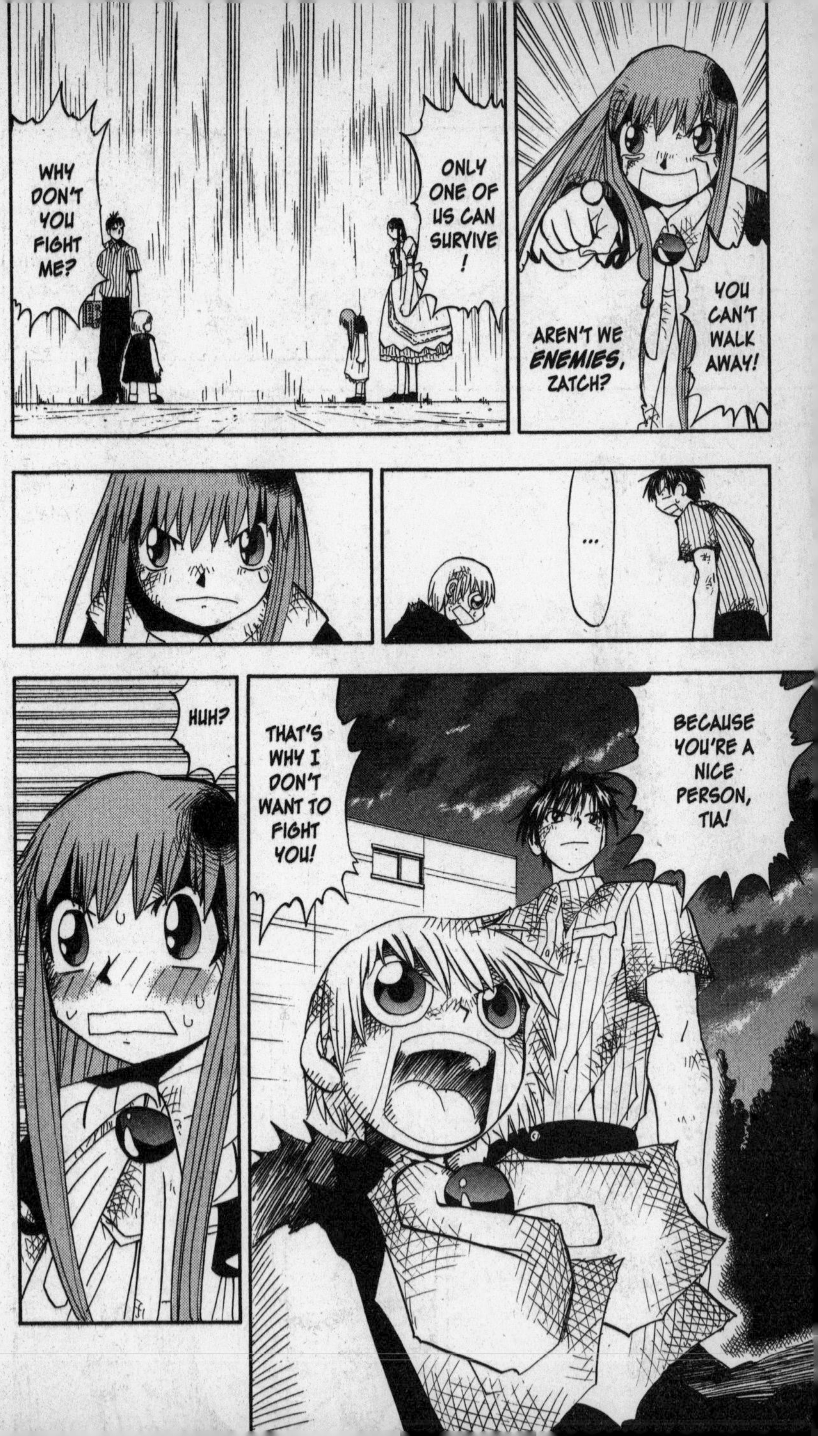
YOU CAN'T WALK AWAY!
AREN'T WE *ENEMIES*, ZATCH?
ONLY ONE OF US CAN SURVIVE!
WHY DON'T YOU FIGHT ME?
...
BECAUSE YOU'RE A NICE PERSON, TIA!
THAT'S WHY I DON'T WANT TO FIGHT YOU!
HUH?

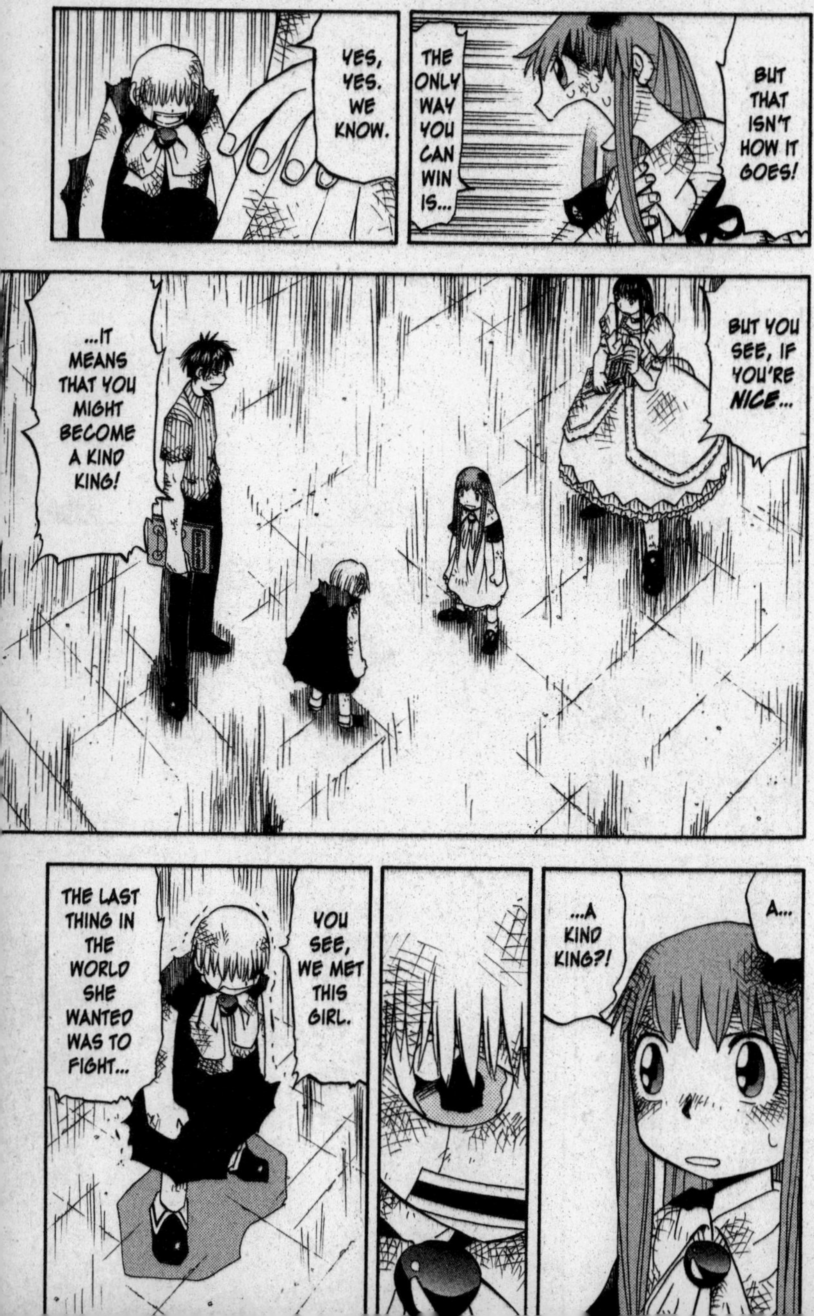
BUT THAT ISN'T HOW IT GOES!
THE ONLY WAY YOU CAN WIN IS...
YES, YES. WE KNOW.
BUT YOU SEE, IF YOU'RE NICE...
...IT MEANS THAT YOU MIGHT BECOME A KIND KING!
A...
...A KIND KING?!
YOU SEE, WE MET THIS GIRL.
THE LAST THING IN THE WORLD SHE WANTED WAS TO FIGHT...

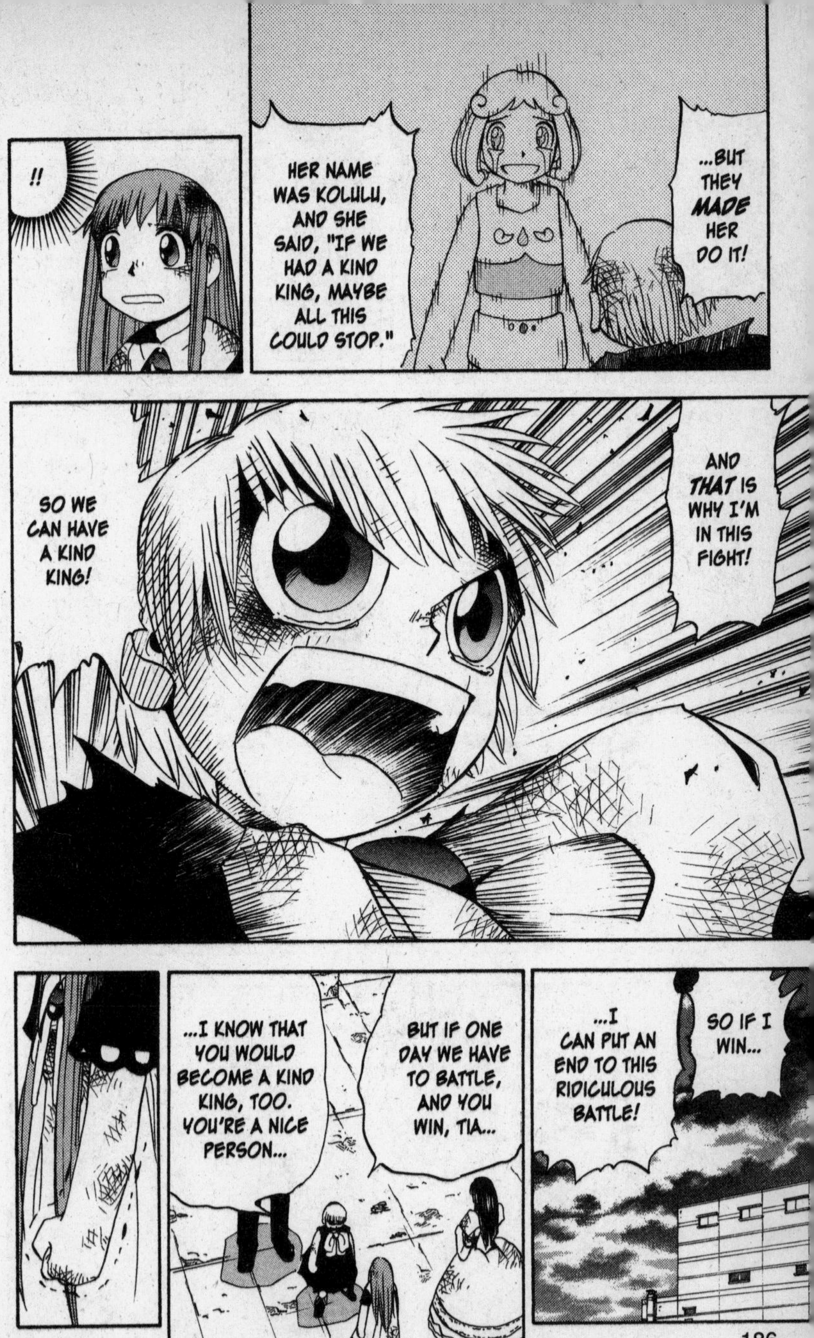
...BUT THEY *MADE* HER DO IT!
HER NAME WAS KOLULU, AND SHE SAID, "IF WE HAD A KIND KING, MAYBE ALL THIS COULD STOP."
!!
AND *THAT* IS WHY I'M IN THIS FIGHT!
SO WE CAN HAVE A KIND KING!
SO IF I WIN...
...I CAN PUT AN END TO THIS RIDICULOUS BATTLE!
BUT IF ONE DAY WE HAVE TO BATTLE, AND YOU WIN, TIA...
...I KNOW THAT YOU WOULD BECOME A KIND KING, TOO. YOU'RE A NICE PERSON...

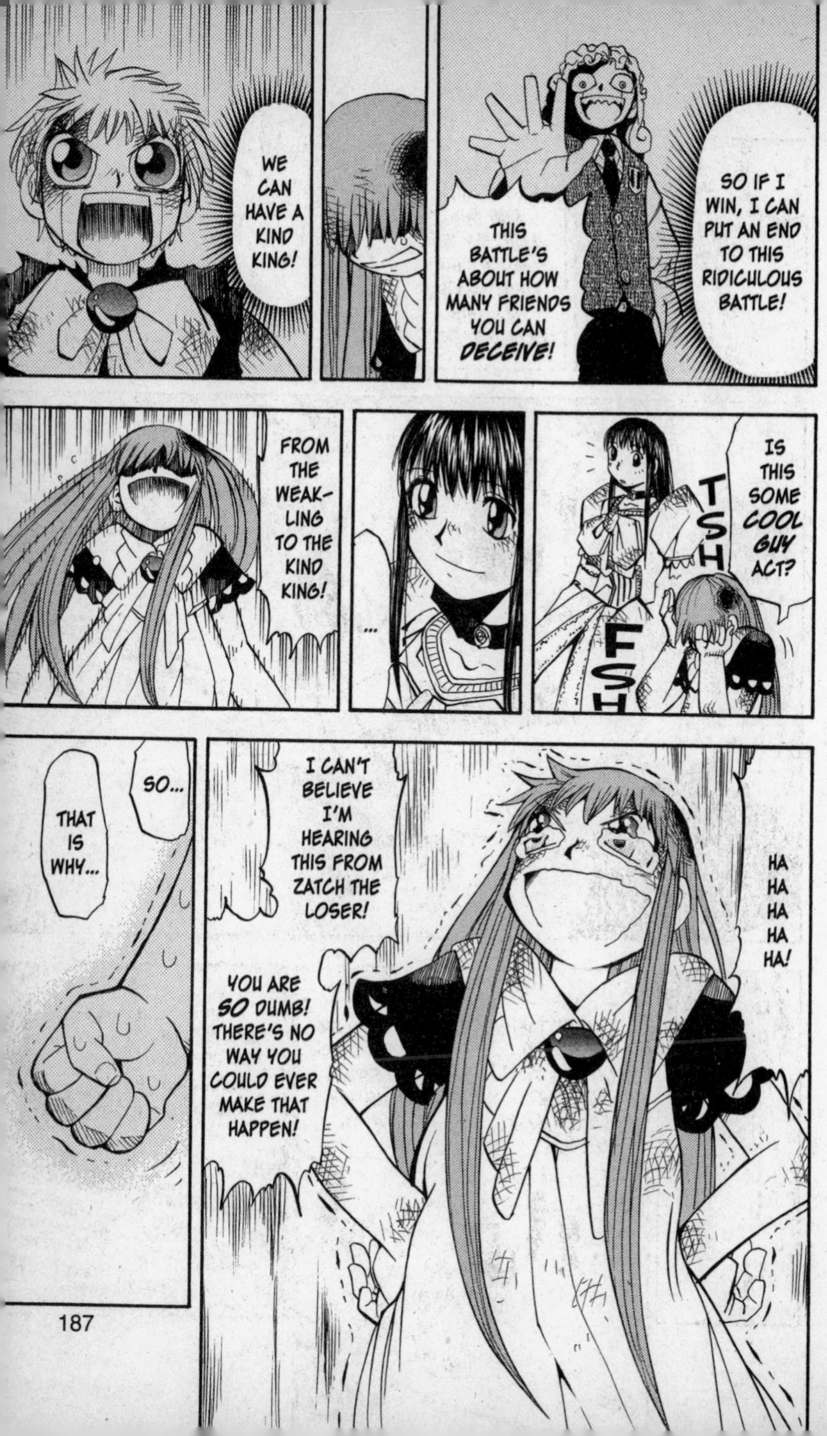
SO IF I WIN, I CAN PUT AN END TO THIS RIDICULOUS BATTLE!
THIS BATTLE'S ABOUT HOW MANY FRIENDS YOU CAN *DECEIVE!*
WE CAN HAVE A KIND KING!
IS THIS SOME *COOL GUY* ACT?
TSH
FSH
...
FROM THE WEAKLING TO THE KIND KING!
HA HA HA HA HA HA!
I CAN'T BELIEVE I'M HEARING THIS FROM ZATCH THE LOSER!
YOU ARE *SO* DUMB! THERE'S NO WAY YOU COULD EVER MAKE THAT HAPPEN!
SO...
THAT IS WHY...

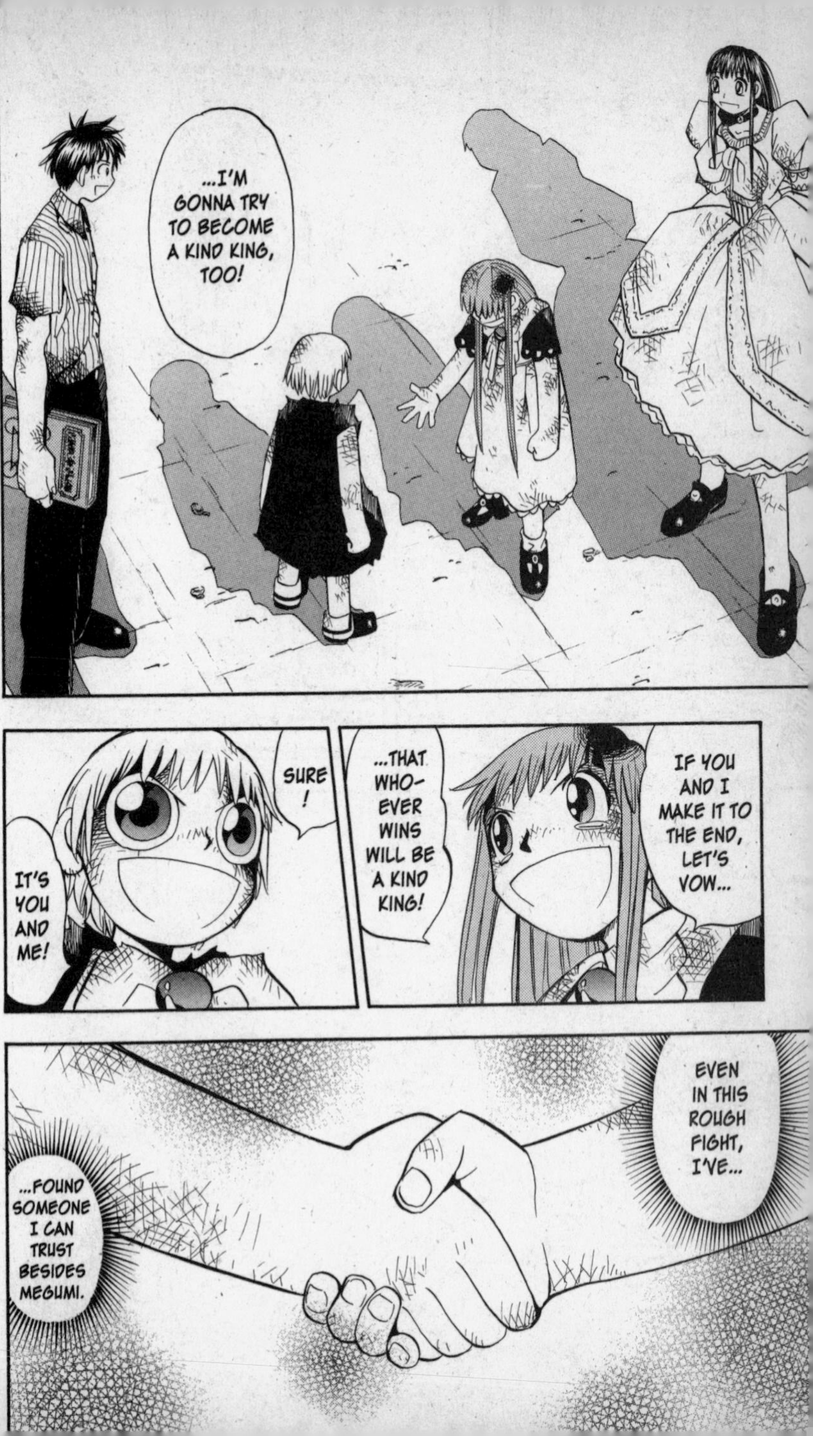
...I'M GONNA TRY TO BECOME A KIND KING, TOO!
IF YOU AND I MAKE IT TO THE END, LET'S VOW...
...THAT WHO-EVER WINS WILL BE A KIND KING!
SURE!
IT'S YOU AND ME!
EVEN IN THIS ROUGH FIGHT, I'VE...
...FOUND SOMEONE I CAN TRUST BESIDES MEGUMI.

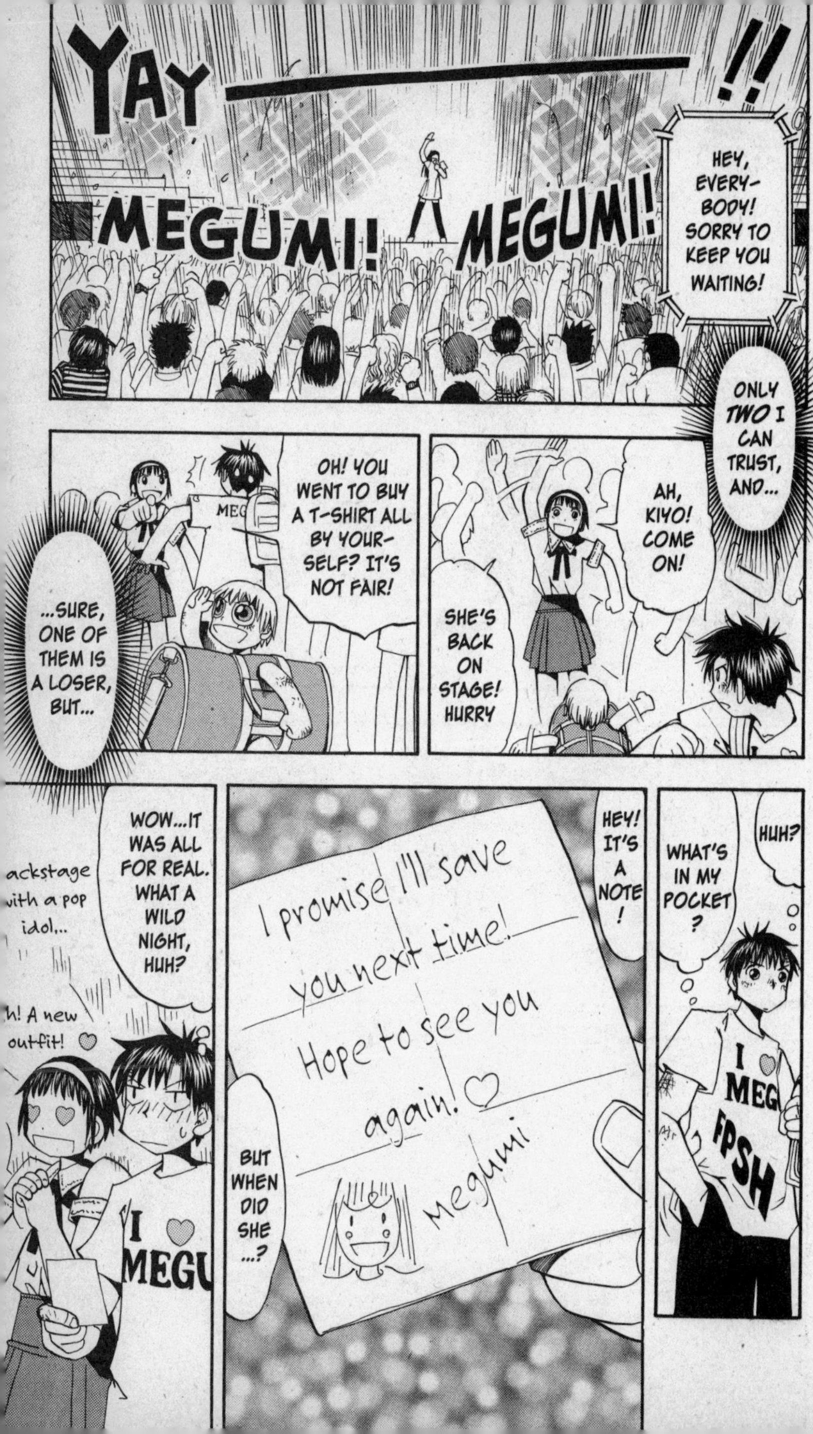
YAY——!!
HEY, EVERYBODY! SORRY TO KEEP YOU WAITING!
MEGUMI! MEGUMI!
ONLY TWO I CAN TRUST, AND...
AH, KIYO! COME ON!
SHE'S BACK ON STAGE! HURRY
OH! YOU WENT TO BUY A T-SHIRT ALL BY YOURSELF? IT'S NOT FAIR!
MEG
...SURE, ONE OF THEM IS A LOSER, BUT...
HUH?
WHAT'S IN MY POCKET?
I ♥ MEG FPSH
HEY! IT'S A NOTE!
I promise I'll save you next time! Hope to see you again! ♡ Megumi
BUT WHEN DID SHE ...?
WOW...IT WAS ALL FOR REAL. WHAT A WILD NIGHT, HUH?
ackstage with a pop idol...
h! A new outfit! ♥
I ♥ MEGU

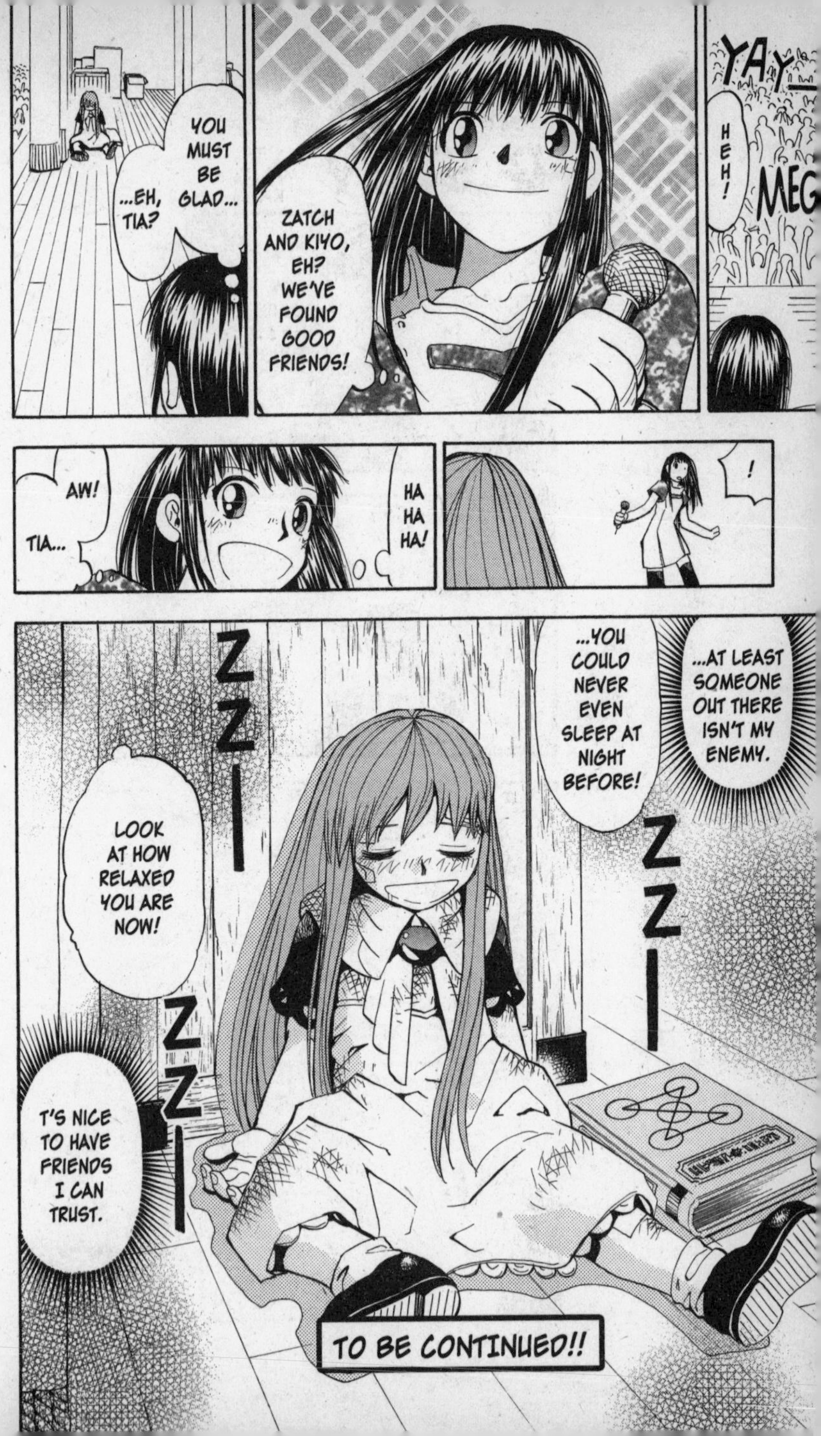
YAY
MEG
HEH!
ZATCH AND KIYO, EH? WE'VE FOUND GOOD FRIENDS!
YOU MUST BE GLAD...
...EH, TIA?
!
HA HA HA!
AW!
TIA...
...AT LEAST SOMEONE OUT THERE ISN'T MY ENEMY.
...YOU COULD NEVER EVEN SLEEP AT NIGHT BEFORE!
ZZZ
LOOK AT HOW RELAXED YOU ARE NOW!
ZZZ
T'S NICE TO HAVE FRIENDS I CAN TRUST.
ZZZ
TO BE CONTINUED!!

ZATCH & SUZY

BY MAKOTO RAIKU

WOW, SUZY... MEGUMI SURE HAS A LOT OF FANS, HUH?
YEP!
SO CUTE, AND SHE CAN SING, TOO!
TMP
TMP
I'VE GOT A SECRET TALENT OF MY OWN, YOU KNOW!
WOW! FOR REAL? CAN I SEE IT?
I'M DRUNKEN MASTER. SEE?
A CHARMING HONG KONG JOKE
WAH WAA-A
WAH

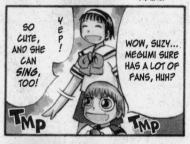

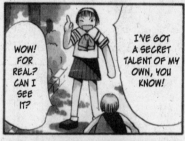

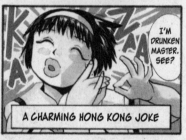

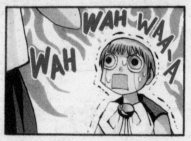

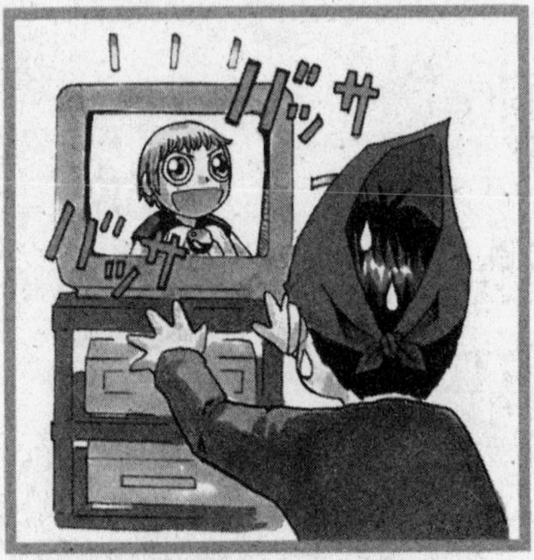
バッサ
バッサ

MAKOTO RAIKU

You can now see Zatch in a TV commercial! It's only thirty seconds, but still... I was so excited to see him running around on a TV screen! It made me so happy. I'm gonna have to make Zatch even more active in the manga version, too.

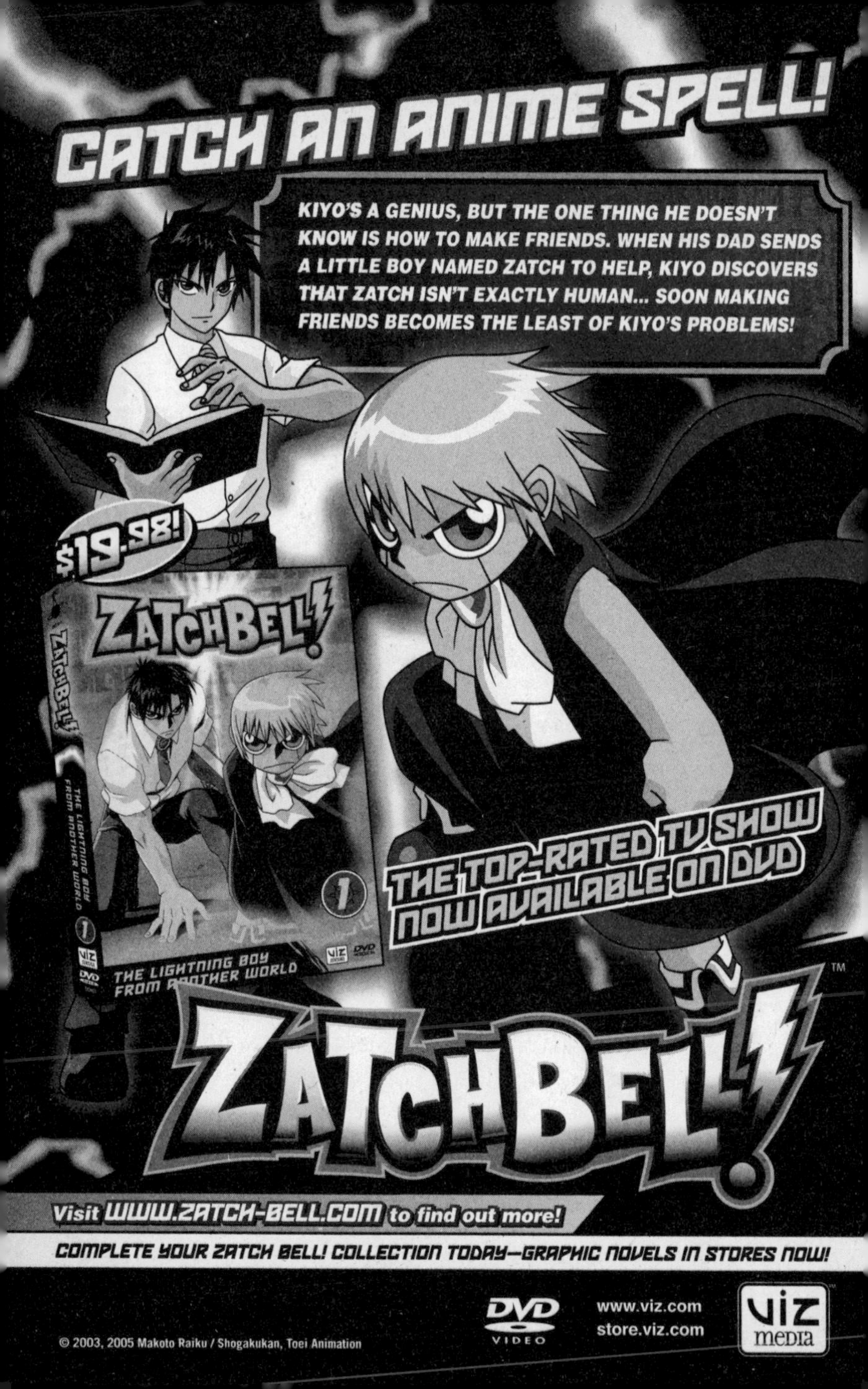
CATCH AN ANIME SPELL!
KIYO'S A GENIUS, BUT THE ONE THING HE DOESN'T KNOW IS HOW TO MAKE FRIENDS. WHEN HIS DAD SENDS A LITTLE BOY NAMED ZATCH TO HELP, KIYO DISCOVERS THAT ZATCH ISN'T EXACTLY HUMAN... SOON MAKING FRIENDS BECOMES THE LEAST OF KIYO'S PROBLEMS!
$19.98!
ZATCH BELL!
1
THE LIGHTNING BOY FROM ANOTHER WORLD
THE TOP-RATED TV SHOW NOW AVAILABLE ON DVD
ZATCH BELL!™
Visit WWW.ZATCH-BELL.COM to find out more!
COMPLETE YOUR ZATCH BELL! COLLECTION TODAY—GRAPHIC NOVELS IN STORES NOW!
DVD VIDEO
www.viz.com
store.viz.com
VIZ media
© 2003, 2005 Makoto Raiku / Shogakukan, Toei Animation

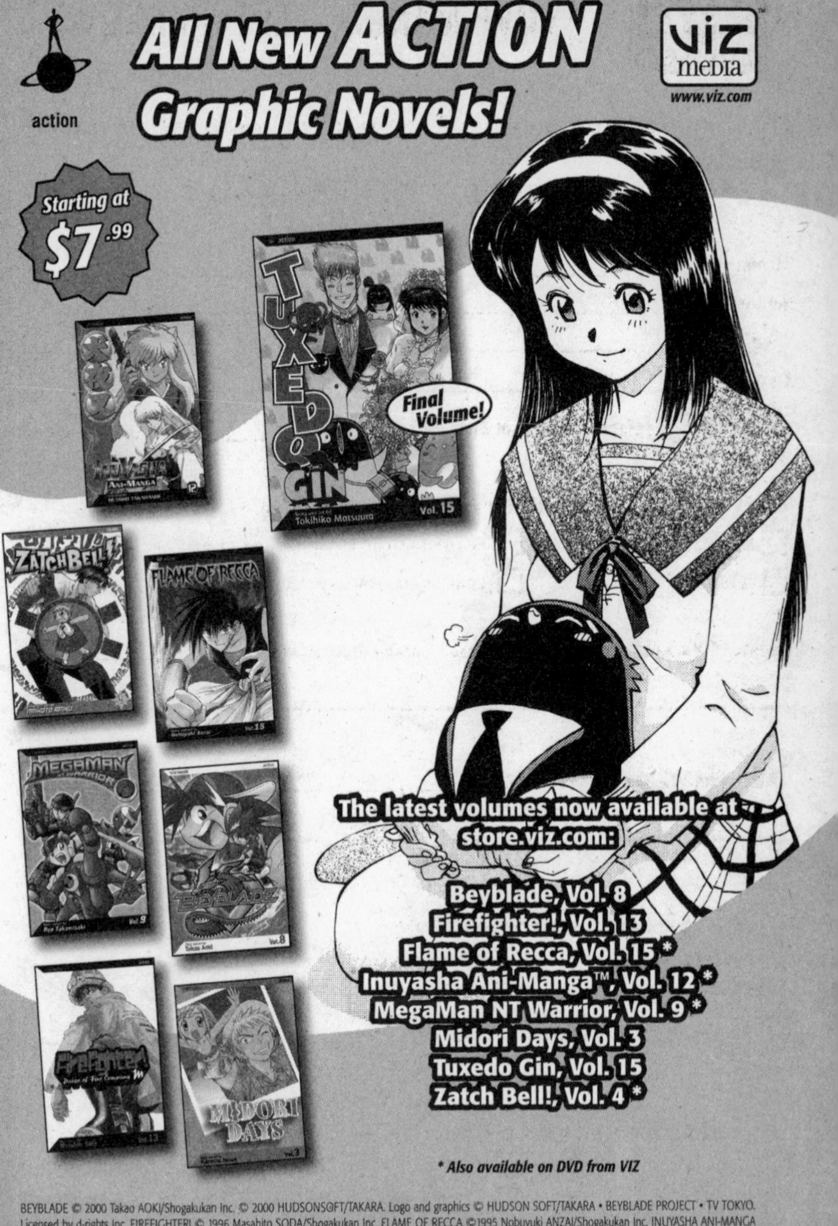
action
All New ACTION Graphic Novels!
VIZ media
www.viz.com
Starting at $7.99
Final Volume!
The latest volumes now available at store.viz.com:
Beyblade, Vol. 8
Firefighter!, Vol. 13
Flame of Recca, Vol. 15 *
Inuyasha Ani-Manga™, Vol. 12 *
MegaMan NT Warrior, Vol. 9 *
Midori Days, Vol. 3
Tuxedo Gin, Vol. 15
Zatch Bell!, Vol. 4 *
* Also available on DVD from VIZ

LOVE MANGA?   LET US KNOW!

☐ Please do NOT send me information about VIZ Media products, news and events, special offers, or other information.

☐ Please do NOT send me information from VIZ Media's trusted business partners.

Name: _____

Address: _____

City:_____ State:_____ Zip:_____

E-mail: _____

☐ Male   ☐ Female   Date of Birth (mm/dd/yyyy): ___/___/_____   (Under 13? Parental consent required)

What race/ethnicity do you consider yourself? (check all that apply)

☐ White/Caucasian   ☐ Black/African American   ☐ Hispanic/Latino

☐ Asian/Pacific Islander ☐ Native American/Alaskan Native ☐ Other: _____

What VIZ Media title(s) did you purchase? (indicate title(s) purchased) _____

_____

What other VIZ Media titles do you own? _____

_____

Reason for purchase: (check all that apply)

☐ Special offer   ☐ Favorite title / author / artist / genre

☐ Gift   ☐ Recommendation   ☐ Collection

☐ Read excerpt in VIZ Media manga sampler   ☐ Other _____

Where did you make your purchase? (please check one)

☐ Comic store   ☐ Bookstore   ☐ Grocery Store

☐ Convention   ☐ Newsstand   ☐ Video Game Store

☐ Online (site:_____)   ☐ Other _____

How many manga titles have you
(please check one from each column)

MANGA
- ☐ None
- ☐ 1 – 4
- ☐ 5 – 10
- ☐ 11+

- ☐ 5 – 10
- ☐ 11+

How much influence do special promotions and gifts-with-purchase have on the titles you buy?
(please circle, with 5 being great influence and 1 being none)

1 2 3 4 5

Do you purchase every volume of your favorite series?
☐ Yes! Gotta have 'em as my own ☐ No. Please explain: ______________________

What kind of manga storylines do you most enjoy? (check all that apply)

☐ Action / Adventure	☐ Science Fiction	☐ Horror
☐ Comedy	☐ Romance (shojo)	☐ Fantasy (shojo)
☐ Fighting	☐ Sports	☐ Historical
☐ Artistic / Alternative	☐ Other ______________________	

If you watch the anime or play a video or TCG game from a series, how likely are you to buy the manga? (please circle, with 5 being very likely and 1 being unlikely)

1 2 3 4 5

If unlikely, please explain: ______________________

Who are your favorite authors / artists? ______________________

____

What titles would like you translated and sold in English? ______________________

____

THANK YOU! Please send the completed form to:

NJW Research
42 Catharine Street
Poughkeepsie, NY 12601

Your privacy is very important to us. All information provided will be used for internal purposes only and will not be sold or otherwise divulged.